Never A Dull Moment

**Hassler Whitney,
Mathematics Pioneer**

Hassler Whitney: 1907 - 1989

This photo of Hassler Whitney was taken by his daughter Sally
Whitney Thurston in April of 1973 during a family hike to Sunfish
Pond in New Jersey's Delaware Water Gap Recreation Area.

AMS/MAA | SPECTRUM

VOL **93**

Never A Dull Moment

Hassler Whitney, Mathematics Pioneer

Keith Kendig

MAA PRESS

An Imprint of the AMERICAN MATHEMATICAL SOCIETY

Providence, Rhode Island

For additional information and updates on this book, visit
www.ams.org/bookpages/spec-93

Library of Congress Cataloging-in-Publication Data

Name: Kendig, Keith, 1938- author.
Title: Never a dull moment: Hassler Whitney, mathematics pioneer / Keith Kendig.
Other titles: Hassler Whitney, mathematics pioneer
Description: Providence, Rhode Island: MAA Press, an imprint of the American Mathematical Society, [2018] | Series: Spectrum; volume 93 | Includes bibliographical references and index.
Identifiers: LCCN 2018023363 | ISBN 9781470448288 (alk. paper)
Subjects: LCSH: Whitney, Hassler. | Mathematicians–United States–Biography. | AMS: History and biography – History of mathematics and mathematicians – General histories, source books. msc | History and biography – History of mathematics and mathematicians – 15th and 16th centuries, Renaissance. msc | History and biography – History of mathematics and mathematicians – 17th century. msc | History and biography – History of mathematics and mathematicians – 18th century. msc | History and biography – History of mathematics and mathematicians – 19th century. msc | History and biography – History of mathematics and mathematicians – 20th century. msc | History and biography – History of mathematics and mathematicians – Biographies, obituaries, personalia, bibliographies. msc | History and biography – History of mathematics and mathematicians – Schools of mathematics. msc | History and biography – History of mathematics and mathematicians – Universities. msc
Classification: LCC QA29.W484 K46 2018 | DDC 510.92 [B] –dc23
LC record available at https://lccn.loc.gov/2018023363

This photo of Hassler was taken using a large-format camera
that he built from scavenged parts. He's atop the Aiguille du
Roc ("Needle Rock"), one of Mont Blanc's Chamonix peaks.
His brother Roger took the photo when Hass was 14.

Contents

Preface

Hassler Whitney never seemed to have a dull moment—his wheels were always turning. He might be climbing in the Alps, drawing geometric figures to get intuition about a math problem, puzzling over a better fingering in a violin passage, flying to Holland to judge ice-skating contests, or turning his Christmas present pictured on p. 292 into an even more awesome challenge.

Hass—he preferred being called that—was like a force of nature. Within five minutes of meeting him, he already put me as cellist in a string quartet. He changed the way I think and do math, and his continual work with examples soon defined the way I teach. And he greatly broadened my musical horizons.

I first met Hass in 1965 and knew him for more than 20 years. I once casually mentioned to Don Albers, former Director of Publications and editor at the MAA, that there ought to be a biography written about Whitney, since he was such an interesting character. Don jumped at the idea. "Do it! He's a true icon of American mathematics! He needs and deserves a biography." That planted a seed. Robion Kirby, a leading topologist, gave me further encouragement when he asked me to write a biography for his online, free collection of mathematical biographies, *Celebratio Mathematica*. My contribution turned out to be just a few pages, but it got me started. The idea of a book-length biography on Hass kept marinating in me, but I wanted to capture something a little deeper about Whitney. As a little boy, the Scottish physicist James Clerk Maxwell often tried to analyze mechanical devices and would ask "What's the go of it?" In this book, through examples and stories, I've attempted to uncover and share what it was that made Whitney tick—his "go."

Two things I've learned: First, Hass always worked on what caught his fancy and seemed significant; second, he was a highly geometric thinker. He would draw lots of little diagrams and pictures and learn from them. He'd organize his results and formulate conjectures. Although the germs of his proofs were generally geometric, in the interests of rigor he habitually translated arguments into algebraic terms when writing things up for an article. Much of the driving intuition never shows up in the formal article, and his papers generally have a reputation as difficult reads. They remind me of those hard, dark brown lumps issued to GIs during WWI. You drop one into a cup of boiling water and after ten or fifteen minutes you get a good cup of coffee. One lump could make 20 or 25 cups. Many of his papers are like those lumps.

How, then, to write a biography that includes the ideas of his most important work? The answer is certainly not to condense his already tightly-written articles. Excluding his two books and published abstracts, his total published page count comes to 1,187. But his work almost always started from a perfectly understandable geometric germ plus some sensible hunches. He then explored his guesses with lots of concrete examples and built up intuition suggesting the answer and how to get to Q.E.D. In this book we illustrate a big theorem in simple cases and then sketch the basic idea of how it can be proved. Pictures are an invaluable aid here, just as they were with Whitney. In fact, in writing this book I often created a string of pictures that serve as a trail of bread crumbs leading to the end result, with text becoming the tissue connecting these pictures. It has been my goal to give an appreciation of what Whitney accomplished, and in general terms, how. Since historical context is often important, I take a few side trips to fill that in, too.

    This book contains lots of stories and paints his mathematical accomplishments in broad strokes. We sometimes present more detail and delve a bit further into Whitney's strategy toward establishing his results, but skipping such areas won't disrupt the main flow of his story, and we'll alert the reader in these cases. References in the bibliography are provided for experts. The aim of this book is to tell some of the surprising stories and facts about him, introduce readers to his ideas, and reveal some of his geometric insights. Full proofs of some of his most important results can involve a multitude of details, and Hassler knew only too well that the devil is in the details. In this book, the devil gets only an occasional cameo appearance.

    It is a pleasure to acknowledge the help, advice, and support from many people. In the MAA, not only was Don Albers an early cheerleader for this biography, but his careful reading of the manuscript has resulted in many valuable suggestions. Steve Kennedy, Don's successor at the MAA as Acquisitions Editor, as well as Jennifer Quinn, have been equally supportive, and Jim Tattersall together with the other members of the Spectrum Board have all offered extremely helpful advice. In the final stages of the manuscript, Underwood ("Woody") Dudley worked his magic, giving the book a meticulous reading; he made the biography flow more smoothly and pointed out errors as well as various inconsistencies. I am greatly indebted to him. In addition, Hassler's five children—James Whitney, Carol Whitney, Marian (called Molly) Melhuish, Sarah (called Sally) Thurston, and Emily Whitney—as well as his widow Barbara Osterman, have all shared with me stories, reminiscences, and insights that help to paint a fuller picture of Hass. Also, my great appreciation goes to Beth Whitney Thomas, the daughter of Hassler's oldest brother Simon: Her detailed knowledge of dates and facts about the large Whitney clan was crucial in keeping these things accurate. I also want to express a huge "Thank You" to Sally. As the Whitney family archivist, she has preserved correspondence to and from Hass spanning some 40 years, as well as hundreds of family photos. She spent innumerable hours sifting through printed photos and family slides, sending me photographs of dozens of them from which

I'd make final selections. She also provided many stories and insights about Hass that could come only from a close family member, and these helped fill out a fuller picture of him. Importantly, she also read multiple versions of the manuscript, correcting mistakes and checking with other family members when necessary. Her very generous time and sharp eye for detail has greatly improved the book. Finally, I am greatly indebted for input on the AMS side from Sergei Gelfand and Christine Thivierge, as well as Kerriann Malatesta, whose careful and thorough work transformed my manuscript into a beautiful volume. My heartfelt thanks to all!

Keith Kendig
September 2018

Permissions & Acknowledgments

The AMS is grateful to the following individuals and organizations for providing photographs and for permission to reproduce copyrighted material. While every effort has been made to trace and acknowledge copyright holders, the publishers would like to apologize for any omissions and will be pleased to incorporate missing acknowledgments in any future editions.

American Mathematical Society

Figure 5.2, p. 45: George Birkhoff.
Figure 10.16 (top right), p. 130: Solomon Lefschetz.

Martha Benezet

Figure 18.2, p. 241: Louis P. Benezet.

ETH-Library Zurich

Figure 10.16 (bottom left), p. 130: Heinz Hopf. Credit: ETH-Library Zurich, Image Archive/Photo Ammann (Zurich)/Portr_07480.

John Heymann

Figure 22.9, p. 310: Hass and Barbara, June 1988.
Unnumbered, p. 332: Family dinner the night before Sally's wedding.
Unnumbered, p. 333: Hass playing piano at Sally's wedding, June 1988.
Unnumbered, p. 337: Barbara with Hass making his typical hand gestures.
Credit: All photographs by John Heymann.

Islapedia

Figure 2.3, p. 14: Ferdinand Hassler.
Figure 2.4, p. 16: The USCSS Hassler three-masted schooner.

Keith Kendig

Figure 7.15, p. 73: Ball and stick model of the propane molecule C_3H_8. Figure created in POVRAY software by author Kendig.
Figure 19.1, p. 253: Kodak stereo camera. Credit: Photo by author Kendig.
Figure 21.2, p. 285: Commodore computer. Credit: Photo by author Kendig.
Figure 22.1, p. 292: Labyrynth game. Credit: Photo by author Kendig.

The Mathematisches Forschungsinstitut Oberwolfach

Figure 10.16 (bottom right), p. 130: Pavel Aleksandrov. Credit: Konrad Jacobs. Source: Archives of the Mathematisches Forschungsinstitut Oberwolfach, used under the Creative Commons License Attribution Share Alike 2.0 Germany.

Figure 16.20, p. 216: René Thom. Credit: Gerd Fischer. Archives of the Mathematisches Forschungsinstitut Oberwolfach, used under the Creative Commons License Attribution Share Alike 2.0 Germany.

NOAA

Figure 2.5, p. 17: The NOAA Ferdinand R. Hassler.

Public.resources.org

Unnumbered, p. 347: Kansas mill explosion, 1947. Credit: Public.resources.org used under the Creative Commons Attribution 2.0 Generic License.

Shutterstock.com

Figure 22.10, p. 311: Mt. Dent Blanche, Pennine Alps, Valais, Switzerland.

The Shelby White and Leon Levy Archives Center, Institute for Advanced Study

Figure 16.2 (left), p. 199: Abraham Flexner. Credit: Photographer unknown. From the Shelby White and Leon Levy Archives Center, Institute for Advanced Study, Princeton, NJ.

Figure 16.2 (right), p. 199: Caroline Bamberger Fuld. Credit: Photographer unknown. From the Shelby White and Leon Levy Archives Center, Institute for Advanced Study, Princeton, NJ.

Figure 19.11, p. 264: The common room at the Institute. Credit: James Stephens, Photographer. From the Shelby White and Leon Levy Archives Center, Institute for Advanced Study, Princeton, NJ.

Figure 19.12, p. 265: André Weil. Credit: Hermann Landshoff, Photographer. From the Shelby White and Leon Levy Archives Center, Institute for Advanced Study, Princeton, NJ.

Figure 20.3, p. 280: The Institute woods. Credit: James Stephens, Photographer. From the Shelby White and Leon Levy Archives Center, Institute for Advanced Study, Princeton, NJ.

Figure 22.5, p. 304: The Institute pond. Credit: Photographer unknown. From the Shelby White and Leon Levy Archives Center, Institute for Advanced Study, Princeton, NJ.

Figure 22.6, p. 307: Whitney Hassler, 1981. Credit: Hermann Landshoff, Photographer. From the Shelby White and Leon Levy Archives Center, Institute for Advanced Study, Princeton, NJ.

Sally Whitney Thurston

Cover photograph/unnumbered, p. v: Hass, age 14, atop the Aiguille du Roc.

Frontispiece photograph: Hass, April 1973.

Figure 1.1, p. 1: Hass, four months old.

Figure 1.2, p. 2: Hass, age 2.

Figure 1.3, p. 3: Hass and cat.

Figure 1.4, p. 4: Hass and geese.

Figure 1.6, p. 7: Letter to Aunt Margaret.

Figure 2.1, p. 9: Josepha Whitney (center left); Hass (bottom).

Figure 2.6, p. 19: Caroline feeding Hass.

Figure 2.7, p. 20: Hass and Roger, ages 4 and 6 (left); 35 years later (right).

Figure 2.8, p. 21: Hass and his siblings, 1920.

Figure 3.1, p. 24: Hass and Lisa.

Figure 3.2, p. 30: Passport photo of Hass, Josepha, and Lisa.

Figure 3.3, p. 31: Hass and Gaston Clerc.

Figure 3.6, p. 35: Hass, shortly before entering Yale.

Figure 4.1, p. 40: Hass's passport photo, 1930.

Figure 4.2, p. 42: Brock, 1930.

Figure 5.1, p. 44: Hass, around the time that he wrote his four-color papers.

Figure 8.8, p. 92: Hass, around the time he introduced matroids.

Figure 14.9, p. 187: Hass, about the time of the strong embedding theorem.

Figure 15.5, p. 195: Hass, shortly after his work toward the war effort.

Figure 16.1, p. 198: Hass, around the time he joined the Institute.

Figure 16.19, p. 215: Hass, Mary, and Sally.

Figure 17.8, p. 226: Molly's wedding photo showing Hass's five children and groom Hugh Melhuish, 1963.

Figure 22.4, p. 299: Hass playing the viola.

Figure 22.7, p. 308: Hass's four-voice round.

Figure 22.8, p. 309: Mary, Emily, Sally, and Hass.

Unnumbered, p. 314: Hass and newborn Sally.

Unnumbered, p. 315: Hass and Sally, age 2.

Unnumbered, p. 316: Hass and Emily, age 4 (top); one year later (bottom).

Unnumbered, p. 317: Hass, Emily, and Sally at the beach.

Unnumbered, p. 318: Molly, Josepha, and Carol (top); Molly, Hugh, and Brock (bottom).

Unnumbered, p. 319: Hass bouldering.

Unnumbered, p. 320: Carol, age 14, rock climbing.

Unnumbered, p. 321: Molly rappelling.

Unnumbered, p. 322: Molly on trip to Sierra Nevada, 1971.

Unnumbered, p. 323: Molly and Emily in the Sierras.

Unnumbered, p. 324: James mountain climbing.

Unnumbered, p. 325: Carol playing guitar.

Unnumbered, p. 326: Molly playing flute.

Unnumbered, p. 327: Brock with Carol, James, Molly, and the family dog, 1945 (top); James, Carol, and Molly seven years later (bottom).

Unnumbered, p. 328: Carol, Brock, Hass, and the family dog, 1945.

Unnumbered, p. 329: Mary and Hass on their wedding day, January 1955.

Unnumbered, p. 330: Hass and Mary cutting wedding cake (top); Hass and Mary sharing wedding punch (bottom).

Unnumbered, p. 331: Sally, Mary, Hass, and Emily at the airport, 1962.

Unnumbered, p. 334: Hass and Barbara at their wedding reception, February 1986.

Unnumbered, p. 335: Family playing music and dancing at Hass and Barbara's wedding.

Unnumbered, p. 336: Amber playing chess.

Unnumbered, p. 338: Carol, Emily, and Sally reading.

Unnumbered, p. 339: Carol and Sally.

Unnumbered, p. 340: Hass, Anne, and Jamie.

Unnumbered, p. 341: Hass and Sally picnicking.

Unnumbered, p. 342: Hass, Emily, and Sally enjoying the mountain view.

Unnumbered, p. 343: Hass and child at the beach.

Unnumbered, p. 344: Hass enjoying his surroundings.

Credit: Family photos courtesy of Sally Whitney Thurston.

Wikimedia Commons

Figure 2.1, p. 9: Simon Newcomb (top left); William Dwight Whitney (top right), Credit: Wikimedia Commons.

Figure 2.2, p. 13: Josiah Dwight Whitney. Credit: Wikimedia Commons.

Figure 6.1, p. 48: The map that started it all. Credit: Wikimedia Commons, used under the Creative Commons Attribution-Share Alike 3.0 Unported License.

Figure 9.2, p. 98: Leonhard Euler. Credit: Wikimedia Commons.

Figure 10.1, p. 108: Enrico Betti (left); Bernhard Riemann (right). Credit: Wikimedia Commons.

Figure 10.5, p. 114: Henri Poincaré. Credit: Wikimedia Commons.

Figure 10.14, p. 127: August Ferdinand Möbius (left); Felix Christian Klein (right). Credit: Wikimedia Commons.

Figure 10.15, p. 129: Emmy Noether. Credit: Wikimedia Commons.

Figure 15.1, p. 190: Re-creation of the first successful fission experiment. Credit: Wikimedia Commons.

Figure 16.2 (center), p. 199: Louis Bamberger. Credit: Wikimedia Commons.

Figure 16.3, p. 199: Fuld Hall. Credit: Wikimedia Commons.

Figure 20.1, p. 270: Harish-Chandra. Credit: Wikimedia Commons, used under the Creative Commons Attribution-Share Alike 4.0 International License.

Figure 20.2, p. 272: Walter Gieseking. Credit: Wikimedia Commons, used under the Creative Commons Attribution-Share Alike 4.0 International License.

Figure 22.3, p. 298: Bach, Beethoven, Wagner, Schubert, Mozart, and Chopin (pictured clockwise from top left).

Unnumbered, p. 348: Karl Weierstrass. Credit: Wikimedia Commons.

CHAPTER 1
Some Snapshots

A sampling of quotes, and some photos

Before Hass could talk:

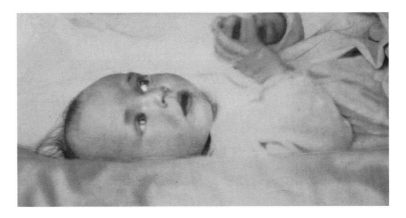

Figure 1.1. Hass, four months old.

"But Mother, I NEED another piece of chocolate cake!"

After four-year-old Hassler's nonverbal entreaties were going nowhere, he blurted this out. These were his very first words. When he at last began talking, it was usually in complete sentences.

"If it weren't for school, I'd have time for the things I really want to do."

Although Hassler was home schooled for much of his childhood, he felt that contending with school prevented him from doing things that seemed much more important. For example, a high point of each month was receiving his copy of the magazine *Popular Science*. It had informative articles that he digested, and sometimes there were suggestions for making interesting mechanical devices. School interfered by limiting the time he could spend on making such devices.

Figure 1.2. Hass around two.

"Here's my ticket, sir."

While waiting for his train ride back home, 12-year-old Hassler found a garden snake. He took a liking to it and decided to take it home. On the train, as the conductor came around, Hass hid the snake under his shirt and carefully gave the conductor his ticket.

"Of all the people in the world who never touched foot on any of Switzerland's mountains, I probably know the most about them..."

In 1921, the Whitney family, minus the three oldest children who by then were on their own, began a two-year visit to Switzerland. Hassler, 14 years old, was still being home schooled. The main goals set for him were to learn French the first year, German the second, and continue with piano lessons both years. But Hass had a much more lofty idea: Conquer the Swiss Alps! Exciting images of climbing to the top of peaks filled his youthful soul, and to prepare for this new life he thoroughly studied all the facts, figures, and maps of the Alps he could get his hands on. It was shortly before boots finally hit rock that he made the above statement.

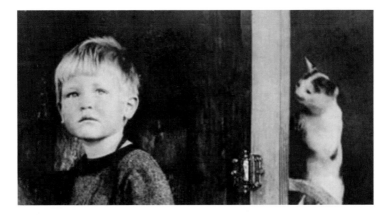

Figure 1.3. Hass loved animals, and they loved him. A couple of years after this photo was taken, Hass made it clear that he didn't like fish, but was served it anyway. On those occasions, little fingers would drop pieces of fish onto the floor under the table, and this cat was more than happy to remove the evidence and keep the matter secret.

"I want big pictures!"

Just as he had imagined, the views from Swiss mountain peaks were spectacular. Hass wanted a large format camera so he could capture the expansive vistas. Because of his experience with projects in *Popular Science*, he'd become quite good at building things, and was able to make a camera using scavenged parts. It turned out to be 41 1/2 inches long, much too long to fit in his backpack. He reconstructed it so it could be disassembled into parts, each at most one foot long. The picture on the cover of this book is Hass on the Aiguille du roc (Needle Rock), at 11,174 ft, and is one of the peaks in Mont Blanc. It was taken by Hassler's brother Roger in August, 1921 using the homemade camera when Hass was 14.

Hassler slinked away, hoping the great man would just forget the incident.

As a freshman at Yale, Whitney had petitioned the math department to skip Calculus I but needed Chairman Pierpont's signature. When Whitney handed him the request, Pierpont roared at him, "Certainly not! You'll start with Calculus I like anyone else!" Hassler never took Calculus I, or any other calculus, ever.

"This is pure genius!"

Pierpont, three years later, remarking to the class about Whitney's ingenious solution to a homework problem. Pierpont, it turned out, had indeed forgotten the calculus incident.

Figure 1.4. Hass feeding some geese, about two years before taking home a garden snake.

"What am I gonna do? I just can't remember things!"

As an undergraduate, Whitney was a physics major. To get a running start before entering graduate school in physics, he decided to blitz through some of his old physics notes. He found that he'd forgotten most of what he had learned. Seeing the ominous writing on the wall, he decided to try mathematics instead.

"I feel sorry for my students."

When it came to classroom exposition, Hass commiserated that he lacked the golden touch that seemed to come so naturally to James Pierpont of Yale or Saunders Mac Lane and George Birkhoff of Harvard.

"I could never jump into the middle of a research area—I'd never keep up with the others. I just do my own thing."

Hassler, explaining why he avoided certain areas of research.

"I never wanted to make graph theory my life in mathematics. I wanted to do *real* math."

Hassler wrote his Ph.D. thesis on the four-color problem, mostly because he found the problem so irresistible. But he felt that he really wanted to work with the sort of functions he had learned about in physics such as polynomials, trigonometric functions, exponential functions, and so on.

Figure 1.5. In the days when the picture of Hass feeding geese was taken, a Model T Ford would have been a common sight. Often called a "Tin Lizzie" or a "flivver," this marvel could go as fast as 45 MPH on a good road. But with just 20 HP, going up a steep hill often required using its lowest gear, which was reverse. That meant turning the car around and going up the hill backwards.

"You did WHAT?!"

Hass seldom blew up, but when his athletic 12-year-old daughter Molly bragged about how she climbed up their huge sugar maple and touched the very top leaf, that was too much. She had no protection against falling. He loved his children and could be very protective.

"90% or more of most children's time spent on math is wasted."

Hassler's estimate, based on a dozen years of working with children in math classes. Most of that time, he said, doesn't help the child towards real or useful goals.

"Float up. Ooze back down."

Hassler's advice on mountain climbing.

"Music continually runs through my head."

Hassler's remark after an evening of playing quartets at his home.

"Sorry. I was thinking about Pontryagin[1] duality."

Hass got completely lost while playing first-violin in an easy section of a Schubert string quartet. To our puzzled looks, he gave the above apology. If music continually ran through his head, duality in mathematics was also very much part of his nervous system—it seemed he was always on the lookout for it, and many of his important results centered around some form of it.

"Let's do it!"

It was a little after midnight, and we'd had an especially long and intense evening playing string quartets. As the players were about to put their instruments away, I jokingly quipped "Let's play *Death and the Maiden*"—well-known as one of Schubert's longest and most demanding quartets. To everyone's surprise, Hass pounced on the idea: "Let's do it!" It was hard to dampen Hassler's enthusiasm, and we played the first movement. After that, Hass turned the page, obviously expecting to continue. We wound up playing it all, and Hass dropped me off at my apartment somewhat after 1 a.m.

"Parallel lines meet at the added point at infinity in the projective plane..."

Hassler's third wife Barbara, an artist, was giving a short course on perspective, and during one lecture Hass stood up and began explaining to everyone its mathematical background. Nobody understood, and Barbara ended up kicking him out of her class.

"I am in the fourth grade in school."

Hass attended a small school in which the second, third, and fourth grades all met in one room. As likely the brightest student in that room, he identified with the most advanced ones, and as his letter (Figure 1.6) to Aunt Margaret reveals, he thought of himself as "a fourth grader." Margaret was the youngest of three sisters. The middle one, Emily, was a professional pianist whose beautiful playing ignited Hassler's early interest in music. The oldest, Marian, taught German at Vassar and gave Hassler his first exposure to a different language.

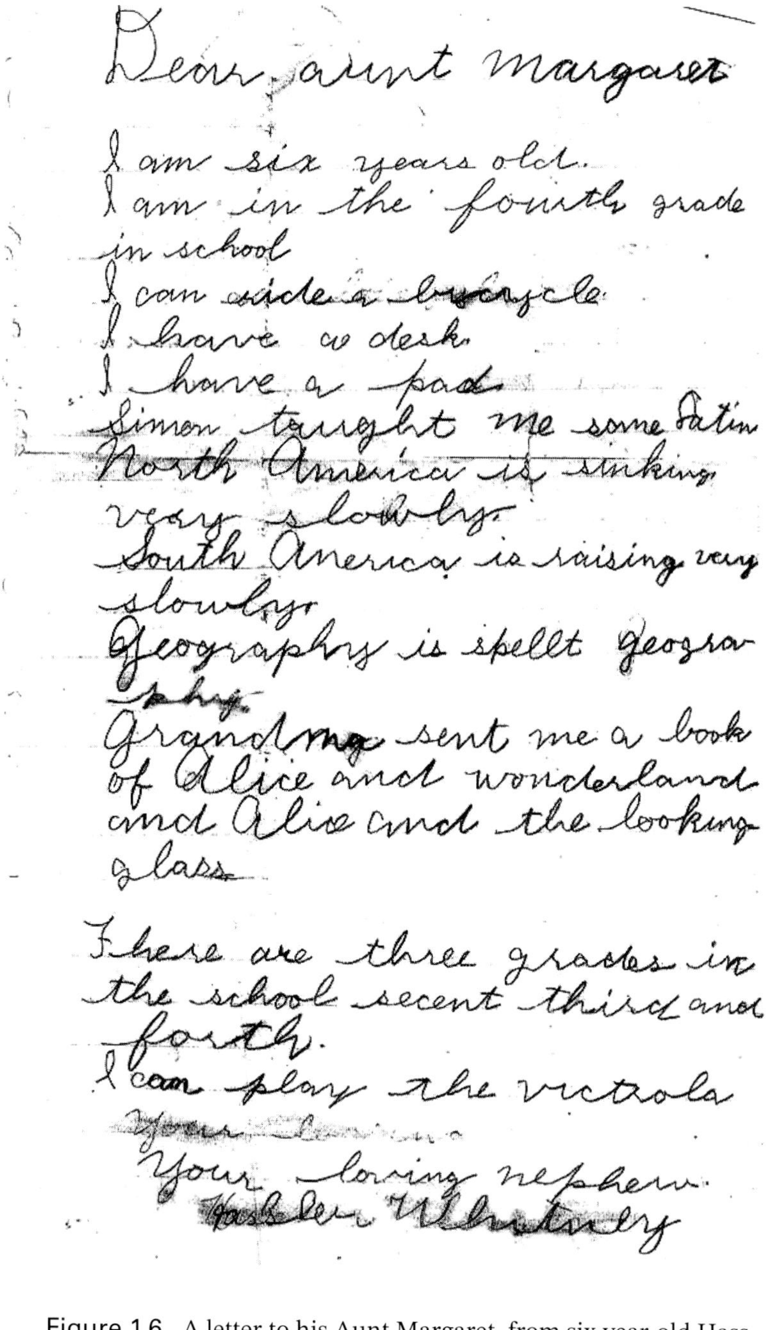

Dear aunt Margaret

I am six years old.
I am in the fourth grade
in school
I can ride a bicycle
I have a desk.
I have a pad
Simon taught me some Latin
North America is sinking
very slowly.
South America is raising very
slowly.
Geography is spellt Geogra-
phy
Grandma sent me a book
of Alice and wonderland
and Alice and the looking
glass

There are three grades in
the school secent third and
forth.
I can play the victrola

Your loving nephew.
Hassler Whitney

Figure 1.6. A letter to his Aunt Margaret, from six-year-old Hass.

CHAPTER 2
How Hassler Chose His Genes

Simon Newcomb

William Dwight Whitney

(Anna) Josepha Whitney

Edward B. Whitney

Hassler Whitney

Figure 2.1. From bottom to top: Hassler, his parents, his grandfathers.

2.1 Hassler's forebears

When the name "Whitney" is mentioned, most people think of the Whitney Museum in New York, or Mount Whitney in California—at 14,505 ft, the highest mountain in the continental United States. The Whitney family is actually huge, with scores of prominent people. Hassler's branch of the U.S. family began with John Whitney (1589–1673), who in 1635 sailed from London and settled in Massachusetts. He and his several sons quickly established both social and financial prominence and the name has had an enduring presence in the U.S., especially in New England. As for the Whitney Museum, it was founded by Gertrude Vanderbilt Whitney. The very wealthy Gertrude Vanderbilt married industrialist Harry P. Whitney (not related to Hass), and she eventually established the Museum. As for Mount Whitney, it was named after Josiah Dwight Whitney, a great uncle of Hassler.

We now give brief sketches of Hassler's mother, father, maternal and paternal grandfathers, along with his great uncle of Mount Whitney fame. We also include a sketch of Hassler's namesake, Ferdinand Hassler.

Simon Newcomb (1835–1909). Simon, Hassler's maternal grandfather, was a famous astronomer and a scientific giant by any measure. A citation accompanying a medal he received from the Astronomical Society of the Pacific says "…he has done more than any other American since Franklin to make American science respected and honored throughout the entire world." There are some remarkable similarities between Hassler and Simon. For one, Simon was entirely home schooled. His father was a schoolmaster in Canada and gave young Simon a solid general foundation for further study. Early on, Simon and Hassler were both strongly attracted to physics: When Simon was about 20, he studied Newton's *Principia Mathematica*, and this interest in physics evolved into his stellar career in astronomy, as well as a distinguished reputation in mathematics—he wrote 318 titles in astronomy, 35 math papers, and served two years as president of the American Mathematical Society. Actually, Simon was something of a polymath and also wrote influential papers in economics. He and Hass both spoke fluent French and German. Both loved to travel. Hass was a devoted mountain climber who eventually took up daily jogging. Simon was a devoted walker, covering several miles each day, and substantially more distance on Sundays. At 70, Simon climbed to a chalet high up on the side of the Matterhorn, a feat almost unheard of for anyone his age. Both Hassler and Simon usually avoided social talk. When a conversation bored Hass, he'd often say, "Well, well…" and the conversation was over. Simon's wife would from time to time host social get-togethers, and guests would often want to meet the famous scientist, asking, "Where's Simon?" The reply would run something like, "He's in his library, and you can wander in if you want. But be advised: The professor does not do small talk."

Simon wrote several books, including a half-dozen popular ones in astronomy. By the end of his career he was considered the most eminent living scientist in the United States. When he died at 74, he was buried in Arlington National Cemetery with full military honors. President Taft and dignitaries from several foreign governments attended the funeral.

Josepha Newcomb Whitney (1871–1957). Simon Newcomb had three children—all girls, with Anna Josepha the middle one. She called herself Josepha from childhood on. She was mostly home schooled, and her father, famous both as an astronomer and as a mathematician, gave her an especially extensive mathematical education. She was in turn extremely supportive of Hassler's early scientific and mathematical interests, and with her strong background, was able to read many of Hassler's mathematical papers. She studied art at the Art Students' League in New York and became a prolific artist known especially for her renditions of large, stately trees in the southern United States. Judging from the many carefully rendered diagrams and figures Hassler included in his early letters to various family members, his mother must have had some artistic influence on him.

Josepha, like her father and like Hassler, was very strong-minded and wasn't afraid to express herself. She energetically fought for women's causes and was active in the suffrage movement. In 1912 she organized the first Cornwall meeting in support of voting rights for women. Also, when young men went to war in 1917, she felt that women ought to fill the void left in the labor force. When told that women weren't strong enough to replace them, she got a job on an assembly line to prove her doubters wrong. After a few weeks, additional women were hired on that line. A few years later she realized that most Connecticut courtrooms were all-male, and at a high profile trial involving a pregnant woman, she gathered up a small army of women supporters and marched in protest every morning, creating such a disturbance that the trial had to be moved to another town. Soon after that, women were admitted to juries in Connecticut. She increasingly turned to politics and eventually became a member of the Connecticut State Legislature.

William Dwight Whitney (1827–1894). Hassler's paternal grandfather, William Dwight Whitney, was a linguistic scholar. An exceptionally bright youngster, he entered Williams College in Williamstown at 15, graduating three years later. He subsequently worked for several years at a bank in Northampton, and then in 1849 assisted his older brother Josiah Whitney for a few months on a geological survey of the Lake Superior region. The next year he went to Germany for serious study. He began writing papers, then several books on language as well as grammar textbooks on English, French, German, and Sanskrit. His reputation steadily grew, and he was given a professorship in Sanskrit at Yale when

27, adding comparative philology a few years later. He became secretary to the American Oriental Society in 1857, eventually becoming its president in 1884. He had six children; one of them, Edward Baldwin Whitney, was Hassler's father.

Edward Baldwin Whitney (1857–1911). Hassler's father, Edward B. Whitney, graduated from Yale at age 21, went to the Columbia Law School, and was admitted to the New York bar when 23. He became a very active Democrat, organized the National Association of Democratic clubs, and was a delegate to the 1892 National Democratic Convention held in Chicago. He caught the attention of President Grover Cleveland, who was re-elected in 1892. Cleveland appointed Edward Assistant U.S. Attorney General in 1893. While in Washington during this time, Edward met Josepha, who was quite the flirt in her earlier years; the older, shy Edward found himself helplessly charmed by the beautiful southern belle. They shared political interests to a T and were soon engaged. At 39, he married 25-year-old Josepha, and they had seven children. After his stint as Assistant U.S. Attorney General, he returned to New York to practice law. He was extremely hard-working, fair-minded, and independent in his thinking. At his core, he was one to contribute to the overall community. In working on cases, he absorbed even the most minute details and revealed a highly acute mind. His legal understanding was broad and jurors found his explanations—sometimes lectures—not simply informative, but educational in a deep way. Making money as an end in itself meant little to him, and he often offered his services for free. Despite his mindset toward the public good, he was quite introverted, but those few who penetrated Edward's shell found a loving and delightful man. Edward was always far more a judge than a lawyer, and this inner nature came to fruition when he was appointed Judge to the New York Supreme Court in both 1909 and 1910. Unfortunately, Edward was physically frail throughout his life, and in the winter of 1910, before even starting his 1910 appointment, he caught a cold that turned into pneumonia. He never recovered, and died on January 5, 1911.

Josiah Dwight Whitney (1819–1896). Josiah entered Yale University in 1836 and studied the sciences, including chemistry and mineralogy. He graduated in 1839 and the next year became an assistant in a survey of New Hampshire's geology. He intended to enter Harvard Law School, but then heard a lecture by geologist Charles Lyell. Lyell had become famous for advocating the theory of uniformitarianism, which says that the earth's geology is largely the product of slow-moving forces acting over millions of years and still operating today. In short, uniformitarianism means geological evolution. Lyell had an enormous influence on Charles Darwin, and now was about to change Josiah's life. That single lecture so inspired Josiah that he dropped all plans for law school and made geology his life's calling.

Figure 2.2. Josiah Dwight Whitney.

He studied science in Europe for the next five years. Upon returning to the U.S. in 1847, he joined a small team making a federal survey of the Lake Superior land district in Michigan, which seemed destined to become an important iron and copper mining center. With his study abroad and another three years' experience during the survey, he turned to writing a book, *Metallic Wealth of the United States*. The book soon became highly regarded and widely referenced, and in 1855 Josiah was given a professorship at the Iowa State University. Six years later he was designated as the State Geologist of California. His mission? Carry out a comprehensive geologic survey of California. "Comprehensive" meant the survey was to include not only geology, but geography, botany, zoology, and paleontology. With generous state funding together with his high reputation, he was able to assemble a dream team of leading experts in these areas. On the geology side, it was determined that the highest point in the continental U.S. was in California's Sierra Nevada range, and the team named the mountain for Josiah: "Mount Whitney." (Alaska became a state in 1959, and now the 10 highest U.S. mountain peaks are all in Alaska.)

Whitney wrote another book, *The Yosemite Book*, which appeared in 1869. It served as a helpful travel guide to Yosemite Valley and in it he proposed turning it into a national park. He was one of the very first people to urge this. Whitney eventually joined Harvard's Department of Geology and in 1874 opened the School of Mines. He remained Professor of Geology at Harvard for the remainder of his life.

Figure 2.3. Ferdinand Hassler.

Ferdinand Hassler (1770–1843). Few people have heard of Hassler's name-sake, Ferdinand R. Hassler. He was related to Hass through Simon Newcomb: Simon's wife was Mary Caroline Hassler, and her paternal grandfather was Ferdinand Hassler. (Hass's sister Caroline was a namesake of Mary Caroline.) Ferdinand played a critical role when the United States was becoming an important economic power. Trade with other countries meant oceanic shipping, and in those days that involved some 20,000 vessels and 200,000 men. Strong winds and storms would frequently force sailors to take down sails and cast anchor to wait out the weather. Often these ships would drift off course, and when they finally did make it near U.S. shores their captains were often unable to find the actual port of destination because the maps of the day were so unreliable. President Thomas Jefferson saw that if our country expected to continue developing as a trading partner we needed accurate and reliable coastal maps, so in 1807 he asked Congress to establish a national Coast Survey. Requests soliciting the most reliable way to carry out such a survey were distributed to the most qualified scientific minds in the United States. Of the many plans submitted, Ferdinand Hassler's was considered the best. He had been trained by exceptionally able scientists in Europe and had just completed a detailed trigonometric survey of much of Bern, Switzerland. His plan seemed solid and tested. Bureaucratic wheels turned slowly due to inadequate finances and a general lack of appreciation by Congress for the many requirements of the job such as purchasing expensive precision instruments from Europe and training assistants. Hassler had been officially appointed Superintendent of the U.S. Coastal Survey, but only in 1832—during Andrew Jackson's presidency—did actual work begin. Just why did those bureaucratic wheels take over two decades to finally turn?

Part of the answer probably has to do with Hassler's particular personality. He was considered brilliant, eccentric, highly individualistic, and very prickly. Also, outrageously absent-minded. He married a well-educated wife who was friendly, social, and a good singer as well as an excellent pianist. She was also totally unsuited to domestic life. So, for example, Ferdinand took it upon himself to bake the family bread, and with nine children, that meant 11 people. He taught mathematics at Union College in Schenectady, New York, and would sometimes show up to class with white flour all over his coat. Didn't bother him at all.

His mother tongue was German, and he spoke English with a very heavy accent. Here is a snippet of the article "Ferdinand Hasslar—First Superintendent of the Coast Survey" appearing in the March, 1879 issue of *Harper's New Monthly Magazine*. The magazine spells his name Hasslar, but he himself used "Hassler."

…On one occasion a committee from Congress waited upon him in the office to inspect his [Coast Survey] work.

"You come to 'spect my vork, eh? Vat you know 'bout my vork? Vat you going to 'spect?"

The gentlemen, conscious of their ignorance, tried to smooth his ruffled temper by an explanation, which made matters only worse.

"You knows notting at all 'bout my vork. How can you 'spect my vork, ven you knows notting? Get out of here; you in my vay. Congress be von big vool to send you to 'spect my vork. I 'ave no time to vaste vith such as knows notting vat I am 'bout. Go back to Congress and tell dem vat I say."

The committee did "go back to Congress" and report, amid uproarious laughter, the result of their inspecting interview.

When Hon. Levi Woodbury was Secretary of the Treasury under Jackson, he and Hasslar could not agree as to the compensation to be allowed the superintendent, and Hasslar was referred to the President at whose discretion the law placed the settlement of the dispute.

"So, Mr. Hasslar, it appears the Secretary and you can not agree about this matter," remarked Jackson, when Hasslar had stated his case in his usual emphatic style.

"No Sir, ve can't."

"Well, how much do you really think you ought to have?"

"Six tousand dollars, Sir."

"Why, Mr. Hasslar, that is as much as Mr. Woodbury, my Secretary of Treasury, himself receives."

"Mr. Voodbury!" screamed Hasslar, rising from his chair and vibrating his long forefinger toward his own heart. "Pl-e-e-n-ty Mr. Voodburys, pl-e-e-n-ty Mr. Everybodys, for Secretary of de Treasury; v-o-ne, v-o-ne Mr. Hasslar for de head of de Coast Survey!" and erecting himself in a haughty attitude, he looked down upon Jackson in supreme scorn at his daring comparison.

President Jackson, sympathizing with a character having some traits in common with his own, granted Hasslar's demand, and at the close of the next cabinet meeting told the joke, to the great entertainment of the gentlemen present.

Over time, under Mr. Hassler's direction large sections of the east coast were accurately surveyed, at last resulting in reliable maps and far fewer maritime problems. His work has been given well-deserved tributes: In 1870, the Coast Survey ordered the construction of "USCSS Hassler," an iron-hulled survey ship designed for charting waters of the Pacific coast and Alaska (Figure 2.4). Also, in 2012 NOAA commissioned a state-of-the-art, twin-hulled 124-foot coastal mapping vessel, the Ferdinand R. Hassler (Figure 2.5).

Figure 2.4. USCSS Hassler was a three-masted schooner with a 125 horsepower engine. It was built in 1870 on the centennial of Mr. Hassler's birth.

Figure 2.5. The NOAA Ferdinand R. Hassler is a high-tech survey ship equipped with high-resolution scanners that can produce three-dimensional pictures of the sea floor. This research ship not only helps NOAA carry out nautical charting, but aids in mapping marine habitat and finding sunken artifacts.

2.2 Early family influences

One of Hass's fondest memories from early childhood was having fun jumping on his indulgent dad's stomach. Hassler was the second youngest of six living children (not counting firstborn Sylvia, who died in infancy): Bill, Caroline, Simon, Roger, Hassler, and Lisa. Besides his mother, there were three other people who were especially important to Hassler in his early years: Aunt Emily, his sister Caroline—six years older than Hassler—and his brother Roger—two years older than Hassler.

Hassler's Aunt Emily. Hassler's father had three sisters, and it was the middle of them, Aunt Emily, who played an especially big role in Hassler's life. Hassler's father died $2\frac{1}{2}$ months before Hass turned four, and two months before Hassler's sister Lisa was born. The newly widowed mother moved from Cornwall to New Haven where all three sisters lived under a single roof. Her sisters-in-law had no children of their own and they would be a most welcome support system. After all, Josepha had a large family, and Edward had left her with only a small income which was only modestly supplemented through her artwork.

Josepha bought a house within easy walking distance to theirs. Emily was an accomplished pianist; her wonderful playing inspired young Hassler, and he was soon picking out tunes on her piano. Although there was no piano in his own home, fate intervened: One day Josepha was talking to a neighbor, telling him that she had an extra icebox from the move and wanted to sell it. It turned out he needed exactly what she had, but had little money for it. Any chance she might need his piano, which was hanging around, mostly unplayed? A swap was made, and Hass got a baby Steinway grand at home to practice on! His aunt's influence went beyond the piano, for often the house was filled with chamber music, and that evolved into one of Hassler's great loves. Later, he began to study the violin and eventually the two of them would play violin-piano sonatas. She lived to 94. The oldest of the three aunts, Marian, was a professor of German at Vassar. She was determined and conscientious, and even though in those days neither cars nor roads were at all worry-free, she would drive from New Haven to meet her classes in Poughkeepsie 75 miles away, logging several hundred miles each week. She lived to 85.

Hassler's oldest sister, Caroline. Six children grew up in the Whitney family. Caroline was the oldest, and was six when Hassler was born. She formed an especially strong bond with him. She was proud of her brother and was always extremely supportive of him. She was fascinated with his little science projects and encouraged his interest in physics and math. In his early teenage years, Hass was exploring and discovering things—mostly on his own—in what today we call precalculus, and when in Switzerland during that time he wrote long, detailed letters to her describing his day-to-day thoughts, insights, and things he simply wondered about. She served as a vital sounding board for him. She became a Professor of Economics at Columbia University. Like Hass, she was extremely independent-minded: She was the first woman to refuse an invitation to join Phi Beta Kappa, saying that was inappropriate for an economist. Though her married name was Barsky, she always went by her maiden name, a rarity in those days. She died in 1938 from complications of pregnancy.

Hassler's brother, Roger. Hassler's brother Roger was two years older than Hass, and the two were best friends from childhood on. As young teenagers, Roger and Hassler were constant companions in learning to climb Switzerland's inspiring mountains.

Roger ultimately became a physician, and both followed similar academic routes in that they did their undergraduate work at Yale and graduate work at Harvard. The two remained close all their lives, and through the years went on numerous climbs around the world. In many ways their personalities complemented each other: Hass was more the introvert while Roger was more outgoing. As a professional mathematician, Hass mostly worked alone, and nearly all his

Figure 2.6. Caroline feeding Hass.

papers are singly authored. With the exception of close friends and family, he
tended to be somewhat taciturn. Roger made friends easily and very often would
grab pen and paper to write a friendly note to this friend or that, just to say "Hi!"
and ask how things are going. They both enjoyed the outdoors, but Hassler was
drawn more to mountain climbing, while for Roger the appeal was broader. In
addition to mountain climbing, Roger was very much into gardening and grew
flowers and vegetables. A carefully tended compost pile was a thing to treasure.
Both Hass and Roger taught their children what was closest to their heart: Hass
spent time on math with all his children, and all of them were introduced to rock
climbing or mountain climbing as well as music. Roger loved the night sky with
its stars and taught his two children many of the constellations. On winter nights,
he would sometimes awaken them so they could see the Northern Lights in the
early morning hours. He would often build outdoor structures with them, and
these experiences gave his daughter Annie so much confidence that as an adult
she tackled building her own house. She writes that "When we were little, my
brother and I would sit with him in his big blue chair, one on either side, and he
would read to us, night after night, while Mom knitted and listened, too. *The Tall
Book of Make Believe* was a favorite." Hassler's daughter Sally has similar memories: "Dad would read to my sister Emily and me nearly every night before we

Figure 2.7. Hass and Roger at 4 and 6 years, and 35 years later in the Alps.

went to bed. He read the entire Laura Ingalls Wilder series—starting with *Little House in the Big Woods*. Emily and I would sit on either side of him on the sofa and I loved hearing him read to us. When he started this series I couldn't read yet, but by the end I could, and I would sometimes follow along with the words, still really enjoying having him read it." One thing is clear: The two brothers' professional lives were genuine reflections of their inner nature—math and science with Hass and the human caring as a physician with Roger. Sadly, Roger died at age 60 in a mountain-climbing accident in Peru.

2.3 Hassler's other siblings

Figure 2.8 shows all six children in the Josepha Whitney clan.

William. He earned an undergraduate and a Law degree from Yale and initially became a partner in a New York law firm. He later was admitted to the British bar and argued cases in front of both the U.S. Supreme Court and the British House of Lords.

Figure 2.8. Hassler and his siblings, taken about 1920. Left to right: Roger, William, Lisa, Caroline, Hassler, and Simon.

Lisa. She attended Vassar College and became a widely known artist. She worked for a few years in Essex, Connecticut, and finally settled in South Carolina's Myrtle Beach.

Simon. He got an undergraduate degree and a Ph.D. in economics from Yale. His main love was education and teaching. From 1942 to 1948 he was the director of Deep Springs College, a small ranch school in California, and from 1956 to 1961 was the chief economist of the Federal Trade Commission in Washington. He then taught at Rutgers University, New York University, and Iona College.

CHAPTER **3**
Growing Up

Young Hassler's formative years, with stories

3.1 Hassler's first bit of research

Hass learned to multiply numbers when he was about eight or nine. At one point the teacher gave a hint about memorizing the multiplication table: Whenever you multiply by 9, the answer's digits always add up to 9. That is, in any of 9, 18, 27, 36, …, 81, the digits sum to 9. Hassler thought this was amazing.

He began to experiment with 9 times larger numbers such as 9 times 10, 11, 12, 13, …, and found that summing the digits until you get a single digit still always ended up giving 9. He also tried really big numbers, like 9 times 8213, and the phenomenon held even for those. He thought about this for a few days, and finally convinced himself that it was always true, no matter what big integer you multiplied 9 by. In what can aptly be called "curiosity-driven research," he wondered what would happen if he used 8 instead if 9. When he tested the idea by multiplying 1, 2, 3, ... by 8, he discovered that instead of always summing to 9, the sum decreased. That is, 8×1 gives 8, $8 \times 2 = 16$ gives 7, $8 \times 3 = 24$ gives 6, and so on. He obtained an endlessly-repeating cycle: 8, 7, 6, 5, 4, 3, 2, 1, 9, 8, …. When multiplying by 7, he got another sequence that went down by 2: 7, 5, 3, 1, 8, 6, 4, 2, 9, 7, …. Symmetrically, if he multiplied by 10, which is 1 more than 9, the sequence went up by 1: 1, 2, 3, …. Multiplying by 11 (2 more than 9) gave a sequence that increased by 2. Young Hassler was excited by finding these regularities, and he always regarded this as "my first little bit of mathematical research." Over a half-century later he looked back on the experience as distinctly formative, and that somehow he was like a little toy train car that—perhaps accidentally—got placed on tracks and started moving forward. He felt that schools should do more to set youngsters on little tracks so they could move forward, too, and experience some of those same emotions.

Figure 3.1. Hass with his sister Lisa, shortly after his "first little bit of mathematical research." Lisa attended Vassar and, like her mother, became an artist.

3.2 Capturing his imagination

During Hassler's early teens, the magazine *Popular Science* played a large role in his development as a budding scientist. He eagerly awaited each month's issue and would devour its contents. The magazine became for him an important source of ideas, inspiration, and general science information. Each issue ran around 150 pages; it had well-written articles and a good selection of drawings and photographs. The magazine's articles on general science, technology, and practical engineering were meant to inform and inspire. Its formula may not have worked for all, but it certainly did for Hassler. Its articles left lifelong impressions—they introduced new horizons, different ways of viewing the world, and different ways of thinking.

Some of the articles asked, "What if?" What if we had telescopic eyes that could magnify images a thousandfold or more? Others quantified and compared:

How much horsepower does Jack Frost need to spread frost throughout New York City in one night? Another article entitled "How Big Can They Build Them?" talked about building airplanes larger than theory says is possible and exposed an error in applying theory. Other articles connected the unlikely, like a searchlight so powerful that it melts lead. Many of the mental templates used in the articles would informally resurface in his own conversation decades later.

Here are some short condensations of the sort of articles that he read.

Popular Science June 1920

If the Eye Were a Telescope

The magnificent cluster of stars in Hercules, which appears merely as a speck of light, but which to the eye of telescopic power would resemble a bursting rocket. Suns of many colors are in this swarm.

If the Eye Were a Telescope (June, 1920). If the night is dark and very clear, we are able see some 3,000 stars, ranging from bright jewels to just barely discernable flecks of light. Some of those flecks hold great surprises, one example being the Hercules Cluster. If we had telescopic eyes that could magnify a thousand times, we would discover that this almost vanishingly small bit of light is actually a huge globe made up of a vast swarm of stars—many suns like ours, and countless others that are hundreds of times larger. No two suns would have exactly the same temperature, so no two would have exactly the same color. With telescopic eyes, we could also see Saturn with its beautiful rings. If we constantly turn up the telescopic power so our field of vision sees ever tinier portions of the planet, our eyes receive fewer and fewer photons, and what we see eventually fades away to nothingness! And our moon? Seeing it rising would be an unforgettable experience: A gigantic disk majestically rises, and in a few minutes a full moon would nearly fill the sky. It would be hard to believe that such an enormous body could long remain in the sky and not fall toward us. Craters that seemed so small and insignificant to our naked eye become huge and menacing. We could also clearly see the red planet Mars, and during some months of the year we could witness its glistening white icecaps slowly melting away as weeks pass, only to reappear months later.

Rings of dust and meteorites surround the globe Saturn. To see them without a telescope would be one of the greatest sights permitted the eye of man.

If Jack Frost Could Be Put to Work (January, 1921). Jack Frost's job is to make ice. If we look at what he does in New York City alone, his gigantic ice-plant there uses energy 300,000 times faster than man's combined energy use throughout the entire world! The key to making this comparison is using a *unit of energy*, one example being the British Thermal Unit, or BTU. It takes 144 BTUs to melt one pound of ice at 32 degrees. That energy could come from the sun, from a fire, from surrounding water or air. No matter, it's always 144 BTUs that are needed. The reverse is true, too. A perfectly efficient refrigerator needs 144 BTUs of energy to turn one pound of water at 32 degrees into ice. Jack Frost, on the other hand, works on a far grander scale. In 1918, there were four days in which the amount of rain on New York City totaled 1 inch—quite a bit of water because the area of New York is the same as a square 17.5 miles on each side. Think of the water as being one inch deep in a huge pan. Now Jack Frost can easily freeze this pan of water during just a single night. The energy his ice-plant uses for this is staggering—64 trillion BTUs! In making the ice, where does all the energy removed from the pan of water go? Although you might not realize it, that removed energy heats up the surrounding atmosphere. That is, the air warms up somewhat as the water freezes. Jack does his job overnight, so that tells us the *rate* of energy use. If a hundred-pound weight is lifted five and a half feet in one second, that's one horsepower, or 1 HP—a very respectable feat for a well-conditioned man. An automobile with a 90 HP engine is therefore quite strong. An actual calculation shows that Jack Frost, doing an overnight rush job on his pan of water, works at the rate of nearly a *trillion* horsepower—more exactly, 916,403,891,235 HP. That would be equivalent to more than 10 billion 90 HP automobiles using all their capacity to freeze water. All the automobiles in the world don't add up to even a tiny fraction of 10 billion!

How Big Can They Build Them? (October, 1920) During the war [WWI], our government desperately required larger aeroplanes, and aeronautical engineers were instructed to design larger craft, no matter what limitations theory put on size. This at once pitted two huge forces against each other: theory versus practice. Theory says that if you double the size of an aeroplane, increasing every dimension by a factor of two, then the surface area—basic to wing surface and lifting ability—goes up as the square, that is, by $2^2 = 4$, but mass, just like volume, goes up as the *cube*, this often being called the "Law of the Cube."[1] That means doubling the size increases the weight by a factor of $2^3 = 8$. Such a rapid increase in weight puts a serious restriction on aeroplane size, because lifting ability can't keep up with the faster increase in weight. But despite this law, today giant machines of the type the government envisioned now routinely "wet their wings in the misty clouds." What happened? Where did theory go wrong? The answer is that in applying the Law of the Cube, the theoreticians made an unwarranted assumption. The Law of the Cube applies when the larger model is *an exact replica of the original.* That means the shape is exactly the same, and all the materials used are the same, too. But in the practical world, we don't have to make these assumptions! We can use lighter materials and change the shape of the aeroplane to make it more streamlined. That's what the engineers did. They succeeded, with the result that they became more reliable, could carry heavier loads, and fly longer distances. We learned that with theory, we need to keep the underlying assumptions in mind, and that in the real world those assumptions may not always be necessary.

Why Does Iron Rust? (June, 1920)   Of all the metals in the world, iron is the most used and the most useful. In fact without it, civilization as we know it would not be possible. But if not protected, rust can reduce any piece of iron to a useless powder, ruining the largest steel bridge or the mightiest ship. But exactly how does rust occur? What is actually needed to form rust? Iron is a pure element, while rust is a chemical combination of iron and oxygen. There can be varying amounts of oxygen in rust, making different varieties of it, and there can also be other elements involved such as hydrogen or carbon. To begin the rusting process, we need both oxygen and water. Now dry air contains oxygen but no water, so iron won't rust in dry air. A piece of iron could lie in a dry desert for years and not get rusty! At the opposite extreme, pure water with no oxygen dissolved in it will not rust iron, either. Ordinary water from a lake or stream contains oxygen, and fish depend on it to live. But if you drop a piece of iron into a capped jar full of water that has been distilled to remove all oxygen, and if you leave no air pocket at the top, then that iron would remain rust-free indefinitely. One way to prevent rust is to coat the iron with a good barrier against water and oxygen, such as a high quality paint. Another way that has proved successful is to build a very large tank with many layers of thin, perforated iron and slowly pass water through these layers. These layers are there exactly to get rusty, and are replaceable. Making rust requires oxygen, so dissolved oxygen in the entering water gets used up as the water passes through the layers of iron, rusting it on the way. The rusting process takes time, but with a very big tank, water can easily stay in the tank for a day or two, and when it finally does leave the tank, it has very little oxygen left in it. So oxygen in the entering water rusts the replaceable layers of perforated iron instead of the iron pipes in your home!

So Powerful Is This Searchlight that It Melts Lead (June, 1920).   How does a searchlight work? When current passes through a conductor like a piece of wire, it heats the wire somewhat, and if the resistance is greater, it heats it up more. The tungsten filament in the newer light bulbs has a great deal of resistance, and passing house current through the filament heats it so much that it becomes white hot, giving off light. When you turn on a searchlight, the "filament" starts off as two touching carbon rods that vaporize some carbon where they touch. The rods are gradually separated up to about four inches, the arc between their ends still conducting current and giving off a tremendous amount of light—much more than a tungsten filament. As the carbon vaporizes the gap between the rods increases, so the rods must be continually slowly moved together to keep the separation at only four inches. The intense light rays emanate from the arc in all directions, and these are reflected off the searchlight's parabolic mirror to create a straight beam of light. This beam is so intense that objects even miles away can be illuminated or "searched for." Early models generated nearly six million candlepower, equivalent to about six million candles all burning at once, but an inventor, Mr. Elmer Sperry, has improved the design by more precisely aligning the two rods, and in addition making them rotate along their long axis so the carbon is burned off more evenly. He now has a searchlight generating over a *billion* candlepower. If you place a bar of lead in the beam's path 12 feet away from the arc, the beam will melt the lead!

35 miles. In May of 1921, 14-year-old Hassler traveled to Switzerland with his mother and younger sister Lisa for a two-year stay. His brother Roger was already there, and the three other siblings, all older, were by that time living independently. Hassler kept a diary to record events, feelings, and impressions during the exciting trip. He noted facts, numbers, comparisons, and conversions. He was tremendously fascinated with the awesome steamship *Orbita* that carried them across the Atlantic, and his diary provides a look at how his mind worked. He notes that the ship was "over 550 feet long and nearly 70 feet wide, weighed over 15,500 gross tons, and its engines generated some 18,000 horsepower. The engine room was 30 feet below the water, and there was a huge staircase going from a glass-topped ceiling down to the bottom of the engine room." In a letter to his aunts dated May 29, 1921, he repeats this information and includes a detailed drawing of the cross-section of the staircase and engine room, reporting that he made the trip all the way to the bottom, where it was unbelievably hot. Back up on deck, he calculates that it would take a line of horses 35 miles long to generate the same power that the ship's engines do. He learns that the ship uses 120 tons of fresh water each day, and converts that, saying it would take a person 250 years to drink that much water. He is taking large numbers and converting them into dramatic visual terms.

3.3 Life in Switzerland

Hassler's mother Josepha believed it was important for her children to have exposure to the wider world and see other ways of life. As for Hassler's education, the idea was that he would learn French the first year, German the second, and continue his piano lessons both years. Hass did in fact become fluent in both languages and once commented that at one time he spoke French better than

English. But the Hassler you see in the passport photo in Figure 3.2 had another, far more intense goal. He dreamed of climbing the beautiful Swiss Alps with his brother Roger, and he was already absorbing as much information as he could about them from as many sources as he could find.

Figure 3.2. Passport photo with Josepha and sister Lisa, when Hass was 14. Hass was headed to Switzerland for a two-year stay, and at the time of this photograph was eagerly looking forward to climbing in the Alps.

He had carefully studied other climbers' routes, the kinds of difficulties each route posed, and various reports of various climbers' experiences. Hassler's mother, always supportive, made an important contact: Gaston Clerc in Switzerland was an experienced mountain climbing coach who thoroughly "knew the ropes." It was arranged for him to give both Hassler and Roger climbing lessons. He also gave Hass French lessons the first year. The contact was especially fortuitous because Clerc's wife was an accomplished pianist and give Hassler piano lessons during his two years in Switzerland.

3.4 Some math in Switzerland

From early on, Hass was attracted to numbers, quantity, and measuring things. Letters from his teenage years were filled with references to the depth of snowfall, the time it took to hike a certain route, and the altitude of various mountains. He

Figure 3.3. Here's Hass, above his coach Gaston Clerc. This candid photo was taken shortly after Hass arrived in Switzerland.

kept a dairy and faithfully noted how long he slept each night. Numbers and measurement were very central to his nature. It is no surprise, then, that when his sister Caroline gave Hass a slide rule as a going-away gift before he left for Switzerland, the rule seemed absolutely magical to him. How could its sliders with numbers marked on them actually multiply numbers? The instructions that came with the slide rule were clear about how to use it, but not at all clear about why it worked. The instructions did mention logarithms, and he knew the most basic thing about them: If x and y are two numbers, then

$$\log xy = \log x + \log y.$$

He eventually concluded that the x and y must be the actual numbers printed on the sliders, and that $\log x$ and $\log y$ must be physical distances. Because the total length of two straight sticks abutting each other is the sum of the sticks' lengths, that must correspond to the "+" in $\log x + \log y$. An example of his basic logic is depicted in Figure 3.4: To multiply 2 times 3, put the left edge of the top slider over the "2" on the bottom scale. As the picture suggests, the physical distance from "1" to "2" is log 2. In the same way, the physical distance from "1" to "3" is log 3, and by moving the slider so as to effectively abut two sticks, their total length is log 2 + log 3. According to the basic log formula, this length log 2 + log 3 is also log(2 · 3), or log 6, and any printed number x is at distance log x from the beginning. So it's the printed "6"—the answer—that's at that distance log 6.

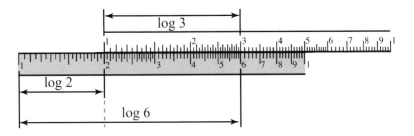

Figure 3.4. Multiplying 2 times 3 using a slide rule.

log 2

Once in Switzerland, his curiosity about the slide rule led to further thought, and his understanding of it began to grow. He realized that the results are never perfectly accurate, because you can see only so closely, and besides that, the scale lines have thickness to them—the magic rule has limitations! Could *he*, Hassler, do better than the slide rule? He decided that accurately finding log 2 would be an excellent test of his own powers. According to the slide rule, it should be a little over 0.3, but how much over? Was there some way to find the value exactly, getting a better answer than his slide rule could? He cooked up a plan of attack. If you multiply 2 by itself a bunch of times to get 2^n, then the logarithm of that is n log 2, while if you multiply 10 by itself a bunch of times to get 10^m, that has a very simple logarithm, just m. His strategy was to keep doubling 2 until you get some 10^m. At that point, n log 2 = m means that log 2 = m/n. But as he doubled 2 over and over again, he realized that the last digit cycles on forever as 2, 4, 8, 6, 2, 4, 8, 6, …. On the other hand, any 10^m ends with all zeros, so his plan hit a wall. He certainly didn't know this observation essentially proves that log 2 is irrational! Seeing that he couldn't obtain an exact answer, he backtracked to getting a good approximation. He got somewhat close when n is 10, 20, 30, 40, but after filling page after page with powers of 2 and always missing his goal of beating the slide rule, he finally gave up. He really tangled with this problem and gained a lot of respect for it. Increasingly things were happening in math that seemed mysterious to him.

He frequently wrote to Caroline about such matters. She was his favorite sounding board as his imagination roamed around numbers and other mathematical ideas. In one letter to her he mused: "What are the logarithms of negative numbers? Do they have any relation to imaginary numbers? If they haven't, I should think they would be pretty useful anyway." Later, he began to wonder why certain graphs have "excluded regions." Even the parts to the left and right of a circle's plot are excluded, aren't they? Is it because of imaginary numbers, again?[2] He was meeting more and more mysteries, and his subconscious was becoming prepared for answers.

Graphs and a bug. It delighted Hass to see that abstract combinations of symbols as in polynomials could be pictured geometrically. He would make up a polynomial and use his slide rule to compute points on its graph, then connect the points to get the full graph. When he stumbled upon $y = 1/x$, something weird happened—the graph (a hyperbola) broke up into two parts. Could he make up things to plot that broke up into *three* parts? Or even more parts? In a long letter to Caroline written over a few days, he chronicled his progress in this, and his understanding was clearly growing. A little later he stumbled upon a different idea: Replace y by y^2. Now, suddenly, the graph is symmetric about the x-axis. In exploring this idea, he happened to plot $y^2 = x^3 + x^2$, and to his surprise, he found it looked like a bug's head together with two antennae coming out! He'd been fascinated by bugs and crawly things for some time, and now an equation could replicate some of that. He was on a roll, and wanted some way to give the bug a body. He eventually realized that if you plot $f(x, y) = 0$ and $g(x, y) = 0$, then the union of the two plots is given by the plot of $fg = 0$. So by appropriately multiplying equations, he was able to add an ellipse-shaped body to the head, as shown in Figure 3.5. Using this same idea, he could add small circles or ellipses to represent dots of the kind you see on a ladybug.

3.5 Mostly a handbook

Hass returned to the States in 1923 and had just one more year before college. His hankering for measuring things now extended to finding lengths of various curves. By this time he knew that calculus could help in finding lengths, areas, and volumes. He owned a calculus book, but never had the slightest inclination to sit down and read it or do exercises in it. For him, the book was a resource, a handbook that he could use to help solve problems that interested him. One such problem he thought about was this: "If an ant crawls along one arch of the sine curve $y = \sin \pi x$, how far has it traveled?" After setting up the correct integral, he found that nowhere in the table of integrals at the back of the book was there anything that could solve the problem for him. He ended up with an approximation, using his slide rule to get the lengths of small pieces of the curve

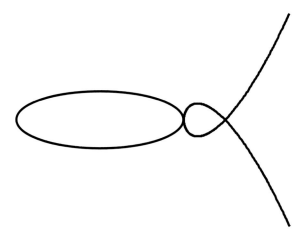

Figure 3.5. Through experimentation, Hass found that if he chose polynomials $f = y^2 - (x^3 + x^2)$ and $g = (x+3)^2 + (4y)^2 - 4$, then $fg = 0$ gave him this "bug," made up of an alpha-shaped curve for its head and antennae, together with an ellipse for the body. The bug's equation is therefore the product of f and g, $[y^2 - (x^3 + x^2)][(x+3)^2 + (4y)^2 - 4] = 0$.

and adding them up. Experiences of this sort made him quite a bit wiser than students who would read about arc length, do the book's problems, get the right answers, take a test and receive an "A". He once said, "They come away thinking they can find arc lengths! Gee, the book carefully avoids problems where things don't work out, so the students see only those rare examples where things can be solved nicely. They can go the rest of their life having a totally unrealistic view."

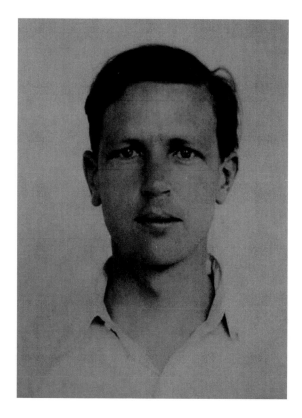

Figure 3.6. Hass shortly before entering Yale.

CHAPTER 4
Hassler Goes to College

As a physics undergraduate, a life in mathematics was totally off his radar screen, and during that time Hass actually took just one math course. After graduating, he had a crisis of confidence in physics and realized he needed a plan B for his life. Plan B? Try math in graduate school.

4.1 Professor Pierpont

Hass entered Yale in 1924 when he was 17 and characteristically tried to leapfrog whenever possible. He figured he should start with Calculus II instead of Calculus I. After all, he had already used his calculus book to help him solve a good number of problems that he had found interesting. All he needed was a signature from James Pierpont, the mathematics department chairman and at that time the most distinguished name in mathematics at Yale. He approached Pierpont and handed him the form to be signed. "Certainly not!" Pierpont roared, "You start with Calculus I like anyone else!" Defeated, Hass slinked away, hoping that somehow the great man might just forget the incident. As it turned out, he did. But Hass never took Calculus I. Or Calculus II. Or any other calculus. After all, he was a physics major, not a math major. For some years his sister Caroline had seen Hass working on real-world and physical problems, and shortly before entering Yale, she said, "Hass, you're so good at physics, I think Physics I would be a waste of time for you!" and encouraged him to enroll directly in Physics II. This involved a placement examination, which he took. The exam asked almost no questions about things he knew, and it seemed there was a good chance he hadn't passed. He enrolled in Physics II anyway, and sat at the back of the class, hoping no one would notice him.

He always expected the professor would approach him, saying that he needed to withdraw from the class. After a few weeks and feeling a bit safer, he got up the nerve and asked if he was still in the class. He got his answer: "There was no way we could pass you on that exam, but you seem to be doing OK in this class, so I decided to let you stay." So that was that. As a physics major, Hass took lots of physics courses, but never Physics I.

Fast forward to 1928, his senior year. It turned out that Professor Pierpont was giving a graduate course in complex variables. The famous man had a reputation for being a forceful, clear, and entertaining lecturer, and questions Hass had wondered about years ago—things like logarithms of negative numbers and those mysterious "excluded regions" he encountered in plotting certain curves—all these mysteries seemed to center around imaginary numbers. He still had no solid answers, and it seemed that Pierpont's course might be just the thing! This time there was no form for Pierpont to sign, so having taken absolutely no math courses at Yale, Hass enrolled in the course.

Pierpont didn't seem to remember him, and that was good. Besides, it was a graduate course, and that usually meant no exams. One day, however, Pierpont happened to ask one student where he studied mathematics. "Johns Hopkins" comes the answer. "Ah, so it's really not your fault. It's your former teachers." Then he gets on a jag, and asks student after student, even Miss Kool, the gorgeous Chinese student. Then he looks right at Hass and asks "And you?" The ax was falling: Hass had taken zero math courses at Yale or any other college. He stammered out what seemed to be the safest answer: "I—I—I studied by myself." Pierpont immediately went into roaring mode: "You studied by yourself! THAT'S the way to learn! Look at Riemann—how did he learn mathematics? He studied by himself. Look at Weierstrass[1] —how did *he* learn? He studied by himself. That's how you really learn mathematics, studying by yourself!" Hass could hardly believe his ears. What Pierpont just said was softening years of guilt. He was getting it from the top, that his approach to math wasn't so awful after all.

A week or so later, another ax fell: Pierpont gave a homework assignment due the very next class meeting. The assignment: Give an example of a function that wasn't analytic. Hass had no idea what an analytic function was, except for a vague notion that it had something to do with being smooth, like the way the graph of a polynomial looks, with no jumps or angles. It seemed that a function having a jump or angle somewhere ought to work, but Pierpont would certainly never ask a question that obvious, and if Hass turned in an answer like that, he'd probably be the only one with an answer that dumb—all those other kids had taken a bunch of math courses. Somehow, Hass had to cover himself. He got the idea that if he came up with a function that was nowhere smooth, he might survive another day. He reasoned, "It ought to be bad at every point. Suppose I make it have jumps. Well, I can't have big jumps everywhere, but it could jump at every integer or something like that. And then, why don't I put in more jumps—smaller jumps in the middle of them." So he started putting in smaller jumps in the middle, and then passed to the limit in the x-direction. He wrote up his argument as carefully as he could, and handed it in. At the next class meeting, Pierpont walks in with the graded homework, and goes directly to Hass. He has this faraway look, and begins, "Mr. Whitney, you ought to be studying real variables with Wilson. I have never before seen an example worked out like this. This is pure genius!" There were no exams, and Hass got through the course intact. The course grading system was on a 400-point scale. When he finally got up the nerve to open the envelope containing the course grade, he saw that Pierpont had given him 400. Later, when Hass was teaching at Harvard, every so often he would visit Pierpont at his home, and they always had a pleasant chat. Never, ever, did Hass remind Pierpont of that very first encounter about skipping Calculus I.

4.2 For Hassler, a road less traveled

At Yale, Hassler majored in music as well as physics. He had earned his degree in physics, but wanted one in music as well. That took him another year of undergraduate work.

> Classical music was a huge part of Whitney's life. He initially studied the piano, but after being greatly moved upon hearing a late Beethoven string quartet, he decided he wanted to play in a string quartet. Although he had studied the violin for a time, he now began to focus on it seriously, and somewhat later he took up the viola. In those days Hassler also did a great deal of composing, and as a teenager he even directed some school stage productions. When he was 21, his *Fantasie for Orchestra* won a monetary award for the year's best original composition at Yale. That extra year spent getting a music degree proved to be far more consequential than Hass had ever guessed: His memory for facts in physics had never been outstanding, and during that additional year he forgot even more of his undergraduate physics—something that soon persuaded him to shift his direction in life.

But he'd made his career choice—theoretical physics—and had been accepted into the Harvard Graduate School in physics. Before starting the program, he decided to spend three weeks in the summer of 1930 to breathe in and absorb the atmosphere of physics and mathematics in Göttingen, Germany. As a sophomore he'd taken a graduate course entitled "General Theory of Mathematical Physics" and had kept his voluminous notes filling up five binders. He took these with him since it seemed that refamiliarizing himself with them would give him a running start at Harvard. He felt comfortable in Göttingen and immediately made friends with the not-yet-famous Paul Dirac. The two shared time puzzling over

Figure 4.1. A physicist here, a mathematician a few weeks later. This is the 1930 passport photo taken before his fateful trip to Germany.

little problems in number theory. After a week of enjoying himself, it was time to blitz through those five binders. Day 1: He was astonished to discover he had forgotten nearly everything in the notes. Day 2: Things still weren't coming back to him. Day 3: Ditto, but he still had nearly two weeks. After additional days of struggling, a horrible reality was beginning to descend upon him: In physics, you have to remember stuff, and it seemed he actually had no head for that. Half way through the second week, he essentially threw up his hands in despair and asked himself, "What am I gonna do?" He definitely wasn't enjoying this, and he began taking serious stock of himself. What were his stellar moments? His worst moments? Certainly the top man in the Yale math department saying that he was learning mathematics the same right way that Riemann and Weierstrass did, and telling the class that the everywhere-discontinuous function he invented was "pure genius"—those were big, stellar moments. His worst moments were in required history courses. He had nightmares about not being able to remember things for an upcoming history exam. (These actually continued for years.) And what did he really love to do? A fellow student at Yale had once mentioned the four-color problem, stating that using at most four colors, you can color any map so that neighboring countries always have different colors. It absolutely fascinated him, and he greatly enjoyed thinking about the problem in odd moments. It grew into a sort of recreation. Plus, no one had ever solved it, so there was a carrot dangling in front of him. Looking back on what he was good at and what he enjoyed, it seemed that thinking about mathematics problems was a possibility. After perhaps the most uncomfortable few days in his life, Hassler made a decision: He would embark on a road all but untravelled by him: His life would be in mathematics, not physics. Toward the end of his career he reminisced, "I have always regretted my quandary, but never regretted my decision."

Deciding on a career in mathematics wasn't the only major development for Hass in 1930. He also married Margaret Howell. She was nicknamed "Brock" as a child, liked it, and as an adult always used that nickname. She was a multi-talented Radcliffe music student with a gift for architecture. She designed several houses in the area where she and Hass eventually settled down, including their own. They had three children: James, Carol, and Molly. James became a mathematician and a developer of geometric software used in computer-aided design. Carol became an ethnomusicologist and more recently a specialist in canine behavior. Molly studied physical chemistry and has spent 40 years defending sustainability and consumer interest against the growth agenda of the electricity monopolies in her adopted country of New Zealand.

Figure 4.2. Hass married Brock in 1930.

CHAPTER 5
Early Days at Harvard

After seeing that he and physics were not an ideal match, as a mathematics grad student Hass followed his heart and pursued his love—the four-color problem. In doing this, he discovered an inner talent: By considering numerous concrete examples and organizing his results, he found he was able to formulate and prove theorems. His eventual Ph.D. thesis results got published in important journals.

Once at Harvard, Hass began thinking intensely about the four-color problem. He put it into a different form: He replaced each colored country by a colored capital, with two countries being contiguous exactly when there was a road between their capitals that passed through no other country. Essentially, he was thinking about "colored graphs." In this form the goal was to color the capitals using at most four colors so that the road between neighboring countries would always connect differently colored capitals. The four-color problem had totally grabbed him, and although he enrolled in courses and attended them, his real effort was spent thinking about his absolute favorite problem.

5.1 George Birkhoff

Hass worked by himself for many weeks on the problem, making countless drawings. He drew capitals using colored pencils, wrote down observations, organized them, drew conclusions, made conjectures, tested them, and proved some results that appeared to be new.

Of course his main aim in going to graduate school was to get a Ph.D., and he needed an advisor for that. He asked around and soon learned that George Birkhoff fit the bill—Birkhoff had done some work on the four-color problem. So Hass paid him a visit and showed him the results he had obtained. Birkhoff immediately saw that Hassler, completely on his own, had come up with some insights that Birkhoff himself had totally missed. Birkhoff in turn shared with Hass some of his own insights he'd gotten earlier, and the two fell into a symbiotic friendship. Hass says in a letter, "Birkhoff, more than anyone else in the world, thinks the same way I do." Every so often, Hass would drop by and show Birkhoff

43

his latest results. After a while, Hassler felt he'd progressed far enough on the problem to warrant writing up his results as his thesis. Birkhoff went over the top with enthusiasm: "With what the two of us have here, I estimate there's a one in five chance that we'll prove the four-color conjecture!" Hass was more cautious, and felt a proof was at least 50 years away. He wasn't far off—Appel and Haken announced their computer proof in 1976, just 46 years after Whitney's guesstimate. The two crucial Appel-Haken papers, totaling nearly 140 pages, appeared in 1977 in the *Illinois Journal of Mathematics* ([**AH1**], [**AH2**]).

Figure 5.1. Hassler around the time he wrote his four-color papers.

Upon receiving his Ph.D. Hassler got invaluable input about his next step. Birkhoff advised him, "Write up the high points of your work right away, and submit it to the *Proceedings of the National Academy of Sciences.* Neither of us would want someone to anticipate your results. Then, after that, write up a more complete account with full proofs, and submit that to the *Annals.*" Hass had his work cut out for him, but by following his inner urgings and arriving at new results about a problem he loved thinking about, he ended up with two papers in those excellent journals. Earlier, Birkhoff had gotten him an Instructorship at Harvard paying $3,000 for the year. Now, he wrote an exceptionally strong letter recommending Hass to the position of Assistant Professor at Harvard for the three years 1934–1936, with wages of $4,000, $4,300 and $4,600—not bad numbers in those days.

Figure 5.2. Hassler's thesis advisor, George Birkhoff.

Hass got an apartment near campus with room for a piano. He learned to cook in a very rudimentary way, and turned a daily regimen of scrambled eggs and peas into theorems. His teaching schedule consisted of just a calculus course and one on differential equations. Hass had launched. No longer was he a scared student sitting at the back of the room, afraid to be noticed.

During this period Whitney bought a Corona typewriter, writing to his mother how pleased he was to get $10 off because it had been slightly used as a floor model. Over the next three decades, papers that transformed chunks of mathematics were written on this bargain machine.

Whitney worked very intensely during this period. His head was filled with ideas that he struggled with to transform into theorems. He wrote mathematics quickly, and he apologized in a letter to his mother that doing this was proving ruinous to his handwriting. (Actually, it never got any better.) He would work at an almost feverish pace for long periods, then fall into a solid sleep of 10 or more hours. During one winter, he commented that "The only exercise I get is running around looking at different thermometers, and opening and closing windows for fresh air."

Figure 5.3. Teaching a differential equations class at Harvard.

CHAPTER 6

The Four-Color Problem: Some History and Whitney's Contributions to It

This chapter gives some history of the four-color problem and a short sketch of what Hassler himself accomplished during his graduate years.

6.1 A little history of the four-color problem

To state the four-color problem (today a theorem!), let's make some definitions:

Definition. A *map* is a division of the plane or the sphere into connected, non-overlapping regions that we call *countries*, and we'll say that two countries are *contiguous* if they share a common border containing at least a topological arc.[1] The four-color conjecture then says:

> **Any map can be colored with at most four colors so that contiguous countries never receive the same color.**[2]

In 1852, a 21-year-old law student Francis Guthrie was coloring a map of the counties of England, shown in Figure 6.1. (Counties there are analogous to states in the U.S.) He realized that he could color that map with no more than four colors, and—after some experimentation—the same seemed true for any other map. He had recently taken courses from the well-known mathematician, logician, and beloved teacher Augustus De Morgan, and had great respect for him. Since his brother Frederick was currently enrolled in one of De Morgan's classes, Francis sent his observation to De Morgan via Frederick. De Morgan had never heard of this map-making conjecture and it was right then that the problem caught fire.[3] No counterexample seemed to occur to De Morgan, and within a day, he wrote to his colleague and mathematical powerhouse Sir William Rowan Hamilton about it.

Hamilton wrote back that he wouldn't be working on the problem anytime soon—perhaps his lightening-quick mind did not see an obvious proof or counterexample. But De Morgan continued mentioning the problem to others, and a

Figure 6.1. The map that started it all.

number of mathematicians spent time on it, including the American mathematician and logician Charles Sanders Peirce who gave the problem serious thought during the 1860s and remained interested in it for the rest of his life.

De Morgan also found a receptive ear in Arthur Cayley, who thought about the problem on and off for several years. After more than a quarter century, Cayley had gained a number of insights but no solution. Finally, at a meeting of the London Mathematical Society in 1878, he asked whether anyone had in fact solved the four-color problem. Nobody there had, and no one knew anyone who had. So the next year Cayley himself published a paper outlining some of the difficulties he had encountered in trying to settle the conjecture, and gave some advice on how it might be approached. Later that year Alfred Kempe (1849–1922) became inspired by Cayley's paper and developed the method that has evolved into what we today call "Kempe chains." He used this method to at last—apparently—prove the four-color problem. Cayley liked what he saw and suggested Kempe publish the paper in the *American Journal of Mathematics.* Kempe did, and subsequently found two simpler arguments resulting in two more papers. Kempe thereby gained a good measure of fame and it seemed that the Four-Color Beast had at last been conquered.

A few years after Kempe's three papers, the young English mathematician Percy Heawood became enamored of the problem and carefully studied Kempe's work. By 1890 Heawood, then 28, realized that Kempe had failed to account for one possibility in using his chains, and that single observation meant, quite simply, that the whole proof came crashing down. In his paper, Heawood was almost apologetic for uncovering the problem, and Kempe saw right away that he had indeed spotted a serious gap. Finding that he was unable to salvage his proof, Kempe concluded that the problem Heawood spotted was fatal—his "11-year-old proof" was never a proof. Much of Kempe's standing has been restored through the years: His chains can be used to solve the five-color problem, and they turn out to play an essential role in the eventual computer-aided proof of the four-color problem.

As for Heawood, he devoted much of the rest of his 93-year life to cracking the four-color problem. He did in fact rigorously and correctly prove that five colors work. But four? That remained beyond anybody's reach at the time.

The four-color problem has to do with maps on a sheet of paper, or on a globe that can be punctured and then topologically stretched out so it lies on a plane. A map that can be topologically drawn on a plane is called *planar* and forms a graph, likewise called planar. The boundaries of the map's countries are edges, and points where three or more different boundaries meet are vertices.

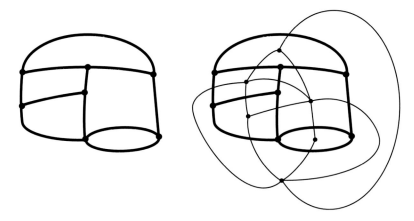

Figure 6.2. The heavily drawn lines are the boundaries of hypothetical countries. As a simplification, instead of coloring countries often having very jagged borders, we can represent the country by just its capital—a single point, or vertex within the country—and color that. By running a road between the capitals of bordering countries, we create the "dual" of the original map, in which the road is an edge of the dual graph. The coloring problem is thus tranformed into assigning colors to the vertices of a graph in such a way that any two vertices connected by an edge have different colors. In constructing the dual, the area surrounding all the countries (think "ocean," for example) is also regarded as a country with a capital. The graph with lightly drawn edges is the dual of the graph with heavily drawn edges.

Gabriel A. Dirac was a mathematics professor in Denmark, and in a 1963 entry of *The Journal of the London Mathematical Society* he wrote of Percy Heawood: "In his appearance, manners and habits of thought, Heawood was an extravagantly unusual man. He had an immense moustache and a meagre, slightly stooping figure. He usually wore an Inverness cape of strange pattern and manifest antiquity, and carried an ancient handbag. His walk was delicate and hasty, and he was often accompanied by a dog, which was admitted to his lectures. His transparent sincerity, piety and goodness of heart, and his eccentricity and extraordinary blend of naiveté and shrewdness secured for him not only the fascinated interest, but also the regard and respect of his colleagues."

Whitney recognized that the four-color problem came down to studying special sorts of graphs—planar ones. However, a planar graph may have edges crossing at nonvertex points. These are sometimes called "accidental crossings"—a square with its two diagonals is a basic example—but a graph being planar means you can topologically redraw it, always maintaining the original vertex-edge relationships, so that the new graph no longer has accidental crossings. However, not all graphs are planar—Figure 6.3 shows an example of each kind, planar and nonplanar.

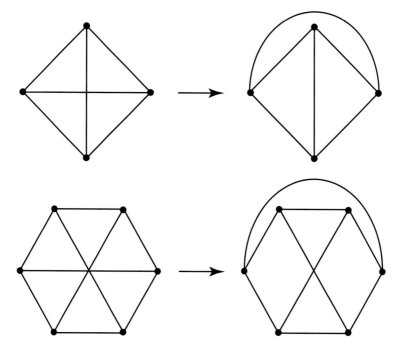

Figure 6.3. The top graph has an accidental crossing, but the graph is planar, since stretching the horizontal edge over the top vertex removes the accidental crossing. The bottom graph also has an accidental crossing, but it turns out that despite any amount of edge stretching, an accidental crossing always remains, meaning the graph is nonplanar.

6.2 What did Hassler accomplish?

In studying graphs, Whitney established several new and important results leading to his Ph.D. thesis. Here are descriptions of three of them. More details for all three results appear in the next chapter.

He gave a criterion for a graph to be planar—that is, drawable in a plane with no accidental crossings. Maps of countries are essentially planar graphs, but because there are many nonplanar graphs, it's important to have a way of deciding whether a graph is planar or not. The first criterion for planarity was discovered by the Polish mathematician Kazimierz Kuratowski (1896–1980) who published his criterion in 1930. Whitney discovered a quite different criterion two years later, and both are important in graph theory. Whitney's planarity criterion essentially says that a graph G is planar if and only if it has a "combinatorial dual," a concept introduced by him and defined on p. 68. His criterion means that if a graph has a combinatorial dual, it is an appropriate graph to study vis-a-vis the four-color problem. Conversely, any graph associated with a map of countries is guaranteed to have a combinatorial dual. It turns out that the definitions of combinatorial dual given on p. 68 insure that the top graph in Figure 6.3 has a combinatorial dual, and that the bottom graph doesn't.

He discovered a big class of cyclic graphs. Whitney knew that working on the four-color problem meant making progress in graph theory, so he set about exploring it. He did some reading and research on what was known, and did his own thing in what was already classic Whitney style: Draw lots of pictures, explore countless examples, and organize results. There was one interesting problem that seemed to have only scattered answers: "What graphs have Hamiltonian cycles?" In a graph, planar or not, a Hamiltonian path is a connected route of edges going from vertex to vertex in such a way that all vertices are visited *exactly* once. If there's a closed path or loop visiting each vertex just once, that path is called a Hamiltonian *cycle*, and one can call such graphs "cyclic." These paths and cycles are named after the brilliant Irish mathematician Sir William Rowan Hamilton who studied them and subsequently devised what he called the "icosian game": Find a Hamiltonian cycle for the 30-edge graph comprising the skeleton of a dodecahedron (a polyhedron with 12 faces). Like Rubik's Cube, the game has solutions, but they're not easy for the beginner to find. Not all graphs have Hamiltonian cycles, but Whitney wondered if he could find some large class of graphs that do. His answer was yes. In fact he found a very large class, and his success represented a breakthrough in graph theory.

He greatly simplified calculating Birkhoff's chromatic polynomials. Whitney's Ph.D. advisor George Birkhoff, in his late twenties, asked, "In how many different ways can we color a map using n colors?" Birkhoff found that the answer is always given by a polynomial function, and he called it the graph's "chromatic polynomial." Since this polynomial captures some of the essential information in a graph, he hoped that because our knowledge about polynomials is so vast, there could be a chance that bringing this knowledge to bear on the four-color problem might yield important progress. He worked out formulas for the coefficients of the polynomial for any graph G, but his formulas require looking at each subgraph of G, so if there are n edges in the graph, that means looking at 2^n subgraphs. Therefore actually calculating G's polynomial often imposed a virtually insurmountable problem since a graph with, say, 15 edges would entail examining $2^{15} = 32,768$ subgraphs. Birkhoff's formulas did, however, help in establishing several central properties about graphs. Whitney's big contribution was finding a way to drastically reduce the number of subgraphs that required checking. Along with that, he uncovered unsuspected and enlightening geometric meaning to those coefficients. We say more about this in the next chapter.

CHAPTER 7
Whitney and the Four-Color Problem: A Closer Look

We now give more detail on the four-color problem and the progress Hass made on it during his graduate years. This period was formative for him, and this chapter sheds light on how working on this problem was basic to his developing the "classic Whitney style" of research. Since the chapter contains more detailed mathematics, the reader may wish to skip it. That won't disrupt the overall narrative of the story.

7.1 Early results of Hassler

Take a map with any finite number of countries. Instead of drawing it on a piece of paper, suppose we draw it on a flat sheet of rubber. We can stretch, shrink, twist, or otherwise topologically contort the piece of rubber, yet all the essential information about any coloring of the map is preserved. Here, *topological* means two things:

- "Separated points remain separated." To a topologist this means that in contorting, we don't let distinct points come together and touch, as would happen if, say, we pinched together the north and south poles of a rubber sphere, or squeezed its equator down to a point.
- "Near together points stay near together." This means that in contorting, we don't rip the piece of rubber and just leave it that way. It *is* OK to sew the ripped edges back together exactly, as when a Möbius strip is cut along its short dimension, one edge given a 360° twist, and then reattached.

The four-color problem is topological—any coloring of a map on a piece of rubbery paper is basically unchanged when we topologically contort it. Countries' borders and the points where different borders meet form a graph before and after the change. Officially, at the abstract level, a *graph* consists of a set of vertices (or *nodes*) and a set of unordered pairs of these vertices. At the concrete level, a *graph drawing* is a drawing in which each point is represented by, say, a dot, and an unordered pair of vertices is represented by an arc or line segment connecting the two points of the pair. This is the sense of graph we'll always use:

When we say "graph," we will always mean a graph drawing.

If a graph can be drawn in the plane so there are no accidental crossings (see p. 51), then the graph is called *planar*. In a planar graph with no accidental crossings, the edges naturally form borders of connected regions, and if we call those regions countries, then we're looking at a map. In this way, planar graphs are by nature two-dimensional. Of course we're interested in coloring those countries and as mentioned in Figure 6.2, we can convert a map with colored countries into a graph with colored vertices by taking the dual. This tremendously simplifies matters since a point is much easier to deal with than a country with possibly jagged edges and weird shape, and edges in the dual can be taken to be straight lines or simple arcs.

Here's a little more detail: Make a dot inside each country (always assumed connected) to represent its capital, and if the map has been colored, color the dot the same as the color of the country. For any two countries sharing some common part of their borders, construct a road between their capitals that transversally crosses that common part. These capitals and roads themselves form a graph, and if we've included colors, it's called a *colored graph*. For any noncolored graph, "doing the capital-roads thing" turns out to be a *duality*. For graphs, this means that when we take the new graph and do the capital-roads thing to *it*, we end up with a graph that is topologically the same as the original one, a truly remarkable property of planar graphs. Dualities are ubiquitous as well as tremendously important in mathematics, and many of them have played a big part in Whitney's work. We'll shake hands with a couple more in a moment, but it is now time for some examples of planar graphs and their duals. For now, all graphs will be uncolored.

Examples. Figure 7.1—a slightly fancier version of Figure 6.2—depicts a planar graph having seven vertices and 11 edges and can be looked at as a map of five countries. The area outside the graph is an ocean or a very large landmass and forms a sixth country. This graph could equally well be drawn on a sphere, the size of the ocean or surrounding land mass being larger or smaller depending on the size of the sphere relative to the graph. Since we're looking at things through a topological lens, size isn't relevant. What *does* matter is that in forming the dual to this graph, the surrounding ocean or landmass, which counts as a country, has a capital. The top right drawing shows the construction of the dual; for clarity, it has thinner arcs. Each original country gets exactly one dot or capital, and these six dots are connected by 10 thin arcs (roads) transversely intersecting common boundaries between adjacent countries.

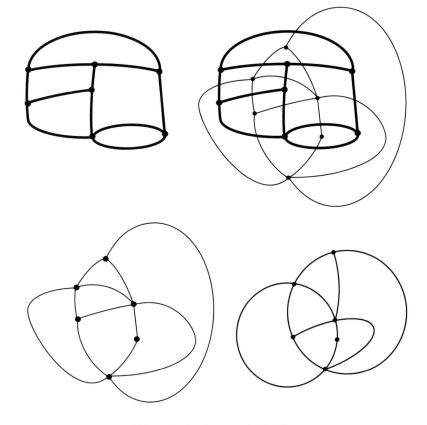

Figure 7.1. Geometric duality.

Counting the surrounding ocean or landmass, this dual graph has seven countries. The dual has been drawn separately in the lower left picture of Figure 7.1, and the lower right picture just neatens up that drawing a bit. We can play this sequence backward to see how the dual of the dual gives the original. The crucial step is in the top right picture. Notice that the capital of the dual's surrounding landmass is the top leftmost heavy dot of the original graph. But this original graph, drawn more heavily, satisfies all the conditions in forming the dual of the dual! We can therefore regard the top left drawing as the original graph, or as the dual of the dual of that original graph. If we wanted or needed to, we could regard either of the lower graphs as the original, and then they would be the dual of their duals.

Graphs have wide use in modeling, and Figure 7.2 is a basic example illustrating this. The figure shows duality applied to a pure series graph, which is drawn more heavily. The lightly drawn graph is its dual. An electrical engineer would say "a pure series circuit is dual to a pure parallel one." In logic, the series graph corresponds to a succession of ANDs, while the parallel one corresponds to a succession of ORs. In elementary set theory, series corresponds to intersection ∩, parallel corresponds to union ∪.

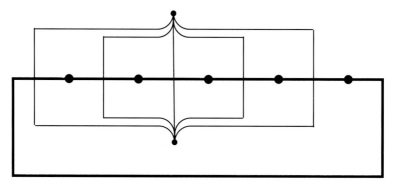

Figure 7.2. Series and parallel circuits are dual.

We know that no more than four colors are needed to color a planar graph. But are four colors ever actually needed? Figure 7.3 depicts three examples in which they are. The differences in these three pictures are topologically only *apparent*—each can be topologically massaged into the other two. In many cases this can be challenging, and topological equivalence is often easier to establish by drawing the dual graph of each map. We have shown the dual of each map directly below it.

In each case, we can look at the dual as the shadow cast on a plane by a wire pyramid. All pyramids are topologically the same. But what about that middle shadow? We see two lines crossing there, so is the graph planar? The important word in defining a planar graph is *can*. If the graph can be drawn in a plane with no lines crossing, the graph is planar. In that middle picture, pull either the horizontal or the vertical line to make it lie outside the diamond. Then no lines in the graph cross, so the graph is planar. In the bottom row, each graph has four vertices; they correspond to the four countries shown in each map. Each graph in the bottom row has six lines, each line corresponding to a road connecting capitals between countries sharing a common border. Finally, each pyramid has four faces—that is to say, each graph in the bottom row, when drawn with no crossing edges, encloses four countries. We see four corresponding (under duality) vertices in the middle and right maps in the top row. But what about the left top map? It should have four corresponding vertices, while we see only three. Often, placing the maps on a globe makes visualizing easier than adding a point at infinity. On the globe, the three large landmasses all meet at one point—say, the south pole—and that point is the fourth vertex.

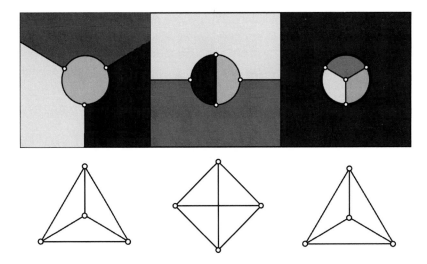

Figure 7.3. Three four-colorings.

In addition to dualizing uncolored maps, we can dualize colored ones too: Just give the capital of a country the same color as the country; and when we dualize that colored graph, color any country the same as the color of its capital.

7.2 How Hassler found Hamiltonian cycles

How did Hass manage to make it so much easier to find graphs having Hamiltonian cycles? In short, he showed that if a graph has a triangulation of the simplest, purest kind, then the graph has a Hamiltonian cycle. His result—the main theorem in paper [6]—says: If a planar graph has an "honest triangulation," then there are Hamiltonian cycles. "Honest" here means that the triangulation consists of just topological triangles—nothing more, nothing less. Specifically:

- There are no loops. That is, no edge ever loops back on itself with its endpoints meeting. An example of a graph having a loop appears in Figure 7.14, (e) on p. 71.
- There are no multiple edges. That means that between any two vertices, there's never more than one edge. An example of a multiple edge appears in Figure 7.14 (f), as well as in Figure 7.1. In Figure 7.1, the top and bottom halves of the ellipse in the heavily drawn graph represent two edges bridging the dots on the ellipse, meaning this graph has one double edge.

Starting from a seed triangle, one can begin doodling, always avoiding accidental crossings, loops, and multiple edges. There are two main ways of doing this to grow the graph. One way is to select an edge, create a new point off the graph, then connect that point with the endpoints of the edge. In the left graph in Figure 7.4, this has been done a few times, starting from the seed triangle at the top. The second way is to connect two adjacent edges and complete them to a triangle, again avoiding accidental crossings, loops, and multiple edges. In the right graph, which extends the left one, this was done twice, adding the two longest, outside edges at the bottom of the graph.

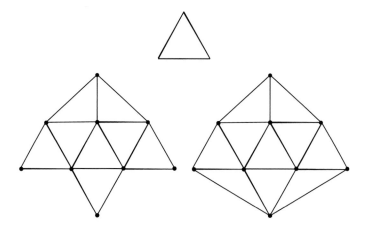

Figure 7.4. Each graph has a Hamiltonian cycle.

Although we were able to add two straight edges in Figure 7.4, sometimes the edges need to bend. In Figure 7.5, the edges *AB* and *BC* can't be connected by a straight edge to form an allowable triangle, but a curved edge works just fine, as we see in the figure. A symmetric counterpart has also been added to the left side of the graph. Finally, the large arc on the right side connects the endpoints of two adjacent edges—one straight and one curved.

His theorem assures us that each graph in Figures 7.4 and 7.5 has a Hamiltonian cycle. In the left graph of Figure 7.4, one way is to start at the top point and cycle around all but one of the outermost edges. (This already connects eight of the nine vertices.) Then go along a horizontal edge, then straight up to the starting point to complete the cycle. The heavily drawn route in Figure 7.6 works for both the right graph in Figure 7.4 and the graph in Figure 7.5.

Since any Hamiltonian cycle in a plane has an inside and an outside, we can pretend that by pumping air into the inside of the curve, the curve pops out to become a polygon which, by massaging a bit, can be considered regular. This gives rise to what Whitney calls a "normal form." To illustrate, the normal form for the path in Figure 7.6 is shown in Figure 7.7. He took any edges on the inside of the regular polygon to be straight lines, and any edges on the outside to be circular arcs.

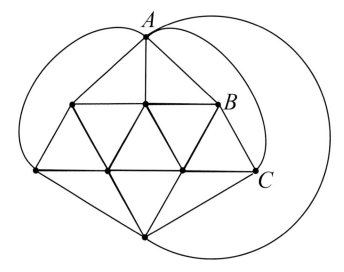

Figure 7.5. This graph has curved edges to avoid accidental crossings, and has a Hamiltonian cycle.

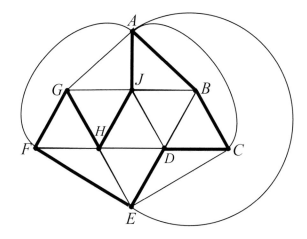

Figure 7.6. A Hamiltonian cycle is drawn more heavily.

7.3 Whitney's planarity condition

The four-color problem has to do with maps on a sheet of paper, or on a globe that can be punctured and then topologically stretched out so it lies flat. Those maps can be looked at as planar graphs, with country boundaries being edges, and points where three or more different boundaries meet being vertices. A planar graph may have accidental crossings—as we've noticed before, a square with

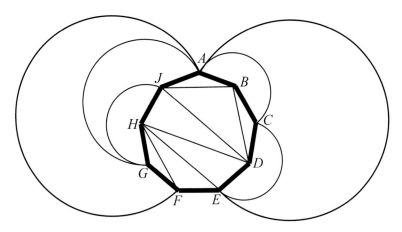

Figure 7.7. Whitney's normal form.

its two diagonals is an example—but a graph being planar means we can topologically redraw the graph, always maintaining the original vertex-edge relationships so that the new graph no longer has accidental crossings. However, not all
graphs are planar, something to remember when applying graph theory to the
four-color problem. Figure 7.8 depicts a nonplanar graph appearing as part of
Figure 6.3 on p. 51.

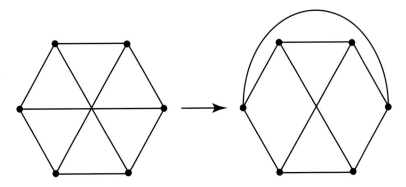

Figure 7.8. Not every graph is planar.

The horizontal edge in the left picture has been stretched upward so it doesn't
intersect the hexagon's remaining diagonals, giving the right picture. However,
we now meet a dead end: No matter how we topologically deform the remaining
two diagonals in the right picture, there always remains an accidental crossing
in the plane. The graph can easily be drawn in $\mathbb{R}^3$ with no accidental crossings,
but not in $\mathbb{R}^2$.

What's needed is some criterion for deciding whether a given graph is planar. Chronologically, the first is due to the Polish mathematician Kazimierz Kuratowski (1896–1980) who published his criterion in 1930. The second is due to Whitney which appeared in 1932, and both are of fundamental importance in graph theory. Hass's proof keys off of Kuratowski's criterion, and Kuratowski's criterion comes down to spotting two particular kinds of subgraphs. Figure 7.9 depicts them.

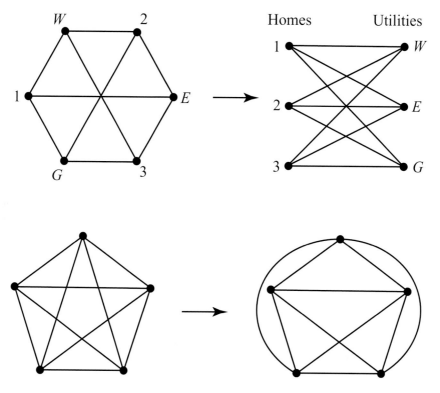

Figure 7.9. The two deciding graphs in Kuratowski's criterion.

The figure shows the left hexagon-with-diagonals picture of Figure 7.8, but with its vertices labeled. Through these labelings, we see that the two top pictures in Figure 7.9 represent the same graph drawing. The one on the right is sometimes called the "utility graph" because it is a representation of three homes 1, 2, and 3 each connected to utilities W = water, E = electricity, and G = gas. The left graph in the bottom row of Figure 7.9 is formed by taking five points as vertices and making all possible connections between pairs of different vertices. The right graph there gives an idea of what happens when we try to topologically redraw edges to remove accidental crossings. After redrawing just two edges, we are already stuck: When we move either of the remaining diagonals so it lies outside the pentagon, that moved edge intersects a previously moved edge. The utility graph edges consist of all connections between three points and another three points, and is correspondingly denoted by $K_{3,3}$. (K stands for the German *Komplete.*[1]) The pentagon graph edges consist of all connections within one set of five points and are denoted by K_5. Both are nonplanar.

Definition. Two graphs are *homeomorphic with* each other provided that, by subdividing some edges of either or both graphs if necessary, they become *homeomorphic to* each other—that is, they become topological copies of each other.[2]

Kuratowski's criterion: *A graph G is nonplanar if and only if within G, there's at least one subgraph homeomorphic with $K_{3,3}$ and/or K_5.*

Whitney's planarity criterion says that a graph G is planar if and only if it has a *combinatorial dual*. This kind of duality was introduced by Whitney and has a decisive advantage over the *geometric* dual. The combinatorial dual is topologically well-defined: Two graphs that are topologically the same have topologically identical combinatorial duals. (This will be clear from the definitions on p. 68.) However, this innocent-sounding fact doesn't hold for geometric duals: Two graphs that are topologically the same may in fact have topologically distinct geometric duals. The reason is that the geometric dual depends on how the original graph is embedded in the plane. Figure 7.10 shows an example.

The two heavily drawn graphs are homeomorphic and their geometric duals are sketched with thinner lines. The heavily drawn graphs each have six vertices, and the way these vertices are connected with edges are topologically the same. But the duals? In the top picture's dual, the number of edges connected to the vertices are 3, 3, 4, 6, while in the bottom dual, the numbers are 3, 3, 5, 5, so the duals must be topologically different.

To introduce the combinatorial dual, look at Figure 7.11. The left picture in the figure depicts a regular polygon, and on the right we see the geometric dual of the polygon. Figure 7.12 shows both the polygon and its dual drawn on a sphere. The edges and vertices of the polygon form the equator; the edges of the dual are semicircles of longitude together with the north and south poles as its two vertices. The polygon and its dual each have the same number of edges, but the two different ways they are connected in a sense represent opposite extremes.

Getting a bit philosophical, we can look at the edges in a polygon as bonds, perhaps atomic bonds between adjacent atoms (vertices). Removing an edge is like cutting a bond, which effectively removes that bond. In the equatorial polygon in Figure 7.12, adjacent atoms are connected with minimal bonding, with just one bond between them. If we cut any bond, the polygon ("molecule") becomes like a length of chain, with two endpoints. Cut an additional bond, and the molecule breaks apart into two smaller ones. Contrast this with the dual; in

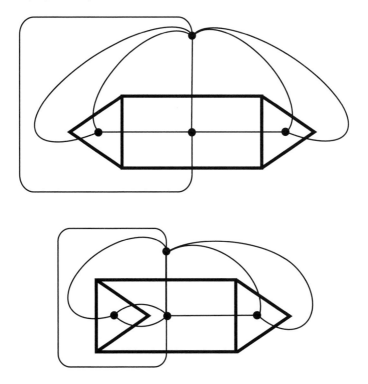

Figure 7.10. Some topologically identical graphs have topologically different duals.

this case the molecule consists of only two atoms, but multiple bonds mean that
these atoms are still held together.

We may go further with our analogy. In Figure 7.12, each edge of the equatorial polygon or cycle can be thought of as not merely crossing a line of longitude,
but actually *cutting* it. The entire equatorial cycle consists of a series of cutting
edges, and together they cut every longitudinal bond, freeing the two atoms at
the poles—breaking up the two-atom molecule into separate, unbonded atoms.
In short, **a cycle of bonds splits up the dual molecule into disconnected
parts.**

Between the equatorial graph and its geometric dual, we can interchange the
roles of "cutter" and "cuttee" so that when an equatorial edge and line of longitude meet, it is the line of longitude that cuts an equatorial bond. Remarkably,
in this dual setup we can continue to say "a cycle of bonds splits up the dual molecule." Let's look at a cycle as what an ant would trace out by walking around
in a closed loop in a general graph: It alternately encounters a vertex, an edge,
a vertex, an edge, …. Let's assume it never visits the same vertex twice, except

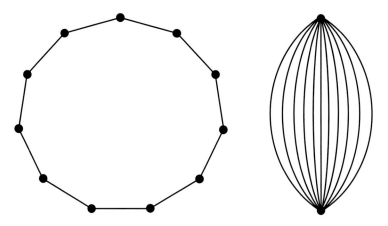

Figure 7.11. The series graph is the geometric dual to the parallel graph.

Figure 7.12. The two graphs in Figure 7.11 are drawn on a sphere.

when returning to the very first vertex that started its journey. It is easy to see that in the right picture of Figure 7.11, a cycle consists of any two edges plus the two vertices connecting them; there are 11 edges and thus a total of $\frac{11 \cdot 10}{2} = 55$ different cycles. In Figure 7.12, any cycle consists of some two lines of longitude together with the north pole and south pole. These two lines of longitude cut two bonds, or edges, of the dual equatorial polygon. In Figure 7.12, we see that the polygon gets broken up into two parts (which can happen in 55 ways) and in each case "a cycle of bonds splits the dual molecule." If two adjacent bonds

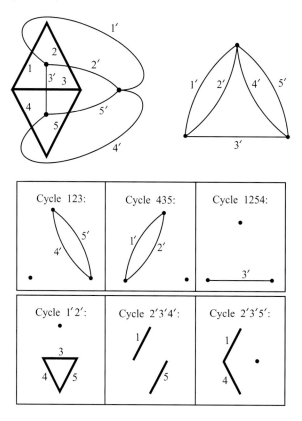

Figure 7.13. "A cycle of bonds splits up the dual molecule" even in the nonpolygon case.

are broken, the circular molecule breaks up into a single atom and one longer chain-like molecule.

This "splitting mantra" is quite general. Let's look at a nonpolygon example. The top left picture in Figure 7.13 depicts a graph G consisting of the two triangles drawn more heavily there. It's not hard to see that there are just three cycles in G: the top triangle (cycle 123), the bottom triangle (cycle 435), and the outer diamond-shape (cycle 1254). The corresponding edges in geometric dual are denoted with primes, and in the upper right picture the dual has been redrawn for easier comprehension. The boxed pictures of the middle row show the split-apart molecules, that is, what's left after removing the bonds or edges corresponding to the three possible cycles in G. Every one of them indeed disconnects the graph, so "a cycle of bonds splits the dual molecule" continues to hold. The bottom row corresponds to picking cycles in the dual. Shown are three representative cycles (the others are counterparts of these three). The corresponding bond cuts (edge removals) in G leave the split molecules shown in the bottom row.

A remarkable fact: The above example generalizes to any connected planar graph G. It has a geometric dual G', and G' is a connected planar graph having the same number of edges as G. Choose either of these graphs—to be specific, let's say G. We let any cycle C in G play the role of the cutter, and let G' play the role of a single molecule, which we think of as a few atoms bonded together in some way. By the way the geometric dual is constructed, each edge of G transversally crosses one edge of G', so that edge of G cuts the associated edge of G'. The punch line: The arbitrarily chosen cutting cycle C in G is guaranteed to split the molecule G' into two pieces. We can argue this way. The cycle C in G breaks up the points or atoms of G' into two sets: the points of G' inside C and the remaining points, which are all outside C. As for the edges of G', C partitions them into three sets: those lying completely inside C, those crossing C, and those lying completely outside C. The points and edges (atoms and bonds) inside C form a subgraph (a part split off from the original molecule), while the points and edges outside form the rest of the molecule. Those crossing edges are the bonds that get broken by the cutting cycle C.

Definition. If S is a set of edges in a connected graph whose removal disconnects that graph, then S is called an *edge-cut set* of the graph.

With the above examples as background, we can now give an official definition of combinatorial dual.

Definition. Two connected graphs are *combinatorial duals* provided that in both graphs, the cycles in one are in one-to-one and onto correspondence with the edge-cut sets of the other.

Here's a more explicit form of the definition:

Definition. Let G be a connected graph with n edges labeled $1, \dots, n$, let G' be another connected graph also of n edges, and let $(\ )'$ denote a one-to-one mapping from the edges of G to those of G'. The edges of G' are thus labeled $1', \dots, n'$. Any cycle C in G maps to a set of edges C' in G'. If, no matter what cycle C in G is chosen, removing the corresponding edges from G' results in a disconnected graph, then G' is the *combinatorial dual* of G.

Note that the above definitions make no reference to the way the graph is embedded in the plane.

Duality fact: If G' is a combinatorial dual of G, then G is a combinatorial dual of G'.

We can now state

Whitney's planarity criterion: *A connected graph is planar if and only if it has a combinatorial dual.*

Here's the idea of a proof. The "remarkable fact" on p. 68 sketches an argument that if a connected graph is planar, then it has a combinatorial dual. So we also need to establish that if the graph has a combinatorial dual, it must be planar. One can reword this converse as "no nonplanar graph ever has a combinatorial dual." To establish that, assume that some nonplanar graph *does* have a combinatorial dual, and obtain a contradiction. By Kuratowski's criterion, any nonplanar graph contains a copy of either $K_{3,3}$ or K_5 (or both). Therefore we will have obtained our desired contradiction if we do these two things:

- Assume $K_{3,3}$ has a combinatorial dual and get a contradiction.
- Assume K_5 has a combinatorial dual and get a contradiction.

We sketch an argument in the case of $K_{3,3}$ (the argument in the case of K_5 is similar). Assume $G = K_{3,3}$ has a combinatorial dual G'. We know from Figure 7.9 that the utility graph $G = K_{3,3}$ has nine edges, and that means the combinatorial dual also has nine edges. We show that the purported dual would need at least 12 edges, our contradiction. We start with something definite about the cycles in $G = K_{3,3}$: Figure 7.9 on p. 63 makes it clear that any cycle must have an even number of edges—that's the only way the starting and ending positions can coincide. There are no 2-cycles, but we see 4-cycles and 6-cycles. Under the assumed duality, cycles map into edge-cut sets, so every edge-cut set in the dual G' has at least four edges, and each vertex in the dual is incident with at least four edges. This means there are at least 12 edges, and we have our contradiction.

7.4 Chromatic polynomials

Kempe's proof crashed in 1890, and it increasingly seemed that a new approach was needed. Not surprisingly, the four-color problem attracted a continuous flow of amateurs since they could understand the problem and at least work on it. But it took more than 20 years before the mathematical community saw a genuinely new approach that seemed to offer some hope. In 1912, 28-year-old George Birkhoff asked, "In how many ways can we color a map using n colors?" He established that the answer is always given by a polynomial function which he called the "chromatic polynomial" of the map, or equally well, of the associated graph. Since the polynomial captures this information about a graph, Birkhoff hoped that because our knowledge about polynomials is so extensive, there could be a chance that bringing this knowledge to bear on the four-color problem might at last yield significant progress.

In this section we give some examples of chromatic polynomials, together with some basic properties that Birkhoff discovered. About 17 years later, Hass made some further progress (representing most of his Ph.D. thesis) and we describe that.

Examples. For a graph G, a *coloring* of G is an assignment of a color to each vertex of G in such a way that different colors are assigned to any two vertices directly connected by some edge. Two colorings of G are *different* whenever the colorings differ on at least one vertex. Thus, for example, a permutation of the same set of colors on a graph in general results in colorings that are different. For a given graph G and set of x different colors, the chromatic polynomial P_G is a polynomial in the variable x such that $P_G(x)$ is the number of different colorings that can be given to G.

To illustrate the idea of chromatic polynomial P_G, we determine P_G for each of the nine graphs in Figure 7.14.

(a) **Graph with no edges.** For a valid coloring of a graph, the color given each vertex need satisfy only that different colors are assigned to vertices directly connected by an edge. Since there are no edges, any coloring is valid. There are x choices at each of six vertices, so the chromatic polynomial is x^6. For a graph with n vertices and no edges, the polynomial is x^n.

(b) **Path graph.** Number the vertices 1 through 6, from left to right. At vertex 1, any of the x colors may be chosen. At vertex 2, any of the remaining $x - 1$ colors are valid. At vertex 3, it's still true that any of the remaining $x - 1$ colors are permitted since vertex 3 doesn't care what color was chosen at vertex 1. Continuing this logic shows that the chromatic polynomial for this path graph is $x(x - 1)^5$. For a path graph with n vertices, the polynomial is $x(x - 1)^{n-1}$.

(c) **Ladder rung graph.** Any rung consists of two vertices connected by an edge, so it can be colored in $x(x-1)$ ways. None of the rungs are connected by edges (not a particularly great ladder!) so each rung is still colorable in $x(x - 1)$ ways, making for a total of $x^6(x - 1)^6$ possible colorings. For a ladder with n rungs, it's $x^n(x - 1)^n$.

(d) **Star graph.** This graph has seven vertices. The center one can be colored in any of x ways, while at each of the other six vertices it's enough to avoid the center's color. That makes the chromatic polynomial $x(x - 1)^6$. For a star with n rays, the polynomial is $x(x - 1)^n$. Notice that a path graph with $n + 1$ vertices has the same polynomial as a star graph with n rays. This shows that topologically different graphs can have the same chromatic polynomial.

(e) **Graph with loop.** Here, a loop means a vertex connected to itself by means of a single edge. But in a graph coloring, the endpoints of any edge must be assigned different colors. Conclusion: Any graph containing a loop cannot be

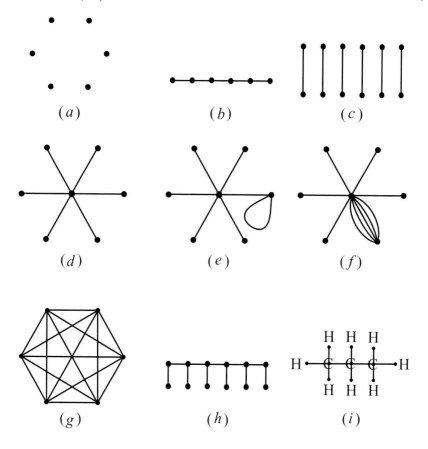

Figure 7.14. Nine different graphs.

colored, so the chromatic polynomial is the zero polynomial. This is another example where topologically different graphs can have the same identically zero polynomial $P_G(x) \equiv 0$.

(f) **Graph with multiple edges.** In any colored graph, replacing an edge by two or more edges does nothing to make that coloring inadmissible. Therefore the graph drawn here has the same chromatic polynomial $x(x-1)^6$ as the star graph in (d). More generally, if a graph G has chromatic polynomial $P_G(x)$, then so does the graph in which any one or more edges of G have been replaced by multiple edges. This shows yet another way in which topologically different graphs can share the same chromatic polynomial.

(g) **Complete graph on five vertices.** In any complete graph K_n on n vertices, every vertex is connected to every other vertex. So once a vertex has been assigned a color, that color can't be used for any other vertex. Therefore the chromatic polynomial of K_5 is

$$P_{K_5}(x) = x(x-1)(x-2)(x-3)(x-4).$$

For $P_{K_n}(x)$, the factors in the product continue on, ending in $(x-(n-1))$.

(h) **Centipede graph.** Although in (h) the unfortunate centipede is lacking most of its legs, the logic for any number n of legs is always the same: In assigning a color to the top left vertex, there are x choices for it, and $x-1$ choices for the vertex below it, as well as $x-1$ choices for the vertex to the right of it; and also $x-1$ choices for the vertex below *it* and also to *its* right, and so on. There are 12 vertices in the drawing; for the first vertex there are x color-choices, and for each of the remaining 11 vertices, $x-1$ color-choices. So the chromatic polynomial for our six-legged centipede is $x(x-1)^{11}$, and for one with n legs, it's $x(x-1)^{2n-1}$.

(i) **Lewis diagram of a family of hydrocarbons.** Sometimes improper colorings can be useful. For example, the world is made up of molecules that can be looked at as graphs, with different atoms being represented by colored nodes, and bonds by (possibly multiple) edges. Familiar so-called "linear alkanes" such as methane, ethane, propane, and so on, consist of only hydrogen and carbon atoms, so assigning one color to hydrogen and another color to carbon produces a colorful graph, but usually not a colored graph. But even with just two colors, the linear alkanes $C_nH_{2(n+1)}$ form a large family of different graphs, all having similar branching structures, with the carbon chain having length n. Their properties gradually change as n increases: At standard temperature and pressure, they are gasses for $n = 1, \dots, 4$, liquids for $n = 5, \dots, 17$, and solids for $n \geq 18$. Their melting and boiling points gradually increase with the number of vertices in the molecule's graph. Just add the suffix "ane" to the roots meth, eth, prop, but, pent, hex, hep, and oct to get the names of the first eight members of the family.

Earlier, we met the two basic graphs that are not planar: $K_{3,3}$ and K_5; all nonplanar graphs contain a copy homeomorphic with one or both of these. It happens that *all* graphs, no matter how fancy, can be embedded in 3-space and, in fact, made to lie with no accidental crossings on some surface of an appropriate genus. The lowest possible genus is called the "genus of the graph."[3] However in nature, even planar graphs such as the alkanes[4] do not actually lie in a plane. Instead, the atoms make angles with each other that force them out of any plane. We see this in Figure 7.15. For longer molecules in the family, the zig-zag pattern in propane continues for the larger carbon atoms, with the hydrogen atoms branching out analogously. Correspondingly, the planar graph in Figure 7.14(i) maintains the same pattern, but simply gets longer.

Figure 7.15. Ball and stick model of propane molecule C_3H_8.

7.5 Properties of the chromatic polynomial

Expanding chromatic polynomials reveals some surprises that lead to useful properties. We state without proof some of these properties. First, here are expansions of the chromatic polynomials for the colorings of seven of the graphs depicted in Figure 7.14. In each case, the terms are arranged from highest degree to lowest.

(a): $x^6 = x^6$,

(b): $x(x-1)^5 = x^6 - 5x^5 + 10x^4 - 10x^3 + 5x^2 - x$,

(c): $x^6(x-1)^6 = x^{12} - 6x^{11} + 15x^{10} - 20x^9 + 15x^8 - 6x^7 + x^6$,

(d): $x(x-1)^6 = x^7 - 6x^6 + 15x^5 - 20x^4 + 15x^3 - 6x^2 + x$,

(e): $x(x-1)^6 = x^7 - 6x^6 + 15x^5 - 20x^4 + 15x^3 - 6x^2 + x$,

(f): $x(x-1)(x-2)(x-3)(x-4) = x^5 - 10x^4 + 35x^3 - 50x^2 + 24x$,

(g): $x(x-1)^{11} = x^{12} - 11x^{11} + 55x^{10} - 165x^9 + 330x^8 - 462x^7 + 462x^6 - 330x^5 + 165x^4 - 55x^3 + 11x^2 - x$.

Meditating a bit on these expansions suggests a number of basic properties. Here are some of them; it's instructive to check each property against each expanded polynomial.

- The coefficient of the first term in each expansion is 1.
- The degree of the polynomial equals the number of vertices in the graph.

- The negative of the second coefficient equals the number of edges in the graph.
- The polynomial's order (the degree of the last term) equals the number of components of the graph.
- The signs of the coefficients alternate.
- Except for graphs with no edges (when the polynomial is x^n), the sum of all the coefficients is 0.
- As you go from the first term to the last, descending one power of x at each step, there are no gaps; each coefficient is nonzero.
- If graphs G_1 and G_2 are disjoint, then the polynomial of their union is the product of their polynomials—in symbols,

$$\{G_1 \cap G_2 = \varnothing\} \implies \{P_{G_1 \cup G_2} = P_{G_1} \cdot P_{G_2}\}.$$

- A graph is called a *tree* if removing any single edge disconnects the graph. For example, removing any edge of the star in (d) leaves one isolated point plus a 5-ray star. A graph with n vertices is a tree if and only if its polynomial is $x(x-1)^n$.
- Suppose the number of terms in the polynomial is m. Round $m/2$ down and add 1, and call that q. The sizes (absolute values) of the coefficients increase up to the qth term. The increases may not always be strict, and sometimes the increase may continue beyond the qth term.
- If the coefficients of the polynomial are a_i, then $a_{i-1} \cdot a_{i+1} \le a_i^2$. When you plot the points (i, a_i), you get a graph that is sometimes called "logarithmically concave."

7.6 The "coefficients challenge"

In each of graphs of Figure 7.14, the chromatic polynomial was pretty easy to find. But if we randomly choose a few points on a piece of paper and then randomly connect them with nonintersecting edges to make a planar graph, actually getting that graph's chromatic polynomial will nearly always prove to be a major challenge. Most graphs do not easily give up their polynomial, and without a good strategy, the amount of computation can be overwhelming. After investing a great deal of effort in finding the polynomial for some randomly created graph, it becomes easy to appreciate how powerful some of the above properties are.

   Even a graph having a small number of vertices and edges can find a way of being uncooperative. As an example, let's look at the humble square—a graph G with four vertices and four edges. Suppose we have a palette of x colors. What's $P_G(x)$? To make things visual, hang the square like a mobile with one vertex at the top, two midway down, and one at the bottom. Start at the top vertex. Clearly there are x choices of color there. There are therefore $x - 1$ choices for the left vertex as well as $x - 1$ choices for the right one. Now for the bottom vertex: Since the color of the top vertex is now available, doesn't that mean there are $x - 1$ choices for the bottom? It does if the right and left vertices happen to have been colored the same. But perhaps two colors were used for those two! Then there are only $x - 2$ choices. (How easily the plot thickens…) What do we do?

Since there are four vertices, the leading term of the polynomial is x^4. Since there is no constant term, the polynomial has the form $x^4 + ax^3 + bx^2 + cx$. We definitely need at least two colors, so one way of conquering the problem is to carefully count all ways of coloring the square using first 2, then 3, then 4 colors. Substituting the values 2, 3, 4 for x would then produce three linear equations in the unknowns a, b, and c, and we could solve for them. If two colors are used, there are just two different ways to color the square graph. Some careful book-keeping shows that a palette of three colors leads to 18 possible colorings. Using extremely careful bookkeeping reveals that with four colors, the number jumps to 84. The hard part here is not solving the system of three linear equations—a calculator or software makes that straightforward. It's getting those numbers like 18 and 84 exactly right. Our list of properties proves to be useful in this case since it allows us to avoid finding those numbers! Here's how: First, a is the negative of the number of edges, so $a = -4$. We also know that all the coefficients sum to 0, so $1 - 4 + b + c = 0$, meaning $c = 3 - b$. We've already found that when $x = 2$, the number of colorings is 2—that is, $P_G(2) = 2$. This leads to $9 = 2b + c$ which, with $c = 3 - b$, gives $b = 6$ and therefore $c = -3$. Therefore

$$P_G = x^4 - 4x^3 + 6x^2 - 3x$$

is the chromatic polynomial of the square graph. We never had to find 18 or 84. (Oh, by the way, $P_G(3)$ is indeed 18, and $P_G(4)$ is 84.) The arguments we used to find the polynomials in Figure 7.14 are not even up to finding the polynomial for a simple square graph! And had we not realized that coloring both sides differently was a possibility, we might have thought $x^4 - 3x^3 + 3x^2 - x$ is the polynomial. In fact, for values of x greater than 2, this always gives too large an answer.

Although our properties serve beautifully for the square, they actually re-move only two equations. What about, say, graphs having 10 or 15 vertices? The properties are enlightening, but they're no magic bullet for finding $P_G(x)$. The problem calls for additional cleverness.

7.7 An illuminating strategy

Birkhoff, in his late twenties, worked out formulas for the coefficients of the poly-nomial for any graph G. The catch here is that his formulas require looking at each subgraph of G, so if there are n edges in the graph, that means looking at 2^n subgraphs. This was no leap in actually calculating G's polynomial—a graph with that many edges would still entail examining 2^n subgraphs, and that number grows very fast with increasing n. Whitney made a huge contribution here, find-ing a way to drastically reduce the number of subgraphs that required checking. In doing this he uncovered unsuspected geometric meaning in the coefficients, and that represented an additional breakthrough. We now briefly describe his method, and then apply it to find the polynomial of the square graph in an en-tirely different way. After that, we illustrate Whitney's method with several other examples.

What is Whitney's method? Suppose a graph G has n vertices. List the cycles in the graph G and then break each cycle by removing from it any edge you wish to create a corresponding *broken cycle*. Now look at the set of edges S_1 taken 1 at a time, then the set of edges S_2 taken 2 at a time, and so on. Count any set of i edges in S_i exactly when that set doesn't contain any of the above broken cycles; for each i, call the total we get this way m_i. Then his big result is

$$P_G(x) = x^n + \sum_{i=1}^{n-1} (-1)^i m_i x^{n-i}.$$

Chromatic polynomial of the square graph using Whitney's method. For the square graph, the number n of vertices is 4 and the number of edges r is also 4. There's just one cycle (consisting of all four edges). Remove any one particular edge E to make the broken cycle B, so B consists of three specific edges of the square. Edges taken one or two at a time certainly can't contain B, so they all get counted. Let's go ahead and count them! Edges taken one at a time are simply single edges, and there are four of them, so $m_1 = 4$. As for edges taken two at a time, there are $\frac{4!}{2!2!} = 6$ of these unordered pairs, so $m_2 = 6$. What about edges three at a time? There are $\frac{4!}{3!1!} = 4$ of these triples, but one of them happens to be that one broken cycle B that we created, so that's not counted. Therefore $m_3 = 4 - 1 = 3$ giving

$$P_G(x) = x^4 - 4x^3 + 6x^2 - 3x.$$

This derivation is very short and shows the geometric content of each coefficient.

Another quick example: For an octagonal graph G, the method gives $m_i = \frac{8!}{i!(8-i)!}$, except that it's 1 less for m_7. So the polynomial is

$$P_G(x) = x^8 - 8x^7 + 28x^6 - 56x^5 + 70x^4 - 56x^3 + 28x^2 - 7x.$$

Notice how this polynomial satisfies the properties listed previously: The degree is the number of vertices, the coefficients add up to 0, the first $\frac{8}{2} + 1 = 5$ coefficients increase in magnitude, $m_1 = 8$ is the number of edges, the lowest degree is 1 corresponding to G having just 1 connected component, and from the highest to the lowest degree, all coefficients are nonzero.

Of course most graphs have more than one circuit; as an example, consider the graph G in Figure 7.16, a square together with one diagonal edge.

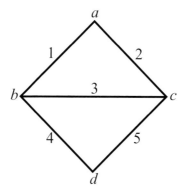

Figure 7.16. A square with one diagonal edge.

This graph has $n = 4$ vertices, $r = 5$ edges, and 3 cycles. These cycles are the upper and lower triangles $(1, 2, 3)$ and $(3, 4, 5)$, as well as the square $(1, 2, 4, 5)$. There are thus three broken cycles, which we'll take to be $B_1 = (1, 2)$, $B_2 = (3, 4)$, and $B_3 = (1, 2, 4)$. We now do our edge-counting thing, counting any set of i edges toward the number m_i if and only if none of the three broken cycles is in the set.

- m_1: All three broken cycles have at least two edges, so no single edge can contain any of them, so all five single edges are counted, making $m_1 = 5$.
- m_2: The total number of edges taken 2 at a time is $\frac{5!}{2!3!} = 10$, but $B_1 = (1, 2)$ and $B_2 = (3, 4)$ can't be counted, so $m_2 = 10 - 2 = 8$.
- m_3: The number of unordered triples—edges taken 3 at a time—is $\frac{5!}{3!2!} = 10$. Any triple containing $B_1 = (1, 2)$, $B_2 = (3, 4)$, or $B_3 = (1, 2, 4)$ is excluded from the list of the 10 triples:
  (1,2,3): excluded
  (1,2,4): excluded
  (1,2,5): excluded
  (1,3,4): excluded
  (1,3,5): OK
  (1,4,5): OK
  (2,3,4): excluded
  (2,3,5): OK
  (2,4,5): OK
  (3,4,5): excluded
  There are four marked OK, so $m_3 = 4$.

For this graph, the summation in Whitney's formula

$$P_G(x) = x^n + \sum_{i=1}^{n-1} (-1)^i m_i x^{n-i}$$

runs up to $n - 1 = 3$, so we've found all the m_i; the chromatic polynomial of Figure 7.16 is therefore

$$P_G(x) = x^4 - 5x^3 + 8x^2 - 4x.$$

This derivation is longer than for the polygons above, but it shines a light on the geometry of the coefficients. Finding the polynomial for a graph can be something of an art form, and this graph's polynomial can actually be found more quickly using stepwise logic (which for an arbitrary graph seldom works). With a palette of x colors, there are x choices for the top vertex a, $x - 1$ choices for the left vertex b, and because of the horizontal edge, exactly $x - 2$ choices at c. The color at d can be the same as that at a, but must be different from the two unequal colors at b and c, leaving $x - 2$ choices at d. Multiply out $x(x-1)(x-2)^2$ and we get $x^4 - 5x^3 + 8x^2 - 4x$.

At an extreme, tree graphs have no cycles at all, so there's no checking or eliminating. For example, the chromatic polynomial of the 6-vertex path graph in Figure 7.14 (b) was shown there to be $x(x - 1)^5$, and its expansion is

$$P_G(x) = \sum_{i=0}^{5} (-1)^i \binom{5}{i} x^{6-i}.$$

This agrees exactly with what Whitney's method gives. A path graph with n vertices and $n - 1$ edges has polynomial

$$\sum_{i=0}^{n-1} (-1)^i \binom{n-1}{i} x^{n-i}.$$

We can always assume each graph is connected since the polynomial of the disjoint union of connected graphs is the product of their polynomials. However, Whitney's method works even if the graph isn't connected. As an example, consider a two-rung ladder similar to the ladder in Figure 7.14 (c). The number of vertices is $n = 4$, and there are no cycles so no broken ones and no cases to eliminate. Therefore $m_1 =$ number of edges taken 1 at a time is 2, $m_2 =$ number of edges taken 2 at a time is 1, and since we can't take two edges 3 at a time, we have $m_3 = 0$. This means that the chromatic polynomial for the two-rung ladder is

$$x^4 - 2x^3 + x^2,$$

which agrees the expansion of $x^2(x-1)^2$, the formula in Figure 7.14 (c) for $n = 2$.

These examples provide some flavor of Whitney's method. The original paper [8] in the *Proceedings of the National Academy of Sciences* includes the necessary arguments for his formula and is pretty easy to read. His thesis, written up as a paper in the *Annals* [24] goes into substantially greater detail.

7.8 The siren, the stubborn beast!

Birkhoff's hope in developing chromatic polynomials was that they would prove to be a link connecting the four-color problem to the vast amount of established knowledge about polynomials. And in Birkhoff, the problem had a brilliant and persistent adversary—he thought about the problem on and off during most of his professional life. Of the many properties Birkhoff obtained about chromatic polynomials, one is a real standout. It is this inequality applying to any map of N countries:

$$P_G(x) \geq x(x-1)(x-2)(x-3)^{N-3}.$$

This simple, concise inequality tells us that given a palette of, say, $x = 10$ colors, any map of five countries can be colored in at least $10 \cdot 9 \cdot 8 \cdot 7^2 = 35,280$ different ways. Even with just a five-color palette, it says that same map can be colored in at least $5 \cdot 4 \cdot 3 \cdot 2^2 = 240$ different ways. His is a simple, beautiful and powerful result. In particular, with a palette of $x = 4$ colors, the inequality tells us that any N-country map can be colored in at least $4 \cdot 3 \cdot 2 \cdot 1^{N-3} = 24$ ways! The heart-breaker: He was able to prove this inequality for every value of x *except* 4. Birkhoff admitted at one point that he had probably invested too much time on The Problem.

Whitney, too, kept an interest in the four-color problem throughout his life, but from a more circumspect distance. During the 1960s the German mathematician Heinrich Heesch, inspired by some arguments Kempe had used in his unsuccessful attempt at the problem, was formulating a very different method of attack: Using a computer to check a large number of critical cases. In those days, few computers had enough power to see this approach through, but using the pioneering ideas of Heesch, the mathematician Yoshio Shimamoto in 1971 discovered an approach that seemed amenable to computer testing. Rumors quickly spread that the four-color problem was about to be cracked. A Cray computer, after 26 hours of ultra-fast computing, cast doubt on Shimamoto's approach, but a very careful analysis by graph-theorists saw no logical flaw in his method. There was, however, always the possibility of a bug in the computer program. In the world of graphs, Whitney and the British mathematician William Tutte were considered the foremost experts of the day. (Tutte was also a brilliant code breaker during WWII whose contributions helped shorten the war. In this respect he was in about the same league as Alan Turing but not as well known.) Both Whitney and Tutte smelled something a bit off in the whole Shimamoto approach, and soon concluded that if his method of attack were valid, then a ridiculously simpler proof could be had, a proof so simple that it defied common sense. They wrote lengthy accounts ([118], [120]) that made it clear: At that point, at that time, the four-color problem was still unsolved. But Heesch, Shimamoto and some colleagues—including Appel and Haken—felt they were on to something, and persisted. In 1976, Appel and Haken finally conquered The Beast; their groundbreaking papers are [AH1] and [AH2].

All this leaves an uncomfortable question. Are chromatic polynomials worth anything? They were, after all, introduced for just one purpose—cracking an unsolved problem. Are they good for anything else? It seldom happens that a coherent mathematical theory ends up with no practical applications, and that's true of these polynomials. We close this chapter by sketching two applications, giving a little flavor for how the polynomials can be used.

Avoiding cross-talk. Suppose, in a certain region of the U.S., the Federal Communications Commission (FCC) grants x different frequencies over which n physical TV stations may broadcast. Stations that are sufficiently far apart from each other can use the same frequency without interference or "cross-talk," while stations close together must use different frequencies. Different frequencies are like different colors. Stations then correspond to vertices of a graph and stations close together are connected by an edge to exclude them from having the same color or frequency. An appropriate assignment of channels to stations corresponds to finding a valid coloring of a graph, and the chromatic polynomial $P(x)$ of the graph tells us how many ways there are to assign x broadcast frequencies to the stations' channels. The smallest x giving a nonzero value of the chromatic polynomial then determines the minimum number of frequencies (channels) needed to satisfy the restraints imposed by no cross-talk, a number very important to the FCC.

Assigning time slots for speakers. At a conference, suppose speakers are to give 50-minute presentations. The speakers must be assigned time slots, and often different presentations are part of a series or are closely related, meaning participants may want to attend all of them. Therefore such presentations shouldn't be scheduled at the same time. We can model this problem by letting each presentation be a point of a graph, and time slots by colors. Points are connected with edges exactly when a time conflict is to be avoided. The chromatic polynomial then gives us a handle on possible scheduling arrangements. If the minimum value of the polynomial is too large, we would be asking for too many time slots to accommodate scheduling restrictions.

Generally, in applying colored graphs, the idea is to connect two vertices by an edge whenever two corresponding possibilities are mutually exclusive. A familiar example of this occurs in completing Latin squares where no column or row can contain the same number (color) twice; or in Sudoku, where the number of colors is nine and no column, row, or any of the Sudoku's 3×3 grids can contain any of the nine colors more than once.

CHAPTER 8

Whitney Discovers a Big Brother to the Matrix: The Matroid

In learning and discovering things about graphs, Hass began to realize that graph theory has surprising similarities with linear algebra. By the time his work with graphs tailed off and he began turning his attention to manifolds, he had formed a good notion about the underlying concepts of graph theory and decided to write a paper laying out his central ideas. He gave the name "matroid" to the new object capturing the essence of these ideas. He considered this paper to be a sort of abstract summation of what he had been involved with so intensely during the previous two or three years.

8.1 Some analogies and examples

To get some feeling for what matroids are, we begin by describing four ways in which they capture similarities between graph theory and linear algebra. Each description's title is in boldface. Further examples will then naturally lead us to a definition of general matroid.

Graphs and vector spaces. The graphs Whitney worked with consist of finitely many points together with edges connecting some or all of them. He realized that a graph G has a basic linear algebra analog: a vector space V generated by a finite collection C of vectors in some surrounding space. A vector is like an edge, and its base point and tip are like vertices. Whitney wrote the vectors of C as columns of a matrix, the number of rows being the dimension of the ambient space and the number of columns being the number of vectors in C. However, the abstraction Whitney was after consists of more than vectors or a matrix; it also includes *all the bases* of V formed from the finitely many vectors of C. In naming this larger structure he went from matrix to "matroid." The suffix "oid," is from the Latin "oides" meaning "similar to" or "resembles," but often the suffix connotes something more general or more extensive, as in ellipsoid, paraboloid, hyperboloid, and, in his case, matroid.

Edges and vectors. In both a graph and in a vector space, we can use edges or vectors to go from one point to other points. This is clear in a graph. From now on we assume the graph is connected, meaning that any two points in the graph are connected by at least one unbroken path made up of edges. In a vector space, the familiar picture depicting the sum of two vectors based at $(0,0) \in \mathbb{R}^2$ as the diagonal of a parallelogram can be redrawn by moving the base point of one vector to the tip of the other, which brings out the continuous-path aspect we see in graphs, and this idea extends to any finite number of vectors in the plane. Figure 8.1 shows five vectors in $\mathbb{R}^2$ added in this way to get their sum $v_1 + v_2 + v_3 + v_4 + v_5$. This extends in the expected way to any set of vectors in the matroid's finite collection of column vectors in $\mathbb{R}^n$.

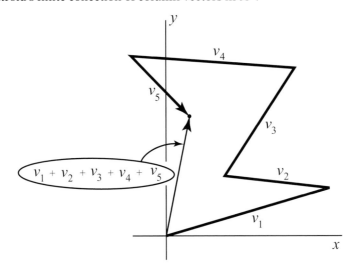

Figure 8.1. The "continuous path" method of adding vectors.

Subgraphs and subspaces. Any set I of vectors $\{v_1, \dots, v_m\}$ chosen from C generates a subspace $S \subseteq V$. In the algebraic sense, "generates" means that any arbitrarily chosen vector v in S is some linear combination of vectors in I. In the geometric sense, it means that by adding appropriate scalar multiples $r_i v_i$ of each $v_i \in I$, we can create a polygonal path ending at the tip of any chosen vector v in S. Figure 8.2 illustrates an example in the plane—just draw lines through v parallel to v_1 and v_2 to create a parallelogram. The approximate multiples required for v_1 and v_2 are then read off the picture. Here's the graph theory analog: A set I

of edges $\{e_1, \dots, e_m\}$ chosen from a graph generates some subset S of that graph. "Generates" in this setting means that any two points in S are connected by an unbroken path of edges selected from I. In both the linear algebra setting and the graph setting, we say that I *spans* S.

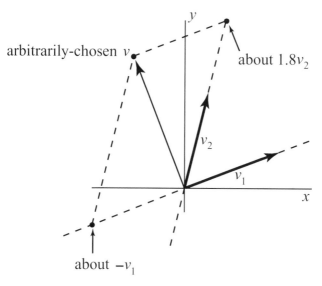

Figure 8.2. We can read off from the figure the required multiples of v_1 and v_2 to get an arbitrary vector v.

Independence in graph theory and linear algebra.

In both linear algebra and graph theory, the notion of "set of independent elements" is fundamental. We've just seen that any set I generates a subspace of V or a subset of a graph. In each case, the set I is *independent* provided that removing any member of I results in this smaller set generating a strictly smaller subspace $S \subsetneq V$ or smaller subset S of the graph. As an example in the linear algebra setting, the columns of the matrix

$$\begin{pmatrix} 1 & 0 & 0 & 1 & 0 \\ 0 & 1 & 0 & 1 & 1 \\ 0 & 0 & 1 & 0 & 1 \end{pmatrix}$$

represent five vectors in $\mathbb{R}^3$. Let's denote them by $v_1, \dots, v_5$, and let I denote the subset $\{v_1, v_2, v_3\}$. Then I generates a 3-space, while any two members of I generate just a plane, so the set I is independent. On the other hand $\{v_1, v_2, v_4\}$ generates the (x, y)-plane, and if you remove v_1, then $\{v_2, v_4\}$ still generates that plane, meaning $\{v_1, v_2, v_4\}$ is not an independent set. In general, any set that is not independent is called *dependent*.

Example. The left drawing in Figure 8.3 depicts a 3×5 "grid graph." Its $3 \cdot 5 = 15$ vertices are connected by a total of 22 edges. In the right drawing, the 14 heavy edges represent a subset I of the graph, and these edges span the graph because we can go from any vertex to any other vertex in the graph by driving along the heavily drawn edges.

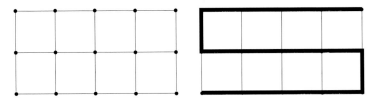

Figure 8.3. Left: a 3×5 grid graph. Right: the grid graph together with a spanning subset.

Now what if we remove, say, the right vertical edge from I? Doing this cuts off communication between the bottom and middle rows of vertices using edges in I as roadways—there's no road connecting any vertex in the middle or top row with any vertex in the bottom row. In fact, this decrease in accessibility occurs whenever we remove any one edge from I, so I in Figure 8.3 is independent.

Example. In either the linear algebra or graph setting, if an independent set I is as large as possible (that is, if it's maximal), then I is called a *basis* of V or the graph. We denote a basis by B. In linear algebra, this is familiar. Figure 8.4 shows nine different bases for our 3×5 grid graph; in each case, the basis elements are drawn more heavily.

For any of these bases there is exactly one path connecting any two points of the grid graph. The graph is connected and each of these bases is itself a connected subgraph of it. However, if we make a system of roadways in which all edges and vertices of our grid graph are used, then there are many paths between any two points. When the system of roadways is restricted to having just the edges in any of its bases B, then there's just one path. In this sense, we may say that any of these subgraphs B is *minimally connected*: Removing any single edge in any basis B disconnects B into two parts. This is true even if the edge is the first or last in a path—in that case, one of the parts is an isolated point since a graph consists of edges and vertices.

Example. In our grid graph, suppose some edge e outside B is added to B. This larger set of edges still generates the grid graph but is no longer independent, since removing e doesn't result in generating a smaller graph.

This is of central importance:

Fact. Adding any single edge to any graph in Figure 8.4 always creates a loop in the graph. This turns out to be true of any basis in any graph.

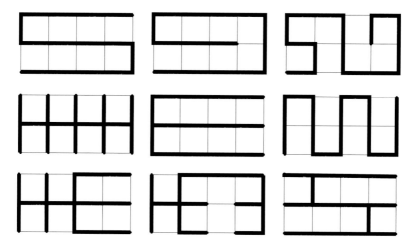

Figure 8.4. Nine bases of a 3×5 grid graph.

In just the same way that two points on a circle determine two different routes going from the first to the second point, a loop means there are two different edge-paths between any two vertices of the loop. So as we destroy independence by adding an edge, we can no longer be assured that there exists just one path between any two points of the graph. This gives a nice characterization of graph bases:

Fact. If a set of edges in a graph spans that graph, then the set is independent if and only if the set contains no loops.

Example. There's a vector space analog to the above characterization of independence in terms of no loops. Here's the idea: Algebraically, vectors $v_1, \ldots, v_m$ are independent if and only if the only way a linear combination $a_1 v_1 + \cdots + a_m v_m$ can be zero is if all the a_i are zero. This says something geometric. Look again at Figure 8.1 on p. 84, but imagine that those five vectors are in $\mathbb{R}^5$. In a 5-space, if $v_1, \ldots, v_5$ are linearly independent, then you can stretch or shrink each vector v_i by a signed factor a_i all you want, but you can never get the final vector $a_1 v_1 + a_2 v_2 + a_3 v_3 + a_4 v_4 + a_5 v_5$ to loop back to the origin—it ends up at the origin only if it never left it! That's just a geometric way of saying that since the v_i are independent, every a_i must be 0. Of course in this scenario the only loop you get is the trivial loop. But if we look at Figure 8.1 as it is actually drawn (with the vectors in $\mathbb{R}^2$), then with $v = v_1 + v_2 + v_3 + v_4 + v_5$, the nontrivial linear combination $v_1 + v_2 + v_3 + v_4 + v_5 - v$ gets represented geometrically as the loop in Figure 8.1, but with the final vector's direction being reversed. Of course, these 2-vectors form a dependent set. With this geometry in mind, we can analogously say that in any vector space, a set $\{v_i\}$ of vectors is independent if and only if you can never create a nontrivial loop like that in Figure 8.1 by stretching or shrinking the v_i and adding them.

8.2 Two basic properties

Here are two basic properties that our vector space and graph examples share:

(a) Each basis is *maximal.* One can alternatively say that no basis can properly contain another basis or that no two bases are comparable.

(b) If B_1 and B_2 are two bases, you can throw away any element $e_1 \in B_1$ that you wish, yet there will always exist some replacement element $e_2 \in B_2$ so that $B_1 - e_1 + e_2$ is a basis. This is known as the *exchange property.*

Property ((a)) is clear from the definition of basis, and it is not hard to see the exchange property ((b)) for a vector space. The situation for a graph is probably less familiar; looking at a few cases gives the basic idea.

Examples. The top row in Figure 8.5 shows an example of an exchange: e_1 is arbitrarily selected in B_1, and our choice of $e_2 \in B_2$ leads to $B_1 - e_1 + e_2$, which is minimally connected and has no loops. However, not every choice of $e_2 \in B_2$ leads to a new basis, and the second row in this figure is an example of this. Here, $B_1 - e_1 + e_2$ isn't connected so it can't be a basis, and it also contains a loop. Figure 8.6 shows three more examples of the exchange property.

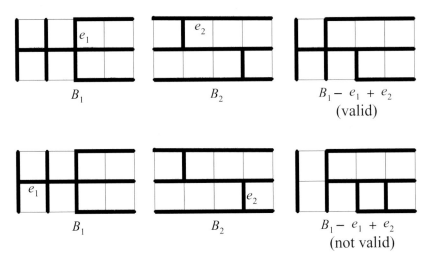

Figure 8.5. One valid and one invalid example of the exchange property.

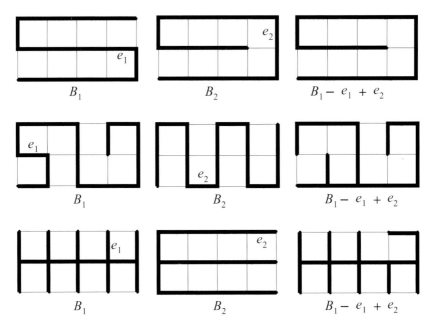

Figure 8.6. Three valid examples of the exchange property.

8.3 Main definition

Notation. In both the linear algebra and graph theory settings, let E stand for the set of building-block elements—either the column vectors of a matrix or the edges of a graph, and let B denote a typical basis chosen from E. Finally, let $\mathcal{B}$ denote the set of all bases formed from the elements of E.

Definition. In both the linear algebra and graph theory settings, a *matroid* is a pair $(E, \mathcal{B})$ consisting of a finite set E of elements and the (finite) collection $\mathcal{B}$ of all bases, where E and $\mathcal{B}$ are assumed to satisfy ((a)) and ((b)) above. That is, each basis is maximal, and the exchange property holds.

In the above definition, condition ((a)) being satisfied is actually an assumption. There happen to exist mathematical constructs satisfying ((a)) but not ((b)), but these are not matroids. Although a linear algebra or graph theory setting is assumed in our definition, the definition extends in a natural way to encompass, for example, simplicial complexes as well as the points and lines in certain projective spaces.[1]

8.4 Dual matroids

Duality is ubiquitous in Whitney's work—it was very much part of his mindset. One of his most frequently cited results from his early period is his planarity theorem, saying that a graph is planar if and only if it has a combinatorial dual. (See p. 69.) Important though this result is, it's a fact that many graphs fail to have a combinatorial dual—those that aren't planar. It's hard to believe that Whitney rested easy with such a state of affairs. What's the right way to look at things so that *any* graph has, in some natural sense, a dual? He found that by extending the concept of a graph to something larger and more complete, there was a natural duality just waiting for him. That more inclusive and complete notion turned out to be the matroid of a graph—larger because it contains not just the edges of the graph, but all the graph's bases. Whitney uncovered the dual of a matroid, and that includes any matroid, not just matroids arising from graphs or vector spaces.

We touch on this important concept just enough to whet the appetite by giving two concrete examples of a matroid dual, with pictures to illustrate. Let's begin with a definition.

Definition. Let $M = (E, \mathcal{B})$ be a matroid. For any $B \in \mathcal{B}$, the dual B^* of B is the set-theoretic complement of B—that is, $B^* = E \setminus B$. Let $\mathcal{B}^*$ consist of the duals of all $B \in \mathcal{B}$. Then the *matroid M^* dual to M* is $M^* = (E, \mathcal{B}^*)$.

Note. Frequently, in forming the dual, E in $(E, \mathcal{B}^*)$ is actually some other edge set having the same number of edges as E, and we can write this other edge set (essentially a copy of E) as E^*. In this case it is natural to write $M^* = (E^*, \mathcal{B}^*)$.

Example. Any graph extends to a matroid by defining E to be the graph's edges—or a copy of them—and $\mathcal{B}$ to be the set of all bases of the graph. This first example is both simple and revealing: a polygon. Figure 8.7 shows a hexagon considered as a graph G, and its dual G^*. (One can think "series" versus "parallel.")

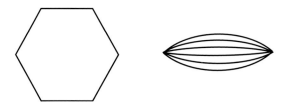

Figure 8.7. A hexagon (series) and its dual (parallel).

A subset of our hexagonal graph G is a basis B if, for any two vertices of G, there exists exactly one path of edges from B connecting them. It's easy to see that a typical basis of G is $G \setminus e$, where e is any single edge of G. The moment you put e back in, you complete the subset to the full polygon, meaning you lose uniqueness—there are two different paths connecting any two vertices. Therefore to extend G to its matroid, supplement the set E of G's six edges by the set $\mathcal{B}$ of G's six bases $B_i = E \setminus e_i$ $(i = 1, \dots, 6)$, to form $M = (E, \mathcal{B})$.

The dual of $M = (E, \mathcal{B})$ extends the dual G^* of G. In forming G^*, we place one point in each of the two regions into which G divides the plane, then connect these two points by an arc passing transversally through each edge e_i of G. This sets up a one-to-one and onto relation between the six edges of G and these six arcs. These edges and arcs are depicted in the left and right sketches in Figure 8.7, and we assign the name e_i^* to the arc in G^* associated with the edge $e_i \in G$. In this sense, we write $E^* = E$. As for $\mathcal{B}^*$, G^* has only two vertices, so any single edge is a basis of G^*. Therefore $\mathcal{B}^*$ simply consists of the six arcs appearing in Figure 8.7, and M^* consists of two sets E^* and $\mathcal{B}^*$ made up of six arcs each. It might appear to be a coincidence that taking the complement of a 5-edge basis in the hexagon gives precisely the corresponding 1-edge basis of G^*, but Whitney had tapped into something deep, because his notion works much more generally.

Calling M^* the dual of M means that M^{**} should be M. To check this, note that G^* in Figure 8.7 divides the plane into six regions, so there's one arc transversally crossing each edge of G^*, making a total of six arcs, which we can enumerate so that $E = E^* = E^{**}$. Each basis of $\mathcal{B}^*$ consists of a single edge, so each base in $\mathcal{B}^{**}$ consists of the complement of this—five edges. All of these 5-edge bases are in $G^{**} = G$ and they're exactly the six bases we originally identified, each being the hexagon minus one edge. From this, we see that $M^{**} = M$.

Example. We now look at a decidedly less trivial example of a planar graph: two identical squares sharing one edge. Once again the set-complement of a basis in the graph will give the corresponding basis in its dual. Because the graph is planar, we can draw its dual and check for ourselves that this correspondence holds; Whitney in [53] proves this remarkable fact for all planar graphs. Then, for a nonplanar graph such as K_5 or $K_{3,3}$, we simply *define* each basis in the matroid dual as the corresponding complement of a basis in the original.

In Figure 8.9, the two-square graph is drawn more heavily and the dual G^* of G is sketched more lightly. Edge 1 in G corresponds to arc 1 in G^*, and so on, so in forming the dual matroid M^*, we may identify E^* with E. Below this appears G^* redrawn in a prettier form. G has six vertices, so each basis has $6 - 1 = 5$ edges. G has seven edges, so some elementary combinatorics tells us that there are $\dfrac{7!}{5!2!} = 21$ basis candidates. Figure 8.10 lists all 21 of them, but six are crossed out since each of these contains a loop. Each of the remaining 15 possibilities turns out to be a basis, so these are *all* possible bases, and they therefore form $\mathcal{B}$ of G's matroid. Since each basis contains five edges and G has seven edges, each basis consists of all seven, minus some two. Under each picture, the two that are eliminated appear as an ordered pair, and doing this gives the 21 possibilities a natural organization. Each pair directly says what the complement of any basis is. The dual graph G^*, with its edges appropriately numbered, appears at the top in Figure 8.11.

Figure 8.8. Hass, around the time he introduced matroids.

Since G^* has three vertices, each basis of G^* consists of two edges, and it's easy to decide when an edge-pair actually forms a basis: any pair not forming a loop! This eliminates the three loops $(1, 2)$, $(1, 3)$, $(2, 3)$ as well as their primed counterparts $(1', 2')$, $(1', 3')$, $(2', 3')$. Note that in Figure 8.10, these six pairs correspond exactly to the six pairs listed under the crossed out pictures. Just as $\mathcal{B}$ consists of 15 bases, so also $\mathcal{B}^*$ consists of 15 bases, and they're sketched in Figure 8.11.

We now have two complete pictures of matroids: Figure 8.10, after removing all crossed-out entries, shows both E and $\mathcal{B}$ for the matroid $M = (E, \mathcal{B})$ of G, and Figure 8.11 shows E^* and $\mathcal{B}^*$ of the dual matroid $M^* = (E^*, \mathcal{B}^*)$ of G^*. We leave it for the reader to check that once again, $M = M^{**}$.

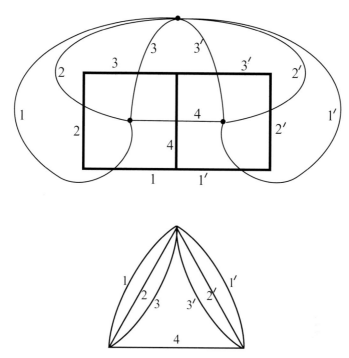

Figure 8.9. A less trivial graph (drawn more heavily) and its dual.

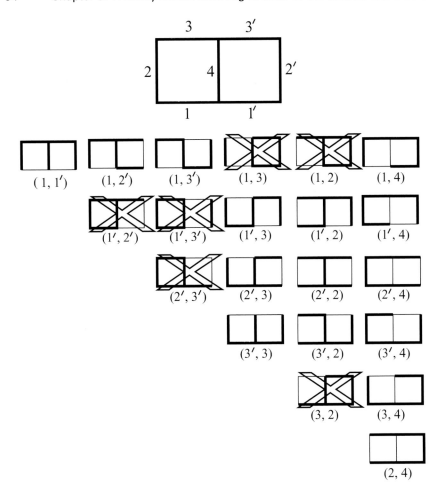

Figure 8.10. From the 21 five-edge basis candidates, six have loops, leaving 15 actual bases.

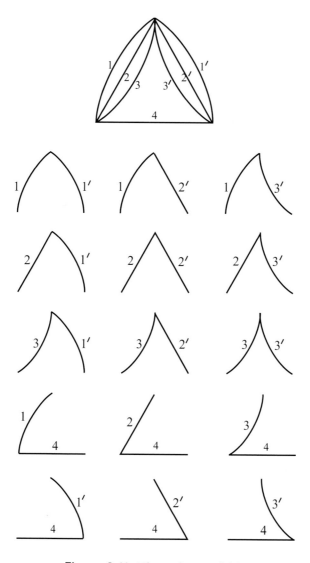

Figure 8.11. The 15 bases of $\mathcal{B}^*$.

CHAPTER 9
Topology: Its Beginnings

Whitney made decisive contributions to what is today one of the most powerful tools in topology—"cohomology." The path leading to it is long, twisted, and contains surprises. This chapter is a stroll along that path up to just before Riemann enters the scene. The next chapter recounts some of the tumultuous developments leading up to algebraic topology. Then in Chapter 11 we meet one of the fundamental contributions Whitney made to algebraic topology.

9.1 Euler: A new way of thinking

Mathematical historians generally agree that topology began with Leonhard Euler's solution in 1737 of the famous Königsberg seven bridges problem. Along the road from Euler's beginning to the discovery of homology and cohomology, we shake hands with a few of the mathematicians and their history-making topological contributions helping us get from then to now. First, Euler.

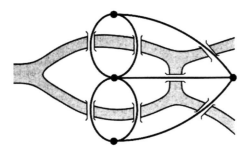

Figure 9.1. North and south land masses and two islands defined by the river through Königsberg were connected by paths and bridges.

Leonhard Euler. Figure 9.1 depicts the layout of the rivers and bridges of Königsberg when Euler worked on the problem. The city was founded in 1254 and lies on the Baltic Sea; it was the capital of the German province of East Prussia in Euler's day. The figure shows a river running through the city, dividing it into northern and southern sections, as well as into two islands in the river. Seven bridges were constructed allowing for easy travel between the four land masses, and formed a natural and scenic way for people to take walks. For years there was an unanswered question about the healthful pastime: Was there some route going over each of the seven bridges exactly once? If so, nobody had chanced upon it. As luck would have it, a young 29-year-old mathematician was living in St. Petersburg and had struck up a friendship with Carl Ehler, the mayor of Danzig in Prussia. They corresponded rather frequently, and in some of his letters the mayor mentions the seven bridges conundrum. In 1736, Ehler finally asks Euler directly, *Was there, or wasn't there, a route crossing each of the seven bridges exactly once?* Well, Ehler was no mathematician, and Leonhard had to set him straight. Euler replies, "This isn't a problem in mathematics, so I'm not the person you should ask." The solution, he explained, involved no more than straight reasoning. After thus clarifying matters for the good mayor and offering no hint about the actual answer, Euler, despite himself, began musing about the peculiar problem, a problem he initially called "banal."

Figure 9.2. Leonhard Euler.

He eventually realized that it was a problem in what Leibniz called the "geometry of position," in which distances were not involved. This realization initiated an evolution in Euler's thinking, and in what was really remarkable for the time, he began discarding quantitative considerations—the sort of considerations that made up the very soul of the day's mathematics. The areas of the land masses didn't matter. The length of the bridges didn't matter. In fact, nothing seemed to matter except how the bridges were connected to the land masses. After discarding just about everything central to mathematics as he knew it, Euler was left with what we would today call a graph theory problem. The biggest difficulty was breaking out of a confining quantitative mind-set, and once that major step had been taken the rest of the story flowed naturally. That very year, he conquered the Königsberg problem and presented his solution to the St. Petersburg Academy. The publication process was slow, but his article appeared five years later in [E].

In Figure 9.1, drawn in over the sketch of the four land masses is a graph with four vertices and seven edges. Since the sizes of the land masses don't matter, each land mass has been reduced to a single point or vertex, and the seven bridges connecting them become the seven edges connecting the vertices. This graph represents what remains after discarding information not essential to analyzing the problem. Although Euler's published solution reads as if he were looking at such a graph and pointing out its salient features, nowhere in any of his writings do we see a single graph like the one in Figure 9.1! In the seven-bridges question, Euler's answer did corroborate what the denizens of Königsberg had guessed—*there's no path going over each bridge exactly once*. Actually, Euler did more than that. He proved a more general result about any connected graph by presenting exactly two scenarios in which there exists a path going over each bridge just once. If neither of these is satisfied, then there is *no* path covering each edge exactly once. (Königsberg falls into this last case.)

One scenario: Suppose the number of edges meeting at each vertex is even. Then for any choice of vertex, there is at least one path starting and ending at that vertex and covering each edge exactly once. Any such path is therefore a cycle. This is a Hamiltonian cycle, which we met on p. 52.

The other scenario: Suppose the number of edges meeting at each vertex *isn't* always even. Then the only way that there can be a path covering each edge exactly once is when there are *exactly two* vertices where an odd number of edges meet. If we start from either of these vertices, then we are guaranteed at least one path covering each edge exactly once, and every such path must end at the other vertex. Any such path is therefore *never* a closed loop; it's a Hamiltonian path, but not a Hamiltonian cycle. (See p. 52.) As a simple example, consider the graph with two vertices and three paths running between them. Starting at one vertex and walking once along each of the three paths means ending up at the other vertex.

Neither of these scenarios is satisfied in the seven-bridges question, because an odd number of edges meets at each of the *four* vertices. Therefore there exists no path crossing each of the bridges exactly once.

Euler's solution to the problem about graphs is an honest theorem in topology, but it involves only dimension 0 (vertices) and dimension 1 (edges). Some 14 years later, Euler discovered another topological pearl, this time involving not only dimensions 0 and 1, but also dimension 2 (faces). This is his famous polyhedral formula.

Euler's Polyhedral formula. A polyhedron having V vertices, E edges, and F faces satisfies

$$V - E + F = 2.$$

Stating this beautiful topological formula was one thing, but Euler discovered that proving it was quite another. Although he verified it in a number of cases, an argument acceptable to him proved elusive. After about two years, he came up with reasoning that seemed adequate, but it took another 40 years before the French mathematician Adrien-Marie Legendre gave the formula a completely rigorous proof.

About the word "Topology"

Euler used Leibniz's Latin term *"geometriam situs"*—the "geometry of position"—to refer to his work on the seven-bridges problem. Gauss became interested in topology about 80 years later due to its connections with electromagnetism, but chose not to publish anything on it. However, his strong interest in topology greatly influenced at least two of his students, Bernhard Riemann and Johann Listing, and in 1847 Listing wrote the first extensive publication on topology. Its title can be translated from German as *Preliminary Studies in Topology* but was actually a long essay of musings on topology, with special attention to knots. Today's familiar name is from the Greek, *topos* + *logy* and it appeared in print for the very first time in this monograph, though Listing used it in a letter to an old high school teacher a decade earlier. All this was well before Poincaré's revolutionary works on topology, written from 1895 to about 1905, where he calls topology *Analysis Situs*. This Latin form endured for another generation, and only when Solomon Lefschetz used "topology" in the late 1920s did this name finally stick.

9.2 Two little-known but important contributors

Simon-Antoine-Jean L'Huilier. L'Huilier is hardly a household name in mathematics, but he filled in a key step in topology's development. Like Euler he was Swiss, and early on found a clear calling in life as a mathematician. An uncommonly bright youngster, he caught the attention of a wealthy relative who believed Simon would make an ideal man of the cloth, and a large fortune could be his simply for saying "yes" to a career in the church. But the youth already knew his own heart and was not about to trade away a future life in mathematics for riches. He proved to be a star in secondary school and went on to the Calvin Academy in Geneva, Switzerland where he fortuitously had one of Euler's students—Louis Bertrand—as a math teacher. L'Huilier's writing skills soon became apparent to his teachers, and at one point his physics teacher asked the blossoming student to enter a competition for writing a physics textbook to be used in Polish schools. To him, the writing part was fine, but he asked, "Could it be in mathematics, instead?" The competition did include mathematics, and he entered it at once. The young man won, and for many years his mathematics text—a primer on arithmetic—was used in Poland. He later wrote two more primers for Polish schools, one on geometry and another on algebra.

From Bertrand, Simon soon discovered Euler's works, including the famous bridges paper and Euler's polyhedral formula $V - E + F = 2$. He thought about these and related results for much of his long professional life, and at one point corrected an error in Euler's proof of the bridges problem. He also felt something was amiss in the polyhedral formula. Did it actually apply to *any* polyhedron? He realized that Euler's formula was valid for any polyhedron drawn on a sphere, but what about polyhedra drawn on, say, a torus, which is a sphere with one handle? Or a sphere with two handles? Or more generally, g handles? Just counting vertices, edges, and faces showed that the formula needed revision to account for polyhedra on surfaces Euler hadn't considered. It was L'Huilier who replaced $V - E + F = 2$ by

$$V - E + F = 2 - 2g.$$

As an interesting historical note, calculus students and teachers around the world write *lim* hundreds of times each day. That's L'Huilier's notation; he was one of the first to consider two-sided limits. In 1795 L'Huilier, then 45 years old, entered a competition for the position of mathematics chair at his former school. He won, succeeding his old mathematics teacher Louis Bertrand in Geneva. He remained as chair until he retired at age 73, and lived to nearly 90.

Johann B. Listing. Listing is an all-but-forgotten near-giant in the annals of topology. His insights helped pave the way for later progress, yet his mathematical accomplishments were barely recognized in his day and only now are beginning to get some of the credit they deserve. What's his story?

Figure 9.3. Simon-Antoine-Jean L'Huilier.

Johann was an only child of a financially struggling family. An especially bright boy, he showed an early, remarkable aptitude in art that caught the attention of the directors at the Städel Foundation in Frankfurt. Johann Friedrich Städel was a wealthy banker and patron of the arts, and one of his Foundation's aims was promoting the education of artists. The Foundation's support allowed Johann to receive a solid early education. Johann moved on to traditional schools upon turning eight and was already beginning to develop into a polymath, quickly picking up mathematics, science, and at least four languages. When he later entered the Gymnasium, the Städel Foundation once again gave him generous support toward what was meant to be an art major. Listing's preference was by then for mathematics, but the good people of the Foundation looked the other way, and Listing studied pretty much what he wanted. This support continued as he entered Göttingen University, his spongelike mind picking up chemistry, geology, physiology, and anatomy as well as physics and mathematics. As luck would have it, he found himself in mathematics classes taught by Gauss, who soon recognized an unusual talent in Listing. Gauss asked him to join his circle of mathematical friends, and a few years later, Gauss became Listing's doctoral adviser. The two remained close throughout Gauss's life. As for his personality, Listing was social and witty, kind-natured, a loyal friend to many, and had no enemies.

Figure 9.4. Johann B. Listing.

So whatever was the problem? Why the almost total neglect and lack of recognition of at least some of his topological insights? A few of the reasons: He did not publish much, and to compound this, he had an obscure way of writing. He would typically dwell on minutiae at the expense of giving any overall picture and that provided little for potential readers to hook on to. He would become involved in other scientific areas and simply forget about mathematics for long periods of time, even years. He was part of the academic world, but would take virtually no part in the political games that came with the territory. He was apparently bipolar, with manic and depressed periods. He most certainly did not inherit financial skills from his parents, and built up heartbreaking debts. His wife was equally inept, unable to work within anything approaching a family budget. Besides that, she seemed to endlessly find herself on the wrong side of the law. It's a wonder the poor man accomplished anything at all. Except that he was a genius.

What *did* he accomplish? Why is he an important figure in the development of topology? It seems almost certain that Listing received a strong topological impetus from Gauss, who had investigated electrical and magnetic fields and their flow lines, and it's easy to imagine how these ideas from Gauss made their way into Listing's first monograph. Written in 1847, the monograph discusses at length spirals of various kinds, and mixes up these discussions with botanical analogies—tendrils found in different plants, and spiral arrangements found in many plants, leaves, petals, seed arrangements, and so on. Often in a plant one sees a series of parallel spirals, sometimes closely and other times loosely spaced. As an example, the seeds of a sunflower are arranged in an even number of parallel spirals, where "parallel" means differing by an angular rotation about the center. He also considered the world of surfaces: If we take a long strip of paper and give it several 360° twists, then paste the ends together, the edges form two parallel helices or spirals. If we give it instead an odd number of 180° twists before pasting, then we get one continuous spiral. Listing also discussed what happens when the twisted strip is cut lengthwise, down the middle of the road—when it is that we get linkage, when we get one or two pieces, and so on. He finds that after cutting lengthwise a strip given three 180° twists, we end up with a paper trefoil knot. The idealized trefoil knot is a mathematical curve; in the real world, it's made from, say, a rope or a thin flexible cylinder. Figure 9.5 depicts such a knot.

Figure 9.5. A trefoil knot.

Listing then considered more general knots. These were all very new ideas, and of course his strips with an odd number of 180° twists are topological Möbius strips. Why the name Möbius? Möbius discovered his strip a few months after Listing, but Möbius was a better known mathematician, and also clearly explained that the surface is one-sided, something Listing did not do.

He wrote a second monograph 14 years later, in 1861, and here he had insights presaging some game-changing advances in topology. As one of the most important examples, in Euler's polyhedral formula

$$V - E + F = 2,$$

Listing wondered where, exactly, does that 2 come from? The reason must lie deeper than "It just turns out that way." He ultimately concluded that counting only 0-dimensional vertices, one-dimensional edges, and two-dimensional faces leaves out the obvious: The polyhedron additionally cuts out two three-dimensional pieces—the inside solid of the polyhedron, and everything in 3-space outside the polyhedron. If you were to denote by S the number of pieces of 3-space defined by the polyhedron, then the formula takes the more satisfying form

$$V - E + F - S = 0.$$

For example, for a tetrahedron—a pyramid with a triangular base—these numbers are $V = 4$, $E = 6$, $F = 4$, $S = 2$, so that $V - E + F - S = 0$ becomes $4 - 6 + 4 - 2 = 0$.

Of course written this way, the formula suggests that for other cases the values of V, E, F, and S could be quite different, but if the insight is right, one should always have $V - E + F - S = 0$. His monograph includes some examples, and while his definitions are unusual and sometimes contorted, the basic idea of the formula is there. He broke through to one higher dimension and set the stage for alternating sums associated with topological manifolds of arbitrary dimension.

CHAPTER **10**
Topology Grows Into a Branch of Mathematics

From 1850–1930, topology really burgeoned. Here, we meet some of the players from this period who had especially far-reaching influences: Bernhard Riemann, Enrico Betti, Henri Poincaré, and Emmy Noether. The ideas they introduced led to successive revolutions, and topology began to play an increasingly larger role in other branches of mathematics. But realizing topology's potential required new concepts and tools, and some of those are more technical. Since we talk about a few of them here, some readers may want to skim over or just skip this chapter. That won't affect the overall narrative of the book.

10.1 Bernhard Riemann and Enrico Betti

Riemann, one of the all-time giants in mathematics, became interested in topology through his thesis advisor Carl F. Gauss, who himself thought about electromagnetic fields. Riemann had absorbed his mentor's interest in topology through its physical connections with electric and magnetic lines of force. A few years after receiving his Ph.D., Riemann by chance met Enrico Betti in Göttingen and the two become friends. Riemann subsequently visited Betti in Italy on a number of occasions, and during these times he and Betti discussed potential theory, elasticity, theory of functions and, very important to the future of topology, the notions of connectivity and genus. When Riemann was 37, he caught a vicious cold that he couldn't shake off. His health was always precarious, so he thought that visiting Italy, with its warm weather, would be better for him than enduring the upcoming winter in Germany. That was how a serious collaboration arose: Riemann stayed near the University of Pisa where Betti was teaching, and their friendship flourished.

Riemann and Betti were interested in connectivity; essentially, the "connectivity number" is the largest possible number of cuts before further cutting would

Figure 10.1. Enrico Betti and Bernhard Riemann.

necessarily break up the space into two pieces. For example Figure 10.2 shows a surface of genus two, and it can withstand up to four cuts—the four circular ones shown—and still stay in one piece, making the surface's connectivity number 4.

The reason it remains in one piece under all this cutting is that none of the four cuts actually contains any surface material, so none is taken away when you cut the surface along the loop. It turns out that after making these four cuts, the surface (made of rubber, say) can be stretched out so it lies flat on a table top. After that, the only kind of cut possible will look like the small oval loop in the figure. That loop is completely different from the others: It contains surface material, so when you finish cutting around the oval, the inside of the oval just falls out, separating the surface into two pieces.

Riemann also approached connectivity as a way to solve a nettlesome problem in graphing polynomials. In plotting a polynomial equation $p(x, y) = 0$ such as the circle $x^2 + y^2 - 1 = 0$, the strange thing was that even such an ordinary, everyday example wasn't even a function! A function has just one y-value for every x, while this circle has *two* y-values for every $x \neq \pm 1$. That's true even to the right or left of the circle—by just doing the algebra, we get two imaginary values. In fact, plugging in complex values from *any* $x \neq \pm 1$ still gives two (usually complex) values! Those exceptions $x = \pm 1$ are the two "join points" where the top and bottom halves of the circle meet. To deal with this, Riemann took a finite number of concentric spheres, made slits, and reconnected the freshly cut edges. For example, if the cut edges in the inner sphere are a and a' and those

Figure 10.2. Some cuts on a surface.

directly above in the outer sphere are b and b', then glue a to b' and a' to b. This is depicted in Figure 10.3.

If there are several such slit pairs, the connectivity number generally increases. Riemann shrank the complex plane to the "Riemann sphere," took two concentric such spheres, made a slit in each from $x = -1$ to $x = 1$, and interchanged edges as above before pasting so that an edge on one sphere joined an edge on the other sphere. We say today that he created a *Riemann surface*. By doing this, Riemann essentially created a satisfactory domain for the circle's equation so that to each x point on the Riemann surface there corresponded exactly one y point. For polynomials of high degree in y, one can get many concentric spheres, many pairs of points like the pair for the circle, many slits, and many switch-and-join operations. Bottom line: This process can create Riemann surfaces of high genus—that is, with many holes and therefore high connectivity number.

Riemann made several visits to Italy for his health, each time visiting Betti, and among other things they discussed how to extend connectivity numbers to higher dimensions. The philosophy of cuts used for surfaces should be much the same. For a surface, a loop counts toward the connectivity number if it doesn't contain any surface material. A key word here is "contain." In the plane—or "Flatland"—what sort of topologically smooth figure can contain something—maybe a prisoner? The answer: a topological circle. That's all the boundary that is needed, assuming all life takes place within Flatland. The same thing holds if you live on the surface of a sphere, because a loop drawn on the surface traps

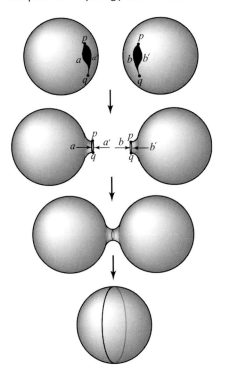

Figure 10.3. Joining two slit spheres.

anything inside it. But for a three-dimensional manifold sitting in some higher-dimensional space, the floor and walls need to be two-dimensional and serve as the boundary of a three-dimensional living space or container. To ensure that the prisoner can't escape from such a cavity, its walls need to be closed with no escape holes, and that means it can't have a boundary. One possible candidate for such a cavity is a topological 2-sphere. The sphere forms the walls for the living space within the bubble. A more interesting living space would have walls forming a closed bounded orientable surface of genus g—a sphere with g handles. Once inside a cavity with these walls, he's trapped. As with Flatland, we assume that all life takes place within the three dimensions of the manifold. The manifold may be sitting in a higher-dimensional space, but everything stays in the 3-manifold.

Now for the big question: Can you cut along the walls of such an appropriately situated cavity in a three-dimensional manifold, and still not break the manifold into two pieces? For that to be possible, the cavity can't contain any of the three-dimensional material. It would need to be empty, in just the same way that four of the loops in Figure 10.2 are empty, and for exactly the same reason: To keep the manifold in one piece, the cavity can't contain anything—otherwise, when you cut it out and set it away from the manifold, some of the manifold would go along with it. Although few people can visualize a 3-manifold sitting in some higher-dimensional space, we can attempt to convey some of the flavor through working by analogy and examples.

Let's begin with "multiplying together simple topological spaces." Place an ordinary (empty) circle on a table top and to each point of the circle, glue the origin of a vertical line $\mathbb{R}$. No two lines touch, and these infinitely many parallel lines form a cylinder. By thus placing the circle in the (x, y)-plane and the lines—all parallel to the z-axis—in a new dimension, we create the "product" of the circle and line, which we can denote by $\mathbf{o} \times \mathbb{R}$, or equally well, by $S^1 \times \mathbb{R}$, where S^1 denotes a one-dimensional sphere (a circle). This construction is illustrated on the left in Figure 10.4.

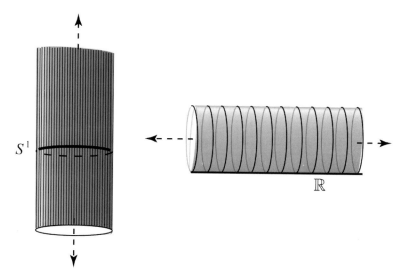

Figure 10.4. In the picture on the left, passing a vertical line through each point of a horizontal circle creates the cylinder $S^1 \times \mathbb{R}$. The picture on the right shows a circle passing through each point of a horizontal line $\mathbb{R}$, creating the cylinder $\mathbb{R} \times S^1$. These are topologically the same—that is, $S^1 \times \mathbb{R} = \mathbb{R} \times S^1$. This is a special case of a general fact: *Topological multiplication is commutative.* If we replace $\mathbb{R}$ in the right picture by a circle so big that all vertical circles are disjoint we get a torus. A torus is in this way the product $S^1 \times S^1$ of two circles.

This circle represents a topological loop in the cylinder, and the loop does not surround any of the two-dimensional manifold material. Let's mimic this idea, but one dimension higher. Place a two-dimensional sphere (like a beach ball) in (x, y, z)-space, and to each point of it glue the origin of a line $\mathbb{R}$, each line always parallel to a new axis going into the fourth dimension. Let's call this new direction the t-axis. So in 4-space, we've created the cylindrization of S^2. This is also a product, $S^2 \times \mathbb{R}$. The dimension of any product like this is the sum of the dimensions of the factors, so this product has dimension $2 + 1 = 3$. This 3-manifold contains the sphere S^2, and like the loop S^1 in $S^1 \times \mathbb{R}$, S^2 is a bubble not containing any of the 3-manifold material. In a sense that Poincaré later made clear, the loop in $S^1 \times \mathbb{R}$ is the only "independent" such empty loop, meaning that the Betti number counting the number of independent voids is $\beta_1 = 1$ for the cylinder. Similarly, the sphere in $S^2 \times \mathbb{R}$ is the only independent void or cavity in that 3-manifold, so we say that for $S^2 \times \mathbb{R}$, $\beta_2 = 1$. Although this 3-manifold sits in 4-space, by a little sleight of hand we can force it into 3-space where we can better appreciate it. To do this, notice that $\mathbb{R}$ can be topologically shrunk down to an open interval I. For example, in the x-axis, map each point x to $\frac{0.05x}{|x|+1}$. The image of this map is an interval I just 0.1 long. Therefore that infinitely long cylinder $S^1 \times \mathbb{R}$ becomes a cylinder $S^1 \times I$ only 0.1 long. We can play this trick on $S^2 \times \mathbb{R}$ to get $S^2 \times I$. Because $\mathbb{R}$ has been so severely shrunk, and since in forming a product the only thing that really matters is that all copies of $\mathbb{R}$ or I are disjoint, we can pass each tiny I through each point of the sphere S^2, always keeping the intervals disjoint. This creates a thickened sphere—think of a clay ball with a big bubble in the middle. With one such empty hole, we again have $\beta_2 = 1$ for this 3-manifold.

We next consider a more sophisticated example of a 3-manifold that truly lives in a higher-dimensional space. For this we provide no sleight-of-hand; the reader will have to be trusting. We begin with a familiar lower-dimensional example, an ordinary torus. As suggested in Figure 10.4, this may be looked at as a product of two circles, $\text{o} \times \text{o} = S^1 \times S^1$. The horizontal circle could be so big and the vertical ones so small that the product looks like an inflated inner tube sitting on a table top and touching the surface in a circle. Actually, this picture is cheating a little bit because each circle lives in a plane, and under products, dimensions add. That means the torus is really a $1 + 1 = 2$-dimensional manifold living in $2 + 2 = 4$-space, and we are quite lucky that we can force a torus into 3-space—a piece of luck that most people are not aware of. There are two "independent" loops on the torus not containing any two-dimensional torus material, similar to the fancier example shown in Figure 10.2 on p. 109 showing four independent such loops. The notion of product allows us to go up a dimension, from a product of two circles to a product of *three* circles. This triple product $\text{o} \times \text{o} \times \text{o}$ has dimension $1 + 1 + 1 = 3$, and it sits in $2 + 2 + 2 = 6$-space. The three subproducts of three circles taken two at a time are independent closed two-dimensional submanifolds—each a torus—and as it turns out, each of these three tori forms a void or cavity containing no material from the 3-manifold O × O × O. These three torus-cavities represent all the independent three-dimensional voids, similar to the two loops on the ordinary torus representing all the independent two-dimensional voids. The dimension of the walls or boundary of each of these three-dimensional voids is 2, and we write $\beta_2 = 3$. Stretching far beyond anyone's ability to visualize, the product of a dozen circles yields a 12-dimensional manifold; there are 12 products taken 11 at a time, giving $\beta_{11} = 12$.

In the examples we've seen so far, the boundary of the void or cavity has always been of dimension one less than the dimension of the manifold. For instance, the torus has dimension 2, and the loops on them have dimension 1. In fact, the torus itself is a two-dimensional boundary for the emptiness inside, meaning there's a two-dimensional Betti number for the torus, and that one cavity gives $\beta_2 = 1$. There is also a Betti number β_0; for convenience, this is taken to be the number of component manifolds, which is 1. So the suite of Betti numbers for the torus is $(\beta_0, \beta_1, \beta_2) = (1, 2, 1)$. What Betti did was work out a suite of Betti numbers for orientable, closed, bounded manifolds of arbitrary dimension—a lofty goal and a history-making accomplishment. As it turned out, flaws and subtle gaps in his work were eventually discovered, so the chapter had not been completely written.

The transformative mathematician Henri Poincaré happened to need topology for his work on the qualitative theory of ordinary differential equations involved in studying the three-body problem (like the earth, sun, and moon), and turned his attention to Betti's work. He recast what Betti did, putting it on a potentially more solid foundation and opening up a whole new area of mathematics, *homology theory*.

10.2 Henri Poincaré

In counting voids or cavities, we have used the term "independent" loosely, never making a formal definition. Yet this notion plays a key role in arriving at the notion of Betti number since the total number of independent cavities is taken as that number. Therefore it is important to know what we're talking about, and Poincaré gave us a clear and workable answer.

Let's begin with Figure 10.6 on p. 115. Of the three loops shown, two of them contain no torus material, so are of the type counting towards the Betti number β_1. Does each count? That is, are they independent? It's easy to see that there are infinitely many loops of just this type, so a "yes" answer doesn't make sense. In some way, these two loops that don't contain any torus material must be equivalent. Now in the realm of numbers, two numbers are equal exactly when their difference is zero, and Poincaré applied this idea to loops. The difference

Figure 10.5. Henri Poincaré.

of two numbers is equal to one of them plus the negative of the other, and this idea has a beautiful analog in the world of loops. First, what's the negative of a loop? Notice that all these loops have arrows drawn on them. That is, each has been given an orientation. If C is an oriented loop, then we'll simply say that $-C$ is C, but with the arrow reversed. That is, $-C$ is given the orientation opposite to that of C. Now in the figure, let's name the top oriented loop C_1. For the bottom loop, let's say that the translate of C_1 to that new position is C_2. However, notice that we've reversed the orientation, so the oriented loop sketched in the figure is $-C_2$. Therefore in analogy with numbers, to prove that C_1 and its pure translate C_2 along the torus are equivalent, we want to show that $C_1 + (-C_2) = 0$. What we are doing here is looking at the union of two oriented loops as their sum, so the top and bottom loops in the figure can be written as $C_1 - C_2$. Now, what is 0? The only loops counting toward the Betti number are ones containing no surface material. That means the middle squarish loop in the figure doesn't count toward the Betti number, and we call any such loop a *zero loop*.

Now let's add all three loops in the figure, whose union can be written as $C_1 + 0 - C_2$. To do this, think of an ant walking along the top loop—say it starts

Figure 10.6. Adding these three oriented loops gives the zero loop.

on the back side of the torus, where the loop is dashed, and walks in the direction (orientation) given by the arrow. It soon comes to where the squarish loop meets the top loop. For clarity, there's a tiny separation, but the paths are meant to coincide. Not only do they coincide, but they do so with opposite orientation. Part of the genius in this approach is that these two oppositely oriented path segments cancel, resulting in a gap. So the ant makes a turn down the long rectangular path, always faithfully following the arrows. At the bottom, once again, two paths have been erased, and the ant doesn't even see this erased part, so continues its walk along the bottom loop, still following the arrow. The ant makes a closed circuit this way. Now let's focus on this circuit. Let the two long rectangle sides slide down toward the rear side of the torus. A little thought shows that this topological loop on the rear side is essentially like the original rectangular loop drawn in the figure, in that it encompasses torus material. That is, it's the zero loop! Therefore

$$C_1 + 0 + (-C_2) = C_1 - C_2 = 0,$$

which is what we needed to prove to establish that two purely translated loops are equivalent:

$$C_1 \simeq C_2.$$

That's of course true for *all* pure translates of C_1. Therefore we can justifiably elevate C_1 to the status of the one independent loop out of all these translates.

The translates we have been talking about are sometimes called the *meridian* circles of the torus, and the argument above tells us there's exactly one independent meridian loop on the torus. Orthogonal to these meridians are the circles of *latitude*, and an entirely analogous argument shows that of them, there is exactly one independent circle. So one meridian and one latitude circle constitute two independent void-containing loops on the torus. These turn out to be the only such independent loops, and we accordingly write $\beta_1 = 2$.

Now there are lots of other loops we can draw on a torus, and if one meridian and one latitude circle are chosen to be the two independent ones, then *every other loop on the torus should be expressible as a combination of these.* This is indeed the case, and the combination looks remarkably like the linear combination of vectors, except we use entire loops, so the coefficients are integers instead of, say, real numbers. That is, if we denote the independent meridian circle by M and the independent latitude circle by L, then every closed oriented curve drawn on the torus is equivalent to $mM + nL$, where m and n are integers (including zero and negatives). In this way Poincaré brought a truly powerful and far-reaching simplification to the subject. We don't present proofs, but a few examples give a good sense of things.

As one example, suppose that as we travel once around a circle of latitude, we loop around in the other direction four times. (If we instead went around a hundred times, the result would look something like a slinky whose ends are brought together to form a slinky on a torus.) We can topologically massage this four-versus-one looping by bringing the meridian loops closer together, as suggested in the pictures in Figure 10.7.

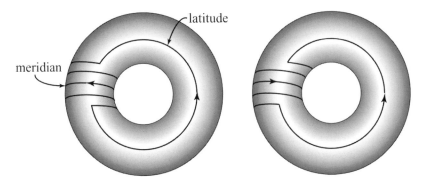

Figure 10.7. Multiple windings in the same direction can be regarded as a single winding-with-multiplicity. These pictures depict multiple windings in the meridian direction. These meridian windings have opposite orientations, and the multiplicities correspondingly have opposite signs.

If we continue this bringing-together process so that all four loops are actually right on top of each other, then these four loops can be thought of as one loop with multiplicity 4. This is essentially the same idea as when we look at the zeros of a polynomial such as

$$(x - a)^3(x - b)^5(x - c)^2$$

as the formal "point chain" or simply "chain" $3a + 5b + 2c$; here, the zeros a, b, and c are regarded not as numbers but as points in $\mathbb{R}$ or $\mathbb{C}$, and those points, written with coefficients to denote multiplicity, are chained together with plus signs. If we agree that the arrows in the left sketch of Figure 10.7 each represent the positive orientation for the meridian and latitude circles, then we can express the winding loop in the left picture in chain form as $4M + 1L$. In the right picture, the meridian arrow has been reversed, so relative to our agreement, that winding loop is the chain $-4M + 1L$. This approach brings a wonderful simplicity to what would otherwise look like a bewildering array of various ways of drawing loops on a torus.

Another possibility is that as we wind around a number of times in the meridian direction, we wind around some other number of times in the latitude direction. For example, we might go around an odd number of times in the meridian direction while going around twice in the latitude direction. The ends of the curve don't meet the first time around the meridian direction, but do on the second. Figure 10.8 depicts the idea, where the combination is written as $-(2n - 1)M - 2L$. This could also be written as $(1 - 2n)M - 2L$. One can draw analogs for any two relatively prime integers, resulting in a lot of interweaving of curves on the torus. But algebraically, it's expressed in a clear, simple, and suggestive way.

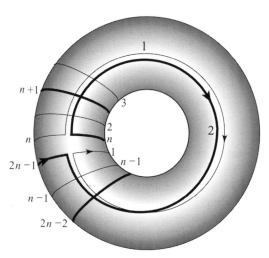

Figure 10.8. This complicated-looking winding can be written as $(1 - 2n)M - 2L$.

The many possible curves on a torus have a natural parametrization as a plane lattice consisting of points (m, n), where m and n are integers. Each lattice point represents all curves equivalent to each other. Let's observe a few things about these lattices:

- In Figure 10.7, the left picture corresponds to the point $(4, 1)$; the right picture, to $(-4, 1)$; the curve in Figure 10.8 corresponds to $(1 - 2n, -2)$.
- There are four natural bases $(\pm 1, 0)$ and $(0, \pm 1)$ of the lattice, but they are not the only bases. As an example, for any integer q, $(1, 0)$ and $(q, 1)$ is also a basis since subtracting $q(1, 0)$ from $(q, 1)$ gives $(0, 1)$. So either curve in Figure 10.7, together with a single circle of latitude, form a basis.
- The fancy windings $pM + qN$, where p and q are relatively prime, correspond to something having an easy geometric description: In the lattice, the lattice's origin $(0, 0)$ can "see" the point (p, q), in the sense that there are no other points between the origin and (p, q) to obstruct the origin's vision.
- A point such as $(25, 11)$ corresponds to a chain of 25 meridian loops $(25, 0)$ and 11 latitude loops $(0, 11)$.
- For the two-holed torus depicted in Figure 10.2 on p. 109, there are four basis elements for loops containing no surface material. Any closed curve C on this surface is equivalent to an integer linear combination of these four basis curves. Any such C is represented as a single point (n_1, n_2, n_3, n_4) in the lattice $\mathbb{Z} \times \mathbb{Z} \times \mathbb{Z} \times \mathbb{Z} = \mathbb{Z}^4$. This generalizes to a sphere with g handles: A basis consists of $2g$ curves, none containing any surface material; any closed, nonintersecting curve C' on this surface is equivalent to an integer linear combination of these $2g$ basis curves; and any such C' is represented as a single point in the lattice $\mathbb{Z}^{2g}$.

In his famous series of papers on topology, Poincaré used triangulated manifolds. This represented another huge step forward in topology. On surfaces, a smooth manifold (such as a sphere, torus, or more generally a sphere with g handles) was replaced by a polytope consisting of triangular faces. Since there were only finitely many such faces, computations and proofs could be carried out at a combinatorial level, and that paid important dividends in greater rigor and generality. Poincaré's idea harkens back to Euler's polytopes and his formula $V - E + F = 2$, except that with Poincaré all faces are triangles, and that means his building blocks are more uniform than the polygonal faces Euler used. This is in no sense a restriction, because any of Euler's polytopes can be triangulated. The reasoning goes like this: On the one hand, every time we add an edge to a polygon face to make a triangle plus what's left of the polygon, we at the same time add a face, so $V - E + F$ remains unchanged. Or, if we add a new vertex to an edge, we've added 1 to both V and E, so $V - E + F$ is still unchanged. A basic fact is that triangulating a manifold doesn't affect its topological properties, nor does the exact form of the triangulation. The triangulation could so fine that the eye would be unable to tell the difference between that and the original smooth manifold. At the other extreme, the triangulation could be so coarse it barely resembles the original.

Figure 10.9 shows a triangulated sphere on the left. The picture on the right shows a hollow tetrahedron. It's topologically the same as a sphere, and with only four faces, is the coarsest possible triangulation of a sphere.

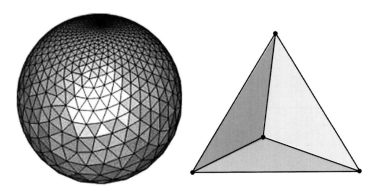

Figure 10.9. A fine and the coarsest possible triangulation of a sphere.

Figure 10.10 shows a triangulated torus. Even with this level of fineness, there are already hundreds of triangles. If you refined this many times over so that the torus would look like a truly smooth manifold, then all the drawings in Figures 10.6, 10.7, and 10.8 would look the same with this fine a triangulation, although it would consist of thousands of faces. Figure 10.11 shows a far coarser triangulation of the torus.

One important advantage of triangulating surfaces is that it easily generalizes to all higher dimensions, with everything remaining combinatorial in nature. To see how to do this, let's look at a triangular face in the following light: The triangle's three vertices can be looked at as the endpoints of three vectors v_0, v_1, v_2, which can lie in any n-space ($n \geq 2$). To get an honest triangle, assume $v_1 - v_0$ and $v_2 - v_0$ are linearly independent, which is to say they don't lie along one line. The entire triangle—vertices, edges, and all interior points—is then the smallest *convex set* containing the three vertices. We explain.

A set is *convex* if whenever two points are in the set, then so is the line segment connecting them. The smallest convex set containing any set S is called the *convex hull* of S. Therefore the triangle consisting of its vertices, edges, and all interior points is the convex hull of its three vertices. Of all polygons, triangles are the simplest. The dimension of a triangular face is 2, so it's natural to call the convex hull of three points not lying in a line a *2-simplex*, and that's the official

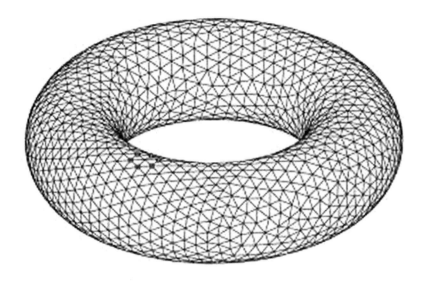

Figure 10.10. A triangulated torus.

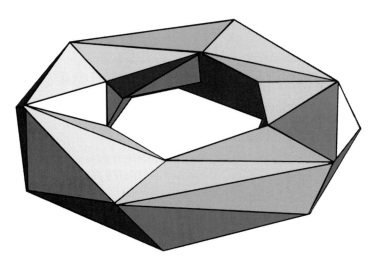

Figure 10.11. A more coarsely triangulated torus.

name we'll use. We can now generalize to other dimensions. In dimensions below four, the definition seems needlessly fancy, but in higher dimensions, where
we humans have serious problems visualizing, it is indeed efficient.

- A 0-simplex is the convex hull of one point. (A 0-simplex is therefore just a point.)
- A 1-simplex is the convex hull of two points not all lying on a point. (A 1-simplex is a line segment.)
- A 2-simplex is the convex hull of three points not all lying on a line. (A 2-simplex is a filled-in triangle.)
- A 3-simplex is the convex hull of four points not all lying in any plane. (This is a tetrahedron, shown for example in the right picture of Figure 10.9 on p. 119.)
- A 4-simplex is the convex hull of five points not all lying in any 3-space.
- An n-simplex is the convex hull of $n + 1$ points not all lying in any $(n - 1)$-space.

This brings us to another bit of terminology: Each of the triangulations in Figures 10.9, 10.10, and 10.11 forms a *two-dimensional simplicial complex*—an assemblage or complex consisting of 2-simplices joined together in a natural way suggested by these figures. Dividing up a 3-manifold into an analogous union of tetrahedrons instead of triangles gives a three-dimensional simplicial complex, and we can extend the analogy to get n-dimensional simplicial complexes.

Using simplicial complexes has another big advantage because the definition of simplex immediately allows us to specify subsimplicies having lower dimension. For example, in the triple torus $M = \mathbf{o} \times \mathbf{o} \times \mathbf{o}$, we said there are exactly three ordinary torus-shaped voids each of whose walls or boundaries has dimension 2, so that $\beta_2 = 3$. We said nothing about β_1 for M, which counts up independent voids in M having one-dimensional boundaries. Simplices, fortunately, give us a mechanism for dealing with questions involving lower dimensions. An example gives the idea of how to step down one dimension at a time, and we can go all the way to the empty set, which has dimension -1. Suppose (v_0, v_1, v_2, v_3) describes a 3-simplex (a tetrahedron). One can eliminate any one of the four vertices in four ways, giving four possible sets of three vertices: (v_1, v_2, v_3), (v_0, v_2, v_3), (v_0, v_1, v_3), (v_0, v_1, v_2), and these four sets give precisely the four faces of the tetrahedron. So we've gone down one dimension from 3 to 2. Now take any one of the faces, say (v_1, v_2, v_3). Similarly eliminating any one of the three vertices gives three possible sets of two vertices: $(v_2, v_3), (v_1, v_3), (v_1, v_2)$, and these are the three edges of that face, meaning we've decreased to dimension 1. Now take an edge, say (v_2, v_3), and eliminate either of the two vertices, giving (v_3) and (v_2)—the vertices (dimension 0) at the ends of that edge. Taking away, say, (v_3) from (v_3) leaves the empty set. This is the gist of stepping down the dimension ladder.

We've often decreased dimension in this historical account. For example, the boundary of any topological disk is a loop, which has one lower dimension than the disk. This loop, being a boundary, is closed—there are no endpoints— so *its* boundary is the empty set. In both cases, taking the boundary decreases the dimension. This holds if instead of a disk, we begin with any solid object, say a lump of coal. Dip it in some paint, let it dry, and let the coal itself disappear. We're left with the boundary of the lump, a shell of dimension 2 that surrounded the three-dimensional lump. The shell, like the loop, is closed, so its boundary is the empty set. It turns out we can play this game in any dimension; the boundary of an n-dimensional object has dimension $n - 1$, is closed, and has the empty set as boundary.

Our previous torus examples teach us something else. Many loops, such as a latitude or meridian circle, are not the boundary of any disk in the surface, and that was an especially important distinction since it is those types of loops that count toward the Betti number. Since we're replacing smooth surfaces by polytopes made up of triangles—and higher-dimensional analogs of this—we need a way of taking the boundary not just of surfaces, but in any dimension. For example, how can we be certain that within a complicated simplicial complex in 150-space, the boundary of the boundary of any 47-simplex is the empty set? For the triangle, we know its vertices and therefore its three edges. But the boundary of any edge consists of two points, so for all three edges, we seemingly end up with six points—clearly not the empty set! These points must somehow cancel, and canceling suggests that some negatives need to cancel positives. This leads to one of the most crucial aspects of using simplices in topology. *We orient them!* Orientations come in two flavors—positive and negative—and with that, the possibility of canceling. Orienting simplices turns out to play an important role in combinatorial topology. We now show how this works for a concrete 2-simplex such as the one in Figure 10.12.

We give the 2-simplex $v_0v_1v_2$ an orientation by just ordering its vertices. In the figure, we see that ordering the vertices as they appear in $v_0v_1v_2$ endows the 2-simplex with a counterclockwise orientation. And as we also see from the figure, this orientation induces a natural orientation on each of the edges, so we correspondingly assign the edges the vertex-orders v_0v_1, v_1v_2, v_2v_0. Along each edge, we've written that edge as a two-element chain of "oriented points." Arguing physically for a moment, one can think of the orientation given the 2-simplex as a rotation of a fluid in the shaded area. This fluid induces in a natural way a flow in each edge. Looking at, say, the bottom edge, the fluid is drawn from v_0 and flows into v_1. In that spirit, we assign a minus to the v_0 to express the draining, and a plus at v_1 to express accumulation. If ∂ denotes the boundary operator, we can write $\partial(v_0v_1) = v_1 - v_0$. Of course, each vertex sees incompressible fluid both coming in and going out, so there is no net accumulation or loss at any of the vertices. This is reflected algebraically by adding up what's happening at the three vertices:

$$(v_1 - v_0) + (v_2 - v_1) + (v_0 - v_2).$$

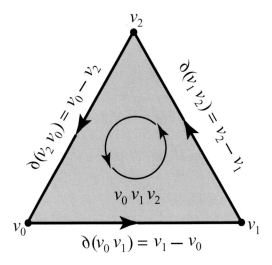

Figure 10.12. An oriented 2-simplex and its three oriented edges.

Physically, we're not surprised: All terms cancel. Writing ∂^2 to denote taking the boundary of the boundary, we therefore have

$$\partial^2(v_0 v_1 v_2) = \partial(v_0 v_1 + v_1 v_2 + v_2 v_0) = (v_1 - v_0) + (v_2 - v_1) + (v_0 - v_2) = \varnothing.$$

Let's up the ante and look at orienting a 3-simplex $v_0 v_1 v_2 v_3$. As with the 2-simplex, a 3-simplex is given by specifying an order on its vertices, so a natural order on them is $v_0 v_1 v_2 v_3$. These four vertices are shown in Figure 10.13.

Viewing the tetrahedron from the outside, assign each of the four faces a counterclockwise orientation. Notice that the lightly drawn circuit on the bottom face is in fact oriented counterclockwise when viewed from a point underneath (that is, outside) the tetrahedron. Since any face is just one point thick, a circle with an arrow on it is still that same circle with that same arrow, no matter where you view it. The arrow determines the face's orientation, so from the bird's eye view, its orientation is $v_0 v_2 v_1$, and viewed from underneath, the orientation is still $v_0 v_2 v_1$.

From Figure 10.13 we can read off each of the four oriented faces; string or chain them together with plus signs and you have the boundary of the oriented 3-simplex. The picture tells us that the boundary—a 2-complex—is

$$\partial(v_0 v_1 v_2 v_3) = v_1 v_2 v_3 + v_0 v_3 v_2 + v_0 v_1 v_3 + v_0 v_2 v_1.$$

The geometric arguments we have used are suggestive in low dimensions, but our geometric intuition in higher dimensions is too limited for trustable results there. We therefore need to recast things algebraically or symbolically in

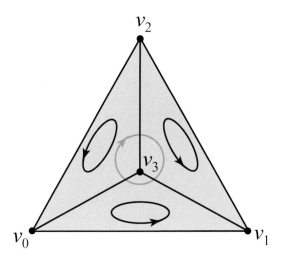

Figure 10.13. Bird's eye view of an oriented 3-simplex.

such a way that extending to arbitrarily high dimensions is easy. This is familiar in linear algebra where vectors, distances, angles, and such are intuitive in dimensions 2 and 3, but where we need algebra to reliably handle higher-dimensional analogs.

We can obtain the same results above by operating on simplices in a certain formal way which, fortunately, is very simple. In describing this formal method we use two ideas.

- Interchanging any two vertices in an ordering of them changes the orientation. For example in the 2-simplex $v_0 v_1 v_2$ in Figure 10.12, switching v_1 and v_2 produces $v_0 v_2 v_1$, describing a clockwise orientation instead of counterclockwise. Here's the general fact: Any odd number of pairwise interchanges in any simplex $v_0 \ldots v_n$ reverses orientation, while any even number of pairwise interchanges leaves its orientation unchanged.
- The "hat" symbol denotes deletion. For example, $v_0 \hat{v}_1 v_2$ is the same as $v_0 v_2$.

We are now ready to describe the symbolic method for finding the boundary of a simplex. We do this first for the 2-simplex shown in Figure 10.12 on p. 123, and then for the 3-simplex in Figure 10.13. Based on the admittedly sketchy evidence that these two examples provide, we then present a general formula for the boundary of a simplex of *any* dimension, and it turns out that this formula has exactly the properties we need, including this very central one:

For any simplex σ, $\partial^2(\sigma) = \emptyset$.

The symbolic method applied to the 2-simplex in Figure 10.12.
Arguing geometrically, we found the oriented boundary edges of this simplex to
be $v_0 v_1$, $v_1 v_2$, and $v_2 v_0$. These can be combined to express the entire boundary as
a chain or 1-complex:

$$\partial(v_0 v_1 v_2) = v_0 v_1 + v_1 v_2 + v_2 v_0. \tag{10.1}$$

We can get this same chain symbolically by writing

$$\partial(v_0 v_1 v_2) = (-1)^0 \hat{v}_0 v_1 v_2 + (-1)^1 v_0 \hat{v}_1 v_2 + (-1)^2 v_0 v_1 \hat{v}_2. \tag{10.2}$$

This simplifies to

$$\partial(v_0 v_1 v_2) = v_1 v_2 - v_0 v_2 + v_0 v_1.$$

We can turn the middle sign into a plus by interchanging v_0 and v_2:

$$\partial(v_0 v_1 v_2) = v_1 v_2 + v_2 v_0 + v_0 v_1,$$

which after rearranging terms is the same as equation (10.1). The idea: In (10.2),
successively hat each vertex in $v_0 v_1 v_2$ and use the position of the vertex (starting
from 0) as the power to raise (-1).

The symbolic method applied to the 3-simplex in Figure 10.13.
We oriented each face of the 3-simplex counterclockwise, suggesting that the oriented boundary of the 3-simplex $v_0 v_1 v_2 v_3$ is the 2-complex

$$\partial(v_0 v_1 v_2 v_3) = v_1 v_2 v_3 + v_0 v_3 v_2 + v_0 v_1 v_3 + v_0 v_2 v_1. \tag{10.3}$$

Using a recipe just like the above gives

$$\partial(v_0 v_1 v_2 v_3) = (-1)^0 \hat{v}_0 v_1 v_2 v_3 + (-1)^1 v_0 \hat{v}_1 v_2 v_3 + (-1)^2 v_0 v_1 \hat{v}_2 v_3 + (-1)^3 v_0 v_1 v_2 \hat{v}_3$$

$$= \partial(v_0 v_1 v_2 v_3)$$

$$= v_1 v_2 v_3 - v_0 v_2 v_3 + v_0 v_1 v_3 - v_0 v_1 v_2.$$

A little interchanging and term rearranging of this gives equation (10.3).

The general formula for the boundary of a simplex. Taking our cue
from the above two examples, we get this formula for the boundary of a general
simplex $v_0 v_1 \ldots v_n$:

$$\partial(v_0 v_1 \ldots v_n) = \sum_{i=0}^{n} (-1)^i (v_0 v_1 \ldots \hat{v}_i \ldots v_n). \tag{10.4}$$

There are some interesting analogs between using ∂ to denote "boundary of"
and using it for the derivative. See Notes 10.1 and 10.2.

This general formula allows for a quick proof that ∂^2 of any simplex is the empty set:

$$\partial^2(v_0 v_1 \ldots v_n) = \sum_{j<i}(-1)^i(-1)^j(v_0 v_1 \ldots \hat{v}_j \ldots \hat{v}_i \ldots v_n)$$

$$+ \sum_{j>i}(-1)^i(-1)^{j-1}(v_0 v_1 \ldots \hat{v}_i \ldots \hat{v}_j \ldots v_n).$$

If v_i and v_j in the second sum are interchanged, we end up with the negative of the first sum. The entire sum is therefore the 0-chain, which represents the empty set.

Using simplices and simplicial complexes, Poincaré was able to put Betti numbers on a solid footing. Here's a quick, informal description of Betti numbers of any dimension based on his ideas. Let S be a triangulated closed, bounded orientable manifold of dimension n; it is therefore a (finite) simplicial complex. Let c_r denote any chain of r-dimensional simplices in S. The boundary operator ∂ then maps c_r to c_{r-1}. Let's assume r is larger than 0 and less than n. Let I_r denote the set of all r-dimensional chains that are boundaries, each being $\partial(c_{r+1})$ for some chain c_{r+1} in S_{r+1}. Let K_r be the set of all chains that have no boundary, meaning each chain of K_r maps to 0 under ∂. Since ∂^2 sends every simplex to 0, I_r is contained in K_r. On a surface, we can think of a chain in I_r as like the small loop on the double torus depicted in Figure 10.2, bounding some of the surface material. Poincaré called these chains in I_r *homologous to 0*. For purposes of exposition, denote I_r by $A_{r,0}$. If c is some chain in K_r not in $A_{r,0}$ (typified by one of the four nonbounding circles in Figure 10.2), then all chains in K_r that are c plus something in $A_{r,0}$ are mutually equivalent, and we'll call this set $A_{r,1}$. If there's a chain in K_r in neither $A_{r,0}$ nor $A_{r,1}$ (typified by another one of the nonbounding circles in Figure 10.2), then we'll get a further set $A_{r,2}$ of mutually homologous chains. Since S_r is finite, there are only finitely many such $A_{r,i}$, say $A_{r,0}, \ldots, A_{r,\beta_r}$. That number, β_r, is the rth Betti number. The alternating sum $\chi = \beta_0 - \beta_1 + \cdots \pm \beta_n$ is called the *Euler-Poincaré characteristic* and is the generalization to dimension n of Euler's characteristic for convex polyhedral surfaces.

Poincaré noticed and eventually proved a strikingly beautiful result about the Betti numbers of a connected, closed, bounded orientable manifold of dimension n: *The ith and $(n-i)$th Betti numbers are the same.* This is sometimes called "Poincaré duality." It applies, for example, to any n-dimensional "multi-torus," the product of n circles $S^1 \times \cdots \times S^1$. Here, for example, are the Betti number sequences for the products of 0 up through 4 circles:

$$
\begin{array}{ccccccccc}
& & & & 1 & & & & \\
& & & 1 & & 1 & & & \\
& & 1 & & 2 & & 1 & & \\
& 1 & & 3 & & 3 & & 1 & \\
1 & & 4 & & 6 & & 4 & & 1
\end{array}
$$

This pattern continues, forming the Pascal triangle, which so frequently and unexpectedly rears its beautiful head! Poincaré duality also applies to n-dimensional spheres S^n, where the sequences of Betti numbers form a triangle consisting of just the first and last 1s of the Pascal triangle, with all other entries being 0. This says that for all dimensions r larger than 0 and less than n, any r-chain in a triangulation of S^n that's closed (has no boundary) must enclose sphere material. This is an impressive generalization of what we can all appreciate on the familiar sphere S^2—any time you draw a loop on a sphere, that loop must enclose some sphere material. This is very different from drawing a latitude or meridian circle on a torus! One immediate application of Poincaré duality: If the manifold's dimension n is odd, then *the Euler-Poincaré characteristic is 0*. That's because for odd n, there are an even number of Betti numbers, $\beta_0, \ldots, \beta_n$. Therefore β_r and β_{n-r} occur with opposite signs in the alternating sum $\chi = \beta_0 - \beta_1 + \cdots \pm \beta_n$. Whitney and Eduard Čech reformulated Poincaré duality in a more modern cohomological form.

Figure 10.14. August Ferdinand Möbius and Felix Christian Klein.

10.3 Emmy Noether

Poincaré had found a fertile plot of land and populated it with topological seeds. Poincaré worked largely from intuition, making leaps of faith based on examples and calculations, but it was for others to make Poincaré's far-reaching topological insights more organized and various arguments more rigorous. The Dutch mathematician L. E. J. Brouwer, for example, had a strong philosophical bent and helped to organize these insights into a more cohesive whole. Others, including Heinz Hopf, Pavel Aleksandrov, and Solomon Lefschetz, also advanced the frontiers created by Poincaré's ideas.

But it is Emmy Noether's almost accidental contribution to topology that stands as one of the most remarkable examples of cross-fertilization in science. She was already widely known for highly original contributions to abstract algebra—the study of the algebraic essence of familiar objects such as the integers, all fractions, real and complex numbers, the set of symmetries of various geometries, and so on. All these involved one or more operations such as addition, multiplication, or composition, and she studied and extended our understanding of such algebraic properties. In contrast to the other mathematicians just mentioned, she was very far from being a topologist.

As luck would have it, David Hilbert, always a strong supporter of Emmy, insisted that she visit the great mathematical center, Göttingen—she would be well received there. She took his advice. During the 1925-6 Christmas and New Year holidays, she traveled from Göttingen to the picturesque village of Blaricum in North Holland for a vacation and also visited the topologist L. E. J. Brouwer at his beautiful home there. He famously hosted dinners, and one wintery evening he, Noether, Hopf, and Aleksandrov all dined there. Inevitably, the conversation turned to mathematics—that meant topology—and it was then that she heard Hopf and Aleksandrov explain how they and others were extending and rigorizing Poincaré's ideas on combinatorial topology. Emmy, the mathematical outsider at the dinner, first found out about chains, simplicial complexes, boundary operators, Betti numbers, and such from her dinner companions, and her reaction was strong and immediate. One can just hear her exclaiming to the effect, "You're adding chains? Subtracting them? There's a zero chain? And a boundary operator sending chains to chains? *All this is group theory!* And when you add chains, the order of adding them makes no difference? And those simplices in a triangulation ⋯ there are only a finite number of them? You're actually talking about *finitely-generated abelian groups.* And your boundary maps are *homomorphisms of those groups!*[3] Furthermore, those Betti numbers measure the ranks of these groups ... " With her extensive algebraic background, she had plenty to say and she could argue passionately. The others were willing and open-minded listeners, and after being taken completely off guard by her crash course on viewing topology through the lens of group theory, after the last thunder from her

Figure 10.15. (Amalie) Emmy Noether.

bolt of lightning had faded, the topologists realized that their subject was about to change. She had shown them that the toolbox algebraists had developed over the years was there for the taking. After the holidays, she gave a lecture at Göttingen on the advantages and naturalness of recasting topology in group-theoretic terms. Many people attended that talk, and word began to spread. It marked the beginning of a new era in topology.

We sketch just enough here to give some flavor of the changes she introduced. Assume a manifold M has been triangulated into a simplicial complex. Building on Poincaré's ideas, we can add or subtract any two r-dimensional chains c_1, c_2 in this simplicial complex, with the zero-element being the empty chain. For each r, the r-chains form an abelian group C_r with the simplices forming a set of generators for the group. The boundary operator ∂ preserves addition and subtraction: $\partial(c_1 \pm c_2) = \partial(c_1) \pm \partial(c_2)$, and we can write ∂_r for the group homomorphism induced by ∂ that maps C_r into C_{r-1}. Since ∂_r is defined for any

Figure 10.16. Counterclockwise, starting from the top left: The three critical players at "the dinner": Emmy Noether, Heinz Hopf, Pavel Aleksandrov. Solomon Lefschetz also had a great influence on the development of topology around this time.

dimension r, for a triangulated manifold we get a sequence of groups and boundary homomorphisms:

$$C_n \xrightarrow{\partial_n} C_{n-1} \xrightarrow{\partial_{n-1}} \cdots \xrightarrow{\partial_{r+2}} C_{r+1} \xrightarrow{\partial_{r+1}} C_r \xrightarrow{\partial_r} C_{r-1} \cdots \xrightarrow{\partial_2} C_1 \xrightarrow{\partial_1} C_0. \qquad (10.5)$$

The size of each group is not unique—for example, one can divide any simplex into two parts, just as one might divide a triangle into two smaller ones by adding an edge connecting a vertex to a new vertex introduced on the opposite side of the triangle. Now Poincaré taught us that the boundary homomorphisms play two roles. First, the image of a chain c_r under ∂_r is an example of a closed "container" that is actually empty, not containing any manifold material. Those empty ones are what contribute to Betti numbers. And then there are the closed containers that *do* contain manifold material, and which Poincaré called homologous to 0. The sequence (10.5) is perfect for seeing both roles of the boundary homomorphism. Take C_r, for example. ∂_{r+1} is on one side and ∂_r is on the other. These two homomorphisms define two subgroups of C_r: On the one hand there's the image $\mathrm{Im}(\partial_{r+1})$ of C_{r+1} under ∂_{r+1}; on the other hand there is the kernel $\mathrm{Ker}(\partial_r)$ of ∂_r—that is, the set of all elements of C_r mapping to 0 under ∂_r. (When these ideas were first discussed in the mid 1920s, there wasn't even the name "kernel." It was Aleksandrov who made up that name.) Since every element in $\mathrm{Im}(\partial_{r+1})$ is itself a boundary, and because $\partial^2 = 0$, every element in $\mathrm{Im}(\partial_{r+1})$ is in $\mathrm{Ker}(\partial_r)$. That is, the group $\mathrm{Im}(\partial_{r+1})$ is a subgroup of $\mathrm{Ker}(\partial_r)$, so it makes sense to form the quotient group $\mathrm{Ker}(\partial_r)/\mathrm{Im}(\partial_{r+1})$. Here's an official definition:

Definition. $\mathrm{Ker}(\partial_r)/\mathrm{Im}(\partial_{r+1})$ is called the rth *homology group* $H_r(M)$ *of* M.

Each homology group is a finitely generated abelian group. These turn out to be the direct sum of a finite part (having only a finite number of elements) plus some number β_r of copies of the integers $\mathbb{Z}$. This number, the "rank" of $H_r(M)$, is precisely the rth Betti number β_r of the manifold M. It is a central fact that although the chain groups C_r are not uniquely defined, the groups $H_r(M)$ are. That is, these groups turn out to be independent of whatever triangulation you happen to choose for the manifold M. So Poincaré's Betti numbers, in addition to being found through combinatorial means, could now often be determined using group theory and the basic decomposition theorem for finitely generated abelian groups. In many cases this way could be both more efficient and illuminating.

There were further important advantages to working with groups. As one example, the homology groups of nonoriented manifolds such as the projective plane and the Klein bottle are finitely generated and abelian. It turns out that the presence of finite parts in the decomposition of such groups supplies information about orientability or nonorientability. Even further, the group approach meant that a mapping from one manifold into another would be reflected in homomorphisms from the sequence of homology groups like sequence (10.5) of one manifold into those of the other manifold.

CHAPTER 11
Whitney Helped Revolutionize Algebraic Topology

At a 1934 mathematics conference, two major mathematicians proposed nearly identical ways of introducing the notion of product into algebraic topology. Their proposals seemed very significant, but they didn't smell quite right to 28-year-old Whitney. Together with his friend Eduard Čech, Whitney fixed up the definition and their "cup product" soon became a standard part of the burgeoning cohomology theory. The basic takeaway of this chapter is that since there can be different rings having the same additive group, assigning a particular ring to a manifold (versus assigning just a group) is like giving the manifold a tag with more information written on it. Whitney succeeded in properly turning a homology group into a homology ring, thus supplying such a tag. If the reader mainly wants to appreciate just that bottom line, the more technical last three sections of this chapter can be skipped.

11.1 Some perspective

In 1925, the idea of becoming a mathematician was completely off Hassler's radar screen. He was an undergraduate physics major, and for him, mathematics was primarily an aid to solving real-world problems. Calculus and other math books? They served as references for looking up ways to get answers. As an undergraduate, not only did Hass skip taking any calculus, the single course he did take was for just one reason: He wanted answers to some mysteries surrounding excluded regions and complex numbers he'd encountered as a teenager when plotting curves defined by various polynomials.

The decade following 1925 was full of surprises. In 1930, Hass found he didn't have the memory for physics, turned to math—in particular the four-color problem which led him to graph theory—and soon proved some fundamental results in graph theory whose combinatorial nature in turn led to his work in combinatorial topology.[1] During that same decade, progress in topology exploded. All sorts of topological spaces had been discovered and explored. It was known that surfaces like a sphere, donut, and, more generally, a sphere with g handles were classified by the single integer g, but what about all the other ones? There were whole new worlds of topological spaces of arbitrarily high dimension, both orientable and nonorientable. New objects could be created by cutting simpler pieces and pasting them together in various ways. Just as Mendeleyev organized the expanding world of chemical elements through his periodic table, and botanists and biologists sought to classify the universe of different life-forms, in topology the growing size and extent of so many different spaces begged for some classification scheme. How do all these spaces relate?

Classification and organizing is certainly nothing new to mathematics. The ancient Greeks knew and studied rational (that is, ratio-nal) numbers as ratios of two natural numbers. Then came the bombshell: The Pythagorean school proved that $\sqrt{2}$ was not rational. The existence of an irrational number created a major crisis in their quest of understanding the world of numbers, and the situation became radically worse when it was discovered that the square root of *any* prime natural number was irrational. Some centuries later the terrible truth fully descended upon them when Euclid proved there exist an infinity of primes, for that implied an infinity of irrational numbers. They began to turn away from investigating such dark truths about numbers and began working more on geometry. More than two thousand years later it was discovered that there are far more irrational numbers than rational ones—in fact, a whole larger infinity of them. Today, all possible real numbers are known, and are classified by strings of digits, their decimal representations. This classification accounts for all real numbers, and is also one-to-one if we omit expansions ending in all 9s. Furthermore, those nice rational numbers so meaningful to the Greeks appear in a decimal representation as decimals that after some point endlessly cycle, such as

$$41.87368368368368368 \cdots = 41.87\overline{368}$$

$$= 41 + \frac{87}{100} + \frac{368}{999}$$

$$= \frac{4{,}219{,}613}{99{,}900}.$$

So although today we have a classification like the above for real numbers, finding some way to classify topological manifolds has become one of today's burning issues. "Classifying" was initially looked at as tagging manifolds in some way—say, with a set of numbers, so that manifolds that are topologically differ-ent get a different set of numbers. It turned out that using only numbers was too restrictive and that other objects were more natural and powerful. In Chapter 9 we recounted the history-making story of how, at a social dinner, the algebraist Emmy Noether first heard about topological ideas and recognized—and dramati-cally pointed out—their strong algebraic nature. Her dinner companions, topolo-gists Heinz Hopf and Pavel Aleksandrov, realized how finitely generated abelian groups[2] could serve as a potent vehicle for classifying spaces and immediately set to work on this new way of looking at things. Such groups, called *homology groups* (see the definition on p. 131) when applied to topological spaces, soon made the rounds in the topological community, and many researchers began working on them. Progress was so fast that an International Conference in Topol-ogy was arranged and held in Moscow in 1934. This was the very first such con-ference in a mathematics specialty.

The conference was filled with luminaries. The central and by then very fa-mous Heinz Hopf and Pavel Aleksandrov were there, and had already written the first volume of a projected three-volume magna-opus entitled *Topologie*. At 636 pages, volume I was a meticulous treatment of the ramifications of the bur-geoning algebraic topology. The confluence at the conference of so many ideas in the growing study was electric, and new ideas surfaced so quickly that Hopf and Aleksandrov realized that their volume I, hardly off the press, was already outdated and reality dictated that there was no point in continuing with the two succeeding volumes. Many topologists were tinkering with the new homology groups with the aim of making their variations squeeze out more information about the underlying spaces on which they were based. After all, the big goal in all this activity was classifying topological spaces.

> One basic question was always "If two manifolds are topologi-cally different, then are the two associated algebraic homolog-ical structures likewise different?" All too often they weren't; the algebraic machinery was too "coarse" and would let non-identical manifolds fall into the same algebraic bin. So it was not tinkering for the sake of tinkering—the need was very real.

One of the youngest mathematicians at the conference was 28-year-old Hassler Whitney. He attended many lectures and saw for himself what the giants were doing and what new ideas were circulating. To the end of making homology groups better at distinguishing between different spaces, one of the ideas in the air was supplementing any such group with some sort of multiplication to make it a ring, reminiscent of the idea that not only can you add polynomials, you can multiply them, too. Since one can create different rings having the same underlying group, rings ought to be better than just bare groups at distinguishing between spaces. One participant, Andrey Kolmogoroff, gave an explicit way of turning a group into a ring. Kolmogoroff was not alone: In the cauldron of the conference another influential mathematician—James Alexander of Princeton—announced that he, too, had devised basically the same definition. These were exciting developments, seeming to presage turning Noether's groups into rings capable of capturing more topological information than groups.

Whitney heard Kolmogoroff and Alexander's definitions of product, and on the one hand the idea seemed tremendously significant, but at the same time something didn't smell quite right. Whitney had made friends with the Czech mathematician Eduard Čech, and the two of them agreed that the multiplication idea seemed powerful and promising. Besides, the idea came from two very prominent mathematicians. Nevertheless, there seemed to be a problem: If you multiply two sets like a disk and an interval, the result is a solid cylinder—the dimensions add: $2 + 1 = 3$. (In Figure 10.4 on p. 111 we showed how to multiply a circle with a line. Replacing the circle with a disk—a filled-in circle—gives a solid cylinder.) However, Kolmogoroff and Alexander's definition of product didn't do that, instead giving a dimension that was larger than the sum by one. Whitney and Čech puzzled over this problem, and within a few months they had ironed out the difficulty. (The next three sections supply some background, definition, and examples.) By that time, Alexander had already written a paper using his original definition and submitted it to the *Annals*. Upon learning of the Whitney-Čech revision, Alexander immediately saw its advantages. He rewrote and resubmitted his paper, which appeared in 1936.

Whitney and Čech called their multiplication the *cup product* and is today a standard part of algebraic topology. What, exactly, is their cup product, and why is it important? In the remaining three sections of this chapter we explain by doing three things:

- Because the "cup product" depends on the idea of cohomology, we begin with a brief account of cohomology.
- We then say just what the cup product is.
- In the last section we give some examples showing how the cup product can let us distinguish between different manifolds sharing the same homology groups. The cup product turns these identical groups into distinct rings.

11.2 What is cohomology?

The difference between homology and cohomology is in many ways like the difference between a vector space and its dual. Any vector $(a_1, \dots, a_n)$ in a real vector space V can be looked at as something other than, say, a directed line segment or a point in n-space. It can also be viewed as a function mapping $(x_1, \dots, x_n) \in V$

into $\mathbb{R}$, with $(a_1, \dots, a_n)$ being the constants in the function $y = a_1x_1 + \dots + a_nx_n$. The *dual* V^* of V is then the set of all $(a_1, \dots, a_n)$ considered this way as functions. Here are other notations for this that bring out its function aspect: With $a = (a_1, \dots, a_n)$ and $x = (x_1, \dots, x_n)$, $y = a_1x_1 + \dots + a_nx_n$ can be written as $y = a \cdot x$, and also as $y = a(x)$. Another commonly used notation is $y = \psi(x)$.

Now just as V has a natural basis

$$\{\epsilon_1 = (1, 0, \dots, 0), \dots, \epsilon_n = (0, \dots, 0, 1)\},$$

so V^* too has a natural basis

$$\{\psi_1, \dots, \psi_n\},$$

where each ψ_i is the function $\psi_i : x \longrightarrow \epsilon_i \cdot x$. This means $\psi_i(\epsilon_j) = \epsilon_i \cdot \epsilon_j = \delta_{ij}$, where δ_{ij} is 1 when $i = j$ and is 0 otherwise.

We can now introduce cohomology through working by analogy with a vector space and its dual. Let M be a manifold that's been triangulated, thus turning it into a simplicial complex. There are therefore simplices of all dimensions, from 0 through dim M, but for right now let's fix a dimension r and consider only those simplices of that dimension. There are only finitely many r-dimensional simplicies—let's call them

$$\{\sigma_1, \dots, \sigma_n\}.$$

As a first step, think of the σ_i as basis elements, making the analogy

$$\sigma_i \leftrightarrow \epsilon_i.$$

In our chosen dimension, consider the integral chains $m_1\sigma_1 + \dots + m_n\sigma_n$ that make up an integer lattice L—analogous to real chains $r_1\epsilon_1 + \dots + r_n\epsilon_n$ generating a real vector space V. Now in analogy with a vector space V, each element $m = (m_1, \dots, m_n)$ of L can be considered to be a mapping from L to the integers $\mathbb{Z}$: Under this mapping, each lattice point $x \in L$ maps to $m \cdot x \in \mathbb{Z}$. As with a vector space, the dual lattice L^* has a basis of functions corresponding to the basis $\{\sigma_1, \dots, \sigma_n\}$ of L, and by analogy with the ψ notation above we can write this basis of L^* as

$$\{\varphi_1, \dots, \varphi_n\},$$

each φ_i being the linear function $\varphi_i : m \longrightarrow \sigma_i \cdot m$. As before, $\varphi_i(\sigma_j) = \delta_{ij}$. The points of L^* can be written as $m_1\varphi_1 + \dots + m_n\varphi_n$ and are called *cochains*. As with V, V^*, and L, it's not hard to see that L^* forms an abelian group, and for any $\varphi \in L^*$, $\varphi(a_1\sigma_1 + a_2\sigma_2) = a_1\varphi(\sigma_1) + a_2\varphi(\sigma_2)$. In analogy to the r-dimensional group of chains C_r, we write C^r for the group of cochains.

In the last paragraph we assumed a particular dimension r, but everything there holds for any dimension 0 through dim M. That means there's a cochain group C^r for each r. If there were a good analog of the boundary operator ∂, we could then form the analogs of (10.1) through (10.4) on pp. 125-125. There is: the *coboundary* operator, denoted δ. This operator transforms a function φ

of r vertex variables to a function $\delta\varphi$ of $r+1$ vertex variables, thus increasing dimension instead of decreasing dimension the way ∂ does. What we need now is a combinatorial definition of δ allowing for trustable proofs in any dimension. The following definition expresses $\delta\varphi$ of $r+1$ vertices as an alternating sum of φs of r vertices:

$$\delta\varphi(v_0 v_1 \ldots v_{r+1}) = \sum_{i=0}^{r+1} (-1)^i \varphi(v_0 v_1 \ldots \hat{v}_i \ldots v_{r+1}).$$

The sum on the right-hand side looks a lot like the formula for the boundary operator applied to an $(r+1)$-simplex:

$$\partial(v_0 v_1 \ldots v_{r+1}) = \sum_{i=0}^{r+1} (-1)^i (v_0 v_1 \ldots \hat{v}_i \ldots v_{r+1}),$$

and is exactly the formula applied to φ of an $(r+1)$-simplex:

$$\varphi(\partial(v_0 v_1 \ldots v_{r+1})) = \sum_{i=0}^{r+1} (-1)^i \varphi(v_0 v_1 \ldots \hat{v}_i \ldots v_{r+1}).$$

Suppressing the vertex argument, this becomes

$$\delta\varphi = \varphi\partial,$$

showing the essential relation between ∂ and δ. We can now write

$$\delta\delta\varphi = \delta\varphi\partial = \varphi\partial\partial,$$

and because $\partial^2 = 0$, we conclude that also $\delta^2 = 0$.

It is now routine to rework the homology machinery set up earlier to get the cohomological analog of the sequence in (10.5) on p. 130:

$$\ldots \, 0 \xleftarrow{\delta_{n+1}} C^n \xleftarrow{\delta_n} C^{n-1} \xleftarrow{\delta_{n-1}} \ldots \xleftarrow{\delta_{r+2}} C^{r+1} \xleftarrow{\delta_{r+1}} C^r \xleftarrow{\delta_r} C^{r-1}$$

$$\ldots \xleftarrow{\delta_2} C^1 \xleftarrow{\delta_1} C^0. \tag{11.1}$$

There's also an analogy to the definition on p. 131:

Definition. $\mathrm{Ker}(\delta_r)/\mathrm{Im}(\delta_{r-1})$ is called the rth *cohomology group* $H^r(M)$ of M.

The H^rs are abelian groups.

11.3 The cup product

After the above brief look at cohomology groups, we can now define the promised cup product in them.

Definition. For any $\varphi(v_0 \cdots v_r) \in C^r$ and $\varphi'(v_r \cdots v_{r+s}) \in C^s$, the value of the *cup product* $\varphi \smile \varphi'$ on the $(r+s)$-dimensional simplex $v_0 \cdots v_{r+s}$ is

$$(\varphi \smile \varphi')(v_0 \cdots v_{r+s}) = \varphi(v_0 \cdots v_r) \cdot \varphi'(v_r \cdots v_{r+s}). \tag{11.2}$$

On the right hand side we're just multiplying two integers. Integers are associative and distributive and the cup product inherits these properties:

$$(\varphi \smile \varphi') \smile \varphi'' = \varphi \smile (\varphi' \smile \varphi'')$$
$$\varphi \smile (\varphi' + \varphi'') = (\varphi \smile \varphi') + (\varphi \smile \varphi'').$$

Also, note that if either φ or φ' is the 0-function, then

$$\varphi \smile \varphi' = 0.$$

In checking that the cup product does actually turn cohomology groups into cohomology rings we need to insure that the cup product of two cocycles is a cocycle, and that the cup product of any coboundary and any cocycle is a coboundary (which is like saying "in a ring, 0 times anything is 0"). The key to seeing these two facts is the δ-analog of the set-theoretic "Leibniz rule" $\partial(S \times T) = (\partial S \times T) \cup (S \times \partial T)$, discussed in Note 10.1 [p. 354]. This analog is

$$\delta(\varphi \smile \varphi') = \delta\varphi \smile \varphi' \pm \varphi \smile \delta\varphi'. \tag{11.3}$$

The $\pm$ comes from vertex ordering and orientation.

- It's easy to see that the cup of two cocycles is a cycle by using (11.2) and (11.3) and remembering that φ is a cycle exactly when $\delta\varphi = 0$.
- To show that the cup of a cocycle and coboundary is a coboundary, argue this way: Let φ be a coboundary and φ' a cocycle. Is $\varphi \smile \varphi'$ a coboundary? Since φ is a coboundary, we can write it as $\delta\phi$ for some cochain ϕ. So is $\delta\phi \smile \varphi'$ the coboundary δ of something? Try $\phi \smile \varphi'$: $\delta(\phi \smile \varphi')$ equals, by Leibniz's rule, $(\delta\phi \smile \varphi') \pm (\phi \smile \delta\varphi')$. Since φ' is a cocycle, $\delta\varphi' = 0$ and therefore $\phi \smile \delta\varphi' = 0$, leaving us with $\delta\phi \smile \varphi' = \delta(\phi \smile \varphi')$, which is what we wanted. A similar argument shows that $\varphi' \smile \varphi$ is also a coboundary.

All the H^r can be coalesced into a single object H^* by taking their direct sum $H^* = \bigoplus_{r \geq 0} H^r$; a typical element can be looked at as an ordered sequence of elements $(\alpha_0, \cdots, \alpha_r, \cdots)$. This is an abelian group under componentwise addition, and this direct sum can be given a ring structure by using the cup product, where for $\alpha_r \in H^r$ and $\alpha_s \in H^s$, the product $\alpha_r \smile \alpha_s$ is in H^{r+s}. This last property says the ring is *graded* by dimension. This is similar to a polynomial ring under ordinary multiplication being graded by degree.

11.4 Examples

As we've noted, using the cup product to give groups a ring structure has a big payoff because cohomology rings can often capture more of the information residing in a topological space than cohomology groups. It's now time to make good on a promise: Give an example of two different spaces whose *groups* are the same, but whose *rings* are different. This will show that the ring's multiplication can distinguish between the two spaces. For our first space we choose the torus $T = S^1 \times S^1$. We saw earlier that the Betti numbers for it form row 2 of the Pascal triangle: 1, 2, 1, which are the ranks of the corresponding homology groups $H_0 = \mathbb{Z}, H_1 = \mathbb{Z} \times \mathbb{Z}, H_2 = \mathbb{Z}$. Just as the vector space $V = \mathbb{R}^n$ is isomorphic to its dual V^*, so also the homology groups of the torus are isomorphic to its cohomology groups—that is, $H^0 = \mathbb{Z}, H^1 = \mathbb{Z} \times \mathbb{Z}, H^2 = \mathbb{Z}$. Our aim now is to manufacture another space S that is a "counterfeit" of the torus, in the sense that its cohomology groups (without any ring structure) are the same as the torus's. We know that the torus has exactly two independent nonbounding 1-cycles—two holes making H_1 (as well as H^1) isomorphic to $\mathbb{Z} \times \mathbb{Z}$. We create our impostor by starting with a sphere (which has no nonbounding 1-cycles) and artificially adding two nonbounding 1-cycles by drawing two loops, each touching the sphere at a common point. This is shown in Figure 11.1. Homology sees the two loops, doesn't realize they aren't circles of latitude and longitude on a torus, and reports back a rank-2 result: $H_1 = H^1 = \mathbb{Z} \times \mathbb{Z}$. This trickery doesn't change H_0 and H_2 of the sphere S^2, which we saw earlier were both $\mathbb{Z}$, so for both the real and fake torus, $H^0 = \mathbb{Z}, H^1 = \mathbb{Z} \times \mathbb{Z}, H^2 = \mathbb{Z}$. Now let's see what cup products tell us. Let α_1 correspond to a circle of latitude on the torus, and α_2 correspond to a circle of longitude there. Then $\alpha_1 \smile \alpha_2$ has dimension 2, generates $H^2 = \mathbb{Z}$, and therefore is nonzero. Let α_1' and α_2' correspond to the two loops we drew on the sphere. A little calculation shows that $\alpha_1' \smile \alpha_2' = 0$, so these products are different, meaning the rings are different, too.

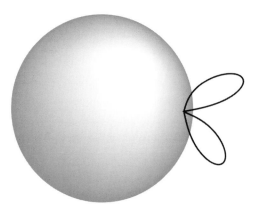

Figure 11.1. A "counterfeit torus."

One can attach additional pairs of circles at that same point on the sphere to create fakes of higher genus, and the cup product will again be able to distinguish real from fake.

Here's a higher-dimensional example showing how the cup product can distinguish between different spaces having identical cohomology groups. One of our two spaces is the "complex projective 2-space," denoted $\mathbb{P}^2(\mathbb{C})$. This space, which has real dimension 4, is one of the truly fundamental spaces in the study of classical plane algebraic curves (that is, curves defined by polynomial equations $p(x, y) = 0$), because $\mathbb{P}^2(\mathbb{C})$ turns out to be the "right" space in which to look at these curves. How so? On the one hand, all finite solutions are accounted for— think of the fundamental theorem of algebra, guaranteeing solutions of $p(x) = 0$ over the complex numbers, but not over the reals. That assumes $p(x)$ isn't a nonzero constant, for then the solution is at infinity. That's precisely where the "projective" part of $\mathbb{P}^2(\mathbb{C})$ comes in, for $\mathbb{P}^2(\mathbb{C})$ adds all points at infinity to $\mathbb{C}^2$: Each complex subspace of $\mathbb{C}^2$ can be looked at as the Riemann sphere minus the north pole, and $\mathbb{P}^2(\mathbb{C})$ adds that point to each subspace and all its translates, so that all "parallel" complex lines intersect at that point at infinity. With the extra space that $\mathbb{P}^2(\mathbb{C})$ provides over $\mathbb{R}^2$ or $\mathbb{C}^2$, all intersections of any two curves defined by polynomials $p(x, y)$ and $q(x, y)$ are accounted for, and when they're counted with multiplicity as we do in the fundamental theorem of algebra, then the curves intersect in exactly $\deg p \cdot \deg q$ points, provided p and q don't share a common factor. This is *Bézout's theorem*, a very beautiful and far-reaching generalization of the fundamental theorem of algebra. For more on this, see [**K1**].

The other space, which we'll call S and is much less important, consists of the four-dimensional sphere S^4, together with an ordinary two-dimensional sphere S^2 tacked on, touching S^4 in just a single point. The sequence $1, 0, 1, 0, 1$ describes the cohomology groups of both S and $\mathbb{P}^2(\mathbb{C})$: From dimension 0 to 4 these groups are $\mathbb{Z}$, 0, $\mathbb{Z}$, 0, $\mathbb{Z}$. However, it turns out that the cup product of two nonzero elements of $H^2(\mathbb{P}^2(\mathbb{C}))$ is a nonzero element of $H^4(\mathbb{P}^2(\mathbb{C}))$, while the cup product of two nonzero elements of $H^2(S)$ is 0.

CHAPTER 12

Whitney's Extension Theorems

When Whitney began publishing mathematics, it was already well known that any function continuous on a closed subset of real n-space can be extended to a continuous function on the entire space. Whitney wondered about differentiable analogs. What if "continuous" were replaced by "differentiable" or "infinitely differentiable"? His answers played a significant role in his becoming a widely known mathematician.

12.1 Searching for that piece of gold

Despite his love for and progress on the four-color problem, Hass never intended to spend his entire career on it. In him was a need to do something he thought was "real mathematics" in the sense of more traditional analysis—something that would involve differentiable functions. After all, he had spent years in physics working with polynomials, trigonometric and exponential functions, and so on, and they were his friends. During this period around 1933–4 he was spending more and more time thinking about differentiable functions in one or several variables and less time on the four-color problem. He began to gain a deeper understanding of real functions and their derivatives and started to keep an eye out for some problem involving differentiable functions whose resolution would be important. It had to be elementary, simply stated, require little extra background to make progress, and involve differentiable functions in some way.

His quarry proved surprisingly elusive: His search was a bit analogous to a beachcomber with a metal detector, except that he found the beach to be much larger than he expected, and it took months before he finally stumbled upon what he wanted: an eight-page article written by William Whyburn ([**W**]). This article, "Non-isolated critical points of functions," appeared in the *Bulletin of the AMS* 35 (1929), pp. 701–708 ([**W**]) and guarantees, for a closed set S in n-space, nonconstant functions having zero partial derivatives at each point of S. The methods used in the paper gave Hass the idea that he might be able to extend the Tietze

extension theorem for continuous functions to certain differentiable ones. In
real n-space $\mathbb{R}^n$, the Tietze theorem says, in part, that a function continuous on
a closed set in $\mathbb{R}^n$ has a continuous extension to all of $\mathbb{R}^n$. The paper inspired
Hassler to ask more general extension questions. Here are two of them:

- If in some sense a function is r-times differentiable on any closed set S of $\mathbb{R}^n$,
  can it be extended to a function that is r-times differentiable on all of $\mathbb{R}^n$?
- If the function is infinitely differentiable on S, is there an infinitely differentiable extension to $\mathbb{R}^n$?

Answers would be significant no matter how they turned out, and in what can
now be called classic Whitney style he considered lots of examples, drew many
pictures, considered various ways of creating extensions, and through persistence
finally got local extensions to match up properly. It was a breakthrough for him,
and a breakthrough for mathematics. He admitted "It wasn't that easy," but in
1934 his 27-page article appeared in the AMS *Transactions* ([44]). Two more articles in the *Annals* ([45], [46]) continued in this vein. 1934 was a good year for
the 27-year-old.

It was Whitney's style to think, argue, and explore geometrically, but when
writing up his results he typically translated the math into an algebraic form with
little reference to his original, intuitive pictures. This was in part because he
submitted articles to journals where it was essential that his arguments be highly
rigorous. It was in the algebraic setting where he succeeded in making algebraic
arguments having an appropriate level of rigor; in fact, in all the 27 pages of the
Transactions paper, there is not a single figure. Although he adopted this method
for most of his papers, in private conversations he was quite different, revealing
his vividly geometric mind. In this chapter we explore the problem in the way
that he typically would have, using concrete examples to progressively lead to a
solution. Along the way we will meet some of the essential difficulties he faced
and how he overcame them, and will give the reader an appreciation of his early
blockbuster result.

12.2 First questions and examples

Let's begin with a very simple example of extending a continuous function—say,
a function continuous on the closed subset $S = [0, 1]$ of the line $\mathbb{R}^1$ and taking on
real values. Here, "continuous" means we can draw its graph without the pencil
ever leaving the paper. To extend it leftward, place the pencil point on the leftmost
point of the graph (which exists because $[0, 1]$ is closed) and just drag further and
further left without ever lifting the pencil. In fact, drawing a nonvertical half
line would do just fine. Similarly for extending it rightward. If the closed set S
consists of two intervals separated by a gap, then one could span the graph's gap

with a line segment connecting the two graph endpoints. It's easy to see how to extend this idea to other closed subsets of the real line.

What if the function on S is differentiable there, and we want to extend it to a function on $\mathbb{R}^1$ differentiable at each point of $\mathbb{R}^1$? To start, let's consider just a first-derivative problem. On a single interval such as $[0, 1]$, we agree that "differentiable at an endpoint" means the appropriate one-sided derivative exists there.[1]   To extend the function f leftward from 0, we may choose a half line whose slope agrees with the right-sided derivative of f there. Likewise, to extend the function rightward from 1, we may choose a half line whose slope agrees with the left-sided derivative there. But if S consists of more than one piece—say, the two closed intervals $[-1, 0]$ and $[1, 2]$—the problem suddenly becomes less trivial. Figure 12.1 shows such an example. We now need to make the left and right slopes at $x = 0$ match up, and ditto at $x = 1$. It's clear that if the extended function is to be differentiable on the whole horizontal axis, line segments are not up to the job.

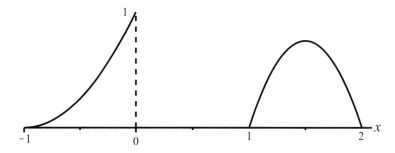

Figure 12.1. How can you differentiably extend this function on $[-1, 0] \cup [1, 2]$ to all of $\mathbb{R}$?

In Figure 12.1, let's say that above the interval $[-1, 0]$ is a section of the parabola $y = (x + 1)^2$, which has slope $+2$ at $x = 0$, and that above $[1, 2]$ is part of another parabola, $y = -3x^2 + 9x - 6$, with slope $+3$ at $x = 1$. One way to solve this problem is by finding a polynomial $p(x)$ for which

$$p(0) = 1; \qquad p'(0) = 2;$$
$$p(1) = 0; \qquad p'(1) = 3.$$

The general cubic $p(x) = ax^3 + bx^2 + cx + d$ is a polynomial with four coefficients, and each of these coefficients can be assigned arbitrary values. In this case, $p(0) = 1$ becomes $d = 1$ and $p'(0) = 2$ becomes $c = 2$. Substituting $x = 1$ then leads to simultaneous equations

$$a + b = -3, \qquad 3a + 2b = 1,$$

having solutions $a = 7$ and $b = -10$. Thus, $p(x) = 7x^3 - 10x^2 + 2x + 1$ defined on $[0, 1]$ connects the two parabolic pieces, with its values and slopes agreeing at the glue joints. To the left of $x = 0$ and the right of $x = 1$, we can extend by simply using half lines of the correct slopes. The result appears in Figure 12.2, with the heavily drawn additions giving a function on $\mathbb{R}$ differentiable at each point there, and extending the original function on $S = [-1, 0] \cup [1, 2]$.

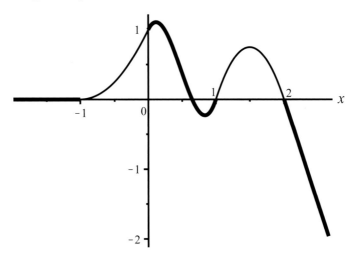

Figure 12.2. The heavily drawn parts extend the function in Figure 12.1 to a function differentiable on all of $\mathbb{R}$.

This general approach can be used for higher derivatives, as well as for any finite number of closed intervals. If the two parabolic pieces in Figure 12.1 were replaced by arbitrary ten-times differentiable functions—that is, members of $\mathcal{C}^{10}$—then for perfect matching there would be 11 conditions at $x = 0$ reflecting values of the 0th through the 10th derivatives there, and another 11 at $x = 1$. These lead to a system of 22 linear equations in 22 variables, those variables being the coefficients of a general polynomial of degree 21. And if there were additional gaps to bridge, there would correspondingly be additional 22-variable systems, one for each gap. All this adds up to considerable work, but in theory it's possible to make such extensions.

So far we've been content to match up only finitely many derivatives. But more generally, there's the question of extending pieces of analytic functions like trigonometric or exponential ones. These entail matching up not a finite number of derivatives, but *infinitely* many, and the method outlined above fails. At this point a really huge problem rears its head: A simple example shows we can't generally bridge gaps between analytic pieces with other analytic pieces because, for example, if you remove part of a cosine curve, there is essentially only one way to extend it analytically—put the removed part back where it was originally. In Figure 12.3, a cosine curve has been cut at $x = 0$ and the right part pushed rightward by one unit. The heavily drawn part depicts a function that does bridge the gap, with all the infinitely many derivatives matching up at the glue joints. This bridging function must actually be defined at the glue joints so that we can take derivatives there. It turns out that the function whose graph is depicted in Figure 12.3 isn't analytic at either of the glue points. A promise: Before the end of this chapter, we'll tell you what the bridging function is, and how we got it.

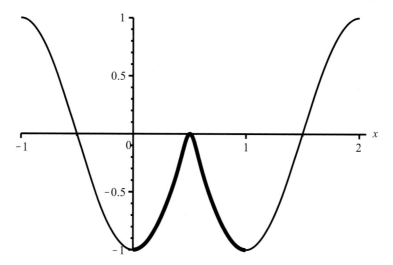

Figure 12.3. The heavily drawn curve represents one possible smooth bridging between the parts of a split cosine curve. Connecting the two lowest points of the split cosine curve with a horizontal line fails to give a smooth extension.

Except in very special cases, bridging analytic pieces requires functions that are infinitely differentiable, yet not analytic. These are the $\mathcal{C}^\infty$ functions. Figure 12.4 depicts that polynomials are more special than analytic functions, which are in turn more special than $\mathcal{C}^\infty$ functions. The class of analytic functions $\mathcal{A}$ is a subset of $\mathcal{C}^\infty$. For a function f to be analytic, the Taylor series[2] of an analytic function f formed from the derivatives evaluated at a point must be f itself, not some other function. The class of polynomials shown in the figure as $\mathcal{P}$ is a subset of $\mathcal{A}$. Polynomials are not only analytic, but all sufficiently high derivatives must be 0. $\mathcal{C}^\infty$ functions are also called *smooth*, so all functions in Figure 12.4 are smooth.

A fair question: Is the set $\mathcal{C}^\infty$ definitely larger than $\mathcal{A}$? That is, is there at least one infinitely differentiable function f whose Taylor series defines a function g

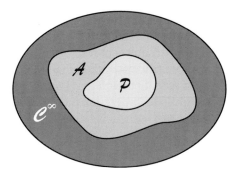

Figure 12.4. Three levels of generality for functions.

not equal to f? Yes. We are about to meet a famous function that is analytic at each point of the x-axis except $x = 0$. It *is* $\mathcal{C}^\infty$ there—all of its derivatives exist (they're all 0 at $x = 0$). But with all derivatives being zero, its Taylor series is identically zero. The series doesn't represent this famous function because the function increases as $|x|$ grows and even has $y = 1$ as an asymptote. The function is

$$y = e^{-1/x^2} \text{ if } x \neq 0; \qquad y = 0 \text{ if } x = 0.$$

Figure 12.5 shows two views of this famous function.

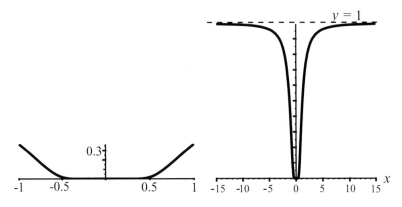

Figure 12.5. Zoomed-in and zoomed-out views of an infinitely differentiable but nonanalytic function. At $x = 0$, the function's derivatives are all zero. Therefore its Taylor series about $x = 0$ fails to represent the function because the Taylor series is $0 + 0x + 0x^2 + \cdots$—the identically zero function.

Not only have we found one function in $\mathcal{C}^\infty$ not in $\mathcal{A}$—that is, a smooth non-analytic function—we've in fact found infinitely many of them, since $y = e^{-1/x^2}$

can be multiplied by any nonzero real number to get a different function in $\mathcal{C}^\infty$ that's not in $\mathcal{A}$. You can get even more of them by simply adding any analytic function you please! Thus, nonanalytic $\mathcal{C}^\infty$ functions represent a rich source of bridging functions, and we'll soon see that there are so many of them that we can bridge gaps between polynomial, analytic, or $\mathcal{C}^\infty$ functions.

As one more example, let $f(x)$ be e^x to the right of $x = 1$, and let $g(x)$ be $\sin(2\pi x)$ to the left of $x = 0$. The heavily drawn curve in Figure 12.6 depicts the graph of one $\mathcal{C}^\infty$-function bridging the gap between f and g. Another promise: Later in this chapter we'll get the graph's actual function.

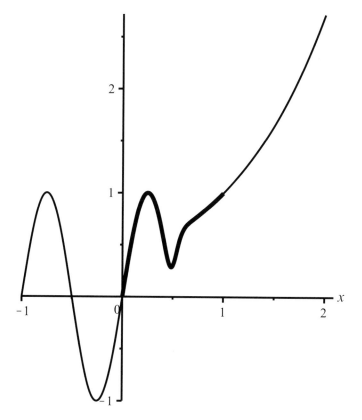

Figure 12.6. A smooth extension of a sine curve to the left of $x = 0$ and an exponential curve to the right of $x = 1$.

12.3 Smooth versus just *looking* smooth

We can turn the graph in Figure 12.2 into one looking even smoother—just re-place its straight-line extensions by the natural parabolic ones, to get the graph in

Figure 12.7. This entire graph looks pleasingly smooth. However in mathematics, smoothness is not just skin deep—it goes all the way to the bone. That is, a function can look nice and smooth to the eye, but have nonsmoothness secretly hiding in it like skeletons in a closet. You may need to open many doors to reach the closet, and opening a door mathematically corresponds to differentiating. So a smooth function is one that, no matter how many times it's differentiated, still looks smooth. That is, it is a member of $\mathcal{C}^\infty$. So what about the function depicted in Figure 12.7? If it is in fact smooth, then all right and left derivatives at $x = 0$ must agree; ditto at $x = 1$. Let's compute: At $x = 0$, the second left derivative of $(x + 1)^2$ is 2, while the second right derivative of the bridging function $7x^3 - 10x^2 + 2x + 1$ is -20. That means our nice-looking function is not smooth at all! Although it no longer matters, the situation at $x = 1$ isn't any better, since the second one-sided derivatives are 22 and -6.

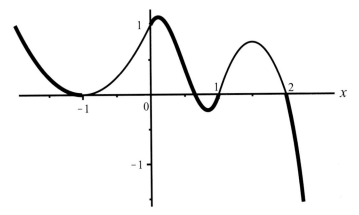

Figure 12.7. The graph in Figure 12.2 looks even smoother when the straight lines are replaced by natural parabolic extensions.

As for Whitney's first bulleted question on p. 144, our foray into extending one-variable polynomial pieces does teach us something: These polynomials are surely differentiable, and we can extend them to piecewise polynomial functions that are also differentiable on $\mathbb{R}$. However, polynomials are not only differentiable, but infinitely differentiable—smooth—and we've just seen that in the above example our polynomial bridging function doesn't give a function smooth on $\mathbb{R}$. It turns out that polynomial bridgings are typically not good enough to give smooth extensions of polynomially defined pieces. Even at the polynomial level, we need functions sharing the DNA of $y = e^{-1/x^2}$. Functions of this type appear throughout Whitney's big papers on extensions ([44], [45], [46]), and we'll show how he used them to extend functions $\mathcal{C}^\infty$ on closed sets of a real space, to a function $\mathcal{C}^\infty$ on all of that real space.

12.4 Extending infinitely differentiable functions

We've seen how different polynomial graphs on disjoint intervals of the x-axis can be patched together, usually with polynomials of higher degree, to form a function on the whole x-axis that at least looks nice at the glue joints. We have also seen that the function

$$y = e^{-1/x^2} \text{ if } x \neq 0; \qquad y = 0 \text{ if } x = 0$$

whose graph is depicted in Figure 12.5 can be used as a smooth function to patch together one-variable differentiable functions more general than polynomials. To see the role this function can play in extending more general smooth functions, let's look at one of the most simply stated and basic cases where this function is used:

> **Extend the function that is identically 0 to the left of $x = 0$, and identically 1 to the right of $x = 1$, to a function that is infinitely differentiable on the entire x-axis.**

For this step function problem, the challenge is finding a function on the closed interval $[0, 1]$ so that all three pieces form the graph of a function infinitely differentiable at every point of the x-axis. One thing is clear: The $\mathcal{C}^\infty$ bridging function can't be analytic throughout $[0, 1]$. If it were, it would continue the function that is zero for all negative x, meaning the function would be identically 0 on the entire x-axis, while it would also continue the function constantly 1 to the right of $x = 1$. It can't do both!

Our exponential function displayed above goes about half way toward solving the problem, but the left picture in Figure 12.5 shows that it rises to only about 0.3 when $x = 1$—too slowly for what we need. But by tinkering a bit in the denominator, we can make the function do what we want: Divide e^{-1/x^2} by $e^{-1/x^2} + e^{-1/(x-1)^2}$ to get

$$y = \frac{e^{-1/x^2}}{e^{-1/x^2} + e^{-1/(x-1)^2}}.$$

When x gets very close to 0, the denominator approaches something nonzero and finite, so the whole quotient approaches 0 essentially as if the denominator were the original value of 1. When x gets very close to 1, the denominator approaches $1/e$, and so does the numerator, so the whole quotient approaches 1 as x approaches 1. Figure 12.8 depicts this function's graph rising from $y = 0$ to $y = 1$ as x goes from 0 to 1.

All derivatives at $x = 0$ remain 0 and fortunately so do all derivatives at $x = 1$. Why is that? The graph appears to be symmetric about its middle point. If

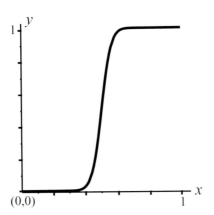

Figure 12.8. The ramp function $y = \dfrac{e^{-1/x^2}}{e^{-1/x^2} + e^{-1/(x-1)^2}}$ is $\mathcal{C}^\infty$ and is an especially useful smooth function.

we can establish that it really is symmetric, then the identical shapes of the graph at each end will tell us that its derivatives at $x = 0$ and $x = 1$ are the same. Here's the proof of symmetry: Replace each x by $(x + \frac{1}{2})$, and y by $(y + \frac{1}{2})$; doing this translates the graph down by $\frac{1}{2}$ and left by $\frac{1}{2}$,[3] to the graph of a function $y = f(x)$. Its graph is symmetric about the origin if and only if $f(x) = -f(-x)$, which is to say if and only if $f(x) + f(-x) = 0$. (Any such function is called *odd*.[4]) Making these replacements and simplifying in fact lead to $f(x) + f(-x) = 1 - \frac{1}{2} - \frac{1}{2} = 0$, establishing symmetry.

The function depicted in Figure 12.8 is not analytic at either $x = 0$ or $x = 1$, but is infinitely differentiable at every point on the x-axis. This solves our basic step problem of extending the function to a $\mathcal{C}^\infty$ (smooth) function that is identically 0 to the left of $x = 0$ and identically 1 to the right of $x = 1$. As a nice bonus, this extension is actually analytic in the interior $(0, 1)$ of the gap. We denote this extended function on $\mathbb{R}$ by $\phi_{0,1}(x)$.

Symmetrically, we get, almost for free, a function $\phi_{1,0}(x)$ on $\mathbb{R}$ that decreases from $y = 1$ to $y = 0$ as x goes from 0 to 1:

$$\phi_{1,0}(x) = 1 - \phi_{0,1}(x).$$

Figure 12.9 depicts the parts of these graphs between $x = 0$ and $x = 1$; the graph of $\phi_{0,1}(x)$ is drawn solidly, the graph of $\phi_{1,0}(x)$ is drawn dashed. By the way $\phi_{1,0}(x)$ is defined, we see that

$$\phi_{0,1}(x) + \phi_{1,0}(x) \equiv 1.$$

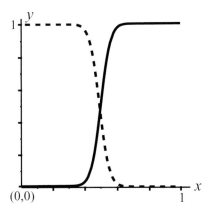

Figure 12.9. The graphs of the $\mathcal{C}^\infty$ ramp functions $\phi_{0,1}(x)$ and $\phi_{1,0}(x)$ sum to the function that is identically 1.

12.5 Exponential bridging functions in action

Can we use these two $\mathcal{C}^\infty$ functions to solve other bridging problems? The answer is not only yes, but *emphatically* yes. As an example, let's dress up the above step problem by replacing the function that's identically 1 to the right of $x = 1$ by $y = e^x$ to the right of $x = 1$. Now the challenge is to find some function that smoothly bridges the function identically 0 to the left of $x = 0$ and our exponential function to the right of $x = 1$. The answer is

$$y = e^x \phi_{0,1}(x),$$

and the way it solves the problem is almost magical. Let's take a look:
When $x \leq 0$,

$$e^x \phi_{0,1}(x) = e^x \cdot 0 = 0.$$

When $x \geq 1$,

$$e^x \phi_{0,1}(x) = e^x \cdot 1 = e^x.$$

So $y = e^x \phi_{0,1}(x)$ correctly matches up the values at the glue joints $x = 0$ and $x = 1$. But what about matching up all *derivatives* at those two glue joints? Let's compute. For the first derivative, Leibniz's rule

$$(fg)' = f'g + fg'$$

gives

$$\left(e^x \phi_{0,1}(x)\right)' = (e^x)' \phi_{0,1}(x) + e^x (\phi_{0,1}(x))'$$

which at $x = 0$ is

$$1 \cdot 0 + 1 \cdot 0 = 0,$$

and which at $x = 1$ is

$$e \cdot 1 + e \cdot 0 = e.$$

This is just what we want. Moreover, since every derivative of e^x is e^x, every one of its derivatives at $x = 1$ is e. The magic continues, for applying the Leibniz rule any number of times and then evaluating at $x = 0$ gives 0, and evaluating at $x = 1$ gives e.

The secret of this good fortune lies in a beautiful generalization of the Leibniz rule, looking much like successive binomial expansions. In Figure 12.10, a symbol like $f^{(m)}$ stands for the mth derivative of f, with $f^{(0)}$ meaning the 0th derivative—that is, f itself. Figure 12.10 shows the result of carrying out successive derivatives.

$$(fg)^{(0)} = 1 f^{(0)} g^{(0)}$$

$$(fg)^{(1)} = 1 f^{(1)} g^{(0)} + 1 f^{(0)} g^{(1)}$$

$$(fg)^{(2)} = 1 f^{(2)} g^{(0)} + 2 f^{(1)} g^{(1)} + 1 f^{(0)} g^{(2)}$$

$$(fg)^{(3)} = 1 f^{(3)} g^{(0)} + 3 f^{(2)} g^{(1)} + 3 f^{(1)} g^{(2)} + 1 f^{(0)} g^{(3)}$$

$$\vdots \qquad\qquad\qquad \vdots$$

Figure 12.10. Coefficients in successive derivatives of a product form the Pascal triangle.

In the figure, the expansion for $(fg)^{(m)}$ starts off with $f^{(m)}g$, and if we let $f(x)$ be e^x and $g(x)$ be $\phi_{0,1}(x)$, then first term becomes $(f)^{(m)}\phi_{0,1}$ which, when evaluated at $x = 1$, gives e. The magic? All succeeding terms in that line involve derivatives of $\phi_{0,1}(x)$, and at $x = 1$, these are all zero! So the first term and all derivatives at $x = 1$ match up. Since $\phi_{0,1}(x)$ is zero to the left of $x = 0$ and 1 to the right of $x = 1$, simply multiplying $\phi_{0,1}(x)$ by e^x solves the problem of extending the given functions on $(-\infty, 0]$ and $[1, +\infty)$ so that the result is a $\mathcal{C}^\infty$ function.

When you think about it, instead of choosing an exponential as a $\mathcal{C}^\infty$ function, we could just as well have chosen a polynomial, or a sine function, or cosine function, or any other function analytic on $\mathbb{R}$. For any of these, multiplying by $\phi_{0,1}(x)$ would define an everywhere $\mathcal{C}^\infty$ function that is 0 to the left of $x = 0$ and the chosen function to the right of $x = 1$. In fact, this extended function is analytic at each point of $(0, 1)$. The function $\phi_{0,1}(x)$ is truly powerful.

One can replay the above arguments to see that the mate to this function—$\phi_{1,0}(x)$—is equally impressive, and with equal ease solves the "mirror" problem. That is, if you have any function $g(x)$ like the ones just mentioned, then $g(x)\phi_{1,0}(x)$ agrees with $g(x)$ to the left of $x = 0$, and morphs in a C^∞ manner to the identically zero function to the right of $x = 1$.

Before meeting Whitney's famous extension result at the beginning of the next section, we need to make an important reality check. Above, we saw the almost magical behavior of $y = e^x \phi_{0,1}(x)$. But when we multiplied e^x by $\phi_{0,1}(x)$, we tacitly assumed that e^x is defined in $[0, 1]$. Of course it is, but in general all we're given to start off with is a function defined and everywhere differentiable in the closed set S—in particular, it need not be defined in $\mathbb{R} \setminus S$. In the above example, if instead of an exponential (or polynomial, or sine, or cosine) function, we chose a function $f(x)$ defined only to the right of $x = 1$, and this function is only C^∞ there, then at this stage of the game, there's nothing to multiply $\phi_{0,1}(x)$ by within the gap $(0, 1)$. But because our C^∞ selection has all orders of right-sided derivatives at $x = 1$, we can use these numbers $f^{(m)}(1)$ to assemble the Taylor series centered at $x = 1$:

$$F(x) = \sum_{m=0}^{\infty} \left(\frac{f^{(m)}(1)}{m!} \right) (x-1)^m.$$

Under mild conditions, this is analytic and defines a nice function in the gap $(0, 1)$. It's as if we're standing at shore's edge $x = 1$ looking toward the left. Without a Taylor series, there's nothing to see in that gap. A Taylor series gives us something concrete between the two shores.

Analogously, suppose we have a function $g(x)$ defined only to the left of $x = 0$, and that this function is only C^∞ there. All orders of left-sided derivatives are defined at $x = 0$, so we can form the Taylor series centered at this other shore, $x = 0$:

$$G(x) = \sum_{m=0}^{\infty} \left(\frac{g^{(m)}(0)}{m!} \right) x^m,$$

and once again, under mild conditions, this is analytic in the gap $(0,1)$. We therefore have two possibly very different analytic functions in $(0, 1)$. We would like to gracefully morph one into the other.

12.6 Taming the clash of the titans

Here we go. Let $g(x)$ be any C^∞ function defined on $S_1 = (-\infty, 0]$ and suppose $f(x)$ is any C^∞ function defined on $S_2 = [1, +\infty)$. (S_1 and S_2 are each closed in $\mathbb{R}$.) Let $G(x)$ and $F(x)$ be their associated Taylor functions. Here's the big result: The function

$$F(x)\phi_{0,1}(x) + G(x)\phi_{1,0}(x)$$

is analytic on $(0, 1)$ and extends f and g to the entire x-axis $\mathbb{R}$. As we move along the x-axis from 0 to 1, $\phi_{1,0}(x)$ picks up $G(x)$ with 100% strength at $x = 0$, and the multiplier $\phi_{1,0}(x)$ diminishes the strength of $G(x)$ to 0% by the time x reaches 1. During this same journey, $\phi_{0,1}(x)$ makes $F(x)$ start off with no strength and increases it to 100% at $x = 1$. So during the trip, the sum $F(x)\phi_{0,1}(x)+G(x)\phi_{1,0}(x)$ morphs from $G(x)$ to $F(x)$. All derivatives match appropriately at $x = 0$ and at $x = 1$ to form a function extending the original one on the closed set $S = S_1 \cup S_2$ to a function on the entire x-axis, which is furthermore analytic on $(0, 1)$.

12.7 Examples revisited

Let's revisit some previous examples. To start, we can now make good on our promises of finding concrete functions that accomplish the bridging.

Figure 12.3 on p. 147. What's the actual function bridging the gap in the figure? Thanks to our morphing functions $\phi_{0,1}(x)$ and $\phi_{1,0}(x)$, we now have an answer:

$$F(x)\phi_{0,1}(x) + G(x)\phi_{1,0}(x).$$

Specifically, this is

$$-\phi_{0,1}(x)\cos(\pi(x - 1)) - \phi_{1,0}(x)\cos(\pi x).$$

This joins the two pieces to form a $\mathcal{C}^\infty$ function, analytic at every point except $x = 0$ and $x = 1$.

Figure 12.6 on p. 149. We can now give a specific function bridging the gap between the sine and exponential functions. In this example, $f(x)$ is e^x to the right of $x = 1$, and $g(x)$ is $\sin(2\pi x)$ to the left of $x = 0$. The heavily drawn curve in Figure 12.6 depicts the function

$$F(x)\phi_{0,1}(x) + G(x)\phi_{1,0}(x) = \phi_{0,1}(x)e^{(x-1)} + \phi_{1,0}(x)\sin(2\pi x)$$

in $[0, 1]$. The union of the three graphs is analytic at all points except $x = 0$ and $x = 1$. These two exceptions mean that the function on the entire x-axis is only $\mathcal{C}^\infty$ there.

Breaking the graph of the famous function at its lowest point. In analogy to breaking the cosine curve at its lowest point, we can do the same with

$$y = e^{-1/x^2} \text{ if } x \neq 0; \qquad y = 0 \text{ if } x = 0.$$

Unlike the cosine curve, it isn't analytic at its lowest point (which in this case is the origin). All derivatives are 0 there, so after translating the right half to the right one unit, both $G(x)$ and $F(x)$ are identically zero in $[0, 1]$. This broken graph function on $S = S_1 \cup S_2 = (-\infty, 0] \cup [1, +\infty)$ gets extended to all $\mathbb{R}$ simply by adding the horizontal line segment $[0, 1]$ to the graph. This extended function is analytic at every point except $x = 0$ and $x = 1$.

What if the pieces to be extended are polynomial? Using the morphers $\phi_{0,1}(x)$ and $\phi_{1,0}(x)$ make solving systems of linear equations unnecessary. For example, we can use them to get a transition which is merely analytic in $(0, 1)$ instead of a polynomial transition. Insisting that the transition be a polynomial means that all Taylor coefficients are zero after some point, while being analytic doesn't require that. Figure 12.11 compares the results of the two methods— our polynomial transition on the left, and the morphers transition on the right. Notice how the morphers transition function both rises and falls more than the polynomial transition. This makes sense since, for example, $\phi_{1,0}(x)$ hugs closely to 1 from $x = 0$ until around $x = 0.3$, so the parabolic piece on the left will continue to rise during this time nearly like the original $y = (x + 1)^2$. Analogously for the other parabolic piece, from around $x = 0.7$ to $x = 1$.

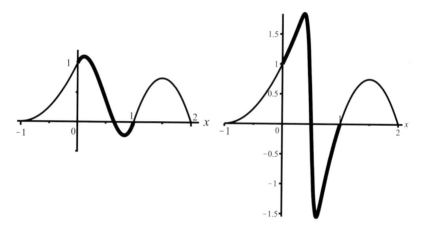

Figure 12.11. The sketch on the left depicts an extension by a polynomial. On the right, the extension is obtained using the morphing functions $\phi_{0,1}(x)$ and $\phi_{1,0}(x)$.

Generalizing from the unit interval. Although we have defined each morpher ϕ to change values over the interval $[0, 1]$, we can create a wide variety of more general examples in which $[0, 1]$ is replaced by $[a, b]$ $(a < b)$. To do this, replace each $\phi(x)$ by the corresponding $\phi\left(\frac{x-a}{b-a}\right)$. This gives a pair of morphers we can use to bridge the gap $[a, b]$. Furthermore, even if we have a large number of disjoint closed intervals whose union forms a closed set S, we can apply a morpher pair to each gap in $\mathbb{R} \setminus S$ to extend a $\mathcal{C}^\infty$ function on $\mathbb{R} \setminus S$ to a function that is $\mathcal{C}^\infty$ on the entire x-axis.

12.8 Beyond the first dimension

Hass found it a real challenge to go beyond the first dimension. He drew picture after picture, but the problem seemed stubbornly intent on putting up a succession of frustrating barriers. His eventual success in 1933 was a real tour de force for the 26-year-old; the following is just enough to give the flavor of his approach.

All the basic ideas in dimension one encountered up to this point have higher-dimensional analogs: a closed set S in Euclidean space; $\mathcal{C}^m$ or $\mathcal{C}^\infty$ functions on S; spaces between components of S; Taylor series;[5] morphing functions that resolve clashes between different Taylor series defined over the same region. But in higher dimensions the borders of the "oceans" separating the components of S require a lot more attention because even in dimension two, these borders are not just isolated points, but curves that can have a lot of wiggles. In dimension one, the gaps between components are just intervals, and morphing took place in the gaps. But what, and how, to morph in higher dimensions?

In going from morphing functions on an interval to morphing functions in higher dimensions, Hass found it most promising to replace "intervals" by "coordinate n-cubes." To simplify exposition, let's assume we're working in the plane, so n-cubes are squares with horizontal and vertical edges. Now look at Figure 12.12. Here the components S_1 and S_2 are simple—just disks. If we wish to smoothly extend to the whole plane smooth functions F on S_1 and G on S_2, Hass saw that the easiest way is to tile the ocean—the plane minus S—with nonoverlapping squares. Because the boundary of S will generally have curves and wiggles, such a tiling will require using ever smaller tiles—their sizes approaching 0—as we approach that boundary (the two circles bounding the disks in Figure 12.12).

Roughly, the overall philosophy Hass used in creating an extension is to first shrink each cube about its center so its linear dimension goes down by, say, half. Doing this creates room to morph. In dimension two, shrinking the tiles creates little roadways between them—room that allows appropriate morphers to do their thing. On each shrunken tile T_i we then create a function: If P_i is the nearest point in boundary(S) to a particular point Q_i in T_i, then take the function's value at P_i together with all its derivatives and create a Taylor series centered at Q_i in T_i. The devil is in the details, but Whitney very carefully chose things so that any morphed function is smooth. His last step was to create morphing functions that smoothly blend the function values on all the T_i to extend F and G to a function smooth on the entire plane. These functions, though quite complicated-looking, have the same basic DNA as our one-variable morphers in that they're multi-variable cousins to step functions like $y = \dfrac{e^{-1/x^2}}{e^{-1/x^2} + e^{-1/(x-1)^2}}$.

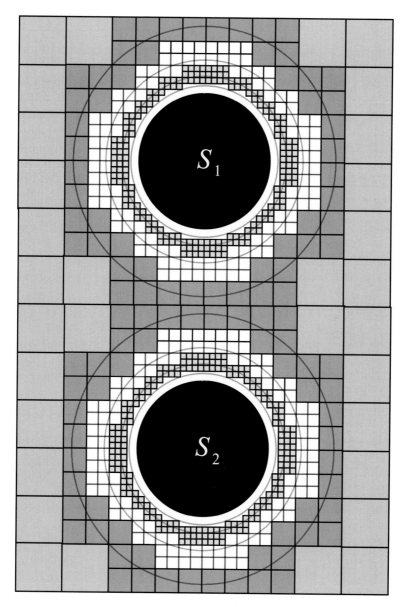

Figure 12.12. Every point of the "ocean" surrounding $S_1 \cup S_2$ is covered by 2-cubes.

CHAPTER **13**
Whitney's Weak Embedding Theorem

Mathematical intuition played an important part in Hassler's work, and when a new, more general definition of manifold appeared in 1932, it seemed to carry with it the possibility of finite-dimensional manifolds that had so many twists and turns that they could not themselves live in any finite-dimensional space. His intuition said that it just wasn't possible, and his proof—the weak embedding theorem—pushed him to the top tier of mathematicians. The theorem you will read about in this chapter can justifiably be called "the grandfather of all embedding theorems."

13.1 Whitney's weak embedding theorem: The main ideas

By 1930 there were several competing definitions of differentiable manifold, and in 1932, Oswald Veblen of Princeton and his doctoral student J. H. C. Whitehead had formalized an abstract definition whose spirit was due to Henri Poincaré. Poincaré needed a more general notion of manifold in studying, for example, the three-body problem in astrophysics. The goal of the new Veblen-Whitehead definition was to unify various ideas of what a finite-dimensional differentiable manifold ought to be as well as to put differential geometry on a more solid footing. Whitney was always one for concreteness, and he as well as others wondered if manifolds satisfying their abstract definition in fact introduced any new objects besides those finite-dimensional manifolds already sitting in some Euclidean space. If it did, then that meant there were two different kinds of smooth manifold: those sitting in some real n-space, and other ones so complicated and darting off in so many directions that no space of finite dimension would be able to contain them. Whitney guessed there were no such wild animals—that any Veblen-Whitehead manifold was tame enough that it could in fact be defined in some Euclidean space of high enough dimension, using patches smoothly glued together on their overlapping parts. As luck would have it, Hassler's work on extending differentiable functions provided some of the essential tools he used to corroborate his guess, and in 1936 he was able to prove that any n-dimensional compact, connected differentiable manifold defined in the abstract sense could be realized as a subset of a Euclidean space of dimension $2n + 1$.[1] This breakthrough connected the abstract with the concrete and radically changed the landscape of differentiable manifolds. Eight years later, using methods from algebraic topology, he was able to prove an even more remarkable result: The embedding dimension could always be reduced from $2n + 1$ to $2n$. A simple case of the stronger theorem would be a fancy knotted loop in a real space of any dimension, the loop being differentiably embedded there. In this case n is 1, so the theorem says there's a smooth mapping between it and, say, a circle in the real plane $\mathbb{R}^{2n} = \mathbb{R}^2$.

The Veblen-Whitehead definition led to this definition customarily used today:

Definition (Whitney definition of an abstract differentiable manifold M of dimension n).

- M has a cover by open subsets U.
- Each U is embedded in the Euclidean space $\mathbb{R}^n$ by means of a smooth, one-to-one map $\phi : U \to \mathbb{R}^n$. The correspondence essentially paints copy of a patch of coordinates in $\mathbb{R}^n$ onto U.
- Whenever any two open sets U_i and U_j overlap, the two coordinate systems painted on the overlap via ϕ_i and ϕ_j are smoothly related, meaning that the vector-valued function $\phi_j \circ \phi_i^{-1}$ is smooth throughout the image in $\mathbb{R}^n$ of that overlap in M. ("Smooth throughout the image" means that $\phi_j \circ \phi_i^{-1}$ is one-to-one and onto there, and that each of the n coordinate functions is infinitely differentiable at each point of that image. You can think of $\phi_j \circ \phi_i^{-1}$ as a spot of glue fastening the overlap together.) Figure 13.1 illustrates the gluing idea.

Here's another basic example illustrating these ideas. Figure 13.2 depicts a closed, compact 2-manifold made up of four open patches U_1, U_2, U_3, U_4. In the left picture, U_1 is the light grey open disk at the center whose boundary is marked by long dashes; U_2 is the horizontally hatched patch extending from about 5 o'clock to 1 o'clock; and U_3 is hatched at an angle, extending from about 11 o'clock to 7 o'clock. Each of these patches is supplied with the usual rectangular coordinates inherited from the underlying plane. U_2 plus U_3 forms an annulus, and in the right picture, this annulus has been turned inside out so that the outer boundary becomes the inner, and vice versa, the dot-dash pattern reflecting this. U_4 in the right picture is the dark shaded open disk, and its coordinates are inherited from the underlying plane. These two pictures define a 2-manifold locally. Each picture tells the story for only three of the four patches, so the definition is not global. This is part of what makes the definition abstract—we are told how

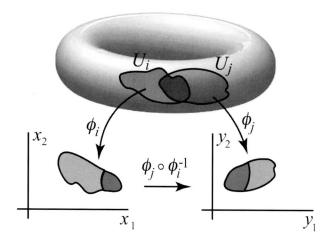

Figure 13.1. The overlapping, dark grey areas of two different local parts of a smooth 2-manifold are glued together using $\phi_j \circ \phi_i^{-1}$.

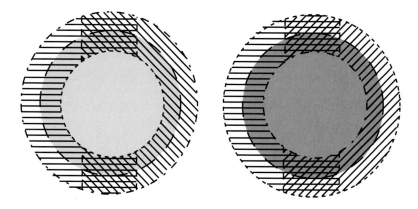

Figure 13.2. Two different local parts of a smooth 2-manifold that we glue together in accordance with the Veblen-Whitehead definition. But is this abstract manifold the same as some concrete smooth manifold sitting in an $\mathbb{R}^N$?

things are put together locally, but with only such local information given, there's no obvious reason why the whole manifold should actually live in some $\mathbb{R}^N$.

To get an initial idea of what's involved in realizing an abstract manifold as a manifold in some $\mathbb{R}^N$, let's try to get all four patches in Figure 13.2 to fit together naturally to make a single object. In Figure 13.3, we're attempting to do that;

however, the dark patch U_4 is giving us a hard time. No matter how far we extend it outward, we still have just an annulus instead of an open-disk patch. The outermost dotted edge actually just represents that we're trying to invert the dark grey disk, and the boundary there is in fact the single point that was originally the center of the disk.

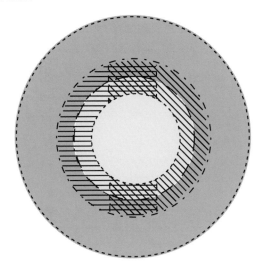

Figure 13.3. This shows an attempt to extend the left picture in Figure 13.2 into a single manifold by adding the fourth patch. In the plane we've inverted the dark disk and drawn it as best we can as an annulus, but with the understanding that its outer boundary actually represents a single point. To make an actual disk, we curl the outer part of the annulus up out of the plane and squeeze the boundary of that outer part to what it represents—a point. This point can be thought of as the north pole of a hemisphere. Curling into a new dimension is generally necessary to realize an abstract manifold as a concrete one in some $\mathbb{R}^N$.

As a solution, we break out of the plane and go into a new dimension. If we curl up the outermost part of the annulus, thus going into the third dimension, then we can extend the patch by simultaneously pulling upward and inward to shrink the outer dotted boundary of the dark shaded region to the point that it represents. We've created a cap that is topologically an open disk, just as it was originally before trying to invert it.

If you think about it, U_1, U_2, U_3 form a disklike base, and U_4 is like a perfectly fitting cake cover over that base. So topologically, our abstract manifold is actually a sphere sitting in $\mathbb{R}^3$! That wasn't obvious from the two pictures in Figure 13.2, and only became clear when we introduced an additional dimension.

In our example, we needed to add a dimension to only one of the four patches. But in other examples it can happen that we need to do this for several patches. As an example, one could give an abstract definition of a Klein bottle as locally defined parts in a plane, similar in spirit to Figure 13.2. But it happens that a Klein bottle needs *four* dimensions to avoid self-intersections and qualify as a card-carrying manifold—so at least two patches would have to curl up from flatness and enter into an additional dimension. Figure 14.8 on p. 186 depicts a typical view of a Klein bottle sitting in 3-space and having a loop as self-intersection.

In going from hunch to Q.E.D., Whitney assumed the worst-case scenario—that *every single patch would have to curl into an additional dimension*. Of course this is nearly always overkill, but it would prove his intuition right. So, for example, if some five-dimensional abstract manifold consists of 100 open patches and smooth mappings between overlaps, then we'd need six dimensions for each of the 100 curled patches, meaning the abstract manifold could be embedded in $\mathbb{R}^{600}$.

Even embedding in such an extremely high-dimensional space was history-making. It made clear that the abstract definition introduced no essentially new objects. Whitney knew that such high dimensions could be improved, and as part of his big paper [68] he drastically whittled down the dimension. After all, a five-dimensional compact connected differentiable manifold M sitting in $\mathbb{R}^{600}$ is a little like a microbe floating in an empty mansion—there's a tremendous amount of unneeded space. Whitney found that he could appropriately choose a succession of projections of M into $\mathbb{R}^{599}$, then $\mathbb{R}^{598}$, and so on, until he got to $\mathbb{R}^{11}$. Now 11 is one more than $2 \cdot 5$, so our five-dimensional manifold can be embedded in $\mathbb{R}^{2 \cdot 5 + 1}$. More generally, [68] tells us that any n-dimensional compact connected differentiable manifold can be embedded in $\mathbb{R}^{2n+1}$.

Whitney strongly suspected he could get the dimension down one more, to $\mathbb{R}^{2n}$, because even a nonorientable 2-manifold like the Klein bottle could, in fact, be embedded in $\mathbb{R}^{2n} = \mathbb{R}^4$. There was other corroborating evidence, too. But going down that one additional dimension caused him a good bit of work. He eventually discovered what is now called the "Whitney Trick"—we describe that in Chapter 14—and eight years after [68], he was able to announce in [87] a general proof that an abstract manifold of dimension n could be embedded in $\mathbb{R}^{2n}$. Today, his original $\mathbb{R}^{2n+1}$ result is known as "the weak embedding theorem" and the $\mathbb{R}^{2n}$ result as "the strong embedding theorem." These embedding theorems have proved to be the grandfathers of a whole host (hundreds, in fact) of embedding results of all stripes.

13.2 Whitney's weak embedding theorem: The idea of the proof

This section is more technical; skipping it won't detract from the narrative.

Whitney proved that for any n-dimensional manifold M satisfying the definition on p. 162, there's a smooth one-to-one map from all of M into some $\mathbb{R}^N$, for N sufficiently large. Now by the definition of M, we know there's a bunch of *local*, smooth one-to-one maps from parts of M—the open sets U of a covering of M—into $\mathbb{R}^n$, but what about a *global* smooth one-to-one map $\Phi : M \to \mathbb{R}^N$? The domains of definition of the ϕ are those (possibly tiny) U, while the domain of definition of Φ is M, the union of all those U, which can be much larger. In one way of looking at the problem, the first order of business is to get the various ϕ to all have M as their common domain of definition. That means smoothly extending each ϕ so that it is defined on all of M. Does this sound familiar? A couple of years earlier, Whitney's first big success in the area of differentiable functions was extending a smooth function defined on a closed set of $\mathbb{R}^n$ so it is smooth on all of $\mathbb{R}^n$. This turned out to be an important tool in creating an embedding.

The approach to making the extension is modeled on what was done in the Whitney extension theorem, and it simplifies matters if we assume from the outset that M is compact, because that means we can assume that the open covering $\{U\}$ of M is finite. In addition, if $\{U\}$ is such a covering, then there's another open cover $\{V\}$, where the boundary of each V is contained in the corresponding U. Pictorially, there is a little moat around V that extends from V out to U. In a manner analogous to what was done in the proof of the extension theorem, for each U, define a smooth morphing function r that is identically 1 on V and trails off smoothly to 0 on the boundary of U. In this way, each $r\phi$ smoothly transitions from being the original ϕ on V to 0 on the boundary of its domain U. Then just extend each $r\phi$ so that it is identically 0 outside U.

The simplest way to illustrate this is in dimension 1, so for this purpose we cheat a little and assume in Figure 13.4 that the manifold M is a closed interval. (There are therefore boundary points, but that doesn't matter in explaining the essential idea.) Depicted in the top picture is M and one of the open intervals $U \subset M$ in a finite cover of M, together with a shrunken version V in each U. In the bottom picture, the 45° line is the graph of a function ϕ from U into the real x-axis. Then ϕ^{-1} paints coordinates onto U; let's call these painted coordinates t. We extend ϕ to the entire closed interval M by setting ϕ equal to 0 outside U.

This above mapping of M into $\mathbb{R}^1$ is not at all a smooth embedding—it's neither continuous nor one-to-one—but we next improve matters. Figure 13.5 shows the graph of a function $x = r(t)$ modeled on what we used earlier in Whitney's extension theorem. In this picture $r(t)$ rises smoothly from 0 to 1

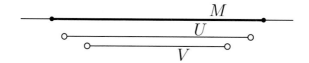

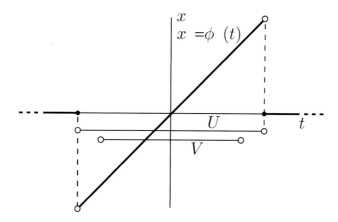

Figure 13.4. The function $\phi(t)$ has a jump, but shrinking U to V creates room to insert a smooth ramp function $r(t)$ so that $r\phi$ is smooth.

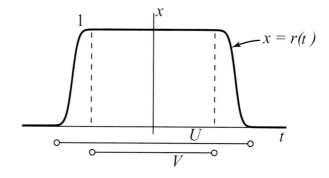

Figure 13.5. The ramp function $r(t)$ rises and falls smoothly in $U \setminus V$.

within the gap or moat between the left end of U and the left end of V. The function remains 1 throughout the shrunken interval V and then smoothly decreases from 1 at the right end of V to 0 at the right end of U.

Figure 13.6 depicts the graph of $r(t) \cdot \phi(t)$. The smoothing function $r(t)$ has taken care of the discontinuity seen in Figure 13.4; the graph of $r(t) \cdot \phi(t)$ is now smooth, is the identity function on V, and is 0 on all of M outside U.

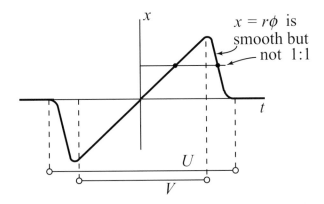

Figure 13.6. The function $r\phi$ is smooth on the entire t-axis, but isn't one-to-one.

It is not yet one-to-one, but a clever trick takes care of that: Instead of mapping merely $r\phi$ to $\mathbb{R}$, map the *pair* $(r\phi, r)$ to a space one dimension higher—to $\mathbb{R}^2$. This mapping is one-to-one on U. The top picture in Figure 13.7 shows this—starting from the left end of U, as t increases, the vector $(r\phi, r)$ sweeps out a circuit. This circuit starts and ends at the origin of the plane because the scalar multiplier $r(t)$ starts and ends at 0, meaning that both components of the vector $(r\phi, r)$ are 0 then. This map is defined on all of M and is smooth there. On U, the map is one-to-one and embeds U into the real plane.

The above scenario can be replayed using an open disk for U instead of an open interval. The bottom picture in Figure 13.7 is obtained by spinning the top picture about the r-axis. U becomes an open disk, V becomes a strictly smaller disk, and the graph in (t_1, t_2, r)-space of the smoothing function $r(t_1, t_2)$ looks like a round mesa with smoothly sloping cliffs.

In place of t increasing, we can cover a patch of (t_1, t_2)-parameter space by a tiny disk growing outward from the center of U. As the growing disk becomes the size of V, $r(t_1, t_2)$ changes from being constantly 1. We are now moving down the smooth cliffs of the mesa, and the scalar increasingly pulls the image toward the origin $(0, 0, 0)$ of (x, y, r)-space.

So far, we've looked at just one U! In general, of course, there will be a good number of U in the covering of M. Figures 13.8 and 13.9 give an idea of what happens for two overlapping open sets, U_1 and U_2. Even two such sets will show the essential engine behind the smooth embedding. Figure 13.8 focuses on the

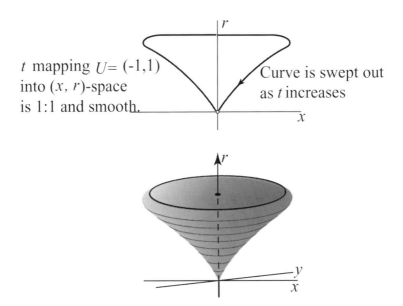

Figure 13.7. The top picture shows the image of the vector function $(r\phi, r)$. The curve is both smooth and one-to-one. The bottom picture depicts the surface of revolution of the curve, and does for a disk-shaped U (dimension 2) what the curve does for an interval U.

overlap. The picture shows U_1 and its shrunken version V_1, as well as U_2 and V_2. The gap or moat between U_1 and V_1 is the same set as the gap between U_2 and V_2. It is in this common moat that we make a smooth transition between U_1 and U_2, and for this, each of these U gets a smoothing function r_i. Their graphs appear at the top of the figure. As t increases, r_1 falls smoothly from 1 to 0 and r_2 rises smoothly from 0 to 1. As in the extension theorem, each r_i is defined on all of M, and if $M = U_1 \cup U_2$, then $r_1 + r_2 \equiv 1$ over M. Now in analogy to the above, let $(r_1\phi_1, r_1)$ embed U_1 smoothly into one copy of $\mathbb{R}^2$ (in Figure 13.9, this is the (x_1, r_1)-plane), and let $(r_2\phi_2, r_2)$ embed U_2 smoothly into another copy of $\mathbb{R}^2$ (the (x_2, r_2)-plane). Figure 13.9 attempts to depict what happens in $\mathbb{R}^2 \times \mathbb{R}^2$: As t advances from the left, the circuit in (x_1, r_1)-space begins to form. When t reaches the left side of the moat, r_1 starts pulling the circuit back toward the origin, but now r_2, which previously had nothing to say, becomes positive and increasing and in $\mathbb{R}^4$ tugs the plot out of the (x_1, r_1)-plane, putting the brakes on the pull toward the origin. As t further increases throughout the moat, the relative effect of r_2 increases, finally hooking up with the circuit for U_2 in the (x_2, r_2)-plane. At that stage, r_1 is 0 and r_2 is 1, and the remainder of the circuit lies strictly in the

(x_2, r_2)-plane. As t continues rightward and approaches the right end of U_2, r_2 itself begins decreasing to 0, and the smooth amalgamation of the two circuits gets completed, as shown in the figure. It is in this way that the larger interval $U_1 \cup U_2$ gets smoothly embedded in a real space of larger dimension.

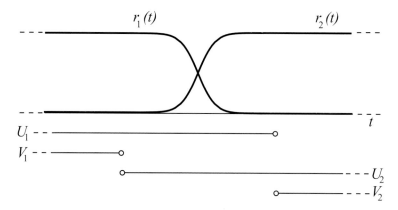

Figure 13.8. $r_2 = 1 - r_1$. $r_1 \equiv 1$ on V_1 and $\equiv 0$ outside U_1. Analogously, $r_2 \equiv 1$ on V_2 and $\equiv 0$ outside U_2. The transitions are smooth in the common moat $U_1 \setminus V_1 = U_2 \setminus V_2$.

Of course for a general compact M of dimension m there will be many open sets U and associated m-component functions ϕ_i, each mapping to $\mathbb{R}^m$, collecting coordinates there and then painting them back on U as a little $(t_1, \dots, t_m)$-coordinate patch there. On each U there will also be an associated shrunken version V_i and a nonnegative scalar function $r_i(t_1, \dots, t_m)$ defined on M having the value 0 at each point of $M \setminus U$. In the transition zone $U \setminus V_i$, r_i smoothly increases from 0 on the boundary of U to positive values on V_i and its boundary. The pair

$$\left(r_i(t_1, \dots, t_m) \cdot \phi_i(t_1, \dots, t_m),\ r_i(t_1, \dots, t_m) \right)$$

smoothly embeds U into its own copy of $\mathbb{R}^{m+1}$. That's the sole purpose of the pair. If there are a total of k sets in the open cover of M, then the embedding of M is defined via $(r_1 \phi_1, r_1, r_2 \phi_2, r_2, \dots, r_k \phi_k, r_k)$.

As we saw before, if M has dimension 5 and is covered by 100 open sets, then each U maps into its own copy of $\mathbb{R}^6$ and with 100 of those, M maps into $\mathbb{R}^{600}$. Even though this is typically very inefficient, this embedding not only clears things up in a history-making way, it also allows us to use all the metric structures in Euclidean space such as tangency, perpendicularity, tangent m-spheres, and more.

Those scalar functions r_i deserve a few more words. Any point of M belongs to finitely many U_i, so if we always take each r_i to rise and fall between 0 and 1,

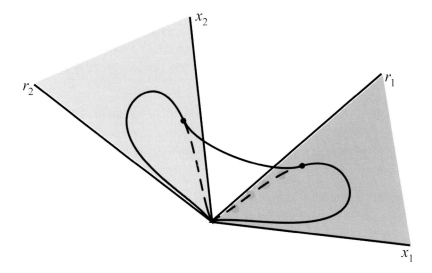

Figure 13.9. As t increases, the image point begins to trace out in the (x_1, r_1)-plane the circuit in the top picture of Figure 13.7, but begins to move out of this plane toward the (x_2, r_2)-plane, where the points eventually trace out the final points of the (x_2, r_2)-version of the curve in Figure 13.7.

their sum at any point would be finite. However, this sum could vary wildly from point to point, so one customarily replaces such an r_i by

$$\frac{r_i}{\sum_i r_i}.$$

At any point of M there are only finitely many nonzero quantities and each r_i stays positive on U_i. At each point of M, the sum of all the r_i there is always 1 since numerator and denominator are then both $\sum_i r_i$. We continue to write simply r_i for the new r_i, and for these we have $\sum_i r_i \equiv 1$. For this reason these new r_i form what is called a "partition of unity," and it allows us to go from the local to the global—in our case, from local embeddings of patches in M to a global embedding of all of M. After dividing by $\sum_i r_i$, an r_i will become smaller, so $r_i \phi_i$ maps to a smaller region of $\mathbb{R}^m$, thus covering a smaller sample of coordinates there. This smaller sample still gets painted back on the same U_i, so in effect the smaller r_i creates a zooming-in on the coordinates in U_i.

Whitney saw that this embedding in something like our $\mathbb{R}^{600}$ example could, by a judicious choice of projections, project down into a much smaller space: Any embedding of an m-dimensional manifold in a high-dimension $\mathbb{R}^N$ could be projected down to an embedding in $\mathbb{R}^{2m+1}$.

To get a sense of how important choosing an appropriate projection is, consider Figure 13.10, depicting a loop drawn on a hollow glass tube. The straight-down projection into the plane of this page is a figure 8. Because it has a cross-point, it is not an embedding of the loop in the plane, but we can choose the projection a little differently: Rotate the tube about the x-axis. After rotating far enough, we encounter directions for which the projection from the original points to the projected points on the plane of this page is one-to-one and smooth. Figure 13.11 shows nine stages, in which the projected image goes from the figure 8 to a circle, which of course is smoothly embedded in the plane.

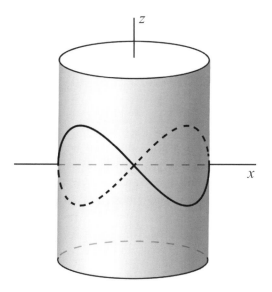

Figure 13.10. Projecting can introduce singularities.

In his proof of this embedding theorem, Whitney likewise chose projections that were one-to-one and smooth, so that a manifold of dimension m sitting in a space $\mathbb{R}^N$, where N is large, would end up in the space $\mathbb{R}^{N-1}$. He was able to apply this successively until he got down to $N = 2m + 1$. The intuition behind his argument was that when N is larger than $2m + 1$, it was easy in such roomy spaces to find a direction so that projecting along that direction to an orthogonal plane of one lower dimension was one-to-one and smooth.

This dimension $2m + 1$ result represented a big step forward. Applied to a Klein bottle (where M has dimension 2), it tells us that the bottle can be embedded in $\mathbb{R}^5$. Whitney, however, knew that the Klein bottle (squashed into 3-space as pictured in Figure 14.8 on p. 186) can actually be smoothly embedded in $\mathbb{R}^4$. This suggested that his $2m + 1$ result was not always the best possible, and in fact

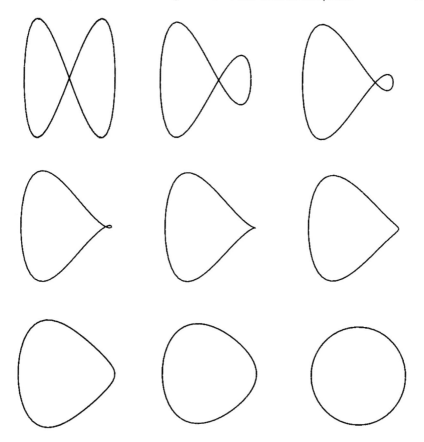

Figure 13.11. By rotating the cylinder in Figure 13.10 about the
x-axis, it will eventually yield a nice, smooth-loop projection.
"Eventually" in this case is about 65°.

all classical examples pointed toward a possible $2m$ result for all manifolds. *That*
one was not so easily disposed of, and kept Whitney thinking about it on and off
for several years. He eventually succeeded, although World War II intervened
and he could not devote his full energies to the problem during that time.

CHAPTER 14

Whitney's Strong Embedding Theorem

Although the weak embedding theorem ensures that any smooth manifold of dimension m can be differentiably embedded in $\mathbb{R}^{2m+1}$, there was a lot of evidence that it could actually fit in the smaller space $\mathbb{R}^{2m}$. Going down this one dimension proved to be a hard nut to crack, but Whitney's intuition was so strong on this that he spent nearly eight years, on and off, trying to establish it. This chapter tells the story of his eventual success.

14.1 His path to success: "The Whitney trick"

Embedding any smooth m-dimensional manifold M into $\mathbb{R}^{2m+1}$ started by finding an embedding of it in a space $\mathbb{R}^N$ of possibly very large dimension N, then successively projecting $\mathbb{R}^N$ into a subspaces $\mathbb{R}^{N-1}$, $\mathbb{R}^{N-2}$, $\mathbb{R}^{N-3}$, ..., so that at each state the projected image is still a manifold. We mentioned in the last chapter that Whitney could easily do this until dimension $2m + 1$. It's in trying to project into dimension $2m$ that serious problems are encountered. An example of two randomly chosen lines in $\mathbb{R}^4$ gives a good idea of what happens. (To keep the exposition simple, let's assume any time we choose a line or other linear object, the choice is random. This avoids atypical situations such as lines coinciding, being parallel, and so on.) There's plenty of free space in $\mathbb{R}^4$, and the lines don't intersect. These two lines form a smooth (but not connected) manifold of dimension $m = 1$, and in this case $4 = 2m + 2$. So we can project one more time: Choose a line in $\mathbb{R}^4$ and project along this direction to a 3-space orthogonal to it. Now the image of the two original lines becomes two (still random) lines in $\mathbb{R}^3$, and of course $3 = 2m + 1$. But when we project just one more time, we get two random lines in the plane, and they'll cross unless we find some way to avoid that.

"Finding some way" is largely what this chapter is about. Since we're working in the world of smooth manifolds, there is a lot of freedom available to us. For example, we can take one of the lines and smoothly bend it into, say, a parabola. A parabola is just as much a differentiable manifold as a straight line, but now, in the bottom picture of Figure 14.1, the parabola intersects in an additional cross-point!

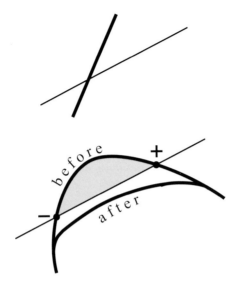

Figure 14.1. Bending the heavy line downward into a parabola can add an extra intersection.

This may sound terrible, but it turns out to be the path to success. Notice that we can take the parabola and continuously push the top part of it downward—always keeping the curve smooth—until the two crosspoints disappear. This curve now has two less gentle bends. In the bottom picture of Figure 14.1, the parts as they appear originally and after the pushing are labeled "before" and "after." This bending and pushing can be looked at as one continuous operation on one of the lines in 3-space before we project everything down to the plane.

Now let's up the ante: Instead of two crossing lines in the plane, let's look at a lemniscate, which also has just one crosspoint. It turns out that smoothly bending or pushing parts of the lemniscate in the plane, never creating kinks or other nonsmoothness, always leaves us with a crosspoint. But look again at the space curve on a cylinder as in Figure 13.10 on p. 172. Remove the cylinder, and now we can smoothly twist the top of the already-warped space curve so that the projection acquires an additional crosspoint and loop. This is not surprising because we could, after all, take a thin wire circle in 3-space, grab two opposite ends, and twist a lot so a projection of it has many crosspoints. However, Figure 14.2 shows creating the extra loop in a more direct way—cutting out a little piece of the original curve and smoothly gluing in another curve already having a loop. We can get the nice result depicted in Figure 14.3 by miniaturizing the separate loop curve shown on the right-hand side of Figure 14.2 and gluing that miniaturized version into the gap. One could use something like the Folium of Descartes or Trisectrix of Maclaurin—either one looks a lot like the loop shown in Figure 14.2. In each case the curve becomes nearly flat away from the loop so it can then be slightly bent to attach smoothly to the rest of the original curve. Whitney found parametric equations for a loop of this sort ([**87**], pp. 222, 223), and they can be easily generalized to a curve in a real space of any dimension.

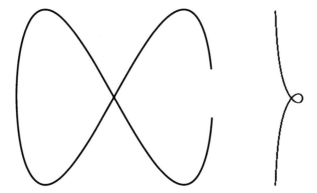

Figure 14.2. Miniaturize the curve on the right and insert it in the gap to give the lemniscate an even number of singularities.

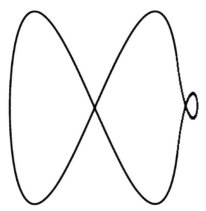

Figure 14.3. The spliced curve has two singularities.

Now we're ready to do our magic. In Figure 14.4, we have reshaped the curve in Figure 14.3 to make it more symmetric, and now we can grab the top middle section between the two crosspoints and push smoothly downward. In the middle picture the crosspoints are approaching each other, and in the bottom they have disappeared, much as they did in Figure 14.1.

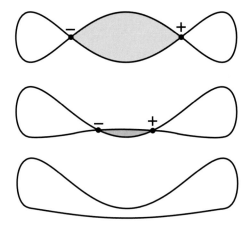

Figure 14.4. The Whitney trick removes pairs of crosspoints.

Sometimes it's not necessary to add an extra loop, but loops generally cancel in pairs, so if for whatever reason we need to remove a crosspoint, add a little loop close to it and then push appropriately (doing this locally and always keeping the curve smooth) to allow the two points to disappear. This Whitney trick, local in nature, may be done several times to take care of crosspoints at various locations on what may be a very complicated curve having many crosspoints.

So far we have looked only at examples of crosspoints in the plane, but the method applies more generally, and that is the reason why both Figures 14.1 and 14.4 show a shaded area as well as a plus and a minus sign next to the crosspoints. The shaded area represents a topological disk bounded by the two arcs between the two crosspoints. Any pushing takes place within the potential manifold, so the disk lies on it and may actually wave around quite a bit instead of lying in a plane. So in pushing, we agree that the changing arcs and points stay on the disk boundary. The plus and minus signs are assigned to the points to give orientations. In Figure 14.1, think of an ant walking along the line segment from its leftmost point to the rightmost. It encounters the parabola-shaped curve from outside the curve and meets the other intersection point from inside. We correspondingly tag the two intersection points with opposite signs. When the points approach each other, one can perhaps think of the points as an electron and positron that annihilate each other when they meet. Carefully assigning orientations to points can be important when working with nonorientable manifolds.

The Whitney trick has to do with moving arcs to shrink to nothingness a loop and two isolated crosspoints on it. But what about higher dimensions? It turns out that the picture in Figure 14.1 can be suitably embedded when working in higher dimensions, and smoothly moving arcs to remove crosspoints will continue to work. This may seem at first to be remarkable as well as somewhat mysterious, but some of the mystery can be removed by looking at simple cases. In analogy to how we began this chapter, let's look at the higher-dimensional analogs of lines—that is, planes and more generally copies of some $\mathbb{R}^n$ sitting in a larger $\mathbb{R}^m$. Again, if we choose our copies of $\mathbb{R}^n$ randomly, we have a very nice and very basic dimension theorem. First, by *codimension* we mean the number of steps down from the top dimension of the space. So in $\mathbb{R}^3$ the codimension of any plane is 1, of any line is 2, and of any point is 3. The codimension of 3-space in $\mathbb{R}^4$ is 1; the codimension of a line in $\mathbb{R}^4$ is 3. The codimension of a copy of $\mathbb{R}^n$ in $\mathbb{R}^{2n}$ is n.

There's a basic dimension theorem we're about to meet. First, we say that when manifolds M_1 and M_2 intersect, the intersection is *generic* provided no arbitrarily small smooth local changes ever change the intersection's dimension. So in 3-space, two unit spheres intersecting in a circle would be generic, but if they intersect in a point (that is, the spheres are tangent) or in a unit sphere (the spheres coincide), then that intersection isn't generic. With this definition and the obvious meaning of codim, our basic dimension theorem reads

Theorem. If $(M_1 \cap M_2) \neq \varnothing$ is generic, then

$$\text{codim}(M_1 \cap M_2) = \text{codim}(M_1) + \text{codim}(M_2). \tag{14.1}$$

Let's look at some examples.

- In 3-space, a sphere and the line through its poles intersect generically, so the codimensions add as $1 + 2 = 3$—that is, the intersection is 0-dimensional and indeed, the union of two points is 0-dimensional.
- In 3-space, let M_1 be defined by $y^2 + z^2 = 1$ (so it's a cylinder of unit radius running along the x-axis) and let M_2 be defined by $x^2 + z^2 = 1$ (a cylinder of unit radius running along the y-axis). Then $\text{codim}(M_1 \cap M_2) = \text{codim}(M_1) + \text{codim}(M_2)$ becomes $\text{codim}(M_1 \cap M_2) = 1 + 1$, telling us that the intersection has codimension 2 and therefore dimension 1. These cylinders do in fact intersect in two crossing circles.
- It's instructive to redo the above example in 4-space with, say, coordinates (x, y, z, t), and let M_1 be the same two-dimensional cylinder of unit radius running along the x-axis. In $\mathbb{R}^4$, specifying this cylinder requires two equations (each one reducing the dimension by one): $y^2 + z^2 = 1$ and $t = 0$. Now let M_2 be the unit two-dimensional cylinder defined by $x^2 + t^2 = 1$ and, say, $z = 0$. These cylinders intersect generically, so $\text{codim}(M_1 \cap M_2) = \text{codim}(M_1) + \text{codim}(M_2)$ becomes $\text{codim}(M_1 \cap M_2) = 2 + 2$, telling us that

the intersection has codimension 4, or dimension 0. That is, in $\mathbb{R}^4$, two ordinary two-dimensional cylinders that intersect generically intersect in only
isolated points.

- In the above examples the intersection is always between two separate manifolds, but that need not be the case. Just as we have a crosspoint within the
connected figure 8 curve, we can manufacture an analogous higher-dimen-
sional example in $\mathbb{R}^4$: Cut down the above infinitely long cylinders in $\mathbb{R}^4$ so
each one is, say, just 10 units long and still intersects in the same set of isolated points. Take two additional bendable sections of a hose and smoothly
attach them to the ends of the intersecting pieces to make a tube looking like
a figure 8 that self-intersects in isolated points. Just as we can look at a figure
8 curve as a projection to a plane of a warped circle in 3-space, we can look
at our self-intersecting tube as the projection into 4-space of a warped torus
in 5-space.

- For randomly chosen subspaces $\mathbb{R}^r$ and $\mathbb{R}^s$ in $\mathbb{R}^{(r+s)}$, the codimension of
$\mathbb{R}^r \cap \mathbb{R}^s$ is $r+s$, which says that randomly chosen subspaces of complementary
dimension intersect in just a point.

- In four of the five examples above, the intersection consists of isolated points,
and it is in precisely these cases that the Whitney trick applies. To use it, to
each isolated crosspoint we need to create another isolated point (as we have
done in Figure 14.3) since the Whitney trick removes point-pairs, not a single
point. Figure 14.5 shows an example already having a pair of intersection
points. The top figure depicts part of a manifold shaped like the cathode ray
tube from an early generation TV. We're looking at it from below, with the
TV screen facing away from us and tilted slightly downward. There are two
arcs, each connecting their two intersection points, and together these arcs
form a topological loop lying in a plane. The curved arc pulls away from
us, dragging nearby points of the two-dimensional manifold along with it.
That's the Whitney trick in action. In the bottom picture, the curved arc has
moved far enough so that the two points of intersection have disappeared.
This action, as always, is performed locally, so that parts of the manifold(s)
away from the points we're removing are not affected. We want this because
there may be many other isolated intersection points, and once we've taken
care of one of them, we don't want anything to affect the status of it or any
other points—we want our march to success to be uninterrupted.

We've noted that two two-dimensional tubes in 4-space intersecting generically do so in isolated points. By taking just one tube and bending it so it self-
intersects generically, the intersection still consists of isolated points, and the
Whitney trick applies in such cases. So suppose we've come to an isolated point
P, and we want to eliminate it on the road to getting an everywhere smooth manifold. When faced with this problem in dimension 1, Figure 14.2 gave us the

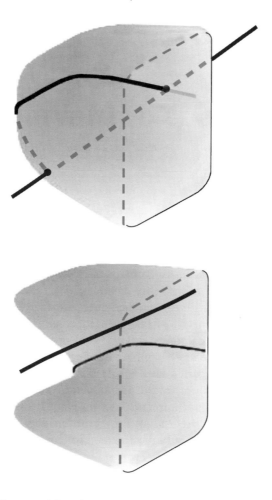

Figure 14.5. The Whitney trick seen on a surface.

recipe—remove a tiny section of the curve and smoothly replace it with a loop having one crosspoint, thus creating a second crosspoint, which then allows us to use the Whitney trick. The two-dimensional recipe is analogous: Around P on the tube, excise a small near-disk or near-rectangle. Now smoothly patch in its place a small object that is smooth everywhere except at one point. You can get such an object by rotating the little loop (such as the Folium of Descartes or Trisectrix of Maclaurin mentioned on p. 177) about its center of symmetry. This object really lives in 4-space, and Whitney works out explicit parametric equations for it (see [**87**], pp. 222, 223), but we can describe in intuitive geometric terms how to make this miniature surface in 4-space that gets flat away from the pinchpoint. (The flatness makes it easy to slightly bend and smoothly attach it to the removed patch.)

Here's the idea: Just as a sphere in 3-space can be thought of as being assembled from a pile of transparencies of growing, then diminishing, circles, in 4-space we can assemble a pile of 3-spaces (each corresponding to t = a constant) having a space curve drawn in it. Let t range from -1 to 1, and start by bending a thin steel wire into an "alpha curve"—one that looks like the letter α. It has one crosspoint. Rest the wire on an imaginary table top, hold one end down, and, as t increases from greater than 0 to 1, steadily raise the other end straight up so the crosspoint separates. The space curve corresponding to each $t > 0$ is smooth while $t = 0$ corresponds to the original loop with crosspoint. Symmetrically, as t decreases from 0 to -1, hold the wire and steadily pull that same free end down through the imaginary table top. Roughly speaking, assemble all these space curves corresponding to t running from -1 to $+1$, and you end up with a surface in 4-space that is smooth everywhere except when $t = 0$, where you have just that one crosspoint. A miniature version of this assembled surface is what you smoothly paste into the hole you cut out of the original self-intersecting tube. In this way we introduce a second crosspoint close to P. The devil is in the details, and this book is not meant to cover them, but the essential idea is that in this and all higher-dimensional cases, you can make things look like the standard picture depicted in Figure 14.1 and then use Whitney's trick to eliminate crosspoints. Applied often enough, you turn what would be a manifold that is smooth—except for those finitely many crosspoints—into an actual manifold that is smooth everywhere.

In particular, Whitney used successive projections to embed a manifold of dimension m into $\mathbb{R}^{2m+1}$. Upon projecting one more time into $\mathbb{R}^{2m}$, you have parts of an m-manifold that self-intersect, and things can be smoothly jiggled to make all intersections generic. These intersecting parts each have codimension m in $\mathbb{R}^{2m}$, which means that the codimension in $\mathbb{R}^{2m}$ of the intersection is $m + m = 2m$—that is, the dimension of the intersection is 0 and thus consists of isolated points. This, as we've said, is just the scenario for which the Whitney trick applies. We thus arrive at the strong embedding theorem, in which any m-dimension manifold assembled from coordinate patches can be embedded into $\mathbb{R}^{2m}$. Whitney published his groundbreaking result in 1944 ([87]).

14.2 Embedding a manifold has important consequences

Whitney's embedding theorems changed the landscape of manifold theory. One reason is that since we are now assured that any manifold sits in some Euclidean space, the manifold inherits a metric from that surrounding space. At any point P of the manifold, it makes sense to talk about things like a point Q being close to P; or the line through P and Q; or the limit line as Q approaches P; or the tangent space to the manifold at any of its points. Since the surrounding space is Euclidean, there's also the vector space of all vectors perpendicular to the manifold at any of its points, and this pointwise orthogonal decomposition played an important role in Whitney's subsequent research.

The metric also means we can define within the tangent space such things as a sphere about P. The same can be done within the orthogonal space. Doing this at each point of the manifold so that the union is smooth yields tangent sphere bundles and normal sphere bundles. One can also form products at each point; these are local products. For example, at each point of a smooth loop in 3-space one can construct a unit interval perpendicular to the loop, the intervals varying smoothly along the loop base space. Globally, there are two distinct topological ways to do this, giving on the one hand a topological cylinder and on the other, a Möbius strip. One can assign a degree of twisting or torsion to each possibility, 0 to the cylinder and 1 to the Möbius strip. This can be recast into the language of spheres: An interval is a 1-ball, and its two-point boundary is a 0-sphere. If the strip is given an even number of half-twists, the 0-spheres form two topological loops; an odd number yields just a single loop; 0 and 1 can naturally be regarded as the group elements of the integers mod 2. It seemed likely that this phenomenon also occurs in higher dimensions, and that there ought to be a way to similarly quantify the behavior. Eventually, a vector over the integers mod 2 captured the torsion information within a more general sphere bundle— essentially a Stiefel-Whitney characteristic class. It is beyond the scope of this book to go into more detail on Stiefel-Whitney characteristic classes, but it is yet another very fundamental area with far-reaching consequences in which Whitney played a foundational role. Those with enough topological and algebraic background may profitably consult the book of Milnor and Stasheff ([**MS**]).

14.3 Duality

Duality played a big part in Whitney's mathematical research. Even in his first musings about the four-color problem, he transformed a geographical map—a planar graph —into its dual and worked with that. A map of countries naturally divides the plane into a simplicial complex, and associated to each r-simplex is a $(2 - r)$-simplex. A country is a 2-simplex, and its associated dual is a $(2 - r) = (2 - 2) = 0$-simplex—a point, which we call its capital. The boundary between two countries is a 1-simplex, and its dual is a $(2 - 1) = 1$-simplex (a road) crossing the boundary transversally. A vertex of the original graph dualizes to the 2-simplex in the new graph that contains that vertex. (This idea is familiar to electrical engineers, who often form the dual of a planar electrical circuit to simplify solving a problem.) He was able to generalize this key idea to simplicial complexes of any dimension n in which associated to any r-simplex is a dual

$(n-r)$-simplex. Importantly, homology of the original complex is essentially the same as of the dual complex, and now Whitney pushed the existing homological frontiers forward. A few years earlier, Poincaré's Betti numbers had been given a group structure by Emmy Noether, and Whitney was able to define a cup product so that the direct sum of groups became a ring, and topological invariants of a manifold could now be expressed in a more natural way using the manifold's ring. This cup product opened up the way for geometric operations on bundles. With the definitions and tools that Whitney now had, he was eventually able to describe characteristic classes of the product of two sphere bundles—a central result now known as the Whitney duality theorem.

14.4 Immersions

Can the dimension $2m$ be improved? Can m-dimensional manifolds be embedded in the even smaller space $\mathbb{R}^{2m-1}$? Whitney found a nonorientable surface of dimension 4 that definitely cannot be embedded in $\mathbb{R}^{2\cdot4-1} = \mathbb{R}^7$ ([**82**], p. 139), but he did show that m-dimensional manifolds can always be *immersed* in the smaller space $\mathbb{R}^{2m-1}$, and this result is known as the *Whitney immersion theorem*. He proved this in [**89**].

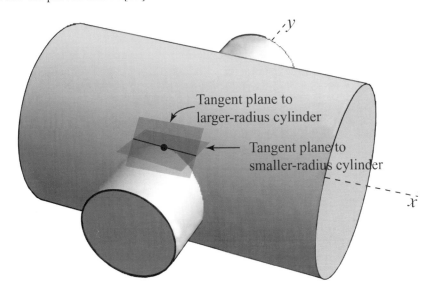

Figure 14.6. At any intersection point of these cylinders of different radii, the two tangent planes are different.

What is an immersion? We can get the basic idea through some pictures. Figure 14.6 shows two circular cylinders in (x, y, z)-space. Let's say one of them has equation $y^2 + z^2 = 4$, so its radius is 2 and its centerline is the x-axis. Suppose the other has equation $x^2 + z^2 = 1$, meaning that this cylinder's radius is 1 and its centerline is the y-axis. How do these cylinders intersect? The cylinders' centerlines are perpendicular to each other, and the cylinders intersect in two bent circles. If an ant were sitting at any point of either of these bent circles, it would see two distinct tangent planes—the planes tangent to each of the two cylinders. These planes intersect in the nicest (meaning most nondegenerate) way that two planes in 3-space *can* intersect: generically. In our case this means they intersect in a line.

On the other hand, if you increase the radius of the smaller cylinder so it grows to have the same radius as the larger cylinder, this new cylinder now has equation $x^2 + z^2 = 4$, and the former two separate bent circles now become two intersecting ordinary (nonbent) circles. These intersections are at two points, where the circles cross at right angles—at $(0, 0, 2)$ and at $(0, 0, -2)$. If the ant walks over to either one of these two crosspoints, it will see that the tangent planes to the cylinders there now coincide—they don't intersect generically, and that's illustrated in Figure 14.7.

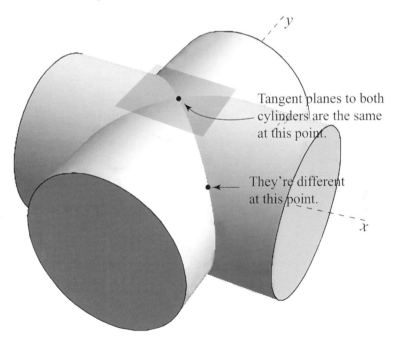

Tangent planes to both cylinders are the same at this point.

They're different at this point.

Figure 14.7. Tangent planes at the intersection of cylinders of the same radii are the same at the top and bottom intersection points.

In the first scenario where the cylinders intersected in two disjoint bent circles, all pairs of tangent planes at each intersection point are as distinct as they can be in 3-space, and we say the two cylinders are *immersed* in 3-space. But when the cylinders both have the same radius, the tangent planes don't always do that—the tangent planes fail to intersect generically at $(0, 0, 2)$ and again at $(0, 0, -2)$. All it takes is one such bad point, and then we say the two cylinders fail to be immersed. In neither case are the two cylinders actually embedded in 3-space, but Whitney's immersion theorem says that since we're allowing smooth changes and warping, we can simply shrink one cylinder to make the radii different, and then the union of the two intersecting cylinders is immersed in 3-space.

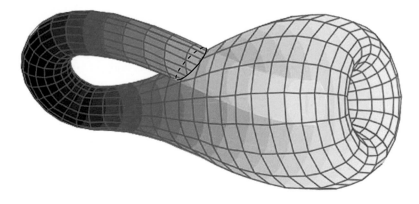

Figure 14.8. An immersion of the Klein bottle in 3-space.

At this point you may protest and say "Well, just move the cylinders far away from each other. Then they'll be embedded, which is even better!" True, but what about trying to embed a Klein bottle in 3-space? Figure 14.8 shows a popular representation of the bottle in 3-space. The bottle self-intersects in a loop, but the way that's happening is much like two cylinders of different radii—the tangent planes at any point of the loop behave nicely, and the Klein bottle is immersed in 3-space. But you can't move the cylinder-like parts away from each other without breaking or tearing the surface. You can't embed the bottle in 3-space, but you can immerse it. It's educational to note that you could massage the immersed bottle so the intersection looks like the intersection in Figure 14.7. Then the bottle wouldn't even be immersed in 3-space.

Figure 14.9. Hass, about the time he published the strong embedding theorem.

CHAPTER 15
World War II

In 1942, Whitney's research life suddenly changed. One afternoon he received a telephone call from the well-known mathematician Saunders Mac Lane, asking if Whitney could help with the war effort. The Blitzkrieg was decimating British cities, and allied defenses were pitiful: It was taking, on average, some 160,000 lb of shells to down a single German plane. The skills of even the best gunners were not equal to the enemy's fast-flying aircraft, so Mac Lane's request was very specific: Could Whitney design a gunsight that could instantaneously determine the right way to aim the gun at a fast-moving target? This chapter tells the story.

15.1 Our nation responds

The Japanese attack on Pearl Harbor on December 7, 1941 immediately united a nation that had been divided on whether to enter the European war. Franklin D. Roosevelt declared war on Japan later that day. Four days later, Germany and Italy declared war on us, and we reciprocated to both within hours. World War II brought many crises to the United States, three of which stand out for sheer size: First, our entire economy flipped to the exigencies of war; second, we began the Manhattan Project. Third, we addressed the dismal response to the German Blitzkrieg, and that underscored the pressing need for much better antiaircraft aiming. It was here that Whitney played a central role. Here are brief sketches of these three crises.

Our economy flipped to the exigencies of war. We suddenly found ourselves fighting wars in both Europe and the Pacific. In less than a month, Roosevelt announced we would produce some 60,000 planes, 45,000 tanks, 20,000 antiaircraft guns, and 6 million tons of merchant shipping. From early 1942 through the end of 1944, the auto industry metamorphosized from manufacturing cars to turning out tanks and armored cars. By war's end, we had built 5,000 ships, five times the number we'd had at the beginning of the war. 1942 suddenly saw the rationing of tires, gasoline, fuel oil, and sugar. Driving for pleasure was banned. Home-building was halted. Highway construction was stopped.

We began the Manhattan Project. The idea of an atomic chain reaction was first proposed by the Hungarian scientist Leo Szilard barely a year after neutrons were discovered in 1932. Nuclear fission itself was discovered in Germany five years later by Lise Meitner, Otto Hahn, and Otto Frisch. Neils Bohr brought the stunning news to the U.S. when he visited here. It was Meitner who first realized that Einstein's famous equation $E = mc^2$ explained the tremendous amount of energy released during fission.

Figure 15.1. A re-creation of the first successful fission experiment carried out by Meitner, Hahn, and Frisch.

Crucially, Enrico Fermi and Szilard found that neutrons were responsible for splitting atoms, and in the process further neutrons were released. This could lead to a chain reaction. $E = mc^2$ would then rear its head, leading to a self-perpetuating stream of energy so great and so sudden that it would represent an explosion of unheard-of intensity. Szilard saw it all, and when he discovered that Germany had halted all exports of uranium, his initial worry turned to consternation. He in fact had reason to worry. Though he had no proof of German activity, it turned out that Werner Heisenberg was in charge of an effort to produce a German atomic bomb. During one experiment a serious accident destroyed much of their equipment which halted progress, and Hitler lost interest. Szilard convinced Einstein to sign a letter to Roosevelt warning about the wartime consequences of inaction. As we know, this ultimately led to the Manhattan Project, which started in 1942.

The pressing need for far better antiaircraft aiming. On September 7, 1940 a fleet of 348 German bombers bombed London from 4 to 6 in the afternoon. Two hours later, a second wave, guided by swaths of flames in London, bombed until 4:30 the next morning. This Blitzkrieg, which soon extended to other British cities, continued until the following May. London was bombed 71 times. Although Britain's ground antiaircraft defense and her Royal Air Force both went into action, it was soon clear that the Nazis were bombing with virtual impunity. It was estimated in October 1940 that it was taking at least 10,000 rounds of 3-inch antiaircraft ammunition for each German plane downed. At 20 shells per minute, an antiaircraft gun would, on average, need to spend over 8 hours of continuous shooting to get one Nazi plane. At about 16 lb per round, that would have been about 80 tons of shells for each plane. It was obvious that at 10,000 rounds per plane, gunners were simply not aiming properly. Although the German aircraft losses continued to grow, a crisis was very much at hand. By the time the raids ended, over a million London homes were damaged or destroyed, and over 40,000 civilians had died from the attacks.

Figure 15.2. A WWII photo showing the great firepower expended in a typically unsuccessful attempt at downing enemy aircraft.

15.2 A critical problem needs a solution

The practical problem was designing a gunsight that could continuously determine how to properly aim the gun at a fast-moving target. The gunsight had to
make minimal demands on the pilot who might be involved in a dogfight and
who may not have any special aptitude for aiming. The sight had to take into
account variables such as the instantaneous distance of the British plane from
the German target, how fast and in what direction the target was moving, as well
as the British gunner's velocity, banking angle, and rate of turn. It needed to
be designed so that the gunner would simply keep the enemy plane within the
sight's target circle, and the sight would do the rest, quickly making the required
calculations and then appropriately redirecting the turret.

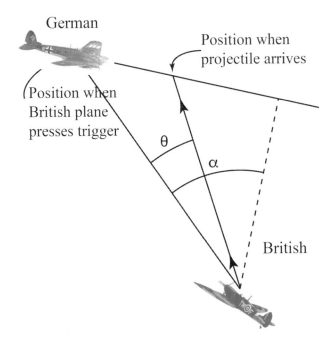

Figure 15.3. All lines and angles are moving in a fast-changing
three-dimensional situation. The theoretical problem is finding
θ with sufficient accuracy. The practical problem is designing a
gunsight that quickly calculates θ and then translates this into
an intuitive form for the gunner.

Solving this and related problems required talented applied mathematicians,
but the United States had a dearth of them. There were a few statisticians at

Princeton and some applied people at Brown and Columbia, but it quickly became clear that to compensate for this shortcoming, a group of powerful mathematicians needed to drop their research in pure mathematics and turn to immediate, practical wartime problems. Surprising names appeared among the eventual members of the group that was called the Applied Mathematics Panel (part of the National Defense Research Committee). At the top in the Panel hierarchy was Warren Weaver, who had expertise in language translation and a talent for administration. Saunders Mac Lane worked with Weaver and was charged with procuring able mathematicians and matching their talents with the wide range of wartime problems. Mac Lane buttonholed a range of people whose specialties were in algebra, geometry, analysis, logic, number theory, topology, or other fields. As a group, they formed a potent force toward aiding the war effort. Just to give an idea of the tremendous change many mathematicians had to make, Mac Lane himself had for years been immersed in abstract math. He helped create category theory and was known for his work in algebraic topology, algebraic number theory, logic, as well as the famous book *Modern Algebra* which he co-authored with Garrett Birkhoff (George Birkhoff's son). But with the war on, his life took a very different track.

What about Whitney? He and Mac Lane were good friends, having spent time together at Harvard as instructors. Like Whitney, Mac Lane earned his B.A. from Yale. He had majored in both math and physics. He knew that Whitney had a good background in differential equations and an aptitude for setting up and solving the kind of problems arising in air-to-air collisions. A phone call was inevitable: Would Hassler volunteer for a position on the Applied Mathematics Panel, specializing in air-to-air rocketry problems? Whitney agreed, and he soon worked out the several differential equations that tied together various rapidly changing distances and angles depicted in Figure 15.3. He pursued his equations' implications for a wide variety of situations, and what he discovered led him to conclusions basic to making improvements in aiming at moving targets. Hassler was asked to report his analyses to the mathematician Mina Rees, head of the mathematics department of the Office of Naval Research and an administrator on the Applied Mathematics Panel. Rees was not familiar with Hassler's talents, and she made it clear that all this analysis was one thing, but the bottom line was, did it translate to actual aiming improvements? Rees and Whitney set up a friendly competition using two flight simulators at a nearby airforce base. In the simulators, waves of enemy planes were to be shot down before they could escape unharmed, mimicking the ongoing tragedies in the actual war. Rees used the common-sense approach most pilots were then employing, and got results much like those pilots were getting: All but two of her planes escaped unharmed. Whitney, using the skills and intuition he had gained through his mathematical

analyses, shot down every last one. There were zero survivors. A suddenly educated Rees recognized that Whitney had "an absolute genius for airplane problems from guidance studies."

The progress Whitney made on gunsights was incorporated in making fundamental improvements to them, making the pilot's job easier, more intuitive,
and far more accurate. In his official report, he writes in a way that nontech-
nical people in the military can understand: "…an important consideration in
assessing a tracking mechanism is the mental effort it requires on the part of the
operator. He may have other matters to attend to at the same time, such as ranging and pressing a trigger. In the heat of combat, one cannot expect a gunner to
go through mental gymnastics." Figure 15.4 depicts a square gunsight with the
approaching enemy aircraft centered in the circle. This gunsight captures the
essence of what he accomplished:

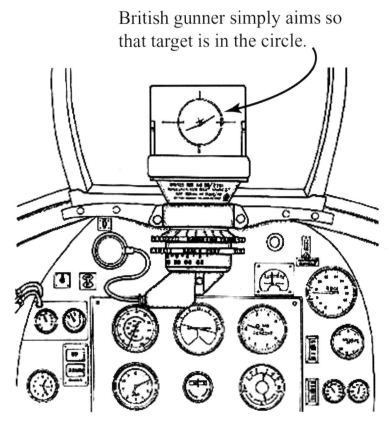

Figure 15.4. With the improved gunsight, the gunner's job was
much simpler and far more accurate.

Figure 15.5. Hass, shortly after his work toward the war effort.

CHAPTER 16

From Harvard to the Institute; Insights on Smooth Mappings

In 1951 Hassler unexpectedly received an offer from J. Robert Oppenheimer to join the Institute for Advanced Study. This would give Hass an unmatched opportunity to work on further projects with essentially no other demands on his time. He accepted, and one fortuitous outcome was his work on singularity-like artifacts that can arise simply from looking at a smooth manifold. These are not actual singularities like crosspoints, sharp turns, or angles, but more like the picture's "horizon," consisting of points that are special due only to the manifold's being viewed from a particular location. But these points can have far-reaching implications. In this chapter we look at some of his groundbreaking insights.

16.1 A new life, new horizons

The Institute for Advanced Study was created in 1930 through the philanthropy of Louis Bamberger and his sister Carrie Bamberger Fuld, with the guidance of the educator Abraham Flexner who became the Institute's first director. The brother-sister team owned the Bamberger chain of department stores based in New Jersey, but sold the chain to Macy's just four months before the 1929 crash. Had they waited, the Institute very well may have never happened. Its permanent home in Princeton is in an idyllic setting where brilliant thinkers are free to pursue their research in whatever direction they wish. The salary is generous and there are homes available near the Institute campus. Whitney would be joining five others in the Institute's School of Mathematics.

Top-tier research mathematicians scattered around the world number in the hundreds, and any one of them would snap up the offer to join the Institute in a heartbeat. So why was Whitney chosen? If you look at the permanent Institute

197

Figure 16.1. Hass, around the time he joined the Institute.

members in any field, it always comes down to their making especially consequential contributions. Einstein changed the way we view a great part of physics. Gödel shocked the entire mathematical community by proving that we can never be sure that mathematics is internally consistent, something everyone else tacitly assumed. Von Neumann was, among other things, a leader in starting the era of programmable computers. Whitney? It is not too much a stretch to view him as a Johnny Appleseed of mathematics in that he planted numerous mathematical seeds that took root and eventually flourished. He was very individualistic and seemed to have some internal sensor that sounded off when he'd stumble upon something having the smell of special significance. His energy, focus, and dogged persistence would then kick in. His innate originality seemed to be enhanced in that he mostly avoided areas that had been plowed through by others. This gave him greater freedom in his approach—he could then establish the basic concepts and direction of development.

Figure 16.2. The Institute founders Abraham Flexner, Louis Bamberger, and Caroline ("Carrie") Bamberger Fuld.

Figure 16.3. Fuld Hall, the main building of the Institute.

Whitney looked forward to his Institute position as an opportunity to finally work on some projects he'd had in mind without having to prepare lectures, grade papers, and so on. Some of these projects will be familiar to those with more topological background.[1]

What's the story about smooth mappings? For much of his life, Hass had worked on manifolds, which have no nondifferentiable points such as crinkles, self-intersections, sharp corners, and the like. As a teenager exploring math, Hass became fascinated with polynomials and their graphs, and wrote long letters to his always-supportive sister Caroline describing the discoveries he was making.

He found that the plots of many polynomial equations could have exceptional, nonsmooth points, called *singularities*. Later, when he started browsing through calculus books, he encountered singularities in lemniscates, roses, cardioids, and cusps. (A cusp is the shape an auto tire leaves in the snow when backing out of a driveway and then going on to the street.) Figure 16.4 shows a few examples.

Figure 16.4. A four-leaved rose, cardioid, the union of four circles, a three-leaved rose, a cusp curve, and limaçon are examples of the sorts of curves with singularities Hass would have encountered when looking through calculus books, or on his own.

So even though his extension and embedding theorems had to do with objects not having singularities, his early experience with singularities left a lasting mark on him, and an important part of Whitney's research at the Institute centered on them. In addition, a new avenue of exploration opened up for him upon realizing that viewing graphs of smooth functions from certain vantage points can reveal what might be called "perceived singularities." This chapter briefly describes what these are, and we look at some of his important work on them. Whitney's breakthrough paper is [**102**], and it eventually led to René Thom's work in catastrophe theory which in turn proved to be a harbinger of today's widely studied nonlinear dynamics and chaos.

16.2 Introduction: Curves and singularities

A set may be a manifold except for points about which things don't look smooth. We see such singular points in curves having self-intersections or cusp points, and as we'll see in the next chapter, Whitney studied these in sets of arbitrary dimension. But he also studied "perceived" singularities that can arise when looking at the object from certain vantage points. Let's briefly look at both types at the simplest level—on curves.

We start with an example of the "objective" kind. Figure 16.5 depicts a lemniscate (looking like a figure 8) which is smooth everywhere except where the curve self-intersects. Line L represents a test line piercing through the curve transversally (that is, not tangentially) at a smooth, or *regular*, point P. If we perturb L a little bit (for example, by translating L slightly to the left or right), the perturbed line still intersects the lemniscate in a single point close to P. In this sense, the behavior of the test line and curve doesn't change under small perturbations of L, and we say that the intersection of the curve with the line is *stable* at P. Now, however, look at a similar test line intersecting the lemniscate at the singular point Q. Translating the line a little to the left or right results in a very different outcome: The point of intersection separates into distinct points.

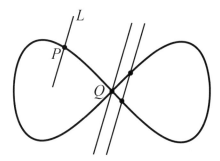

Figure 16.5. A lemniscate has a single objective singularity.

The test line actually intersects the lemniscate in *two* points at Q. That intersection is most naturally regarded as a double point—the line intersects the uphill road part of the lemniscate through Q in one point, and it intersects the downhill road going through Q in another. These two points just happen to be at the same location. When L is translated a bit, the intersections don't remain a double point, and we say "the intersection splits up." If you do this at the center of a rose having many leaves, then there are many roadways through the single point of intersection, and a multiple point of intersection analogously splits up into many distinct ones.

Now let's look at an example of a *perceived* singularity. Figure 16.6 shows a basic example.

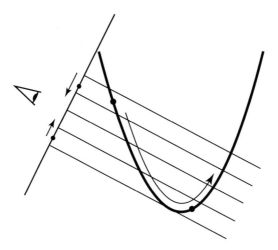

Figure 16.6. A steadily moving point on the parabola appears to stop for an instant at the "horizon"—the point of contact with the viewing tangent line—and an observer perceives that as a singularity.

The parabola is everywhere smooth and therefore has no objective singularities, but the behavior of a test line tangent to the curve shares some of the behavior of the transverse test line through the lemniscate's crosspoint—parallel translation can cause the point to split up into two points. With the lemniscate, for small perturbations of the transverse line through Q shown in Figure 16.5, the only point near Q that splits up is just Q itself. In contrast, the particular point splitting up on the parabola depends on the direction of the test line, since as we roll the tangent line along the parabola, the point of contact changes. We can regard any particular test direction as a viewing angle, and what we see depends on that viewing angle. Any such singularity on the parabola nonetheless possesses a certain stability, in that if we roll the tangent test line to a different viewing angle, then in the new view the new contact point splits up in the same way that the old one did.

One can further highlight the role of the observer by letting a point move along the curve at constant speed, as depicted in Figure 16.6. The line perpendicular to the viewing angle represents a viewing screen, or what is basically the same thing, the retina of the observer's eye. As the point nears the point of tangency, the shadow or projection on the screen slows down and stops for an instant as the point on the parabola crosses the point of contact. The shadow then reverses direction and picks up speed. We again meet stability because another observer, with a different viewing angle, sees behavior that's the same in that the shadow on the screen slows down, instantaneously stops as the point on the parabola crosses the point of contact, then reverses direction and picks up speed.

Let's see what happens when we run this last experiment, replacing the parabola $y = x^2$ by the cubic $y = x^3$. In Figure 16.7, the line of sight we've chosen is never tangent to the cubic, and correspondingly, the shadow of the point slows down and then speeds up, but never stops.

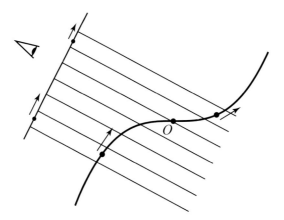

Figure 16.7. From this vantage point, the cubic has no horizon. The observer perceives no singularity and never sees the point stop.

Let's compare that with what happens in Figure 16.8. Instead of seeing no points of tangency, we now see *two* points of tangency. As the point on the cubic moves with constant speed through the left dark grey box, the projection slows down, and for an instant, at the right side of that box, just as the point on the cubic goes through one of the points of tangency, its speed is zero. During the time the point is in the light grey box, the projection has reversed direction, speeding up to a maximum as the point on the cubic crosses the origin O. It then slows to a stop and reverses direction a second time as the point exits the middle box.

This behavior is very different from that of the parabola. What we haven't drawn is the view intermediate between the kind of views shown in Figures 16.7 and 16.8. In the intermediate case, the line of sight is tangent to the cubic at O. From this viewpoint, the projected point slows to a stop at O, then speeds up, continuing in the same direction. But to actually see this, the observer's line of sight must be kept *precisely* tangent to the curve at O. Any deviation from that, and what is seen falls into one of the two scenarios seen in Figures 16.7 and 16.8. In this sense, we can say that the behavior at O on the cubic is *unstable* in much

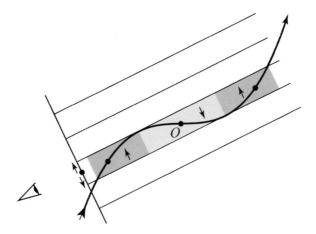

Figure 16.8. The point appears to reverse direction in the light grey box.

the same way that in the real world nobody sees a pencil perfectly balanced on its point—it's always slightly off-balance and naturally falls down. As for the behavior at other points on the cubic, it turns out that if you choose coordinates at a point $P \neq O$ so that the new x-axis is tangent to the cubic at P, then the expansion of the cubic about P looks like that of a parabola, plus a cubic term. Geometrically, sufficiently near P the curve looks like a parabola distorted an insignificant amount by the cubic term.[2] Bottom line: The behavior at P acts like the behavior at any point of a parabola—it's stable.

> One can say that in looking at the world around us, things destroyed by tiny changes will not be seen, which suggests a mantra: **"The visible is the stable."**

We've seen that every point on a parabola is stable, while $y = x^3$ has one unstable point—the point of inflection. In general, analyzing behavior at some point P on other curves always comes down to whether the behavior remains the same when the viewing angle is changed a tiny bit. If the behavior remains the same, the point is stable; otherwise, it's unstable.

The above ideas apply even when the curve is represented locally as a power series instead of just a polynomial. For example, let's consider the unit circle $x^2 + (y - 1)^2 = 1$. As we see from its picture in Figure 16.9, the circle is tangent to the x-axis at the origin.

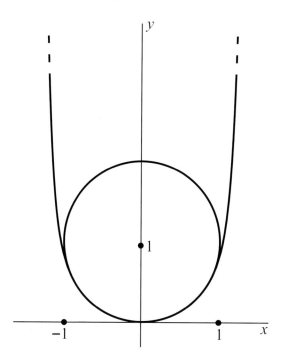

Figure 16.9. No matter how large a number n you pick—it could be a trillion, or much larger—the first n terms of the Taylor series for the bottom half of a circle still define a curve touching the circle in *only one point*—the origin. But if n is huge, the curve will hug the bottom half of the circle extremely closely.

Near the origin, the part of the circle is the graph of a function, and it turns out that this function has a power series expansion about the origin:

$$y = \frac{1}{2}x^2 + \frac{1}{8}x^4 + \frac{1}{16}x^6 + \frac{1}{128}x^8 + \frac{7}{256}x^{10} + \frac{21}{1024}x^{12} + \frac{33}{2048}x^{14} + \dots.$$

All the extra terms beyond $\frac{1}{2}x^2$ pull the bottom of the parabola upward just enough to make it closely fit the bottom half of the unit circle. The $\frac{1}{2}x^2$ gives the expansion a parabolic nature, and very close to $x = 0$, the higher-degree terms are relatively much smaller than x^2, so x^2 strongly dominates. The perceived singularity is accordingly stable at the origin, as well as at all points of the circle.

It turns out that there's a kind of touchstone for stability at a point—whether the curve is essentially a parabola that's been distorted by higher order terms the way $y = x^2 + x^3$ differs from $y = x^2$ near the point $(0,0)$ by amounts approaching zero as x approaches zero. Not surprisingly, the familiar equation $y = x^2$ serves as a normal form for stable behavior.

In the moving point interpretation, we can regard the projection as being plotted on a one-dimensional screen, and as the plotting pen reverses direction, it lays down a second layer of ink over the first. We can look at this as the projection squashing the parabola down onto the screen, forcing the parabola to fold over on itself. The point where the pen reverses direction is therefore often called a *fold point*. We will meet a higher-dimensional analog of this in the next section.

16.3 Going up a dimension: Singularities in smooth plane-to-plane maps

Many of the phenomena we've just seen for curves have analogs in the higher-dimensional setting of smooth mappings from a plane or 2-manifold into a plane. For example, in Figure 16.6 on p. 202, when our line of sight is tangent to the parabola, a point on the parabola moving toward the point of contact P seems to slow to a stop and reverse direction as it passes P. We see the same thing when our line of sight is tangent to a paraboloid. Take a look at Figure 16.10:

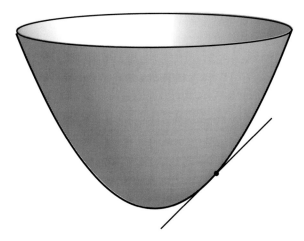

Figure 16.10. A paraboloid. The line is a tangent plane seen edge-on.

That "tangent line" you see is actually an edge-on view of the plane tangent to the paraboloid at the point of contact. The paraboloid is meant to depict the two-dimensional graph in $\mathbb{R}^4$ of a smooth mapping from the (x_1, x_2)-plane to the (y_1, y_2)-plane. If a point on the paraboloid moves steadily away from us and goes past the point of contact, then on our viewing screen (which we take to be this page) the point appears to slow to a stop just as it goes over the horizon. If the paraboloid were transparent, then we would see the point speed up again. If we change our viewing angle a bit, corresponding to rolling the tangent plane slightly, we would again see the same slowing-down and speeding-up phenomenon, and as with the parabola, we say this behavior is stable. The contact point was chosen arbitrarily, and it is easily seen that every point of the paraboloid is stable. In real life, the paraboloid could be replaced by, say, a smooth egg-shaped stone. As we slowly rotate or translate this a tiny bit, we see no big viewing surprises. If we had X-ray vision, we'd see an ant walking past our horizon stopping for an instant and then, like a ball bouncing off a wall, reversing direction as it continues walking. Each point of the horizon is a fold point, again analogous to the parabola example. Whitney found a normal form for this kind of stable behavior in a smooth map from the (x_1, x_2)-plane to the (y_1, y_2)-plane:

$$y_1 = x_1^2; \quad y_2 = x_2.$$

Whitney was able to show that there is only one other stable situation in smooth plane-to-plane maps, and that is where a fold actually begins. In the paraboloid or sphere, there are no starting or ending points for the set of fold points since they constitute the outer edge of what we're looking at, and that's a closed curve. In looking at a sphere, for example, the outer edge of what we see is a circle. In contrast to this, take a look at Figure 16.11:

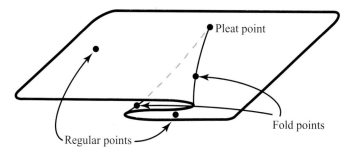

Figure 16.11. This surface has one pleat point and two curves' worth of fold points. All the remaining points of the surface are called *regular*.

This figure depicts fold points, one point where a fold begins, and regular points (all the remaining points). A point where a fold begins is called a *pleat point* or sometimes a *cusp*. If you gently deform the fabric's shape, that pleat point may move, but it still starts the folding situation seen in the picture and is accordingly stable. Whitney worked out a normal form for a pleat point. In his form, origin maps to origin in a smooth map from the (x_1, x_2)-plane to the (y_1, y_2)-plane, and in this normal form, the origin is the pleat point:

$$y_1 = x_1^3 + x_1 x_2; \quad y_2 = x_2.$$

Figure 16.12 is a representation of this mapping in 3-space. The graph, a manifold in 4-space, has been projected along the y_2-axis into (x_1, x_2, y_1)-space, and this projection retains the essential features of the original graph. This figure may not at first seem like a pleat, but it can be made to look like the pleat in Figure 16.11 by greatly compressing the graph along the x_1-axis and rotating the result 90° clockwise about the x_2-axis.

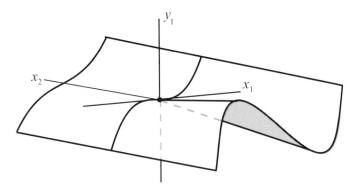

Figure 16.12. This is a normal form for a pleat.

We sometimes see pleats in the everyday world. A torus, viewed as in Figure 16.13, depicts both visible and hidden cusp points. If the torus were made of glass, you would see four of them—two on the left and another two on the right. Looking at the torus from a slightly different angle still shows these cusp singularities; they are stable.

It's fair to ask for an example of an *unstable* point in a smooth plane-to-plane mapping. Figure 16.14 shows one. It's not stable because you could pull rightward on the fabric of the lower fold in such a way that the picture changes into an ordinary fold on the right together with a pleat point on the left.

16.4 Singularities in smooth maps from the plane to 3-space

Whitney also studied singularities of smooth maps from $\mathbb{R}^2$ to $\mathbb{R}^3$, and he found that the only stable singularities in this case are:

- The transverse intersection of two or three two-dimensional sheets. Locally, this is like two planes in $\mathbb{R}^3$ intersecting in a line, or three planes in $\mathbb{R}^3$ intersecting in a point. In appropriate coordinates, the first case can be written in a normal form such as $x = a$, $y = b$. In the second case, a normal form is $x = a$, $y = b$, $z = c$.
- A *pinch point* surrounded by the "Whitney umbrella" in $\mathbb{R}^3$. A normal form for this surface is $x^2 = y^2 z$. It is a ruled surface since it consists of the intersections with planes $z = z_0$ which are lines; for positive z_0, the intersection is

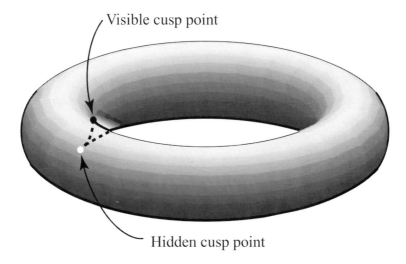

Visible cusp point

Hidden cusp point

Figure 16.13. On a glass torus, you'd see four pleat points.

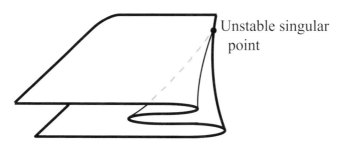

Unstable singular point

Figure 16.14. A pleat point on top of a fold point isn't stable—
a little topological massaging separates the two.

always two lines crossing the z-axis, and as z_0 approaches 0, the smaller angle between the two lines likewise approaches 0. When x and y are both zero,
z can be anything, so the umbrella contains the entire z-axis. The negative
half of this axis looks like an infinitely long handle to the rest of the surface,
giving the entire surface somewhat the appearance of an umbrella. Its equation has this parametric form: If u, v are two independent parameters, then
nearly all of the umbrella can be written as

$$x = uv, \quad y = u, \quad z = uv.$$

"Nearly all," because this form omits the handle. Figure 16.15 shows four
views of the umbrella without the handle.

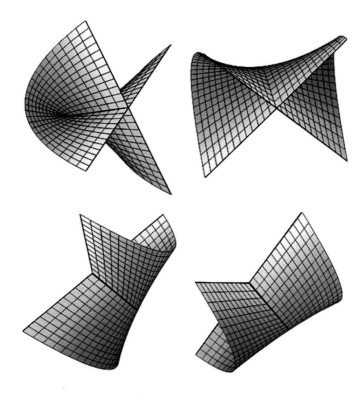

Figure 16.15. Four views of the Whitney Umbrella.

16.5 Some perspective

Nearly everything mathematical that Whitney published ended up as the foundation of something significant and of lasting importance. His 1955 paper ([**102**]) on singularities of smooth mappings is no exception. In this section we give some perspective on where this paper fits in with the larger picture.

In the 1880s, Poincaré studied the three-body problem and more generally, the behavior of Newtonian astrophysical systems. The common assumption before Poincaré's work was that in a system with a big mass M and a number of smaller orbiting objects, a small nudge of any object would result in only small changes in the entire system. Poincaré taught us that quite the opposite can happen. A tiny push on an object can, in the right circumstance, be just what is needed for it or some other object to spiral toward and crash into M, or perhaps leave the system entirely. In either case, a small perturbation in the system has resulted in a big change—the essential spirit of a "catastrophe" or, in later terminology, "the butterfly effect." The differential equations describing such a system cannot be solved exactly, but Poincaré studied their solutions qualitatively. In just the right circumstance there will be one evolution in time of the system *without* that small nudge, and a very different evolution of the system *with* it. The two evolutions can be modeled as two diverging paths in an appropriate space. Their mutual divergence from a common starting point is a "bifurcation." Poincaré coined this term, and is usually credited with discovering the idea.

An important question: Can we distill the essence of bifurcations by finding simple models so that any bifurcation corresponds to one of them? How many models do we need? Whitney's 1955 paper is important because, in part, it establishes that the fold and the cusp are the two main models needed—they turn out to be the ones defining the two most typical types of catastrophe. In this sense, Whitney's 1955 paper ([102]) set the stage for the creation of catastrophe theory, eventually followed by chaos theory.

It was the French mathematician René Thom who built upon Whitney's paper, as well as his own earlier work, to mathematicize sudden changes, or "catastrophes", that occur in nature and everyday life. Such sudden changes are common—think of an avalanche, earthquake, the freezing of pure water at just a smidgeon below 0°C, the bursting of a dam, the collapse of a bridge, the eruption of a volcano, or a collapse of the stock market. By turning the graph in Figure 16.12 on p. 208 90° and interpreting its points as states of a system, the jump from a critical point of a fold or pleat to the surface below (or above) corresponds to a sudden change or catastrophe. Figure 16.16 is a bare-bones representation of his main idea.

In this figure, the bifurcation point lies on a space curve, and this curve projects into the horizontal plane giving a cusp curve as shadow—hence the name "cusp singularity."

Figure 16.17 illustrates one particular physical setup whose parameter space looks like the general situation in Figure 16.16. Figure 16.17 depicts a laboratory table equipped with two blocks that can slide right or left and be held there. Firmly attached to these blocks are the ends of a wooden dowel about two feet long and a quarter of an inch in diameter. We regard the dowel as an elastic medium analogous, say, to a violin bow, which springs back to its original shape after being flexed a bit.

Sliding the blocks apart slightly correspondingly stretches the unbent dowel, putting it under tension, while sliding them together puts it under compression. Figure 16.17 shows the dowel under compression, and we're assuming the dowel buckles upward due to the compression. With the blocks fixed, if a downward force F is slowly increased, then when it reaches a certain critical strength, the rod will flip from bending up to bending down—a classic catastrophe.

Figure 16.18 is an annotated analog of Figure 16.16 for this concrete example. The point $(0, 0)$ represents no tension, compression, downward, or upward force on the rod. The region labeled "Stable region, no catastrophes" corresponds to

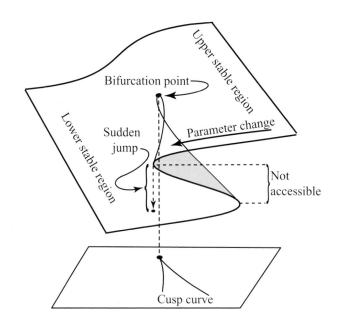

Figure 16.16. This surface encapsulates Thom's main idea of a catastrophe.

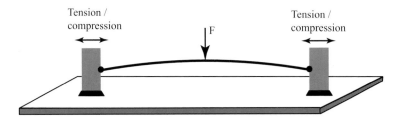

Figure 16.17. As the downward force F increases, the rod will eventually flip to bending the other way—a catastrophe.

the two blocks pulling on the elastic rod, putting it under tension. Under tension, the rod simply stretches along with the increased distance between the blocks. In the diagram, the region below this represents the rod under compression; the further we go down on the diagram, the greater the compression and therefore the greater the bending. The space curve consisting of all critical points passes through $(0, 0)$ and has an upper and lower branch. Points to the right of the upper branch correspond to the rod buckling upward; points to the left of the lower branch correspond to the rod buckling downward. The directly upward projection of the lower branch to the surface is drawn as a dot-dash curve, and at each

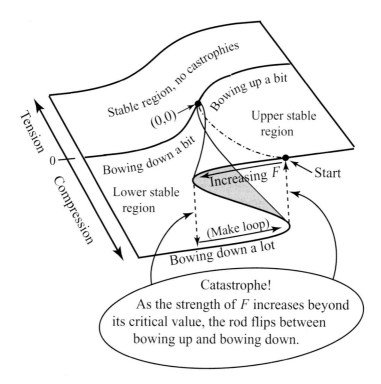

Figure 16.18. Analog of Figure 16.16 for the buckling rod experiment.

point of the curve the force F is zero. Points to the right of this curve correspond to an *upward* force applied to the middle of the rod. Since the rod is already buckling upward, the additional upward force simply increases the bend and we are in the upper stable region, with no catastrophes. Points immediately to the left of this curve correspond to a downward force on the middle of the rod. Analogous observations lead to the lower stable region.

There's a fundamental loop in Figure 16.18. Let's travel around it, beginning at the point labeled "Start." Move leftward on the S-shaped edge along which the compression is constant. The further leftward we go, the greater the downward force, and when we reach the critical strength of F on the upper space curve branch, catastrophe occurs—the rod flips to arcing down. This catastrophe puts us on the lower region, and now moving rightward along the edge corresponds to starting to apply an upward force to the rod. In a way symmetric to what we've just done, when we reach the lower critical point for F, we initiate a catastrophe in which the rod suddenly flips to bending upward. We've just completed a full loop, appearing as a near rectangle on the constant compression edge of the surface.

Thom wrote up his big opus in a 400-page book in French whose translated title is *Structural Stability and Morphogenesis*. (See [**T**].) Thom himself was an enormously well-respected mathematician—before writing this book, he had already founded a whole new branch in topology and had earned the Fields medal, often thought of as a mathematical equivalent of the Nobel prize. Thom casts a very wide net in this book and, not surprisingly, this major work from a major mathematician raised expectations that his ideas would have predictive power in the areas he suggested: biology, sociology, economics, engineering, physics, as well as other areas. The promises implicit in his novel work created quite a stir in the scientific community, which apparently now had at its disposal a qualitative theory of "applied topology" that would at long last give mathematicians and scientists a better handle on nonlinear problems. But its value, as in any applied theory, came down to how good its predictions were, and unfortunately Thom was overly optimistic. In the 1970s the pros and cons of his work were widely and intensely debated, but the initial excitement began to die down as reality seeped in and many of the theory's predictions proved wide of the mark. Make no mistake: Thom's mathematics itself is unassailable, and his theory worked well for certain engineering applications—the buckling of beams and capsizing of boats are just two examples—but in areas too far away from physics and engineering, including psychology and economics, his theory proved to have little or no predictive power. Thom lived through all the ups and downs, and finally had to sum up much of the applied aspects of his work as a "shipwreck."

Importantly, however, his work taught us that in a number of important cases it's possible to get a handle on real-world discontinuities. Sudden and catastrophic phenomena can sometimes be understood mathematically, and together with the rise of fast and cheap computing, this has led to remarkable progress in understanding nonlinear, unstable phenomena. Thom's catastrophe theory, which owed so much to Whitney's 1955 paper, helped lead to studies of chaos and fractals.

In contrast with catastrophe theory which is qualitative, chaos and fractals are quantitative—various parameters are assigned numeric values, and chaos theory is steadily building up its credentials as a useful predictive tool in nonlinear dynamics. As an example, see Strogatz's book [**S2**] for an informative and accessible overview of how far we've already advanced in understanding nonlinear phenomena. The interested reader may get a quick overview of some of the ideas in chaos and fractals in Note 16.3.

Figure 16.19. Hass with Mary and Sally, just after his work on the singularities of smooth mappings.

Figure 16.20. René Thom, who ushered in catastrophe theory.

CHAPTER 17

Are There Decomposition Theorems for Nonmanifolds?

One of the great themes in mathematics is breaking up something big or complicated into smaller, simpler parts. The zero-sets of polynomials of several variables can be complicated indeed, with all sorts of subtle singularities. This chapter gives a brief overview of Whitney's quest of expressing the part of a zero-set around a singularity as the finite union of smooth manifolds.

17.1 Some perspective on decomposition theorems

Decomposition theorems stand alongside other major themes in mathematics such as existence and uniqueness theorems, extension results, embeddings, duality theorems, classification theorems, approximations, analogies and correspondences (for example, tying together Euclidean geometry and algebra via analytic geometry), and others. Decomposition facts abound in mathematics, some being so commonplace we forget or don't realize that that's what they are. Looking at a few of them will lend some perspective on what Whitney accomplished in splitting up a nonsmooth manifold into a finite union of smooth manifolds.

Decimal representations. Every time you write an ordinary decimal number, you're performing a decomposition into at most 9 power-of-ten building blocks. In monetary terms, for example, if you have 9 each of pennies, dimes, one-dollar bills, ten-dollar bills ...—that is, $10 - 1 = 9$ of each monetary denomination that's a power of ten—then you can pay for anything *exactly* with the following simple algorithm: Never overpaying, present the seller with as many of the largest denominations possible. Do the same with what remains to be paid. By continuing this way, you end up with an exact payment. If the total amount due was, say, $381.06, peel off 3 hundred dollar bills, 8 tens, and so on. Reading $381.06 digitwise from left to right essentially carries out this decomposition algorithm, giving chunks of standard sizes. Relative to base ten, this decomposition is unique. In fact, the decomposition is unique relative to *any* choice of base. So, for example, issuing coins in a monetary system based on powers of 5, with coins or paper denominations of 1 cent, 5 cents, 25 cents, 125 cents ..., we could similarly pay any bill using at most $5 - 1 = 4$ of any denomination.

Of the three most famous fundamental theorems in mathematics—the fundamental theorem of arithmetic, the fundamental theorem of algebra, and the fundamental theorem of calculus, two are decomposition theorems.

The fundamental theorem of arithmetic. One form says that any natural number n breaks up into the product of prime numbers $n = p_1^{m_1} \dots p_r^{m_r}$, and these primes are unique up to the order of multiplication.

The fundamental theorem of algebra. This is an analog of the fundamental theorem of arithmetic. Instead of natural numbers, the theorem is about certain "whole" or (w)holomorphic functions—which the theorem assumes are polynomials with coefficients that are complex numbers. The primes are just $x - c_i$, with c_i a complex number, and any nonzero polynomial $p(x)$ breaks up, or decomposes, into a constant times $(x - c_1)^{m_1} \dots (x - c_r)^{m_r}$. These primes are unique up to the order of multiplication.

Coordinates. Writing a point P in $\mathbb{R}^3$ in coordinate form like $(3, -5, 2)$ is really just shorthand for the decomposition of P relative to a basis $\{\mathbf{e}_1, \mathbf{e}_2, \mathbf{e}_3\}$ as $P = 3\mathbf{e}_1 - 5\mathbf{e}_2 + 2\mathbf{e}_3$.

Two ways of expressing a complex number. Any complex number c has two kinds of decompositions: rectangular, $c = x + iy$, and polar, $c = re^{i\theta}$. These in a sense represent opposite extremes because on a sphere having lines of latitude and longitude, a small patch around any point on the equator inherits coordinates that are nearly rectangular, while a small patch around either pole of the sphere inherits coordinates that are nearly polar.

A complex number is also a 1×1 matrix. The above two ways of writing a complex number generalize to decompositions of a square matrix M of any size. For those who know some linear algebra, the rectangular decomposition is entrywise ($M = M_1 + iM_2$), while the polar decomposition can be written $M = HO$, where H is Hermitian symmetric (which is positive definite when M is nonsingular) and where O is proper orthogonal. Geometrically, H performs pure stretching in $\mathbb{C}^n$, while O performs pure rotation. When $n = 1$, H is a positive real number r when nonzero, O is a complex number $e^{i\theta}$ of magnitude 1, and multiplying each point of the complex plane $\mathbb{C}$ by $re^{i\theta}$ stretches all those points (vectors based at the origin) by the positive amount r and rotates them by θ.

Real numbers and Taylor series. In all the above examples the decomposition is into only finitely many pieces. Sometimes infinitely many pieces are required—the decimal representation of most real numbers are of this kind. In the world of functions, representing an analytic function as a Taylor series about a center c uniquely decomposes the function into the sum of building blocks of the form $a_n(x - c)^n$. Infinitely many of these are needed unless the function is a polynomial.

17.2 Decompositions of nonmanifolds

Even before 1942, Hass had the idea that nonsmooth manifolds should somehow break up into a finite union of nice smooth ones. He was chasing after some sort of decomposition theorem for nonsmooth manifolds—that is, taking a nonsmooth set defined by polynomials or analytic functions, and breaking it into the disjoint union of smooth submanifolds joined together in an appropriately coherent fashion. The idea turned out to be surprisingly subtle, and it was only after Whitney joined the Institute that he gave the matter serious time. When he at last wrote his big *opus* on it in 1965, Whitney used the standard term *decomposition*. As a bit of history, before submitting the paper for publication, he asked his wife Mary to look it over. Her reaction wasn't what he expected: "Hass, why on earth all these *decompositions?* I just hate things decomposing! Can't you find some other word?" Hass thought things over, and chose instead "stratifications." So when Whitney partitioned an algebraic or analytic variety into smooth manifolds attaching together in a reasonable way, those smooth manifolds became officially known as *strata*, and the partition of the original variety into disjoint manifolds became a *stratification* of the variety. The terms "strata" and "stratification" have now become standard in the context of such nonsmooth manifolds. (The nonsmooth points are actual singularities mentioned in the last chapter, and in this chapter we always assume any singularity is actual.)

When Whitney gradually moved from the four-color problem to the differentiable world, his early contributions there were on differentiable manifolds—sets that can be taken to be smooth at every point. Later, when he proved his immersion theorem (see pp. 184–186), he worked with surfaces that self-intersect in nice ways. But not all surfaces self-intersect nicely. In fact, nonsmoothness can happen without any self-intersecting at all—think of the sharp point of a cusp curve. Two such curves appear in Figure 17.4 on p. 221, and other examples in Figure 16.4 on p. 200. So it was obvious to him that many naturally occurring objects are *not* smooth at every point, and we should try to understand them. What about the center point of all those roses encountered in calculus? Or the vertex of a cone? One could easily find example after example of sets defined by quite simple polynomials that have crosspoints, sharp points, and other singularities.

Let's begin with a few basic examples of singularities. The left picture in Figure 17.1 shows that the polynomial equation $xy = 0$ defines the union of the x- and y-axes, and the origin is a nonsmooth point in this union. A figure eight curve likewise has a nonsmooth point. The one in Figure 17.1 is a lemniscate defined by $x^4 + y^4 + x^2 - y^2 = 0$.

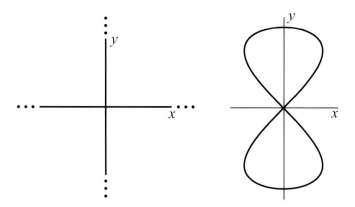

Figure 17.1. Two familiar sets, each having one self-intersection.

Figure 17.2 shows a three-leaf rose, $r = \cos 3\theta$, and a four-leaf one, $r = \cos 2\theta$. Although they are the plots of certain trigonometric functions, they are also the plots of polynomial equations: The three-leaf rose is the plot of $(x^2 + y^2)^2 = x^3 - 3xy^2$ and the one with four leaves is the plot of $(x^2 + y^2)^2 = x^4 - 6x^2y^2 + y^2$.

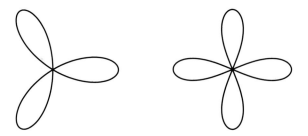

Figure 17.2. The center point of a rose is a singularity in which the curve crosses itself several times.

By making n large, you can make the center of the rose $r = \cos n\theta$ have extreme nonmanifold behavior. For the curious, these can all be defined by polynomials. If $\Re$ denotes "real part of," then when n is even, $r = \cos n\theta$ translates to the polynomial $(x^2 + y^2)^{n+1} = \Re\left[(x + iy)^{2n}\right]$, giving a $2n$-leaf rose. When n is odd, $r = \cos n\theta$ translates to $(x^2 + y^2)^{\frac{n+1}{2}} = \Re\left[(x + iy)^n\right]$, giving an n-leaf rose.

The self-intersections we've seen with roses occur all at one point, but in general, nonmanifold points can be widely scattered. For example, Figure 17.3 depicts a Lissajous figure in which sinusoidal motion of one frequency in the x-direction is combined with sinusoidal motion of another frequency in the *y*-direction. In this case, it's frequency 8 versus frequency 7, and a pen would trace out Figure 17.3 if it moved horizontally with frequency 8 cycles per unit time while at the same time moving vertically with frequency 7 cycles per unit time. The polynomial equation defining it has degree 8 and, as it turns out, because 8 and 7 are relatively prime the number of self-intersections is $\frac{(8-1)(7-1)}{2} = 21$. If one used relatively prime frequencies 100 against 83, the number of self-intersections would be $\frac{(100-1)(83-1)}{2} = 4,059$.

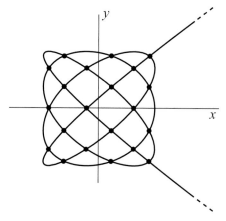

Figure 17.3. There's no upper limit on how many self-intersections Lissajous figures can have.

The cusp is another often-encountered nonmanifold point. In Figure 17.4, the curve on the left has the very simple equation $y^3 + x^2 = 0$. It is unbounded in the real plane, but you can generally force a real curve $p(x,y) = 0$ to be bounded by adding $x^m + y^m$ to p, where m is even and larger than the degree of p. To get the teardrop curve, we've used $m = 4$ to get its equation $y^3 + x^2 + x^4 + y^4 = 0$.

Figure 17.4. Examples of cusp singularities.

Whitney's work on the four-color problem and combinatorial topology meant that cellular decompositions of topological spaces had become second nature to him. All the above examples fit in with the paradigm of a space consisting of a disjoint union of especially simple open pieces of varying dimensions. Some archaeological digging into his research history reveals that by 1942 he had already thought quite a bit about the issue of bad points—singularities— and had concluded that they could have considerable complexity and subtlety. It also seemed they could almost always be split up into a finite number of smooth open sets fitting together nicely. In many cases the pieces join up to form a triangulated topological space, much as in combinatorial topology. (For a little more on combinatorial topology, see note 7.1.)

Figure 17.5 takes the first figure in this chapter—Figure 17.1—and splits each curve up into 0-dimensional and one-dimensional pieces. This provides a first peek at Whitney's approach.

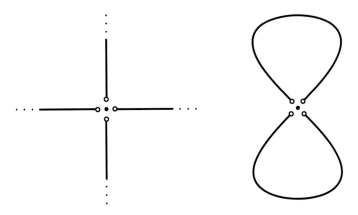

Figure 17.5. Stratifications of the curves in Figure 17.1.

For convenience, let's refer to the general definition of n-simplex given on p. 121, and call a point a 0-simplex and a topological open interval a 1-simplex. Then in Figure 17.2, the three-leaf rose splits up into one 0-simplex and three 1-simplices and the four-leaf rose into one 0-simplex and four 1-simplices. The Lissajous curve in Figure 17.3 splits up into 21 0-simplices and 43 1-simplices. In Figure 17.4, the cusp curve splits into one 0-simplex and two 1-simplicies, while for the teardrop, it's just one 0-simplex and one 1-simplex.

17.3 Higher dimensions

All the curves considered so far are one-dimensional, but every one of the curves in this chapter can be turned into a two-dimensional object in various ways. Here are two common ways.

A trivial way. Pass a copy of the z-axis through each point of the curve sitting in the (x, y)-plane to get a surface in (x, y, z)-space. This process is called "cylinderizing the curve" and indeed, passing a copy of the z-axis through each point of a circle in the (x, y)-plane produces an ordinary circular cylinder in 3-space. Cylinderizing the left curve in Figure 17.1 gives two intersecting planes, while doing this to the lemniscate in that figure creates a surface suggestive of a piece of paper curled around so that each end looks like a figure 8. Cylindrization is trivial for three reasons:

- First, the construction is very easy.
- Second, the equation of the cylindrization is exactly the same as the equation of the curve, but since that equation contains no z-variable, then along with any point (x_0, y_0) on the curve are all points (x_0, y_0, z), where z can be any real value.
- Third, whatever the structure of the singularity in the plane curve, the cylindrization has essentially the same structure.

Making a cone. Another way of turning a curve into a surface is by forming a cone from it: Lift the curve directly up from the (x, y)-plane it is in so that in 3-space, the curve sits in the plane $z = 1$. Now for each point in the lifted curve, pass a line through it and the origin $(0, 0, 0)$. So, for example, if the curve in the (x, y)-plane is the circle $x^2 + y^2 = 1$, then the cone formed from it is an ordinary circular cone consisting of two nappes and looking like two ice cream cones joined at their vertices and facing directly away from each other. Since the cone formed from any plane curve consists of lines through the origin, it is by definition a homogeneous set, and we have *homogenized* the curve in the plane $z = 1$. There's an exact algebraic counterpart to this: To get the equation of the cone in (x, y, z)-space formed from a curve $p(x, y) = 0$ in the (x, y)-plane, homogenize the polynomial by packing each term of $p(x, y)$ with powers of z to make each term have the same degree as the degree of $p(x, y)$. This gives a *homogeneous polynomial* $p(x, y, z)$. Doing this to $x^2 + y^2 - 1 = 0$ produces $x^2 + y^2 - z^2 = 0$, the equation of the cone. This simple method gives the equation of the cone formed from any polynomial curve. So the lemniscate $x^4 + y^4 + x^2 - y^2 = 0$ seen in Figure 17.1 has for its homogenization the cone depicted in Figure 17.6; $x^4 + y^4 + x^2z^2 - y^2z^2 = 0$ is its equation.

Forming the cone from our lemniscate introduces a new layer of complexity: The origin is essentially a singularity within a singularity, something we have not encountered before. This new kind of singularity is reflected when we split the cone into a complex of smooth pieces. These pieces are a point (the origin), two half-lines (one on each side of the origin) and four other connected two-dimensional pieces.

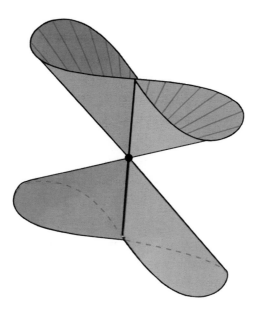

Figure 17.6. Homogenization of the lemniscate in Figure 17.1.

As another example, Figure 17.7 depicts the cone formed by passing lines through the origin and a three-leaf rose. Higher dimensions can lead to more dramatic examples of singularities within singularities. For example, in the union of the three coordinate subspaces of 3-space, any two of the coordinate planes intersect in a singular line, and the three axes (each one being a singular line) all intersect in the origin. So the decomposition becomes one point, six half-lines, and twelve two-dimensional quarter-planes or quadrants (three coordinate planes, each with four quadrants). This example leads to arbitrarily deep nests of singularities—just think of the union of the coordinate $(n-1)$-spaces of $\mathbb{R}^n$!

In striving for a natural decomposition of singularities, what Whitney accomplished takes its place along with other decomposition theorems in mathematics.

17.4 Tangents and stratifications

On September 8, 1942 Whitney gave a short talk at an AMS meeting in which he shared some of his evolving thoughts on singularities. He argued that one could break up a small neighborhood of a singular point into a finite number of smooth manifolds that attach together in a reasonable way. Even at this early stage, he realized that in general there could be all sorts of curious situations that may occur locally, and had concluded that the behavior of tangent spaces near singular points would play an important role. He finally published his ruminations about

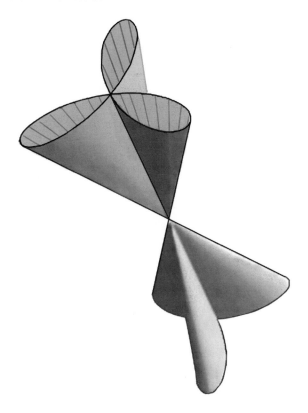

Figure 17.7. Homogenization of a three-leaf rose.

five years later as a two-page article in the *Proceedings of the National Academy of Sciences* ([**91**]). In 1957 he published a 12-page paper ([**103**]) dealing with real manifold complexes—the analog of topological simplicial complexes—in which he applied his ideas to real algebraic varieties. A real algebraic variety is the locus in some $\mathbb{R}^n$ of a finite set of polynomials with real coefficients. He showed that the set of singular points $S(V)$ of any such variety V has dimension strictly less than that of V, and that the set of singular points $S(S(V))$ of $S(V)$ has dimension strictly less than that of $S(V)$, and so on. Using this idea, he partitioned V into a strictly decreasing set of real submanifolds. This was a promising start, but René Thom (whom we met in the last chapter) felt that in an ideal partition, the parts around small neighborhoods of any point in any of the connected submanifolds, should all look topologically the same, preferably having the trivial structure of a topological product. (See p. 111.)

By around 1964–5, Whitney had made a lot of progress with his ideas on partitions and was ready to publish a major work on the subject. This appeared

Figure 17.8. This photo of all five of Hassler's children was taken in 1963 during the time he was working intensively on stratifications. Clockwise starting from upper left, this wedding picture shows James, the bride Molly, groom Hugh Melhuish, Carol, Sally, and Emily.

in a 54-page 1965 *Annals* paper "Tangents to an Analytic Variety," [**113**] and true to his early guesses, tangents near singularities do in fact play a central role.

The conditions needed to insure a good decomposition are a little technical; the reader may safely just skim over the examples and counterexamples below to get a flavor for good versus problematic decompositions.

One of the really major contributions of this paper was Whitney's introduction of conditions (a) and (b). The idea is that if a stratification satisfies them, the stratification will have essentially the nice, intuitive behavior that Thom proposed. They remain today the most successful conditions that assure such behavior, and when they are satisfied the stratification is then called a "regular Whitney stratification," but which is often simply called a "regular stratification." It turns out that condition (b) is stronger than condition (a), so if (b) is satisfied, then (a) is too. In theory, only (b) is actually needed, a fact pointed out by John Mather of Princeton. However, (a) is simpler to check, so if a stratification fails (a), one need check no further.

What are the two conditions? For expository purposes, instead of formal definitions (which appear, for example, in [113]), we capture their basic spirit through examples. Let's start with two spheres intersecting in a circle. The lowest-dimensional stratum in this case is the circle in which the spheres intersect, and the two-dimensional strata are the four open manifolds remaining after the circle is removed.

Condition (a). Let Q be any point on the circle and, in any two-dimensional stratum, let $P_1, P_2, \ldots$ be an infinite sequence of points approaching Q. Let $T_1, T_2, \ldots$ be the sequence of corresponding tangent planes on the sphere, and suppose this sequence converges to a plane T. Then condition (a) says that *the tangent line L to the circle at Q lies in T.* More generally, condition (a) holds if the tangent space to a lower-dimensional stratum at any point Q lies in the limit space of a sequence of tangent spaces T_i as points P_i in any higher-dimensional stratum approach Q.

Condition (b). With $P_i \to Q$ and T as above, suppose $Q_i \to Q$ is another sequence of points Q_i in the circle. Condition (b) says that *if the lines L_i through points P_i and Q_i converge to a line L, then L lies in T.*

17.5 Examples and counterexamples

A major reason that conditions (a) and (b) have remained so important is that they allowed Whitney to prove that any algebraic variety has a regular stratification. This is true not only in the real setting, but also in the complex setting, where the varieties are defined by polynomials with (possibly) complex coefficients, and live in $\mathbb{C}^n$. Furthermore, he proved this for the more general class of analytic real or complex varieties.[1]

Example (The union of two transversally intersecting planes). Within (x, y, z) space, the (x, z)-plane and (y, z)-plane intersect in the z-axis, which is the set of singularities of the union of the two planes. We can look at the union as a complex consisting of four 2-strata (each an open half-plane) and one 1-stratum (the z-axis). An exploded view of this complex is shown in Figure 17.9 and is essentially the cylindrization of the stratification seen in the left picture of Figure 17.5 on p. 222. Is this stratification regular? The origin $O = (0, 0, 0)$ can be taken as a typical point of the 1-stratum. Let $P_i \to O$ be a sequence of points in any one of the four 2-strata, and let $Q_i \to O$ be a sequence of points in the 1-stratum. For each i, the line L_i through P_i and Q_i lies in the limiting tangent space of the chosen 2-stratum, which in this case is simply the (x, z)-plane or the (y, z)-plane. So if the L_i converge to a line L, then L also lies in the respective (x, z)-plane or the (y, z)-plane. Therefore condition (b) is satisfied, and the stratification is regular. The bottom picture in Figure 17.9 depicts how Thom's triviality condition holds: At any point Q in the 1-stratum, the two intersecting planes is the Cartesian product of the z-axis with the union of the x- and y-axes. Such a product can be regarded

as the simplest possible structure, or trivial, and at its heart is meant to describe
the local structure at a point. That is, the strata may warp a little, as would happen
if the planes were actually part of huge spheres—or what is the same thing, what
things would look like in a very small neighborhood about a point where two not-
so-large spheres intersect. Topologically, the structure at an intersection point is
still locally a product.

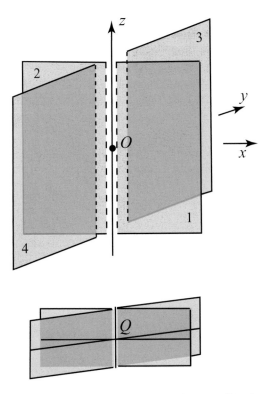

Figure 17.9. The top picture depicts the stratification of the
union of the (x, z)- and (y, z)-planes into four 2-strata and one
1-stratum. The (x, z)-plane breaks up into the two open half-
planes labeled 1 and 2, and the (y, z)-plane breaks up into the
two open half-planes 3 and 4. The 1-stratum is the z-axis. The
bottom picture suggests what Thom's local triviality condition
looks like in this case.

Example (The union of two spheres intersecting in a circle). Pick a point Q in the
circle of intersection. Within some sufficiently small neighborhood of Q, what
we see is almost indistinguishable from the scene of the above example, except

that the planes may not be perpendicular. With only minor changes, the arguments given above show that the stratification into the circle of intersection (the
1-stratum) and the left-over pieces of the union (the four 2-strata) is regular.

Example (The union of several intersecting planes). Instead of intersecting two
planes, consider the variety V consisting of m different planes in $\mathbb{R}^n$, all containing a common line such as the z-axis. This axis is a line of singularities and
the stratification of V consists of $2m$ open half-planes, along with the z-axis. An
argument essentially like the one we used for the two intersecting planes shows
that this forms a regular stratification. Any plane $z = a$ intersects V transversally
(as opposed to tangentially) in m lines, and the Cartesian product of these lines
with the z-axis gives V. We can localize this idea about any point in the line of
singularities so that in a small neighborhood of such a point, if we slightly bend,
twist, or otherwise smoothly deform V a bit, the accompanying stratification and
local triviality continues to hold.

Example (The three-leaf rose and its cone). For an interesting example having a
natural stratification decreasing all the way to dimension 0, look at the three-leaf
rose with equation
$$(x^2 + y^2)^2 = x^3 - 3xy^2$$
and homogenize to get
$$(x^2 + y^2)^2 = (x^3 - 3xy^2)z.$$

The set of singularities of this homogeneous variety, or cone, is the z-axis. However, the origin is a little more complicated than in, say, the cylindrization of
the rose. In this homogeneous variety, the origin becomes in a natural way the
0-dimensional stratum. The remaining singularities form two open half-lines
which we take as the two one-dimensional strata. The rest of the cone consists of
six two-dimensional strata—three above, and three below the origin. The strati-
fied cone is depicted in Figure 17.10.

It is not difficult to show that the stratification is regular. Also, at any point
P of either half-line, it is easy to see we have the same sort of trivial local product
structure—in a small neighborhood of P, the cone is topologically the product of
a little line segment in the z-axis with a little transverse "star" made up of three
crossing small line segments. Do we have this "topologically the same" behavior
at each point of the 0-dimensional stratum? Yes, because there's just one point
in that stratum!

Although every variety defined by one or more polynomials has a regular
stratification, not every stratification of such a variety need be regular, and that
will happen if conditions (a) and (b) aren't met. Whitney himself devised some
clever examples based on what might descriptively be called "alpha curves." One

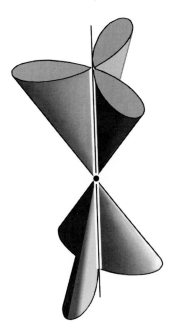

Figure 17.10. A stratification of a homogenized three-leaf rose.

general form for an alpha curve is

$$y^2 = x^2(x + a).$$

The curve crosses itself at the origin, forming a singularity there. The curve crosses the x-axis at one other point, $(-a, 0)$. Figure 17.11 shows alpha curves for three different values of a. The smaller a becomes, the smaller the alpha curve's loop. The two tangent lines to any alpha curve at the origin get closer and closer to being horizontal as a gets smaller.

In fact each tangent line approaches the x-axis as a approaches 0. In Figure 17.12, a is chosen so small that even in the zoomed-in view, we don't see the very small loop at all. What we do see is that the tangent lines have nearly coincided with the x-axis.

Now for two basic counterexamples. One possibility is that both (a) and (b) fail. The other possibility is that only (a) holds. Notice that only (b) holding isn't a possibility; we pointed out above that if (b) holds, so does (a).

Example (Conditions (a) and (b) both fail). Whitney made a cone from an alpha curve. The curve's equation, $y^2 = x^2(x+1)$, when homogenized is $y^2 = x^2(x+z)$ and its surface is depicted in Figure 17.13. Notice that when $x = y = 0$, any value of z satisfies this homogeneous equation, so the z-axis is included in the

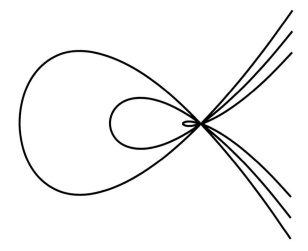

Figure 17.11. Alpha-shaped curves $y^2 = x^2(x + a)$ for three values of a.

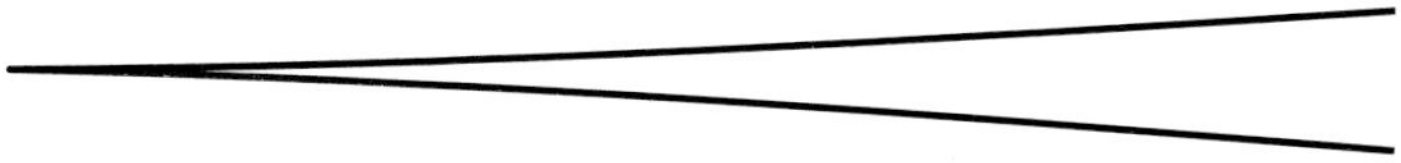

Figure 17.12. For very small $a > 0$, the curve $y^2 = x^2(x + a)$ can have a loop smaller than the thickness of the pen. Tangents at the origin are nearly horizontal.

cone. Figure 17.14 is a bird's-eye view of the cone from a point on the z-axis at, say, $(0, 0, 5)$.

Define a stratification consisting of the z-axis as the one-dimensional stratum, and the connected components of what's left as the two-dimensional strata. Let $P_i \to (0, 0, 0)$ be a sequence of points in the ice cream cone stratum, with the P_i lying directly over the x-axis. That means P_i is of the form $(-x_i, 0, x_i)$. Let Q be the origin in the 1-stratum. Now every plane T_i tangent to the ice cream cone at P_i is the plane $z = -x$ in $\mathbb{R}^3$, so the limit of those planes is just $z = -x$. The punch line of condition (a) fails, since the tangent line at Q to the 1-stratum— the z-axis—is just the z-axis, and that's not contained in the limit plane $z = -x$. Because (b) is a stronger condition than (a) and (a) fails, then (b) fails, too.

Example (Condition (b) fails but condition (a) holds). Whitney gets clever here. The above cone's equation can be written $y^2 = x^3 + x^2z$, but if you bump up the power of z to get $y^2 = x^3 + x^2z^2$, this is no longer a cone, but instead the leftmost points of the alpha curves trace out the parabola $x = -z^2$ in the (x, z)-plane, seen in Figure 17.15.

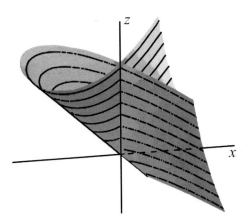

Figure 17.13. Cone defined by an alpha curve.

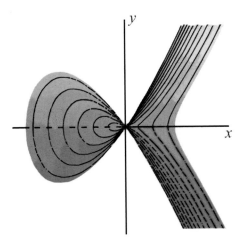

Figure 17.14. A bird's-eye view of the cone in Figure 17.13.

The one-dimensional stratum for this surface is the entire z-axis, and the remainder of the surface breaks up into four 2-strata. Let $P_i \to (0,0,0)$ be a sequence of points in the warped ice cream cone stratum, with each P_i having the form $(-x_i, 0, +\sqrt{x_i})$. Let $Q_i = (0,0, +\sqrt{x_i}) \to (0,0,0)$ be a sequence of points in the 1-stratum. The lines L_i through P_i and Q_i are all horizontal and lie directly over the x-axis, their limit being the x-axis. What about the planes T_i tangent to the warped ice cream cone at P_i? These planes, as they follow the parabola, become more and more vertical as $i \to \infty$ and have as their limit the (y, z)-plane. Because the limit of the L_i is the x-axis, condition (b) doesn't hold. On the other

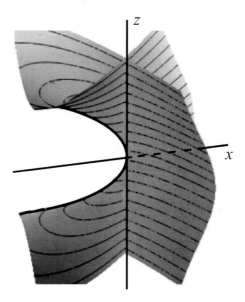

Figure 17.15. A surface for which condition (b) fails but condition (a) holds.

hand, this limit plane contains the z-axis, so condition (a) is satisfied for this sequence $P_i \to (0,0,0)$. With a little more work, we can show that the T_i corresponding to any $P_i \to (0,0,0)$ in a two-dimensional stratum always contains the z-axis.

Figure 17.16. Hass shortly after his work on stratifications. He's in a mountain climbing cabin, and the photo captures his conviviality when among good friends. He's gesturing here the same way as he often did when explaining a logical point.

CHAPTER **18**
After Research

In 1967, Hass visited an elementary school in Princeton to observe how his daughters Sally and Emily were being taught math. He was horrified. "There were so many dead eyes in the classroom...it seemed that here was a group of child slaves being told what to do, led by a master slave who got orders from some lesson plan that had to be followed!" What he saw seemed just the opposite of everything that had led Hass to his own mathematical success. Now older, and seeing younger mathematicians carrying the torch in areas he had begun, the next direction in his life seemed not only natural but compelling: Address the critical problem of nurturing in our future scientists a love rather than a fear of mathematics.

18.1 Whitney tackles an educational crisis

The last big thrust in Whitney's life was addressing problems he saw in mathematics education at the grade school level, especially the early grades. It struck him that these kids were being subjected to a regimen that throttled their natural instinct to think on their own and experience the excitement of making their own little discoveries. To Hass it was clear that preschoolers have a natural ability to think on their own—after all, look at how much these little souls have figured out about the world in their first few years of life! Hass felt that as they enter school, this inborn ability should be nurtured, not discouraged. Instead, math classes too often force kids to depart from their inborn learning instincts and replace it by rote learning. Before this they were never given any "manual" on how to learn in life. Why force one on them now? To Hass, that seemed to go against the grain, and could often lead to a whole new tragedy called "math anxiety." What he himself did as a youngster was guess and play around with problems that he found interesting. There was never any time pressure, and if he made mistakes, he would eventually find them and fix things up. Always proactive, he began spending more and more time in Sally's sixth grade class and ended up running the math part of the curriculum for the final month or so. He started playing little games with the kids. They loved them and the games made them think.

Many mathematicians were mystified by Whitney's sudden switch from doing epoch-making research to "only working with kids." The thing to remember is that he himself was once a kid, and at that time had the good fortune of not being put in a regimented environment. He would get interested in little mathematical puzzles and think about them. No tests, no scores, no grades—just natural curiosity and the good feeling of having figured something out. That's all pretty much the way kids in their early childhood years pick up their native language along with hundreds of other skills. They have a very large and effective learning capacity, so why mess with it and try to substitute that with some sort of regimented learning? In his later years, he reflected back on things. He was successful, no doubt, and as a youth he'd just continued learning and growing in a natural, nonartificial way. In contrast, visit a typical math class in the early grades, and you're not likely to find many sparks of enjoyment or looks of enthusiasm.

Hass soon changed from observer to active participant, and was given a chance to teach math to a classroom of kids. He introduced them to some of the very things he did on his own as a youngster. For example, he supplemented required rote methods for adding, subtracting, multiplying, and dividing with making reasonable estimates. Estimating before calculating was something he did all the time on his own—to him, it was a common-sense, lifetime habit, and forming this habit should pay great dividends to students. After making an estimate, they could then use the computational algorithms they had just learned to check how close they had gotten. Sizes and answers became much more meaningful to students.

Hass eventually pulled his daughter Sally out of the 7th- and 8th-grade math classes, and she remembers Hass giving her math problems he made up at home. She would work on them in the library, puzzling out the answers on her own. She did the same through the last three years of high school. He began extending his activities by running workshops, giving lectures, and writing, all with the aim of helping youngsters rekindle their natural curiosity and desire to explore.

He once commented that a method used in certain Japanese schools seemed to tune in to the curiosity and tremendous natural ability in children. "The teacher would bring in a big box of broken small appliances and an assortment of tools, testing equipment, and supplies. Each group of two, three, or four students would be given one of the broken items. The only directive? Fix it! The teacher would often be amazed at how students would somehow find a way of using logic, exploration, trial and error, or guessing to finally get the thing to work." Hass saw this process as essentially mathematical thinking—it's what he did all his life—and is far more important than learning a lot of mathematics itself. That could come later as kids mature and become more ready for abstraction. When a student got something broken to work through using scientific tools like measuring, running tests, collecting data, and making logical deductions, such success could lead to a sense of confidence and power, setting the student up for further successes. "Contrast that creative scene of children fixing things versus an assembly line where they simply put together the same thing over and over again according to instructions. The second way doesn't help kids grow scientifically or mathematically!" Hass indeed had more than a little skepticism about introducing abstract math ideas too early, and was aware that kids simply don't think the way adults often expect them to.

To make his point, he loved to tell this story: A small child comes home from school, and her dad asks, "What happened in school today?" She answers, "We learned about set theory." Dad: "What did you learn?" "Well, the teacher asked all the girls in the room to stand up, and the teacher said 'You see, that is the set of girls.' Then he asked all the boys to stand up, and the teacher said, 'That is the set of boys.' " They were in the kitchen, and there were some carrots on the table. So the dad picked them up and asked, "These carrots, are they a set?" Answer: "Oh no, they can't stand up!" Hass continued working with youngsters to the very end of his life. At age 81, he drove to an elementary school in Trenton, New Jersey and walked into the Principal's office. "Good morning. My name is Hassler Whitney and I have come to help students learn math." The principal had never heard of him and refused, but he persisted, and finally she gave him her worst math students. They improved so quickly, she was happy to let him teach as many of the other students as he wished.

Hass strongly believed in turning students loose on a problem that could be approached in several different ways. Giving them freedom to choose and find their own path was important. That's the way good scientists work, and it's how kids normally function until they are put into a regimented environment. He abhorred the emphasis put on teaching mechanical algorithms to the exclusion of using common sense when the opportunity arises. As an example, what about subtracting 19 from 45? Well, taking 20 from 45 leaves 25, so subtracting only 19 must mean the answer is 26. That doesn't mean algorithms are useless—often they're the only reasonable way to an answer. But a teacher is doing a real disservice when an algorithm is presented as "the only" or "the proper" method for getting an answer, with the student then expected to follow the given rules whenever any subtraction (or division, etc.) problem arises. All too often, the teacher has no idea at all of why the algorithm works. Whitney would wince at comments like "The process covered in this grade is part of math." Or, "That's just how it's done." Students quickly learn that following those rules precisely and without error, functioning as a good secretary, is the route to a good math score or grade. But when word problems are encountered, following set rules and algorithms no longer reliably works and students, who have just learned that math consists of memorizing rules and following regimented processes, are suddenly flustered. To them, there's now "regular math" (mechanical manipulation of numbers) and "bad, scary math" (problems requiring understanding). Common sense wasn't one of the things the teacher talked about, and panic often ensues.

Using an algorithm should be looked at as a tactical approach to getting an answer, but kids should never be discouraged from trying strategy—that path can be a lot shorter and is often illuminating. If that method doesn't pan out, then try something else, including an algorithm, but an algorithm should be regarded as an option, not a dictate.

Figure 18.1 depicts a handout Hass created in 1974. The challenge: Look for patterns and fill in as many empty squares as you can. Although on the surface this might appear as a somewhat uninspired exercise, it's surprising how easy it is to get caught up in seeing patterns. The teacher might say that the numbers represent how many feet above sea level you are, with a minus in front representing the number of feet under water, as when you're scuba diving to see unusual fish or a sunken ship. This handout can lead youngsters to experience "Aha!" moments in several different ways. For example, filling in certain rows are harder, but the student might realize, as an "Aha!" experience, that by doing columns instead, filling in suddenly gets much easier. Or even go along diagonals. Whitney's advice on this was, "Don't tell them there will be easier directions! The whole thing is for them to discover that on their own, which then gives the student a feeling of his or her own power of discovery."

After the squares are filled in, the kids will see something easy and suggestive in the shaded cross. Then a natural next step is to ask students to try devising their own version of the handout using different numbers, and then they can compare what they come up with. Some of their results can be surprising.

18.2 Louis Benezet and his experiment

Whitney's first encounters with teaching kids were guided in large part by intuition. He felt that his initial impressions of Sally and Emily's math classes could not be far off the mark—it was all too clear that most of the kids found little joy in doing math. How could that ever lead to further gratifying and productive math education? Whitney was by nature proactive, and it seemed imperative to him that something be done; the whole system seemed wrongheaded and called for some truly big changes. Yes, he was well known in mathematical academia, and he was convinced that his cause was valid. But to convince others, objective evidence was needed. He eventually came across a report published in 1935-6 that offered just the kind of approach and evidence of its success that he was looking for. This was the three-part article "The teaching of arithmetic: The story of an experiment" by Louis P. Benezet ([B1], [B2], [B3]). Many of Benezet's ideas

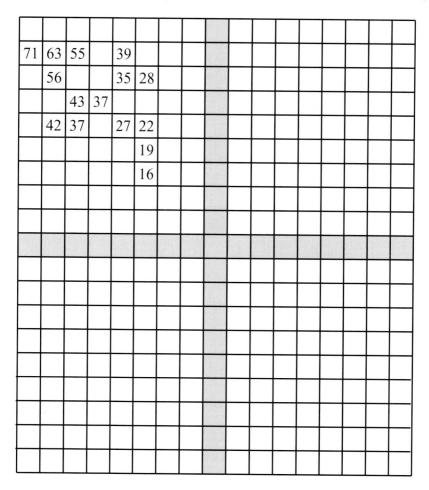

Figure 18.1. A handout devised by Hass in 1974.

coincided exactly with Whitney's, and these became core principles of Whitney's cause. At every opportunity he distributed copies of Benezet's report to others. Here is the story of how this now-famous report was born.

For many years Benezet was the Superintendent of Schools in Manchester, New Hampshire, and one spring day in 1929 he received a letter from another superintendent based in Ithaca, New York. The Ithaca superintendent had a problem: He was often being asked to add yet another course to the curriculum, but nobody ever had any idea about what to *eliminate*. It seemed like the overall curriculum could end up like an old attic stuffed with countless items that nobody had the heart to throw away. Did Mr. Benezet have any suggestions? It turns out that he indeed did, and eventually responded with an eight-page letter. His un-thinkable recommendation? **Eliminate arithmetic from the first six grades!** His aim was to do away with the early introduction of algorithms for adding, subtracting, multiplying, and dividing, especially with long numbers. He em-phasized avoiding purely mechanical drill and manipulation without thought. That should be replaced with reasoning and estimating, encouraging more men-tal work and less pencil-and-paper work. He knew his suggestions amounted to fighting words: He had already encountered a storm of protest from irate parents when, as Superintendent, he eliminated arithmetic from the first two and a half grades. But now the first *six* grades? Was the Superintendent crazy? A crank?

In that letter he had talked the talk, but he realized that if he actually be-lieved what he wrote, then as a professional he needed to walk the walk. He was handling TNT, so it was with the utmost care that he began working to transform his mold-breaking suggestion into reality. It actually amounted to an experiment on the kids. Out of all the primary classrooms in Manchester, he chose just five: three third grades, one combined third and fourth grade, and one fifth grade. In each case the teacher was young and open-minded, and he chose classrooms in districts where the parents were not likely to have English as a mother tongue. Notices to these parents fell under the radar, and the experiment went ahead.

What would the teachers teach in place of arithmetic? Here, too, Benezet had concrete ideas. There seemed to be far too many kids who were backward in both the ability and willingness to express themselves verbally. Here was an area obviously needing improvement—explaining things to others is a skill used every day in every grade—while arithmetic fluency is a skill barely needed in the primary years. So Benezet had teachers in these five classrooms encourage a great deal of oral composition. What happened? We now fast-forward eight months, and quote from Benezet's own report ([**B1**]):

"The children in these rooms reported on books that they had read, on incidents which they had seen, on visits they had made. They told stories of movies that they had attended and they made up romances on the spur of the moment. It was refreshing to go into one of these rooms. A happy and joyous spirit pervaded them. The children were no longer under the restraint of learning multiplication tables or struggling with long division. They were thoroughly enjoying their hours in school.

"At the end of eight months I took a stenographer and went to every fourth-grade room in the city. As we have semi-annual promotions, the children who had been in the advanced third grade at the time of the be-ginning of the experiment were now in the first half of the fourth grade. The contrast was remarkable. In the traditional fourth grades, when I asked children to tell me what they had been reading, they were hesi-tant, embarrassed, and diffident. In one fourth grade I could not find

Figure 18.2. Louis P. Benezet.

a single child who would admit that he had committed the sin of reading. I did not have a single volunteer, and when I tried to draft them, the
children stood up, shook their heads, and sat down again. In the four experimental fourth grades the children fairly fought for a chance to tell me
what they had been reading. The hour closed, in each case, with a dozen
hands waving in the air and little faces crestfallen, because we had not
gotten around to hear what they had to tell."

There were further enlightening comparisons. For example, when the third
graders had advanced to the low seventh grade, Benezet brought a picture of a polar bear on a small iceberg, and in separate sessions, asked the traditional and the
experimental class to write down anything the picture inspired in them. Benezet
found the experimental class responses to be much more colorful and imaginative. The average number of adjectives used in the traditional class was 40; the
average for the experimental class was 128.

Benezet never suggested eliminating *all* math during those years—his idea was to eliminate mindless rote math, for that took up valuable time, gave students the wrong impression of what math is, and was time better spent in other ways. He did indeed advocate introducing numbers, counting, comparing, and estimating, but these should not be abstractions and mere symbols on paper. Rather, such foundational ideas should be introduced using the concrete and real, such as page numbers in a book, telling time, and comparing lengths and areas. Later, the kids could play store and make change with play money. Still later, the class could divide up into groups of three or four kids, each designing an itinerary for an imaginary $500 vacation trip, where day to day car mileage and other expenses had to be taken into account.

How did this change in emphasis affect students' ability to solve simple word problems? Here is one example Benezet used to compare traditional versus experimental classes: Three steamboats go from one port to another 120 miles away, and they all start at the same time. The first steamboat makes the trip in 10 hours; the second in 12 hours; the third in 15 hours. Question: How long did it take until all three steamboats had arrived? In one traditional class of 29 students, 23 of them added $10 + 12 + 15$ to get 37 hours. In the experimental class, virtually all of them got the right answer of 15 hours. The experimental class had developed much further in comprehending what was actually written or spoken, while the traditional class saw three numbers, didn't comprehend the implications of what was stated, and applied in rote fashion their arithmetic skills. Another example highlights the difference even more vividly: A farmer has 21 goats and 6 sheep. How old is the farmer? Many in one traditional class said 27, since that's $21 + 6$. In the experimental class, nobody made that mistake, a typical reaction being "How should I know?"

18.3 A page from my ninth grade

Whitney encouraged teachers to present many everyday arithmetic questions as thought challenges, instead of the teacher instilling the automatic reaction of "use this rule." If an ordinary problem like finding $42 - 18$ is given as a challenge, creative young minds often come up with surprising roads to the answer. Today, I myself would rather think that "$42 - 20$ is 22, so if you take away only 18, the answer must be 2 larger, or 24." I resist grabbing a piece of paper or a calculator, and find this other way quicker. Besides, the touch of logic involved makes it more fun. I never had a teacher teach me this—I learned it one day in the ninth grade, by a nonteacher and out of desperation. Here's the story.

In the ninth grade I had the job of arriving early and working behind the "Administrator's Counter." A student who had missed some school would come in and give me an absence slip filled in by the parent explaining the reason, and

I would then file that slip with the student's overall attendance record. I felt important and learned a lot of unexpected things—which kids had been only a little sick, which ones had something much more serious, and when various girls had red-letter days. One girl approached me between classes and coyly said, "You know too much!" I replied that I thought I knew just the right amount. Mrs. Brown was the big administrative cheese there—she seemed to be everywhere at once—and one day she told me that the cafeteria needed me and I would no longer be working at the Counter. "Talk to Eve," she said.

Eve was fat, jolly, the cafeteria cashier, worked two lines, and was especially easy to talk to. It turned out that doing both lines—the right and the left—was getting too stressful, and that starting next week they'd add a cash register and I would be taking one of the lines. She was very nice and at first this new job sounded great, but then after a few minutes I began to realize that I'd have to find the total for each cafeteria tray, then subtract that from whatever amount was given to me. I couldn't make mistakes, or else someone would complain. And then all those *teachers*—they'd be in line, too. My initial feelings turned into consternation. I said to myself, "I can't do this!" and didn't sleep much that night. My mother suggested a small pad of paper where I could do the arithmetic real fast, but Eve didn't do this, and I would look like a klutz.

The next day I pretty much decided not do this job, and started talking to Eve. She was just so understanding, and said that at first it's scary but becomes easier after awhile. Since I'd already eaten there for two years, I at least knew how much each dish cost. Adding up the total? She said, "Just add up big whole numbers first, and then fix up the pennies at the end." I didn't understand, but she explained, "Suppose somebody has the main dish (45 cents), a salad (10 cents) and dessert (12 cents). Go 45, 55, 65, then count two more—66, 67." I began to see she was just keeping tab of running totals, doing the easy ones involving only nickels and dimes first, then counting any additional pennies at the end. Then she said, "Sometimes I count backwards at the end. The big chocolate cake slice with whipped cream is 17 cents, so I go 45, 55, 75, then go back three pennies—74, 73, 72." I was starting to see her method: 17 cents was really 20 cents less 3. I did want the job, but it seemed like a high-stakes gamble, and I felt very inadequate. She agreed to talk more after school, and she explained how she did the second half of the job, making change. "Suppose the total is 67 cents, and you're given a dollar. I do just the reverse, pennies first: 68, 69, 70, 75, $1—so it's 3 pennies, a nickel, then a quarter!" Her method was new and felt strange, but it was starting to make the job seem at least doable. I practiced on my own quite a bit for the next few days, wondering just how horribly nervous I'd be sitting at the cash register. She counseled me, "Take your time, don't rush, and if you make a mistake, it's not the end of the world!"

My very first day, I tried to be methodical. I used her method, and I began to appreciate a phrase I'd heard from time to time, "hanging on for dear life." My practice had helped, and somehow I made it through. I was exhausted, but in a good sort of way. I wasn't going to quit. And there was a nice perk: With my lunch, I got a free ice cream cone. It was vanilla, the ice cream went all the way to the bottom, and the cone had a chocolate covering with some chopped nuts on top.

After a few weeks, I got to feel a lot easier on the job and I was now known as "a cashier," which was definitely good for my self-image. One girl with beautiful long brown hair and sparkly eyes was especially nice to me, which was another perk. One evening my mom said, "Keith, you get an ice cream cone after you do your lunch job…" I said "Yes!!" and I triumphantly began to explain how this is a really great thing. Then, "Well, it looks like all those cones are putting on some weight. I think you better cut that out." What a downer. It didn't seem fair, but I "forgot" the cone for a couple of days. Then, fate worked a wonder: The girl with the sparkly eyes was buying a cone! In a brilliant "Aha!" moment, I said, "I always get a free cone for being cashier, but I'd like to give you my cone today!" She was obviously touched and lit right up. This was truly excellent, and she got many more free cones. Of course—at least at my school—the news of "the arrangement" spread like wildfire.

The bottom line: I absolutely couldn't have done the job using the pencil-and-paper method I learned in primary school. Eve's method was easy, fast, and became fun. Each day, continually using a little logic with those pennies maybe even made me grow mathematically by a few epsilons.

The longer Whitney worked with children, the more he became convinced that the best time to foster productive approaches to math is in the very early years—say up through the fourth grade. Although he regarded Benezet's account of his experiment as the most important reference to him, there was a close second—Vivian Paley's "On listening to what the children say" [P]. This vividly recounts the ongoing struggles she had with understanding preschoolers' perspectives. Sometimes the students were lively and imaginative and other times fidgety, wondering when the teacher would ever be done with interrupting them. It was humbling to find that despite her best efforts, she so often remained an outsider, unable to connect and become part of their world, making it difficult to teach and nurture them. In desperation she began tape-recording sessions with them, later listening to their voices and reactions, versus *her* voice and reactions. Gradually, several truths emerged. When a discussion touched on fantasy, fairness, or friendship, their interest and participation zoomed, and Paley began calling these "the three Fs." In a fantasy setting, an unfair situation or broken friendship became a matter of urgent attention, and children would reach to their very limits of verbal and mental abilities to argue matters to where reason and justice was at last reached. It is this process that is so central in older students in arguing a problem (a type of fantasy, or made-up situation) through to a solution.

18.4 Why?

Whitney's change from a life of research to a consuming interest in grade school education—especially the very early grades—elicited a wide range of reactions from the mathematical community. Some were mystified and puzzled. Why would a mathematician with such a stellar reputation trade that for math ed? Could anybody remember another case like that? Others were more judgmental: "He simply shouldn't have done that!" The question of *why* is a good one. Thinking about this over quite a few years now, I have some ideas, and knowing Hass over time has possibly provided me with a few helpful insights.

To begin, there was not just a single reason why—there were several. One thing is certain: Mathematics education in the 1960s was very far from ideal, and Hass got a giant dose of reality in seeing how his daughters Sally and Emily and their classmates were being taught math. In visiting their classrooms, instead of youthful energy, healthy curiosity, and genuine interest, he saw a room full of glazed eyes, children turned into robots doing mindless pencil work. Envisioning himself in this environment made the hairs on the back of his neck stand on end. Hass was always proactive, and realized something had to be done—he knew that what he saw was wrong. Yet he was still thinking about stratifications and how to give the subject a proper foundation.

Being older, a slower pace in life gave Hass more pause, even permission to pull back a little from the focus and hard work of pure research. In this connection, in May, 1966, Hass made a comment that really struck me. "I just don't have the energy that I used to. When I was young I had all sorts of get-up and go, but it's mostly not there anymore." That was all; he said no more about it. The completed manuscript of his book *Complex Analytic Varieties*[1] lay on his desk, ready to be sent to Addison-Wesley, but he was basically dissatisfied with it. Its original purpose was to supply a solid foundation for studying singularities beyond his work in stratifications, but the book turned out to be a geometric treatment of complex analytic varieties. He'd worked hard at it, yet he felt its true purpose was mostly unfulfilled. Soon after, I left to spend the summer in California where I was raised. The general idea was that I'd think about some issues in stratification theory, and he would continue along that line, too. When I met him at the start of the next academic year, I asked about his stratifications progress, and he seemed a bit apologetic. "I ... I got involved in something a bit different." He was working on the mathematical foundations of dimensional analysis. This change seemed to give him a breath of fresh air. In retrospect, I think his comment about not having his old energy referred more to the mental energy and focus required for research, rather than to physical energy. After all, he was jogging several miles each day, and still regularly climbed mountains, a joyous challenge that he was still up to even in his 80s. But I believe the intensity required to make further progress in stratification theory was putting him off, and he was getting weary of that intensity. Besides, the daily effort he put into writing his 400-page tome on complex analytic varieties had burned up a lot of mental energy, and he may have questioned whether it had been worth all the effort. Also, he'd planted seeds in a number of mathematical areas, many of these seeds had sprouted, and now young, energetic researchers were making important progress in areas he'd helped create. It was around this time that he approached the Institute administrators and requested that his salary be cut in half. It is not unreasonable to suppose that he wanted more freedom to pursue a less intense research path, and that he felt requesting the smaller pay was the right thing to do.

In retrospect, his comment about not having his former energy seemed to be a harbinger. He had, after all, truly done his thing in discovering new mathematics, and seeing younger people carrying the torch was in some ways a relief. But

Hass was still Hass, and there was no way he would go gently into that mathematical night. A central core to everything he did up to that time in mathematics was that it had to be *significant* and *important*. That core was not about to change. He saw a truly major problem in how youngsters—our future adults—were being exposed to math, and working on a problem of not only national, but actually international scale, was immensely significant and important.

This problem needed to be addressed, somewhat the way various mathematical problems did. But in all this there was also an intense emotional, even protective, component: He had an especially soft place in his heart for animals, children, and mathematics. What he saw happening to children and to mathematics was simply agonizing to him. As he was getting older, his empathetic side was beginning to grow. He revealed this very directly to Anneli Lax, who for years headed up the Mathematical Association of America's *New Mathematical Library* series. She was involved in mathematics education too, and over the years she and Hass had many conversations about educational philosophy. She once asked Hass, "Why did you make the career change?" (See [113].) Hass answered that it was not only for the sake of the children, but also, he said, "to become human."

At the beginning of his career, Hass focused on research like a laser. In the process mathematics got richer, but his family life got poorer. His first wife, Brock, was soon dealing with three rambunctious youngsters, and although there was some hired help, the steady demands on her almost became too much. Hass would spend the better part of each week away from the family, working near Harvard intensely and alone, away from any distractions and family responsibilities. Over time, the relationship between Hass and Brock began to unravel, eventually ending in divorce. Hass was alone for some years. Later, when at the Institute, he met Mary Garfield at a square dance weekend at New Hampshire's White Mountains. (She was a great-granddaughter of President James Garfield.) They soon married, but in time tensions began to develop in this marriage, too. In part, Mary felt isolated in the neighborhood of the Institute and wanted to live in a more family-friendly area. Hass, Mary, and their two daughters worked out a list of pros and cons about moving, and after much discussion it seemed that the overall sentiment was to make a move. They found a house under construction in a development a few miles away, and decided on that. But after a few more years, Mary still felt a void and lack of emotional support in her life. She had been an elementary school teacher and wanted to explore a new career direction, but it seemed that Hassler neither understood nor truly appreciated that. To him, it seemed that she had a nice, comfortable life. Mary's plight, however, increasingly affected Hass—it seemed that yet another marriage was starting to break down. He began looking more and more within, realizing there was a real need to experience his and other people's emotions less filtered through intellect. He and Mary eventually began scream therapy to get in touch with basic feelings, and the two of them would return home quite hoarse after these sessions. Hassler's daughter Molly was very direct about the change: "The difference in Dad was like night and day. So often, he used to be like a stone, but after some months of scream therapy, his face seemed much more normal, friendly, accepting, and *responsive.*" So the therapy made a change, but Mary's career needs still remained unfulfilled. They separated amicably, with Mary returning home for holidays from Brooklyn. But Hass, once again, was alone.

A few years later Hass went deeply into Transcendental Meditation (TM) and for him, the method lived up to what several hundred peer-reviewed studies seem to suggest: It reduced feelings of stress and anxiety and brought about a greater inner calm. (These changes apparently have a physical component: MRI brain scans of many subjects taken before and after TM have found increased mass in areas of the brain affecting emotions, memories, cognition, and empathy, and decreased mass in the amygdala, which is associated with the fight or flight response.) Hass actually held some classes on TM at the Institute, but the administration eventually told him this was not in keeping with the Institute's purpose, and he discontinued them.

There was another aspect to Hassler's career change that dovetailed with his lifestyle: traveling. It was always a significant part of his life—for example, his trip to Switzerland at age 14 was a true high point, and later, vacation was a common theme in letters to his mother when teaching at Harvard. For him, it meant bursting out and traveling. So running various workshops for teachers and students fit in very naturally with this side of him: He regularly held workshops throughout the U.S., in New Zealand, and in Brazil. Beginning in his late 60s he learned Brazilian Portuguese over the course of several years, so that in Brazil he could speak to the teachers and kids in their native tongue.

18.5 The wheel comes full circle

We end this chapter with a synopsis of a half-page article Hassler wrote in the *American Mathematical Monthly* in 1979 entitled "Comment on the Division of the Plane by Lines" ([121]). It illustrates that the method he espouses at the end of his career in 1979 is basically identical to the method he used to make progress at the start of his mathematical career.

Comment on the division of the plane by lines

The purpose of this note is to illustrate what I consider a basic principle in mathematical research: If a problem is difficult, don't be afraid to get your hands dirty. That is, make up various examples, simple and complex, and test out what happens in a rather complete way.

Consider this problem: How many regions are formed by a set of lines in the plane? Start by drawing a number of lines in the plane, and actually look at the counting process. A basic question is: In what order should I count the regions? There are plenty of different choices, so look for a simple one.

If the plane is a large sheet of paper on a table, you might first count the ones furthest up, then move downward. To do this, you could take a horizontally stretched string and move it from top to bottom, counting regions from left to right if several of them are encountered at the same time.

This principle applies very much to teaching math: You learn math best by *doing* it, and especially by *needing* it in some situation. Particularly in the early grades, "dirtying your hands" becomes "act out the story." In this way, there is a much better chance that school children will regain some of the extraordinary rate of learning that they exhibited before entering school.

Figure 18.3. Hass at about 75, with some excited and involved students.

CHAPTER 19
Evolution or Revolution?

Whitney influenced the course of mathematics not only through his many original results; he also had an effect on the lives of individual people. His son became a mathematician; one of his daughters, a specialist in ethnomusicology; another daughter, a biostatistician. Around Hass, many youngsters, once fearful of math, came to experience "Aha!" moments in discovering little mathematical facts new to them. In this chapter, I tell the story of the case I know best—my own—of how he decisively shaped the way I do and teach mathematics.

Hass did not influence me through anything he did deliberately. Rather, he was a powerful role model; I saw for myself how effective his approaches were. There was a large element of luck in how all this happened. Hassler did not readily make close friends, but because he and I both shared a strong love of classical music, the situation was different. Through the medium of string quartets, we mutually made and enjoyed our kind of music, and this music had a direct connection to both our hearts. As a side benefit, I was able to observe him in various contexts and I slowly began to see things more through his eyes. Mathematically, I eventually found my own approach becoming more concrete and example-driven. Our tale starts on my first day at the Institute.

19.1 "I have mail"

Hassler's influence on me began abruptly. The first time I checked my Institute mailbox I discovered a handwritten note signed Hassler Whitney saying that he'd found out I played the cello, and was anxious to meet me and talk over music in town. So I went to his office and knocked on the door. He appeared, and his piercing blue eyes seemed to drill right through me. "Oops," I thought, "not a good time to interrupt him…" I told him I had gotten this note in my mailbox from him, and in less than a second his entire demeanor changed. With a big smile and sparkling eyes, he invited me to take a seat in his office. He explained that in all his 13 years at the Institute (it was then 1965), this was the very first time there was a violinist, violist, and cellist among the members. Since he played the violin, we could have an Institute string quartet! It would meet weekly. On my end, there was just one thing. As a kid, I'd had some horrible experiences playing chamber music—I had been chosen to fill in when the regular professional cellist couldn't make it. That sounded like an honor, but I couldn't count all that well, and I sight-read even worse. The few times it happened, I could hardly wait until the ordeal was over. Now this fellow wants me to experience this every week! No way. I just wasn't going to go through this again, and I had an airtight excuse. "Unfortunately, I left my cello at home in California, so I really can't do this…" His sparkling eyes and smile never faded, and he said, "Oh, that's no problem at all! My sister-in-law will be visiting us in a couple of days. She has a good cello, and I know she would be happy to bring it along and loan it to you." I thought, "Yikes…this can't be happening. Think! Think of something to say!" But Hass had already check-mated me. I mumbled that I had no music stand, no music, no nothing. It was a weak, pitiful response, and in a couple of days Hass brought to my bachelor apartment a cello, a stand, and the music we'd play on Tuesday.

He picked me up Tuesday at 7:50 sharp and drove to his home, where we had our first evening of quartet playing. I was expecting the worst, but to my surprise, I discovered that in a decade one can mature a lot. We started with easy stuff. I found I could count a lot better than before. By evening's end, I found that playing quartets wasn't the terrible ordeal that I'd expected. I was by no means hooked yet—that took another three or four sessions—but Hass had introduced me in a very digestible way to a whole new world. This soon led to a lifelong change in me, and after these many years I still love and play chamber music.

19.2 Larger implications

Although the centerpiece of each music-making evening was playing music, what happened at the end of each evening ended up having even larger implications for me. At the end of each session all four players, together with Hassler's wife Mary, would sit around a large table generously supplied with cheese, crackers, nonalcoholic liquid refreshments, and usually a cake. It all made for a very pleasant time. All four of us players had mathematical background: Kerson Huang, who played second violin, was a physicist at M.I.T., and Mayo Greenberg, the violist, was an astrophysicist at Union College. With these backgrounds, Hass found it very natural to bring up little brain teasers. There were lots of little questions like "Where should you be so the gravitational forces of the earth and moon cancel out?" Or,"If there were no atmosphere on earth, how long would it take for a meteoroid at rest 50,000 miles up to fall to the earth?" But a simple-sounding question could quickly turn into a discussion about what was and wasn't assumed. How would the moon's gravity influence the meteoroid's journey? In retrospect, I see why he so strongly related to some articles he read as a youth in *Popular Science*.

19.3 Hass reverse-engineers

One of the more memorable of these discussions arose when I mentioned that I was taking pictures around Princeton, but not just ordinary ones. I had recently purchased a stereo camera and a viewer, and was having a great time with my new acquisition. The rest of the quartet seemed interested in such pictures and suggested I bring some along next time. I did—camera, viewer, and some of my better slides, all in color.

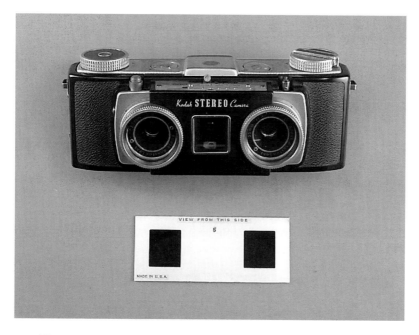

Figure 19.1. Kodak manufactured about 100,000 of these stereo cameras between 1954 and 1959. Below the camera is a mounted stereo slide.

Hass looked at the camera and asked what size film it used. I said it was standard 35mm film, and I usually bought a roll of 36 exposures. He seemed incredulous. "The camera doesn't seem big enough to hold both rolls that size!" I said, "But it uses just *one* roll..." At that, he suddenly saw a problem...if it uses just one roll, then the pictures had to be spaced in a smart way, or else there would be either double exposures or a lot of wasted film. I told him there were never double exposures, and I usually got around 17 stereo pictures from a roll. You could tell that for him, the chase was on. There was clearly some cleverness in how the camera took pictures to use almost all the film without making double exposures, and he just had to see how it did that. He had no interest in opening up the camera—besides, it had film in it—but instead grabbed a piece of paper and pencil and wrote down the numbers 0, 1, 2, 3, ..., 35 to represent individual nonstereo frames, and invited us all to look at them. Was there some way to get a sequence of number pairs corresponding to stereo views that would cover essentially everything on his list? He asked if the film seemed to advance the same amount between successive shots, and I said yes. We all tried this and that for a little while, and he suddenly split up the numbers into three rows, one being the multiples of 3, the next being 2 plus multiples of 3, and the last, 4 plus multiples of 3. Then he circled pairs as in Figure 19.2. There were two frames that never got exposed, but only because the film comes as a strip rather than a continuous loop. Just like that, he had reverse-engineered the secret the camera had quietly held. I was starting to get some ideas of how Hassler thought. It seemed it was always a concrete question that had some subtleties that made you think. His primary focus seldom began in the abstract realm.

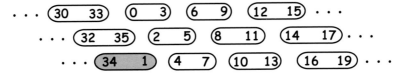

Figure 19.2. Here's how Kodak engineers arranged exposures to minimize waste and avoid double exposures. The top row consists of multiples of 3, with pairings corresponding to the left and right transparencies in a mounted slide. Everything in the second row was 2 more than in the top row, and the numbers in the bottom row were 4 more than in the top. This accounts for all numbers from 0 to 35. Successive stereo shots form the pattern $(0, 3)$, $(2, 5)$, $(4, 7)$, $(6, 9)$, ..., and this pattern was easy to see both visually and numerically. Because the film came as a strip, there's one pair of frames left unexposed, the shaded pair.

As the weeks went by and I experienced more such evenings, his way of thinking was starting to have an effect on me. After reading through the literature on some of the things he had done in mathematics, it became more and more clear to me that he worked with some concrete example containing an essential core at its center, and would keep at it until he really understood it. Sometimes that would lead to a fundamental, new discovery. The process seemed like a cousin to the little puzzles he would bring up after quartets, and it got me thinking. Throughout my years of undergraduate and graduate training in math, my overall direction amounted to ever-increasing abstraction. Now, I meet Hassler Whitney, and he's working in a very different way. There was no question about it—he was the most powerful mathematician I ever knew up close, and he approached things in nearly the opposite way from what I was used to.

19.4 A crucial turning point

One of the most important moments in my life occurred one day in his office, when I happen to mention Bézout's theorem. This basically says that two plane curves defined by polynomials of degree m and n intersect in mn points. Figure 19.3 suggests the idea. In the figure, the ellipse $x^2 + 4y^2 = 1$ has degree 2, and $y = 10x^3 - 5x$ has degree 3, and the two curves intersect in $2 \cdot 3 = 6$ points. When you translate either curve to decrease the number of intersection points, the points don't actually disappear, but move out into complex space $\mathbb{C}^2$ where we don't see them. If you algebraically solve for them, their coordinates turn out to be complex. Should some points happen to coalesce, there's an algebraic way to determine how many piled up. Ditto even for points at infinity.

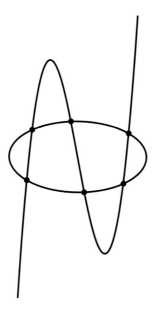

Figure 19.3. One example of Bézout's theorem.

This theorem *is* in fact highly under-appreciated, and he said he had never heard of it. But he was galvanized, jumped up, and went to the blackboard saying, "Let's see if I can disprove that!" Disprove it?! "Waitaminute!" I said, "That theorem is nearly two centuries old! You can't disprove anything… really… " As he began working on some counterexamples at the blackboard, my well-meant words were just so much static. His first tries were easy to demolish, but he was a fast learner and ideas soon surfaced about the complex line at infinity, and how to count multiple points of intersection. After a while, it got harder for me to justify the theorem, and when he asked, "What about two concentric circles?" I had no answer. He argued his way through, and eventually found all four points. Finally he was satisfied, and the piece of chalk was given a rest. He backed away from the blackboard and said, "Well, well—that's quite a theorem, isn't it?" I think I mostly kept my cool during all this, but after I left his office I realized I was pretty shaken. I remember thinking to myself, "Golly, Kendig, you just saw how one of the giants does it!" He'd taken the theorem to the mat, wrestled it, and the theorem won. I had known about that result for at least two years, but I realized that in about 15 minutes he had gained a deeper appreciation of it than I'd ever had. Whitney looked at theorems new to him in terms of a series of concrete examples, and typically developed his own theorems the same way—working from a series of concrete examples. In retrospect, that day represented a turning point for me: I began to think examples, examples. I realized that Whitney worked by finding at least one example that contained the essential crux of a problem, and then working relentlessly on it until he cracked it.

I came to the Institute having nobody in particular to work with. My self-elected mission was to learn and do mathematics, but Hassler was already influencing me in unexpected ways. I realized that my understanding in my field of algebraic geometry was up to that point quite abstract, and the very concrete approach that Hass used was something that was missing in my own education. I came to a turning point. I didn't like the feeling of hanging onto a rope suspended from a blimp, with my feet dangling in mid-air. It felt a lot better to have my feet on the ground, and it seemed that Hassler's feet were always on the ground. I came to a conclusion. I wanted to look at my own field of algebraic geometry in a more concrete way.

19.5 Relearning some algebraic geometry

I decided to look at plane algebraic curves—curves defined by a polynomial equation in two variables, $p(x, y) = 0$. Examples are lines, circles, conics, cubics, and, by clearing denominators, even graphs of rational functions. Graphs of trigonometric or exponential functions aren't included. For example, the exponential $y = e^x$ is the sum

$$1 + \frac{1}{1}x^1 + \frac{1}{1 \cdot 2}x^2 + \frac{1}{1 \cdot 2 \cdot 3}x^3 + \cdots,$$

which continues on forever. So do analogous sums for the sine, cosine, logarithmic, and other transcendental functions. For any polynomial, however, the sum always stops.

It turns out that for algebraic curves, a lot of interesting things happen infinitely far away from a normal vantage point such as the origin. Somewhere I'd read that a powerful tool for understanding such things was to shrink the whole plane down to something finite, like a disk. Any curve in the plane gets dragged along in the shrinking process, so by looking at the edge of the disk we can directly see what's actually going on at infinity.

The big question is, how do you do the shrinking? A uniform approach doesn't work at all, since shrinking distances to merely 1% of their original leaves things a trillion miles away, still very far away. One way is this: Instead of making the shrinking uniform, make it increasingly strong as you go further from the origin. This is quite easy to accomplish for a line: If x is any point in $\mathbb{R}$, then let

$$x \longrightarrow \frac{x}{|x| + 1}$$

be the shrinking function. This makes the point $1 \in \mathbb{R}$ go to $\frac{1}{2}$—that is, the distance from the origin has decreased to just half its original distance from the origin. The point $99 \in \mathbb{R}$ moves to $\frac{99}{100} = .99$, only a hundredth its original distance from the origin, a much more severe shrink. The denominator is doing the heavy lifting here, since it's always larger in size than the numerator. A point really far out, like 999,999, gets pulled in to 0.999999, just a millionth its original distance from the origin—an extremely strong shrinkage. The main fact is that *all the points of $\mathbb{R}$ get squeezed into the interval* $(-1, 1)$. The interval's endpoints $+1$ and -1 correspond to the points at infinity of $\mathbb{R}$. That's why this idea is so helpful—you can gaze directly at points at infinity.

So how about the entire plane? For any point P of $\mathbb{R}^2$ there's a line through that point and the origin, so we do to each of these lines what we did to the x-axis! That is, if P is at a distance d from the origin, then pull P in to $\frac{P}{d+1}$. This squeezes the entire plane into the open unit disk centered at the origin, and the boundary of the disk corresponds to points at infinity. As you might guess, far away points in $\mathbb{R}^2$ that were originally 1 unit apart get squeezed near the disk's boundary like sardines. Two points more than trillion miles apart could end up being less than a trillionth of an inch apart. Figure 19.4 illustrates how this affects parallel lines in $\mathbb{R}^2$: The intense squeezing of points in $\mathbb{R}^2$ far from the origin means that parallel lines get drawn ever closer together toward the edge of the disk. In the figure, they seem to meet at the boundary. They do. Furthermore, topologists "glue together" or identify the two opposite points so that two parallel lines actually meet in only one point, just as any two nonparallel lines do. The disk in which every pair of opposite boundary points are identified or glued together is called the *real projective plane.*

Drawing some familiar curves in the real projective plane can lead to surprises. Figures 19.5 and 19.6 show polynomial graphs after they've been shrunk to fit in the projective plane. In the graph of a polynomial $y = q(x)$, after squeezing the graph into the unit disk, the branches approach the disk's boundary. *But*

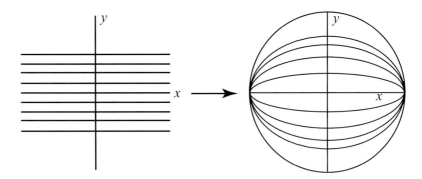

Figure 19.4. Parallel lines in $\mathbb{R}^2$ map to curves approaching the same point at infinity.

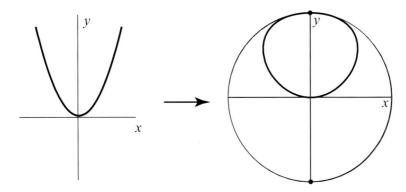

Figure 19.5. The parabola $y = x^2$ and its image in the projective plane.

exactly where? If q's degree is greater than 1, then the y-values grow faster than the x-values—so much so that the branches approach the end of the y-axis. We see this in Figure 19.5 when the degree is even. Figure 19.6 depicts an example when the degree is odd. Since the two opposite vertical points on the disk are identified, the branches in each figure approach one and the same point. This says something nice about the graph of any polynomial $y = q(x)$: Regardless of whether the degree is even or odd, the image in the disk-with-boundary is a topological loop, even when the degree is 0 or 1.

One can incorporate the shrinking equation into the polynomial defining the curve in $\mathbb{R}^2$, and today we have software such as Mathematica or Maple allowing us to easily see an accurate image of the shrunken curve. Back in 1965, doing this could amount to some real work—for example, look at the fancier example in Figure 19.7. The top picture depicts a rational function which, by clearing

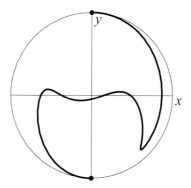

Figure 19.6. Image in the projective plane of a polynomial of odd degree.

denominators, can be cast into the form $p(x, y) = 0$. The actual rational function is

$$y = 1/[(x^2 - 1)(x^2 - 4)]$$

which can be rewritten as

$$y(x^2 - 1)(x^2 - 4) - 1 = 0.$$

The image in the unit disk includes the images of the vertical asymptotes.

19.6 The right environment is crucial

I remembered reading that the curve $y^2 = x(x^2 - 1)$ has genus 1. That struck me, because it didn't seem to make any sense. I knew what genus meant, and that genus 1 meant you had a donut, but the drawing of $y^2 = x(x^2 - 1)$ on the left in Figure 19.8 definitely doesn't look like a donut. Was there some other meaning of genus that I had missed? Since I was in the mode of squeezing various curves into the unit disk, I did that to this curve, and I got the picture on the right in Figure 19.8.

Seeing this curve squeezed into the disk, with its points at infinity on the boundary, offered the first glimmer of hope, because the two ends of the branch shown in the left picture end up at the ends of the y-axis in the disk picture. Those two points are opposite on the disk, so are considered as one and the same point. That branch, drawn in the disk, therefore became a loop. That, together with the other loop certainly wasn't a donut, but if you lay a hollow torus down on a table top so that its bottom touches the table in a circle, then a cleaver vertically slicing the torus into two equal halves leaves two circular cut edges. That didn't solve my problem, but it seemed to offer a clue.

Fortunately, I knew that the nicest theorems about polynomial curves assume a complex context rather than real. For example, if the curve has the special

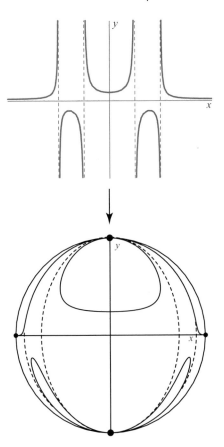

Figure 19.7. Image in the projective plane of a rational function.

form where y occurs to only the first degree, meaning the equation is $y = q(x)$ for some polynomial $q(x)$, then you have the fundamental theorem of algebra which says that number of roots is $\deg q$—that is, the curve crosses the complex x-axis that many times. Repeated roots correspond to higher order crossings, the way the parabola $y = x^2$ touches the x-axis tangentially in a double point. (See [K2] for a more complete story.) So looking at the curve $y^2 = x(x^2 - 1)$ not in $\mathbb{R}^2$ but in $\mathbb{C}^2$ might offer further clues to how the curve had something to do with a donut. But $\mathbb{C}^2$ has *four* real dimensions, and I wasn't able to visualize in four dimensions. I eventually tried looking at what the complex curve would look like within other real planes in $\mathbb{C}^2$. I wrote x as $x_1 + ix_2$, y as $y_1 + iy_2$, and plugged these into $y^2 = x(x^2 - 1)$. The real and imaginary parts of this equation turn out to be

$$y_1^2 - y_2^2 = x_1^3 - 3x_1x_2^2 - x_1; \quad 2y_1y_2 = 3x_1^2x_2 - x_2^3 - x_2.$$

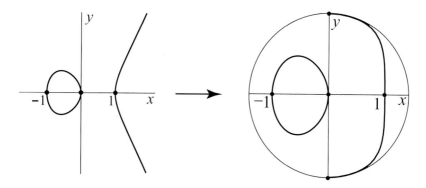

Figure 19.8. Image in the projective plane of a cubic.

When I looked within the (x_1, y_2)-plane, I struck gold. This plane corresponds to $x_2 = 0, y_1 = 0$, and substituting these values into these two equations gave

$$-y_2^2 = x_1^3 - x_1, \quad 0 = 0.$$

Writing the first equation as $y_2^2 = -x_1^3 + x_1$, I realized that its graph is a kind of brother to the curve in the (x_1, y_1)-plane. The left picture in Figure 19.9 shows the two brothers together in (x_1, y_1, y_2)-space, the new curve being dotted. After some thought I saw that both branches headed to the same point at infinity. To my delight, I was able to draw a picture like that on the right—the skeleton of an actual torus!

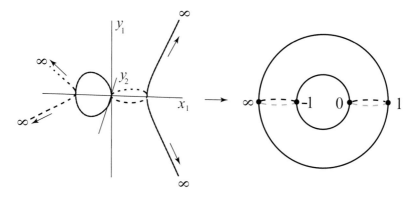

Figure 19.9. The space curve depicted on the left corresponds to time $t = x_2 = 0$, and it falls naturally into four parts, two drawn solidly and two drawn dashed. In complex projective space, these form four topological loops that can be arranged as on the right, making the skeleton of a torus.

This was exciting, and my confidence was growing. I knew that I was looking at only two special planes in 4-space, but the final victory came when I let time x_2 vary. Each value for it gave me a different parallel three-dimensional slice of 4-space. When x_2 is small, the corresponding space curve hugs the skeleton—the curve in the $x_2 = 0$ slice. All positive values of x_2 fill out one-half of a torus, shown in Figure 19.10. All negative values of x_2 fill out the other half of the torus. I finally got it: "YES! The genus of $y^2 = x(x^2 - 1)$ is 1," and I had a wonderful picture to prove it.

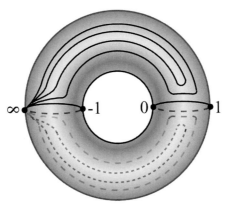

Figure 19.10. This figure shows space curves corresponding to time $x_2 = t$ equal to a few choices of positive constant. All such curves fill out the skeleton to form one half of a torus. The negative constants give curves—not shown—that fill in the other half. The full cubic in complex projective space is therefore topologically a torus.

Later, I sketched curves with several factors, like

$$y^2 = x(x^2 - 1^2)(x^2 - 2^2)(x^2 - 3^2)(x^2 - 4^2)(x^2 - 5^2),$$

which in the real plane looks like a string of loops plus a branch. By mimicking what I had done for $y^2 = x(x^2 - 1)$, I was able to create curves that, when plotted in $\mathbb{C}^2$ together with points at infinity, gave surfaces of arbitrarily high genus.

19.7 A burning question

My understanding of algebraic geometry in more concrete terms was beginning to grow. I knew that complex algebraic curves were orientable and that they were compact in their natural habitat of complex space with points at infinity added. What struck me so much was that if you randomly choose real or complex numbers as coefficients of a polynomial $p(x, y)$, that polynomial would define a compact, orientable topological manifold, and I knew the major fact about them—a single number classifies these manifolds: the genus. Remember, it was reading that $y^2 = x(x^2 - 1)$ has genus 1 that initially led me down this whole path. Now a very natural and important question occurred to me: If I just make up a polynomial of some degree n with coefficients chosen by throwing darts at $\mathbb{R}$ or $\mathbb{C}$, how do I find the associated genus? I thought about this for some days, and could not come up with any answer that satisfied me.

Since Princeton was full of so much mathematical talent, I decided to ask some of my friends at the Institute. I asked maybe four or five temporary members who knew some algebraic geometry, but I couldn't get a straight answer from any of them. I was auditing a graduate course in algebraic geometry at the University and asked some of the students there, but again, no clear answer. *This thing had turned into a burning question.*

19.8 A bad joke

I at last made a huge decision. André Weil, a permanent member at the Institute, was one of the greatest algebraic geometers in the world. If he couldn't answer my question, nobody could. I resolved to screw up my courage and ask the great man. He had a reputation for sometimes being difficult and unpredictable, but he regularly came to the afternoon tea held in the Institute's common room, and that offered a natural opportunity. The next afternoon around 3:30, I saw him standing all by himself with a cup of tea. He seemed perfectly nice and pleasant, and looked as if he could perhaps use someone to talk to. So I went up to him, and he seemed happy to see me. I carefully phrased my question, and at once his eyebrows arched up and his eyes started dancing around. Then he started laughing—"Hee-hee…hee hee!" This is not what I expected. Then it came: "Is this some sort of joke? You don't actually mean this!" OMG, I felt my face changing color, and I sort of stammered out "Yes, I guess a really bad joke…" He didn't answer me, and it seemed he was still assuming it really *was* a joke. But I finally said that I very much wanted to know the answer, that I had thought about it pretty hard. "Hee-hee, don't you know that was one of the first things ever discovered in algebraic geometry?" No, I didn't know that. "So what's the answer?" I asked. Then he replied, simply enough, "If the degree is n, then the genus is $n - 1$ times $n - 2$ by two!" I was feeling terrible, but I got what I wanted, *the formula:*

$$g = \frac{(n-1)(n-2)}{2}.$$

How beautiful. How clear. I thanked him and started to leave. But Weil was not done, and was enjoying things. He commanded me, "Stay right there! DO NOT MOVE!" What on earth was he up to? I saw him quickly talking to some other people, and dragged three or four of them over to me. So we formed a little circle, and he animatedly said, "I want to share something with you. This is Mr. Kendig, here. He wrote a thesis on 'Algebraic Geometry Over Dedekind Domains,' and has read through all of Lang's book on abelian varieties," and maybe he mentions something else. One of the giants he snared is the Japanese mathematician Kenkichi Iwasawa, who was broadly smiling at me and bowing, bowing. Another is Friedrich Mautner who was just taking it all in. "And you know what he just asked me? What the genus is of a nonsingular complex algebraic curve!" Yes, I too was smiling like everyone else—what else is there to do? But I felt like going through the floor. Then, just when I was thinking things couldn't get any worse, I saw Whitney, maybe 20 feet away, looking right at me. Now my very best friend knew what a total jerk I was. Everything was going up in flames. It seemed like an eternity, but was probably only two or three minutes, and then our little circle broke up and I was free to go.

Figure 19.11. The Institute common room, and the scene of the bad joke. Weil was indeed an important mathematician; a bust of him graces the room today.

And go I did. I headed straight for my bachelor apartment, steaming mad and completely embarrassed. I thought and thought and thought. After a long time, a little rationality started to return. *I really had vetted that question.* Look at all the people I asked, temporary members just like me. Weil could have laughed at all of them too. And Iwasawa? He seemed completely friendly and pleasant during the entire time. Whitney? Well, he *was* 20 feet away, so he couldn't have heard exactly what I'd asked Weil. Besides, when I thought back on it, his expression was more one of "So Keith is in with some of the big guys—I guess he must be doing OK!" So I slowly began to calm down. Sure, things weren't the greatest, but not everything was totally bad. One idea kept coming back to me. *I had asked quite a few people, and I never got a clear answer.* What Weil gave me was both clear and beautiful, and I thought everyone should know about such a central, wonderful, and powerful result. If that was one of the first things known in algebraic geometry, then all those people I had asked deserved know that, too. Somewhere deep inside me, something was happening. Was I going to hunt up every person I asked and explain what the wonderful answer was? Reliving those moments with Weil definitely didn't appeal to me. As the jumble in my mind gradually started to clear, a solution welled up: *Someday I should write a book on algebraic geometry, and I would make the beautiful formula for the genus one of the VERY BIG highlights.* That day, that one hour, proved to be the kernel, the germ of a promise I made to myself. It did not happen overnight, but after three or four years I began work on what I hoped would finally be a book. I found it slow and difficult going, and I learned a tremendous amount during the process. Finally, ten years after that fateful encounter, *Elementary Algebraic Geometry* was published in Springer-Verlag's Graduate Series. An updated version was issued by Dover in 2015 ([**K2**]).

Figure 19.12. André Weil.

CHAPTER **20**
Other Happenings at the Institute

The Institute is a cultural crossroads, and meeting new ideas and friends is part of its territory. This chapter gives a few slices of life during my two years there.

20.1 A new friend

Every so often Hass and Mary would throw a party. There were all sorts of finger foods, cheeses and crackers, breads and spreads, always at least one cake, and for those who knew about the "Whitney Special"—a drink made up of equal parts grape juice, orange juice, and ginger ale— the components were there for the mixing. Hass and Mary would invite colleagues from the Institute as well as guests from other walks of life including, of course, music.

Mary's father was at one of these parties, and I fell into a pleasant conversation with him. He was very friendly and easy to talk to, though I had to look up all the while since he was well over six feet tall. At one point we started talking about the permanent members, and he finally asked, "What does it take to become a permanent member? What sort of people are they?" I answered that many of them could be considered "immortals" in their field. They had made contributions that were likely to outlast all our own lifetimes. "Well," he asked, "would you consider someone like Harish-Chandra to be an immortal?" I knew a bit about him; I was once told that the sum total of his contributions was like a great cathedral, and already belonged to the ages. No less than Robert Langlands went overboard in praise of Harish-Chandra, saying he knew of no one else in Harish-Chandra's generation who cast such a wide net and threw so much light on his subject. So I vigorously responded to Mary's very tall father "Oh, yes! Yes! Harish-Chandra is absolutely one of the immortals!" My friend's gaze then turned upward, which I found a bit odd— after all, we were directly talking to each other. Instinctively, I turned around and saw Harish-Chandra looking down right at me, with a slightly embarrassed smile. We shook hands, and were in this way "formally introduced." He and I had crossed paths several times before, but he was always in his own world, paying no attention to me, and

I made no attempt to disturb him. After our "introduction" he always would give me a little nod of recognition when we passed. It was clear that I was, so to speak, on his side, and he seemed to appreciate that. Harish-Chandra considered himself something of an outsider at the Institute and never felt entirely comfortable with a few of the permanent members with whom he worked. Some of those Institute mathematical giants came with equally giant egos, but Harish-Chandra was not at all that way, and some of the mathematical alpha males there intimidated him. A key reason for feeling as an outsider: He was formally trained as a physicist, not a mathematician, and felt that he was in some ways incompletely educated as a mathematician. Despite those feelings, he had a clear philosophical perspective on things and believed his lack of background in mathematics was in a way responsible for the novelty of his work: "On the process of discovery, I have often pondered about the roles of knowledge or experience on the one hand, versus imagination or intuition on the other. I believe there is a certain fundamental conflict between the two, and knowledge, by advocating caution, tends to inhibit the flight of imagination. Therefore a certain naiveté, unburdened by conventional wisdom, can sometimes be a positive asset." Notwithstanding his perspective, he still couldn't always trust some of his colleagues to the point that he would open up personally to them. With me, however, the dynamic was different. He knew how I really felt about him, and I think this played a role in our developing friendship.

In the common room in the main building of the Institute—Fuld Hall—there was a big table always stocked with current newspapers from all over the world. I got into the habit of reading these newspapers around 10 o'clock each evening, and after a few weeks, Harish-Chandra fell into the same pattern. We began to exchange random comments about the day's news and events around the world. As time went on our conversations became a little longer, and finally we actually started talking a little math. He asked me how I decided to go into algebraic geometry. I told him that I had taken a course based on Emil Artin's notes, and was struck by how powerful and beautiful the idea was that algebra and geometry can mirror each other—a sort of natural outgrowth of analytic (or cartesian) geometry. He seemed very satisfied with that answer. I added that it sure wasn't that way with other courses I had taken. He responded with, "For example?" I said that I could never get into a certain course based on Zaanen's book on abstract integration theory, because neither the book nor the teacher offered much in the way of intuition on what the driving force—the raison d'être—was for doing all that theory in the first place. I sort of looked for it myself, but didn't know enough to find it. That seemed to strike a chord with Harish-Chandra. He said, "I once took a course on real analysis, and I felt the same way. This fat book was filled with a seemingly endless stream of theorems and corollaries. How could the author ever come up with all this? It was so intimidating, and it seemed I could never, ever get on top of the book. I tried so hard to find some unifying thread that would connect things—something the book never offered. At last it came to me: The whole course, the whole book, was little more than one big theme and variations on the Heine-Borel theorem." (In its simplest form, the Heine-Borel theorem says that in real n-space, a subset is closed and bounded if and only if every open cover of the set has a finite subcover. This theorem extends to more general metric spaces.) He continued, "When I saw that, I 'got' the course, and both the book and the teacher became less intimidating. That was a real breakthrough for me, and it made me realize that in other branches of mathematics there could be unifying threads—but you have to find them."

He went on. "The same thing is actually true in current mathematical research. You look at all these journals filled with theorem and after theorem after theorem, and it seems like all this mathematics coming down the pipeline is enough to blow you over. But really, all this research is like a big snowstorm, and after the snowstorm you're looking at three or four feet of snow—all very imposing and somewhat overwhelming. That's like what you see in printed journals. But with time that snow melts down, and you end up with just a couple of inches of water. That water is the essence, the core, of what was actually accomplished."

I discovered that we shared a number of things in our formative years. I fell in love with Vincent van Gogh's work when I was about 13, and he did, too. We both became serious dabblers in painting around the same age. As adults, our favorite style in art was Impressionism. Physics was the most important course to me in high school; the same for him. I started out as a physics major in college, and so did he—but I switched to math after just two years, while he went all the way to a Ph.D. in it.

In one of our late night conversations, I said it was a shame that the world's greatest mathematicians and physicists had to be mortal. To me, it seemed like a big waste that even they must eventually die. After all the many things we agreed on, I was surprised when he forcefully disagreed with me. "It wouldn't be at all good for top scientists to live forever. When they're young, maybe they make some important discoveries in a certain field, but science progresses by a series of revolutions, some small and some larger. Very old people, fixed in their thoughts, could act as a drag on the free and uninhibited progress that younger people are set to make. Science remains fresher and more vital with the old ones dying off." Although I could intellectually appreciate his argument, it took me a few years to accept this emotionally.

There are interesting parallels between Harish-Chandra and Hassler. Both were attracted to the arts when young—Harish-Chandra to art and Hass to music—and both kept their interest the rest of their lives. Both wished to understand the physical world and had majored in physics as an undergraduate. Both had a moment of truth when they saw they were better at math than physics. For Hass

Figure 20.1. Harish-Chandra.

it was in Göttingen when he realized he couldn't rely on his memory for facts in physics, but an important teacher, James Pierpont, had made it clear that he had a special talent in math. Harish-Chandra met his fork in the road thanks to his thesis advisor Paul Dirac. Harish-Chandra had already written his Ph.D. thesis on the Lorentz group and then followed Dirac to Princeton soon after that. When in Princeton, Harish-Chandra began looking at his work on the Lorentz group more critically and realized his conclusions in the thesis were based on rather shaky arguments. "I had naively manipulated unbounded operators without paying any attention to their domains of definition. I complained to Dirac that my proofs were not rigorous and he replied, 'I am not interested in proofs but only in what nature does.' This remark confirmed my growing conviction that I did not have the mysterious sixth sense necessary to really succeed in physics and I soon decided to move over to mathematics." It seemed clear that Dirac thought Harish-Chandra had more natural talent in mathematics than in physics, and it was in mathematics where he really belonged. Some of Harish-Chandra's work turned out to be an outgrowth of supplying a more solid mathematical base to some of the intuition-based methods and assumptions physicists were using. The same was true of Hassler, where notions of bending and warping in 4-space led to questions about the deeper nature of such spaces. Could they inherit their properties by being embedded in a higher dimension? Whitney's embedding theorems shed light on this. Much later in his career, Hass decided that when it came to dimension theory, physicists really didn't really understand what they were talking about, and that it was time to give the theory a solid mathematical foundation.

20.2 Hass opens other doors

Halfway through one quartet session the violist announced that he had to leave early because he needed to drive to Schenectady and wanted to arrive at a decent hour. Hass seemed disappointed—he was really into the music-making, and the evening was being cut short. I depended on Hass to drive me and my cello back to my apartment, but Hass had other ideas. He was in a musical state of mind, and he suggested we talk a bit first. Had I ever heard Debussy's string quartet? I hadn't. He had a recording, and played some of each of the four movements. The slow movement, in particular, clearly moved him, and I remember him comparing it to moonlight reflecting off a lake's quiet ripples. I had never quite seen this side of him. A little later he volunteered that Debussy wrote a lot of wonderful piano music and that, in particular, Walter Gieseking[1] was a uniquely gifted interpreter of Debussy's piano works. He said I ought to listen to his recordings. I had never heard of Gieseking, but I had previously discovered Sam Goody's record shop in New York, and Hassler's suggestion immediately gave me a reason to make a bus trip up there.

Sam's was a treasure trove with row upon row of inexpensive 78s, and the shop had already helped expand my musical horizons. Once there, one of the knowledgeable salespeople helped me, and I ended up with four or five Gieseking recordings. Little did I realize what a great impact his interpretations would have on me.

On the bus heading home, I really looked forward to what Gieseking sounded like. But around halfway through the trip, the most incredibly beautiful woman boarded. Being young, male, and biological, I found I simply could not take my eyes off her. The bus was pretty much filled, so she had to walk to the rear for a seat. I said to myself "Wow, you never know when you'll see someone like that!"

I got off the bus at Princeton's Palmer Square and was waiting for a red light to turn green at the corner of Nassau and Mercer Streets. At this point, who should be standing exactly beside me? And she started talking. It wasn't, "Nice evening," or "Are you from around here?" She was simple and she was direct: "I saw you looking at me..." I was caught completely off guard, and with some embarrassment agreed that I had. Her voice was colored by a slight, very pleasing

Figure 20.2. Walter Gieseking.

foreign accent. Then she asked, "Are you walking down Mercer?" Yes, I was, and it became clear that a little company would be appreciated. "How far down are you going?" I said it was to the apartments at the Institute for Advanced Study. "You're at the Institute? ... You must be pretty smart." After a little silence, it was "What are you studying there?" I said it was mathematics. "Oh, then you're really really smart!" Well, I knew what really smart was—those permanent members, and a generous smattering of exceedingly bright temporary people, for example. But this was no time to disagree with this angelic companion. I somehow managed to keep responding to her easy conversation. I was nervous, very nervous. But I knew this was a rare experience that I would remember for a long time.

After a good walk, she (and therefore I) stopped in front of an enormous brick home and she announced that this was her destination. We talked a little longer, and she finally asked if she might give me a little advice. "Advice? What kind of advice?" She answered, "You like girls, don't you?" (Silence.) "You're pretty shy, but you need to meet a girl halfway. I've done almost all the talking, but not all girls do that. If you go halfway, most nice girls will do the same!" Nobody else in Princeton had ever talked to me so directly, but it seemed clear that she was taking my interests to heart.

She wasn't finished. "I'm just house-sitting here while the owners are traveling in Europe. It would be very nice if you would visit me sometime." She considered possible times, finally suggesting this coming Saturday around 6:00. This was all happening so fast, but yes, Saturday at 6:00 would be absolutely perfect. She called herself Aika, which she said was short for Aikaterina. I couldn't quite believe how things were turning out with this statuesque Greek girl with her beautifully chiseled features. What was happening was big. As I turned to leave, she said, "Why don't you bring a bottle of wine?"

As I walked home, I tried to get some perspective on all that had just happened. For one thing, I'd never bought anything from a liquor store—my parents only got sleepy after any kind of alcohol, so it wasn't something I grew up with. Going there and asking for wine was somewhat out of my comfort zone and I rationalized that there was a good chance she would forget she asked about wine, or maybe I would be the one to forget. As a couple of days passed and Saturday drew nearer, it seemed ridiculous to blow this opportunity, and I began to ask myself why *not* get a bottle of wine? There are liquor stores all over the country, and people buy from them all the time. How else would they stay in business? So I decided that I should just do it and, as it turned out, thinking about it was harder than actually doing it. I explained the situation to the guy in the store. He was understanding and suggested something appropriate (translation: somewhat expensive), which I then stored in the tiny refrigerator in my bachelor apartment at the Institute.

The question was, how reliable was she? Would she remember the date? If not, it wouldn't be my fault. I timed things carefully, and arrived very nearly at 6:00. I rang the doorbell, and she answered promptly—the huge carved wooden front door must have been 12 feet tall, and it slowly opened up. She seemed absolutely delighted to see me and the nice bottle I had brought. She made me feel comfortable right from the start. She poured each of us a glass of wine, and she brought out a generous assortment of cheeses and crackers. At evening's end, it seemed that time had flown by, and she suggested we meet again.

We fell into a routine of meeting every week or so. At one point, she suggested walking to Palmer Square and looking for a bar. I had gotten to know her long enough that the newness of the friendship had evolved into knowing her more as a human being having feelings and emotions, not just as an object. When we entered the bar, I never imagined it would be a grand entrance, but six or so guys in there surely did—all these pairs of eyes were fixed on her, and I got the feeling that some of them wondered how on earth this plain guy ever rated such a creation. I realized again what kind of cargo I was with. A couple of weeks later, I figured it was about time for me to make a move—to go "halfway," as she initially put it. She was an outdoorsy type and liked to walk, so I said let's walk up to Palmer Square and I'd treat her to a nice dinner. The Grotto restaurant always seemed to have good vibes coming from it when I had walked past it before, so that's where we went. After being seated, I realized that none other than André Weil was exactly facing me a couple of tables away. He seemed involved talking to two friends at his table. He was severely near-sighted, and it seemed that at two tables away he probably couldn't see me. I just didn't want him coming over and checking out her mathematical bona fides—let's just say they were scant. He soon left, seemingly happy and still conversing with his friends.

Once, during a cheese-and-crackers session in her front room, I wondered aloud if she wasn't somewhat intimidated by her surroundings. The house was a mini-mansion with ornately carved woodwork everywhere, a massive winding staircase to the second floor, stained glass, a huge fireplace adorned with beautiful tilework. It all bespoke considerable wealth. "Oh, no—I'm not intimidated at all!" She explained that she had been married briefly to a very rich Greek shipping magnate, and she was used to and comfortable with such surroundings. She could be very direct with me, so I decided to be direct with her. "So what happened? You're not married to him any more?" She said that he considered her exclusively as a sex object, and he never seemed to get beyond that—hardly a recipe for an enduring relationship. So she had some money from the settlement and had decided to see the world. Before Princeton, it was Acapulco, Mexico. After Princeton, it would be back to Greece, and then who knows where?

Visiting her a few weeks later, a slightly uncomfortable feeling came over me. There were extended silences, and finally she said "In two weeks, I'm leaving for Greece." Just like that, it was going to be over. She invited me to a going away party, and some 15 people showed up. She had more friends than I realized, and I was surprised to see my buddy Lou there. He was a graduate student in biochemistry at Princeton and we often had relaxed, friendly conversations. But tonight, he seemed different—basically, wound up. People just weren't leaving the party, and at 1:30 I said goodbye to her and left. There was a very light drizzle outside, certainly nothing that bothered me. However, within three or four minutes, a car came zooming up to me and then quickly stopped. "Keith, Keith, get in!" It was Lou, even more wound up than before. He explained that Aika got angry at him for letting me walk home "in the rain" and had told him to drive me home. Some weeks later I saw him as his usual laid back self. After a while I asked him whatever was the deal at the party. He had seemed so different that night. He said, "People just wouldn't leave, and they wouldn't leave. It got to be past 4:30 in the morning, and I never could get any privacy with Aika. You see, I was planning to propose to her!" That explained everything. He said he began to realize that it was probably a fool's errand, and finally left at nearly 5:00 without getting close to making any proposal. There were four other guests still there. He was philosophical about it—she was not ready for another relationship, so it was probably best, and he undoubtedly saved himself the embarrassment of a "no."

So the era of Aika was over. She helped me evolve in my feelings about women, and that helped when I finally did meet the future Mrs. Joan Kendig. Joan was a petite, blue-eyed blonde, very intelligent Polish girl whom I soon called "Princess." Over the course of our marriage of over four decades and counting, she has often reminded me that I have always treated her as a real person rather than just an object, the way so many of her suitors had, and that she really appreciated that. So at the Institute, I not only learned some mathematics, but I got a some important education about people. The Institute experience was multi-dimensional.

20.3 "Open!...Open up!"

A few months after the Aika era, another Greek came into my life. Nick arrived at the Institute to work with his fellow countryman, the well-known geometric topologist Christos Papakyriakopoulos of Princeton University. Nick and I thought quite alike in that my geometry oriented brain seemed to mesh harmoniously with his. We also were joggers, and discussed math, jogging, and girls. Mostly girls. Up to this point, I never had said anything about Aika to anyone at the Institute. Her interests were orthogonal to mathematics, and for months I'd just kept it all my own. But Nick and I became quite friendly, and I finally opened up about her. After hearing the story, he seemed appropriately impressed. But then he found out that I didn't have a car. He was just flabbergasted. "How can you expect to do girls if you don't have a car?!" I explained that Aika liked to walk, and that we'd often walk to Palmer Square and hang out there. "Yes, but that's *her*—she's an outlier. Man, you need a car, *bad*. Do you even have a driver's license?" Sure, I had a valid one from California. That was enough for him. "C'mon, we're gonna go to Trenton and get you a car!"

It seemed that in no time, we were in a used car lot. I asked for a transportation car. I didn't want to spend much. The salesman led us to the cheapest car on the lot. "Here's a '55 Caddy—only $99." That car was ugly. I mean, *really* ugly. It was battleship gray with no shine at all. There were places on the sides and back where the paint had chipped off, and below each chip, a vertical rust streak. I asked if I could hear what the motor sounded like. He said that it might not start because it had been sitting there for a long time and no one had bothered to start it. He turned the key, and that ugly beast started up immediately. The motor sounded nice and smooth, and I was beginning to get slightly interested. Meanwhile, Nick reminded the salesman every 15 seconds how ugly that car was. After a long time discussing and arguing, Nick finally wore the man down to $90. Nick slowly shook his head "no," but that model of Caddy had its gas fill cap under the tail light. You pushed a reflector button, and the light popped up, revealing the filling tube. I'd loved that cool feature since my teenage years, and always wished our family had a Caddy like that. So I wasn't ready to let it go. I said, "I'll take the car for $85." Then, in what just may have been the clincher, I added, "Do you really want to have this thing sitting on your lot? The impression it creates is disgraceful, but I'm here, willing take it off your hands." The guy accepted the deal, and soon I was off in my car.

A couple of days later, Hass phoned me, reminding me that he's about to pick me up to go to orchestra rehearsal. A few weeks back he'd talked to the conductor and arranged for me to join the cello section. I found those rehearsals enjoyable. I at once told Hass about getting new wheels, and that maybe this time I should provide transportation. He seemed delighted and eager to see my car. When he saw it he never said a thing about its extreme ugliness. And once you got inside, it really was quite comfortable—more so than Hassler's Plymouth which was a modest but reliable vehicle. On the way to rehearsal, I launched into a demonstration of all the bells and whistles that came with such a premier car: Every window could be raised or lowered with just a push of a button. In those days, the norm was for windows to be hand-cranked, so this was a definite cut above and quite special. Even better, by just pushing buttons you could make the front seat go forward or back, and up or down. Since the front seat was all one piece, Hass was carried along for the seat's demo. He was very nice about all this nonsense. When we arrived at the rehearsal parking lot I opened my door to get out, and Hass said "Open!" Then, "OPEN UP!" I asked, "What's going on? Why are you saying that?" He quipped, "This car has so many features, I was sure that if I just asked it to open, it would understand me and open the door." Hass had this wonderful sense of humor with almost always a twist of cleverness. Over time, the Ugly One proved useful, making life easier in shopping and essential to inviting out girls.

20.4 Dandelion greens

I was raised in the Southern California coastal city of Santa Monica. Our house was just a block away from the Palisades Park, a two-mile stretch on a fairly high bluff overlooking the Pacific Ocean. The park's well-kept pebble paths made it a favorite place for hundreds of walkers, joggers, and, with its many benches, sitters. After a long stretch of studying, it was great to be able to walk down to the park and just decompress, filling my lungs with fresh ocean air.

One cloudy day I was about two blocks from my house when a thunderstorm hit out of nowhere. I had little choice but to run home. I was amazed at how hard it was for me to cover those two blocks. After running just a little while I got so winded and exhausted, it *really hurt*, and I wondered if I was already a candidate for a heart attack. Finally, safe inside but drenched, I couldn't help but think I had to do something about my totally crummy physical condition. Here I was, in my early twenties, and a two-block run had wiped me out. As a result I began to take longer walks. These increased over time, and one day when passing a bridge connecting the park to the beautiful beaches below, I decided to try the bridge and walk along the ocean's edge. After doing this a couple of times, I happened to see my former professor Leo Sario.[2] I had taken a course on differential geometry from him. (We covered every page of Struik's famous book.) He gives me a cheery wave and continues on, jogging with seemingly no effort. He looked to be in perfect physical shape, yet he was easily 20 years older than I. After the third time of his cheery wave, he instead stops jogging and says to me, "How come you're just walking? That's old man stuff! You should be jogging!" With that, he continues his jogging, leaving me slightly shook up. Maybe I just didn't *want* to jog. Maybe I just didn't *need* to jog. That run home was—well, excruciating—and walking was fine with me. The next time we met, he kept on going, but called out, "You should run!" After hearing this three-word reminder a couple more times, I wondered if I should find another route to avoid him. He made me feel bad; he was in terrific shape and I wasn't, but that one experience of forced running had left a really bad taste in me. On yet another day, I see those blue trunks quite far in the distance, heading toward me, and I brace for another three-word lecture. When that pair of trunks gets to within 500 feet or so, just to keep him shut, I decide to do a little flat-foot shuffle. WOW! He comes right at me, throws his arms around me, and *lifts me off the beach.* "Yes! Yes! Wonderful! Marvelous! I am so proud to see you running. Mr. Kendig, keep it up!" I really didn't think I was easily influenced by other people's words, but that reaction did something to me. I tried running a little bit the next few days, and it seemed that I could do with running what I had done with walking: Gradually increase the distance. I had other encounters with Prof. Sario, and he was consistently an irrepressible cheerleader. Once, he surprised me and came from behind to greet me. He courteously slowed down for me, and we jogged together for awhile. He seemed just thrilled, and secretly, so was I. When I could run no farther, he said, "Good for you!! I hope we'll do this again sometime, and maybe we'll go a little farther." The die was cast, and I took it upon myself to conquer what seemed an impossible goal: to have a real, no nonsense jog along the beach. It took me quite a long time, but I felt absolutely triumphant when I jogged an entire mile without stopping. It seemed that progress got faster after that, and within another four or five months, I was up to nearly five miles. By this time, my former teacher became "Leo" and we got so we would jog the entire distance together. This was the closest I had ever gotten to any of my math teachers, and he had done me a really big favor. I was feeling better and more energetic.

When I found out I would be a temporary member of the Institute the coming year, I realized there would be no beach. By that time I had made a daily five-mile jog part of my life, and I didn't want to give that up. I told Leo about that, and he said, "Oh, use the Institute woods!" He had spent time at the Institute and seemed to know all about its surroundings. He promised me that there were good walking paths in the woods that were also great for jogging, and that I could easily put together a five-mile route. As soon as I arrived at the Institute, I checked out the woods, and immediately chose that to be my new jogging experience. (Figure 20.3 shows one of the paths there.)

So I was adapting to and enjoying my new life in Princeton, and jogging my five miles each day. After a time, however, I began to experience a slightly strange sensation after running: It seemed I had to cough and sometimes the coughing was surprisingly hard to stop. It seemed to gradually get worse over the days, and I began thinking, "What am I doing that's so different from what I was doing in California?" One day, walking home through the woods, it struck me that back home I took a vitamin A capsule every day, and that I hadn't ever done that since leaving home. I was into reading about health, and had somehow got it into my head that vitamin A was exactly what I needed. I figured I would have to go to Princeton's Palmer Square and find somebody who carried this magic bullet. Grocery stores probably didn't carry that back then. As I continued walking and naturally looking down at the ground every so often, I saw a solution staring me right in the face: dandelion greens! They were full of all sorts of nutrition, including lots of vitamin A. Even better, they were completely fresh and part of nature. All I had to do was pick some of those greens and eat them. After just one bite, I saw that this bitter stuff was going to be an acquired taste, and resolved to acquire that taste right then and there. *I needed vitamin A.* I looked for greens that were clean, trying dark ones, medium-green ones, as well as younger lighter-green ones. They all tasted awful (some were worse than others), but I kept at it, munching on those little dandies and letting my body absorb all the good stuff in them. I did this for maybe a half hour or 45 minutes, until my belly seemed about half full with this marvelous potion. I was proud of myself. In a new land problems would arise, but you use your noggin to figure out solutions, and I had done that with my vitamin A problem.

As I entered my apartment, I felt rather triumphant; all I needed was time to let my body respond to this treatment, and things would get better. If needed, I could do this each day for as many days as needed! So I felt quite happy— quite happy, until I glanced into the bathroom mirror. *I was horrified!* Chewing and munching on those countless greens had stained my lips green. Not just somewhat green, but *very* green.

This required immediate attention. I pursed my lips together real tight and rubbed them with a bar of soap to remove the unsightly color. This led me to my second installment of horror: The soap didn't touch it. Those dandelion juices didn't just coat my lips, they actually penetrated in and stained them. I tried vinegar. Nope. I tried oil. Nope. I was running out of ideas, but I had some peanut butter and tried that. Nope again. The stain was there, and it wasn't about to go away. I couldn't possibly be seen in public looking like this. Did I want to hear about people saying "…you know, that skinny guy with the green lips…" That was not going to happen. So I made a decision: I was going to stay in my apartment until the green went away. I had no idea how long that might be, but I wasn't optimistic. I had enough food for a few days, so I turned into an unwilling recluse. Finally, on the fourth day, the stain had faded enough that I felt I could enter the real world again. I went to my office, and my office mate, who had not seen me for all this time, says, "What happened? You been sick or something?" I said I'd been a little under the weather. That was true…green lips had made me feel *way* under the weather for all that time. He never seemed to notice the faded green, and soon I was mostly back to normal. By the way, those dandelion leaves actually did help, and my cough subsided nicely. But it was vitamin A capsules from then on. I left those dandelion plants alone for the remainder of my two years at the Institute.

20.5 A lifetime habit

One day Hass and I were looking over his book's manuscript *Complex Analytic Varieties*, and at 2:30 I said I had to leave. This was about the third time I'd done that, and he asked, "What's going on?" I told him I ran each day at 3:00 in the Institute woods with a group of friends. At our next meeting, he said that he'd brought some running clothes to his office, and would like to join us. He was there promptly at 3:00. He ran alone, starting a couple of minutes after we'd begun. Next day I asked him how it went. "Well, I guess mowing the lawn once a week isn't enough. I got pretty winded!" He continued appearing at 3:00 and initially ran alone. After a week or so he started running alongside some of the slower folk. A few months later at a summer chamber music camp held at Bennington College in Vermont, he challenged me to a friendly race. He was tall, had long legs, and the sixty-year-old was now conditioned. He won easily. He had conquered running, saw its benefits, and adopted taking regular jogs for the remainder of his life.

Figure 20.3. The Institute woods proved ideal for jogging. This picture was taken almost exactly where Hass started his jogging career in 1966.

CHAPTER 21

The Unspeakable Was About to Happen

Hassler's influence on the author's teaching style

21.1 Day one...

It was 8:30 on a bracingly cold, clear morning. The air seemed especially clean and pure, and I was on my way to my first day of teaching. By that, I mean my *very* first day of teaching. I had never, ever taught a class before. I had resolved that I wanted to be a good teacher, and had prepared my inaugural lecture with great care. I felt confident as I entered the classroom filled with about 30 students, politely sitting and ready for the start of the semester. The course was on abstract algebra and ran from 9:00 to 9:50 three days a week.

I began with definitions and theorems, stating everything very carefully. My confidence increased and I relaxed a bit. It seemed that I was actually making a go of this teaching thing. Finally, I came to the last theorem of the lecture, and was feeling almost triumphant—no particular glitches or goofs, and I thought my delivery went smoothly. Great. Then I glanced at the clock, and my feeling of success turned to horror. It was only 9:30. I had 20 minutes to go—how could time go so slowly? Or was it that I covered the material much too quickly? Simply put, I had run out of everything I had planned to say. A moment flashed back to me during my time at UCLA. It was in an English class, and one time the youngish teacher said he had nothing more to say, and he let us out. He looked so apologetic; he was a nice person, and I felt sorry for him. In all my years there, this was the one and only time that ever happened to a teacher in class. Now, it seemed that *on my very first day*, the unspeakable was about to happen. I needed an emergency plan and I needed it fast. I paced back and forth in front of the class, trying to figure out what the heck to do. Yes, I kept smiling, and I believe it seemed that I was maintaining my cool, but inside, I was a wreck. Then I saw a lifeline. I decided to ask if there were any questions. Answering questions could take up time, and that would help me out of my hole. So I asked, and immediately everyone started looking at the floor, or the ceiling, or maybe to the right or left. No one looked at me, and there was not a peep from anyone.

"You're sure?" was my pitiful question. Continuing silence was announcing that they were very sure—no questions for the teacher. I continue my charade, pacing back and forth, desperately hoping for some plane B. Plan A was clearly a failure. Is *this* what teaching was going to be like for me? Was I starting off a career as one of the worst teachers ever? Then, somewhere out of my inner depths, came a very simple thought. What was perhaps the most important thing I had learned from Whitney? Did I not learn how basic examples are? Concrete examples? So I say to the class, "OK, we've gone over a bunch of definitions and results. It's time to go over what I've said, illustrating everything with examples!" I start drawing pictures on the blackboard—a straight line, a circle, a series of dots, a lattice, all illustrating different groups. People in the class seemed to wake up and begin to take an interest. How about the plane? What about all the points in the plane with rational coordinates? Before I knew it, it was going on 5 minutes till 10:00, and we were done. I had saved my skin, and a big high point for me is that in this process, two people actually asked questions!

That one moment of realization, remembering the mode of thought Whitney used all the time, was perhaps the most significant in my teaching career. It established my main method of teaching: Work with examples, examples, examples, and make them, along with counterexamples, your friends.

The things I learned from Whitney through observation and osmosis meant that subsequent lectures seemed to run almost by themselves. I found myself using a question-and-answer method that Hass often used in arguing through little problems. For example, was the first quadrant of the real plane a group? Somebody pointed out that it's closed under addition. Great. Someone else countered, "Yeah, but not closed under inverses!" Big victory for that student. OK, let's add in the third quadrant to take care of that—so now we have a group, right? Most agreed, sure, now it's a group. I hesitated. I wasn't so sure about that. *The teacher isn't sure?!* Finally someone noticed that with just the first and third quadrant, if you add one vector from the first quadrant to one in the third, the result could end up in the second or fourth. Brilliant! So we actually need all four quadrants. Those victories were psychologically good for the students, and things got to be more interactive.

All these aspects of teaching were things that naturally flowed out of Whitney's influence on me. He always took a rather dim view of formalizing things too much in mathematics. Seeing concrete examples and making sense of them was much more important to him, and I began to absorb and use this approach in teaching.

21.2 You could hear a pin drop

Fast forward ten years. I was teaching a course in differential equations, and illustrating theory and facts with lots of real-world examples had by then become second nature to me. One of my favorites was the suspended mass-and-spring problem, and the techniques used to solve its equation are the same in spirit as for solving many more general ordinary differential equations with constant co-efficients. In our idealized setup, one end of a spring is firmly attached to the ceiling, and a weight is attached to the other end. If you just leave this setup alone long enough, everything virtually stops moving, with the weight sitting quietly at a position of equilibrium. This setup is illustrated in Figure 21.1.

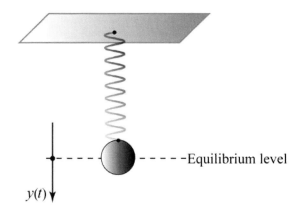

Figure 21.1. Pulling down on the mass and releasing makes the mass vibrate up and down.

If you now move the weight vertically down below equilibrium and let go, the stretched spring pulls the weight upward, and in this way an up-and-down vibration begins. Of course, if you again wait a long time, the vibrations get smaller and smaller because the system loses energy to its surroundings, and the system eventually becomes quiet again.

In all this, there's a grand total of five different quantities:

- The mass of the bob.
- The strength of the spring—how hard it is to stretch.
- How much damping there is. There's less in air, more in a liquid.
- Where the bob starts. That is, what's the initial vertical distance above or below equilibrium?
- The up-or-down velocity given to the bob as it is released.

Only after we know all five of these can we determine the exact motion of the system. That was the challenge of the students in this course—I (or the book) would specify five numbers, and from them they were to find the equation of motion. That is, they had to find the function $y(t)$, where t is time and $y(t)$ is how far below equilibrium the weight is at time t, as depicted in Figure 21.1. I also asked them to plot $y(t)$ so they would get a more visual understanding of the motion. Doing such problems kept them busy. Solving just one such problem could easily take 20 minutes—even longer if the function was a little more complicated and needed more data points to get a decent graph. (This was before the days of graphing calculators.)

As part of making these concrete examples of differential equations more meaningful to the students, we spent some time getting a rough, qualitative sense of what any particular setup would do physically. For example, if the weight was heavy—its mass M is large—and if the spring was weak—that is, its K is small— then the spring is very easy to stretch, so it didn't take much force to stretch it, say, 3 inches. These two things would mean the vibration is slow and sluggish; the wimpy spring couldn't pull up very hard on the massive bob, and so it would take a long time to finally get the weight up to equilibrium. On the other hand, a stiff spring would whip a small weight upwards very quickly, with a resulting fast rate of vibration. And how quickly would the vibration's amplitude decrease due to losing energy to the surroundings? In an ideal setup, there's no decrease in a vacuum, there's some in air, and the decrease is much faster in, say, water. We've talked about three quantities so far—the bob's mass M, the drag D leading to energy loss, and the stiffness of the spring K. The two remaining numbers tell us how the bob is released. Initial displacement tells where the bob is when we let go. We could let it go from rest, or instead give the bob a push up or down as we let it go—the initial velocity. So the students had to use the techniques introduced in the course to put all this information together to solve for and plot the bob's motion.

Enter, now, the main character of this story: the Commodore PET computer. At the behest of my wife's youngest brother, she bought the computer shown in Figure 21.2 in 1980 for $795. With 16K of memory, you could program it in BASIC, and a cassette port at the rear meant you could save your program on tape. I wasn't especially impressed with the computer, and big deal Ph.D. math dude Kendig decided to show its clear limitations right away, just so everyone would get a realistic perspective on things. I asked it to evaluate π raised to the e power—two transcendentals would keep the computer grinding away while I casually enjoyed lunch. What actually happened, however, was that the computer displayed a ten digit answer almost before I had taken my finger off the ENTER key. I was humbled, and it was I who got a realistic perspective on things.

I began to wonder what all this BASIC programming hoopla was about. The very first program I ever wrote in my life was for this computer—enter a number r and make it return the area of the circle of radius r. I got hooked in spite of myself, and began writing fancier and fancier programs. I even got to the point where if I entered the five quantities for the mass-spring problem, PET would return the solution. I was honestly impressed. But plotting? That was beyond

Figure 21.2. My wife bought this computer; it made many calculations effortless and fast.

the capabilities of the computer. The closest it would let me get to specifying a pixel was a round disk about an eighth inch in diameter. Little disks like this were great for playing ping-pong and other screen games, but it was just plain frustrating that I couldn't get to an actual pixel on the screen. Clearly each disk, each letter, each number, was composed of honest pixels, and when you looked at the dot over the letter i, you would see one pixel all by itself. I very much needed to get my hands on those pixels if I was to graph my solutions. I asked all sorts of people and basically got gibberish. I accidentally ran across an advertisement for a small circuit board that a PET owner could buy and install to access the pixels I needed. I jumped at the chance and ordered it right away. Not until many years later did I get up the courage to reveal the actual price to anyone in the family—at nearly $500, it was almost as expensive as the computer itself. I installed it with the utmost care, and that baby worked beautifully. I learned how to program it, and I finally got beautiful plots of solutions to the mass-spring problem. It was, in all honesty, pure joy to see that thing light up pixels on the screen, working from left to right, to give a more accurate plot than anything I could have done myself. An entire plot would appear in maybe five seconds.

I used this many times to check my own work and to see graphically what the textbook's mathematical solutions actually looked like. Then, I got a wild idea. *Why not take this to school and show it to the students?* The PET was pretty heavy, but I put it right beside me in the front seat of my car, with a seat belt around it, drove carefully, and made no sudden stops or turns. When I arrived at school, I put it on an appliance cart I had in my office, and pushed it all the way to my classroom, thirteen stories up in a building two blocks away. When I entered the room a little early, I immediately saw a look of surprise from those students who were already there. Was the teacher gonna show a movie? Or what? To them, it was a TV screen—a computer monitor was unfamiliar to almost all of them. I explained that this was a computer, and that I had programmed it to solve and graph the mass-spring problems they had been assiduously working on. By the time I had it plugged in and warmed up, the room was nearly full, and it was time to start the great demonstration. I asked the students how they did on the last batch of problems. They agreed that things were getting tough, and that it took quite a while to work out each solution, and even more time to get decent plots. Now it was time to let PET spring into action. We chose one of the harder problems, and I typed in the values of M, D, K, and the initial position and velocity of the bob. A second or so after I pressed ENTER, the solution's formula popped up on the screen, and then right below it, a gorgeous plot took shape. The students were just mesmerized. It was a reaction I had never seen before. Then I said, "How about if *you* choose some values for the bob's mass M, the spring's stiffness K, the amount of damping D, as well as the initial position and velocity of the bob?" One student chose M, another K, ... and I entered their five choices into the computer. Before we let PET do its thing, we made a qualitative, rough idea of what the solution should look like. Then I pressed the all-powerful ENTER key, and the solution appeared, followed by its plot. As the students were looking at this incredible performance, you could hear a pin drop.

We did this for the remainder of the class period. You could just sense in the students the tremendous amount of learning and development of intuition that was going on. One student chose a quite high value for D, and we all agreed that this was like putting the whole apparatus into molasses. There would be no vibration—just a slow return to equilibrium—making the system overdamped. PET's solution and plot reflected our guess perfectly. We did problem after problem, and we even took fixed values for M and K and experimented to see what damping D would just barely make the vibration disappear. We compared that with the theoretical answer and saw that we had gotten quite close.

As I walked out of the room that day, I thought two things: (1) If only Whitney could have witnessed the understanding that all those concrete examples could bring. (2) What had happened that day was big, big, big. It possibly represented a trickle that could turn into a rushing river and bring an exciting era to the mathematics department. That was pretty much what happened. Today, students at all levels use desktop computers to enhance understanding and make formulas come alive. It has been gratifying to see engineering students use Maple and Mathematica to solve problems, run "what if" scenarios, and continue to deepen their understanding of the real world.

CHAPTER 22
Sometimes You Get to Know People Through the Little Things

This collection of snippets helps illuminate our subject.

Hass had a mantra: "In mathematics, if you don't know what to do next, draw a picture."

◇——◇

"When you're trying to prove something in math and you keep running into obstacles, that might be because what you're trying to prove isn't true. Try using what you've been bumping against to search for a counterexample."

◇——◇

Hass was very concrete in his approach to math. He would find a specific example containing the essential idea and would work with it until he thoroughly understood it. He got critical insights by working with his example and used those insights to arrive at new results. After cracking the central nut in a new area, he'd often leave it to others to generalize.

◇——◇

Whitney thought very geometrically and drew lots of pictures. When it was time to write up a proof, he would reformulate the geometry in algebraic terms. But almost always his original inspiration was geometric.

◇——◇

He frequently looked for "geodesics" taken in a general sense: an especially short proof or argument, a simple counterexample, as well as the shortest route from one point to another. Somewhat related to this, he tended to leapfrog in life. In college he skipped Physics I and took but one math course, a graduate course on complex variables. From his early teens on, he was an avid mountain climber.

Through the years he gradually dispensed with all but the most essential safety equipment, ultimately using what is today called the "fast and light" technique of mountain climbing.

◇——◇

After a quartet session at his home, Hass asked, "When looking in a mirror, why is it that the right and left sides are reversed? Why not the top and bottom instead? And what's the story if you're lying on your side?"

◇——◇

After another quartet session, it was, "Suppose someone secretly switches the two thermostat controls of a heater blanket. What happens to the couple in bed?"

◇——◇

The Chamber Music Conference of the East is a music camp in which professional musicians coach amateur chamber players. It's held every August on the beautiful campus of Bennington College in Vermont. Hass went each year, and I did too after he introduced me to it toward the end of my first year at the Institute. There are all sorts of amateur chamber music groups—some quite good—and they get coached by experienced teachers hired by the conference. One morning Hass and I were walking to Jennings, the old mansion on the Bennington campus where music coaching takes place, and he suddenly asked, "Suppose a scrabble box contains squares printed with 1s and the operations +, −, ×, ÷, factorial, and exponentiation. If you're allowed to choose five 1s and five operations, what's the biggest number you can make?"

◇——◇

Once Hass and I were eating lunch in Bennington's dining room, and I happened to mention how clever Gauss was as a youngster, when he did the equivalent of adding all the integers from 1 to 100 by looking at $1 + 100$, $2 + 99$, $3 + 98$, $\cdots$— that is, 50 pairs of 101, which add up to 5050. Hass agreed that that was clever. Then, a moment later, he mused, "Suppose the sequence was shorter, like 2 to 99 instead of 1 to 100?" Nipping off the ends like that meant subtracting 1 and 100 from 5050. Hass chuckled, seeing that was 49-49 instead of 50-50. Immediately, the question was "OK, from 3 to 98?" *That* sum was 4848. So he had stumbled on a pretty pattern. And it worked all the way down, so that if we chopped off all but the innermost two digits 50 and 51, the sum is 0101. It even worked the other way, when you make the sequence grow at each end: 0 to 101 gives 5151, −1 to 102 gives 5252, and so on. We finished lunch before asking about what happens after the sum is 9999.

◇——◇

One evening it was time for Hass and me to help Mary with a little kitchen duty, and when it came to putting away the silverware, I stared blankly at the drawer of spoons, forks, and knives. It was a complete jumble and seemed entirely out of character for Hass. He sensed my reaction and explained, "It takes more time to keep everything organized and separate. On the other hand, it takes just about the same amount of time to find a fork, spoon, and knife whether they're organized or not, so in the end, this method saves time."

◇——◇

After the Whitney family moved into their new house further from the Institute, Hass would often use his bicycle instead of driving there. He had since childhood a strong proclivity for measuring things—his diary's entries during his trip to Switzerland on the steamship *Orbita* provides a nice window on that. (See p. 29.) Much later in life, true to form, Hass would measure the distance from home to various destinations. Keeping his bike in a fixed gear, he'd count the number of turns the bike pedal took to make the trip, and then on subsequent trips he would know when he was various fractions of the way there. Measuring was a constant in him.

◇——◇

One Christmas at Hassler's home, he and his son James each received a labyrynth maze as a present. (See Figure 22.1.) The two of them spent most of the morning playing this very challenging game. The playing plane's tilt is changed by turning two knobs, and the object of the game is to continually work the two knobs so the ball bearing makes it all the way from the Start point to the Finish without falling into any of the 59 holes. Of course Hass decided that a better way to play the game is to go from the Start to the Finish points *and back again*. With James also having a labyrynth maze, the two began running races. If there was even a small crack of light where a dull moment might creep in, Hass took care of that by making up a variation: One ball bearing is placed at the Start point, another at the Finish point, and then you play the game forwards and backwards simultaneously.

◇——◇

Whitney had a distinctly contrarian streak and often sought the opposite to the conventional or unwritten norm. As a kid, he learned to roller skate backwards almost as well as he did forwards. Later in life, when encountering a theorem new to him, he would often begin by trying to disprove it, looking every which way for some counterexample. After a period of rough and tumble, he often ended up

Figure 22.1. A labyrynth maze game.

with a depth of understanding that most people never get by merely accepting the theorem and reading through its proof. His approach seemed reminiscent of someone testing the strength of a fabric by trying to rip it. He tested the theorem for strength.

◇——◇

For several years, Deane Montgomery headed the School of Mathematics at the Institute and once said of Whitney: "If you were to ask a good sampling of first-rate mathematicians to list the top ten mathematicians in the world, Whitney would be on nearly everyone's list."

◇——◇

One afternoon at tea in the Institute's common room, Mary was chatting with Lars Ahlfors, the complex analysis luminary. He was a recipient of the Fields Medal the first year it was offered, and wrote the very popular text, *Complex Analysis*. After a while, Hass came over to Mary, and she was glad to see him, saying, "Hi, Hass!" Ahlfors shook Hass's hand warmly: "It's so nice to see you again, Hassler! How *are* you?!" Hass said fine, but looked somewhat confused. Who is this guy? Mary quickly picked up on things and said, "Hass, you remember Lars, don't you?" Lars? Lars? It still wasn't ringing a bell. Then Ahlfors said

"Lars Ahlfors…" Hassler brightened up, saying, "Oh, of course! Sorry." Mary smoothed things over a little, saying, "Lars has a different haircut." Hassler agreed, and then the two settled into a more normal conversation. Later, Hass came over to me, still feeling chagrined, and explained what happened in mathematical terms. "There are so many new people every year, it's hard to keep track, while there are just a few permanent members, so the visitors have a lot fewer people to remember."

When asked a question, if Hass wasn't sure of an answer, he'd politely demur. Once during tea in the common room, a topologist asked him a somewhat technical question in combinatorial topology. Hass replied that it had been such a long time since he had thought about questions in that area, he wasn't the best person to ask. This trait wasn't just in math. The famous French mathematician Henri Cartan was very closely involved in the Vietnam war. For example, he was politically engaged in efforts to free a number of people imprisoned in various countries because of their views on the war. The effects of war struck close to home for him—Cartan's brother was in the French resistance during WWII and was captured and executed. One afternoon at a chamber music get-together Cartan, an excellent pianist, asked Hass his opinion about some aspect of the war. Hass quickly responded, "There are so many things to have an opinion on, but this is one on which I have no opinion at all."

Hass hated feeling trapped in a situation he didn't like and would find some way to adroitly extricate himself from it. Once a number-theorist friend of mine at the Institute invited me to a party and decided to invite Hassler, too. Hass arrived late and quietly sat there, looking pretty bored. In fact everybody was just sitting around, with the conversation going nowhere. People would say something, trying to be a little funny, but as parties go, this dog wasn't hunting. I was starting to feel sorry for Hass and getting uncomfortable about how things were going. After maybe 20 minutes, someone made a quasi-joke about somersaulting, and Hass brightened up. "You mean, like THIS?" He immediately did an impressive somersault, landing right before the door. He stood up and announced that he needed to be somewhere else right about then. And that was that—Hass was free.

In high school or college, Hass almost never read through a mathematics text or worked through the book's problems. Instead, he would either make up his own problems, or run across a problem that intrigued him, and then learn whatever math was needed to solve it. He never functioned in a vacuum.

◇——◇

Hass seldom complimented himself, but one time after quartets at his home, he told us that earlier in the day Mary had stumbled upon his old high-school graduation suit. He tried it on, and although that graduation day was over 40 years ago, the suit still fit perfectly.

◇——◇

Hass was very proactive and acted on things that seemed wrong to him. This certainly had something to do with Hassler's later devotion to early mathematics education, which he found abysmal.

◇——◇

More broadly, if Hass felt that something was wrong, he did something about it, even if that meant going outside his comfort zone. Often it was just little things. For example, he almost never used the Institute for Advanced Study's shuttle going from Fuld Hall to Princeton's Palmer Square and back, but the one time he and I were in the van together, he asked the driver why he used a shortcut instead of the full route given in the Institute booklet. "Oh, I never take that—haven't for years!" The next day, the driver used the full route, and did from then on.

◇——◇

One winter, Hass and I were headed for an 8:00 orchestra rehearsal. It was dark, and as Hass was driving he saw someone walking on the right side of the road. Hass really started reacting, seeing so much that was wrong: "That fellow is making every possible mistake! He's walking *with* the traffic instead of against it. He's walking too far into the road. He's wearing dark clothing instead of light." He probably mentioned a thing or two more. Hass was careful about avoiding accidents and on occasion would dispense advice. He gave me a few driving tips that I still use: There's less tire traction going downhill versus level or uphill since the car's weight is at times less when going downhill, especially if you go fast. One should therefore drive slowly on a downhill curve. Another: After a dry spell, a light rain can turn dust on the road to a slippery coating. Once at a quartet session at his house, the violist put his instrument in the case and closed the cover but didn't snap it shut. Hass pointed out that by habit, you might just yank the case by its handle as you're ready to leave, and the instrument would then fall out onto the floor.

Hassler, by modern standards, was fairly conservative in his musical tastes. In his earlier years he would always listen to operas on Sundays—Wagner was a favorite. He intensively practiced Bach on the piano, and in chamber music we usually played Mozart, Beethoven, Brahms, or Schubert. In his later years, he developed a special fondness for Chopin, and also greatly appreciated Debussy. But twelve-tone or other music in which group theory plays a central role? To him, that just wasn't music. Group theory, he said, can be of great use in mathematics, physics, chemistry, crystallography, and other natural sciences, but to music it seemed basically misapplied.

◇——◇

Hass attended the Bennington Chamber Music Conference to be coached in chamber music, but there's also a scholarship program for composers in which each composer, during the conference, composes a piece that volunteer chamber players would learn and perform. Hass did not like that part of the Bennington experience at all, and one time back home he played some especially strange chords on his piano. "That sounds like something from one of those compositions written during the Bennington Conference!" Then, a moment later, "Oh, no—I forgot!" and he stood up, leaned over the piano and began plucking some treble piano strings with his right hand and playing weird chords with his left. Hass generally didn't criticize others much, but when it came to music he didn't like, he could be disarmingly frank.

◇——◇

Around May, the conference mails everyone a circular listing the current coaches, fees, housing accommodations and such, and the circular's cover always has a photo of some group rehearsing. At his home he showed me the cover of the circular he had just received: It's of a string quartet, and you can see the first violinist's music on the stand. Of course the printed photo, at perhaps 300 dots per inch, means the music is pixilated, so you can't really tell what they're playing. But the challenge of figuring that out caught his interest. He asked me, "What do you imagine they're rehearsing?" Of course I had no idea, but his interest was totally aroused. You could make out that there's a good-sized heading at the top of the page, so they must be on the first page of a quartet. He made out just nine staves on the page, fewer than what's typical, and then he invited me to ponder density. Certain parts of the page are darker, meaning that there must be a run of fast notes at those places. He spotted an upward swoop of darkness at the page's left bottom. Well, he surely knew his Beethoven quartets—those are what sparked his interest in chamber music in the first place—and he blurted out, "Waitaminute—it's got to be Opus 95! Violin I has a big run up the scale in the first movement!" He pulled out his copy of Opus 95, and we compared. There were indeed nine staves, and the big fast-note run was printed on his page just where it appeared on the cover. He seemed satisfied and somewhat delighted by his detective work.

It's fair to ask why one would spend time on such a trivial question, but this opens a little window on how Hass operated. Math is often discovered through making a guess based on incomplete evidence and then trying to verify it. That's what happened here. This was just for fun, but he was typically ready for a challenge, big or little—it just ran in his blood. I'd guess conquering mountain peaks fell into the same category; the spirit of striving toward a goal seemed to be a constant in him. Of course Hass chose with great care which problems to work on in his professional life as a mathematician. In working on such a problem, he'd usually have a hunch, then follow it by exploring many concrete examples and collecting evidence. Using what he learned through working through those examples, he would finally turn to proving his hunch.

◇──◇

Related to the above story is a comment Hass made once about the slide rule, which played an important part in his early mathematical development. "As part of using a slide rule, people always grab hold of the upper/lower rails, keeping them stationary, and move the middle slider. But you could just as well keep the middle slider fixed and move the other part."

◇──◇

A story for algebraists: A cello comes with an end-pin at its bottom, which goes into the floor to keep the instrument from sliding. To protect the floor, cellists often use a little wooden block to stick the end-pin in. Mine was typical: A loop of wire attached to the block went behind the two front legs of the chair, and I always used this. Henri Cartan called it my "inseparable extension."

◇──◇

For music aficionados: In printed music, a movable clef's center of symmetry or "leftward pointer" points by definition to middle C. In Figure 22.2, for example, is the alto (or viola) clef, in which the middle line of the staff is middle C. During a break in an evening of string quartets, Hass mirthfully asked, "In printed music, the notes are always moved up and down to represent pitch. But why not keep all the notes on the same line and put the correct clef before each note?" He left me wondering, "Who else in all the world would have thought of that?!"

Figure 22.2. The alto clef. By definition, its vertical center of symmetry lies on middle C.

◇──◇

Hassler's first instrument was the piano, and he took regular lessons until around the time he entered college. He was especially attracted to Bach and throughout his life worked to master a variety of his keyboard compositions. He had also acquired the rudiments of violin playing. Later on in college, Hassler heard one of Beethoven's late quartets—regarded by many musicians as some of the greatest music ever written—and was so moved by it that he decided to focus seriously on the violin so he could play that and other string quartets. When he was a young professor at Harvard, his children James, Carol, and Molly were exposed to Sunday opera and learned, for example, the intense story of *Tristan und Isolde*. His love for the pure, poetic music of Chopin ran deep; appropriately, his piano music was played at Hassler's memorial service. Portraits of six of his favorite composers are shown in Figure 22.3.

◇──◇

One year at the Bennington music camp, he struck up a friendship with our family physician in California, Dan Weston. Dan was an avid chamber music player and he and Hass got along famously. One summer, out of the blue, Dan phoned Hass and says, "Why don't you come on out to Santa Monica and we'll play Brahms sextets at Keith's house! I'll get some really good players to join us." (Actually, Dan gave free medical service to professional players who would join him in chamber music.) Dan could be very persuasive, and Hass was almost immediately on board. He came, immensely enjoying himself, and his daughter Carol flew in for the occasion. My mom cooked a splendid dinner for everyone, and at one point, Hass took three or four sprigs of parsley and arranged them in a sort of tree on his plate. He said to me, "Oh my—a parsley-ordered set!"

◇──◇

In August, 1971, I was attending the annual chamber music workshop held at Bennington College. The workshop always provided slots of free time between coaching for groups to get together and just read through music for fun. One

Figure 22.3. Clockwise from upper left: Bach, Beethoven, Wagner, Schubert, Mozart, Chopin.

time a woodwind quintet was having a get-together like this. The door was open, and the group sounded very good. Others must have thought so too, because a number of people were standing at the doorway listening. I couldn't see into the room, but enjoyed listening just the same. After 15 minutes or so, the group had finished their impromptu performance and people began to disperse. I see Hass leaving the room, and he seemed extremely emotional—I had never seen him like this before. I must have looked at him somewhat agape, and he said, almost apologetically, "Proud papa..." and kept walking. It was then that I saw his 15-year-old daughter Sally putting away her oboe. So *she* was one of those mellifluous voices! Music was an intense part of Hassler's life, and seeing his young daughter progressing so beautifully, joining so seamlessly with others to create beautiful music—that touched him in a deep way.

◇——◇

Hass was never one to spend a lot on personal belongings, but he once had an opportunity to buy a remarkable viola whose seductive tone proved too much to resist. The instrument was made by the Italian master Matteo Gofriller (1659–1742); Nicolo Paganini owned a Gofriller violin, and Pablo Casals, a Gofriller cello. On one very special occasion, Jascha Heifetz' well-known pupil, Erick

Friedlander, played quartets with us and used his superb Stradivarius violin. A Princeton graduate student played second violin, Hass played his Gofriller and I was on the cello. Beautiful instruments can make beautiful music, and that evening was the most memorable during my time at Princeton.

Figure 22.4. Hass playing the viola. The picture on the wall is by his mother.

◇——◇

Hassler's passion for mountain climbing continued unabated throughout his life. When he was 80, he needed someone with whom to climb his favorite mountain in the Swiss Alps. None of the younger climbers wanted any part of it, but through persistence he eventually found a professional guide. The guide was nearing retirement but was eager to make the ascent. However, well into the climb the guide became more and more winded and finally asked, "Could you please slow down a bit? After all, I'm nearly 65."

◇——◇

Terry Tao of UCLA is one of the brightest math talents today and is sometimes called "The Mozart of Mathematics." In a 2006 interview with the Los Angeles Times, Tao said that a lot of mathematicians liken what they do to rock climbing:

"You want to get to the top of the cliff. But that's not what you focus on immediately. You focus on the next ledge just beyond your reach, because you need to do one clever thing to get up there. And then once you're there, you do it again. A lot of this is rather boring and not very glamorous. But you can't jump cliffs in a single bound."

◇——◇

The Whitney-Gilman ridge on Cannon Mountain in New Hampshire was named after Hassler and his cousin Bradley Gilman; they first made the now-famous climb when Hass was an undergrad at Yale. The Whitney-Gilman ridge has a well-deserved reputation as a difficult climb.

◇——◇

Hassler's daughter Emily particularly enjoyed family mountain trips and did some additional mountaineering with Hass. She said that a lot of people don't "get" the draw of mountain climbing, but she and her dad shared the same feelings about it. She said, "It separated us from the ordinary world and transported us to a special, magical place." I think Hass often felt the same way when immersed in music or math.

◇——◇

Hass took dozens of photos with his home-built camera when climbing various mountains. He had many of these framed and hung them in his offices, both at home and at the Institute. Each was labeled with the name of the location or peak. In this way he was constantly surrounded by many of his fondest memories.

◇——◇

In the summer of 1971 Hass, Mary, Sally, and Emily visited the Grand Canyon en route to a two-week Sierra Club trip in the California Sierras. They arrived late at their hotel near the rim of the Grand Canyon and found there was not a single place open to buy food. With nothing to eat that night, Hass said "I guess we'll just have to tighten our belts!" After a good breakfast the next morning, the foursome hiked down to the bottom of the Grand Canyon and walked around, finally locating a good place to camp for the night. They started hiking back up well before dawn so they'd arrive at the top before it got too hot. As they were making their way up the steep parts of the Grand Canyon, Hass said, "Take it slow so we can keep up the pace." A group of young men passed them and one remarked, "Look at that old man hiking—s-o-o-o slo-o-o-w!" Not long after that, Hass, Mary, Sally, and Emily passed the group, all sitting on a big rock and panting. Hassler's advice of slow and steady paid off.

Each morning in his office at home, Hass would go through an exercise routine—squats, push-ups, pull-ups, and so on, to maintain his body strength as well as flexibility. He felt that doing this was essential to safe and enjoyable mountain climbing. He wasn't afraid to challenge himself: When he was 80, he decided to see how he would fare in a 26-mile marathon. He ran not to win, but just to see how far he could go. At around 20 miles he stumbled on a crack in the sidewalk and began walking. He then decided that at 80, he was a bit too old to run a marathon for the first time, but was quite pleased with how far he had gone.

Hass could be impulsive. His wife Mary had just put on her apron to prepare some dinner, when Hass got a bright idea. "Let's have dinner at the Institute!" The Institute has a very nice restaurant. The menu varies each day, and the food is always good. As a convenience, the restaurant will even keep refrigerated a member's favorite bottle of wine. So Hass, Mary, Sally, and Emily each threw on something warm and piled into their car for the short trip to the Institute. When they arrived, Mary discovered that she still had her apron on. Hassler traditionally paid after eating, but this time he forgot and the cashier came rushing after him saying "Professor Whitney, you forgot to pay!" Hass, embarrassed at his forgetfulness, immediately paid. It was just a time to forget. Going out to the car—a new Plymouth with fresh license plates RPN 573—Hass asked if anyone could think up a good mnemonic for remembering "RPN." It suddenly came to Sally: "RPN stands for Remember, Pay Now!"

The experience as a kid of carrying out projects appearing in *Popular Science* never entirely left Hass, and he would occasionally get the itch to build a little something. On one occasion he constructed a miniature door so their two cats could go in or out of the house on their own. It was hinged at the top, making it easy to push open and it would close by itself. Another time, he thought of a nice project to do with his daughters Sally and Emily: Make a cardboard cylinder and cover it with frosting to create a fake cake. The three of them cut out foot-wide disks and a long rectangle that would wrap around to made a cylinder. With plenty of Scotch tape, they soon had the basic foundation. The three of them whipped together a frosting and applied it. When Mary came home, she was greeted with a wonderful surprise! It became, however, less wonderful when she discovered the thing was a complete fake. She assumed there had to be an actual cake to follow the "surprise." There wasn't. When an idea entered Hassler's head, that idea mostly drowned out everything else, including possible reactions from others. As the years passed, he became increasingly aware of this tendency and became more thoughtful and empathetic.

◇——◇

Mary would periodically get a cold or the flu, running a fever. Although Hass seldom got sick, during one of Mary's bouts she worried that her germs might have spread, and told Hass he'd better take his temperature, just to be sure. Hass said okay. When Mary wasn't looking at him, he winked at his two daughters, put a spoonful of hot chicken noodle soup in his mouth, then put the thermometer in. He took out the thermometer three or four minutes later, and of course it said he had a raging fever. Mary was totally alarmed. Sally writes, "Emily and I, both preteens, were in on the joke and the whole thing seemed incredibly funny. It took a while but, with Hass actually just fine, my mother had to admit that Hass had 'got' her on that one."

◇——◇

Hass was happy and excited to learn that I was about to get married. My wedding to Joan was on Sunday, June 15, 1969 at her godmother's large home; I invited Hass, and he really looked forward to coming. The whole affair was an excellent example of how a beautiful wedding, full of good feelings and warmth, could be had on just a shoestring. I was marrying into a very resourceful and financially prudent family. Hass arrived quite early while everyone was still scurrying around with last-minute arrangements, and picked up on the energy around him. He really related to it all—it had the right vibes and he immediately opened up. Joan's maiden name was Nowicki, and I'd already nicknamed the swirl of two parents and their five energetic kids "Nowickorama." Except for travel, Hass, too, was frugal. He had simple tastes, a rather ordinary car, and got dressed up only for special occasions. In later conversations I realized how impressed he was with the way the family put together an especially beautiful day without financial excesses.

Joan baked a beautiful four tier carrot cake. Being health-conscious, she used honey instead of commercial sugar, but it turned out that the honey had a mind of its own: The frosting refused to set, and the layers kept slipping—as in *slipping all the way off* if you weren't paying attention. It was right in the middle of this evolving fiasco that Hass rang the doorbell, and he came right over to me as I'm struggling, trying to figure out what to do. Somehow I got the idea that a wooden dowel might save the day, and the homeowner went down to the basement and returned with a quarter-inch dowel that looked like it might work. I stuck it straight down through the four layers, Hass watching with great interest. Except for a very few others nearby, it was my little secret, and during dinner I couldn't help but look up every so often to be sure it was holding. That dowel was a trooper. After dinner, it was my job to cut the wedding cake, and of course after cutting the top layer the dowel's end stuck up and then everyone could see it. With subsequent layers, it stuck up even more, but I acted like lots of wedding cakes were made that way. After everyone had tasted the cake, and feeling generally triumphant about things—I'd repeated the vows without a goof, the ring that refused to go on my finger during the vows finally got on thanks to applying one big push, and the dowel had worked for me—I stood up and said, "Everyone in favor of the cake, say 'Aye!' " There was a nice chorus of ayes. Then Hass, totally into the spirit and thoroughly enjoying himself, stood up and dramatically sniffed the cake, announcing, "Ah-h-h, and also the NOSE!"

◇——◇

One afternoon Hass phoned me. He sounded a bit upset, not his usual self. It turned out that he and Mary were going out for the evening, and they needed a babysitter—the one they'd set up suddenly couldn't make it, and all their backups were unavailable. Any chance I could fill in? That was something new to me, but sure, I'd be willing. I found myself getting somewhat nervous as the time got near—I had never babysat before. What, exactly, was I supposed to do? Sally was 11 and Emily 9, so obviously they could put themselves to bed. Should I just read a book on my own? Entertain them? When I arrived, they seemed really happy to see me, which was helpful. After Hass and Mary left, I said something slightly funny, and they laughed, putting me at ease. So telling funny stuff seemed to be the way to go. At one point I told them about the guy who comes in from a downpour and his friend says, "Boy, it's really raining cats and dogs out there!" The drenched guy says, "Yes, I know—I just stepped in a poodle!" The two of them went into gales of laughter, like it was one of the funniest things they'd ever heard. Those two put me completely at ease, and before I knew it, it was bedtime. It ended up being a very pleasant experience.

◇——◇

When Hass threw a party, he always set up a large jigsaw puzzle in his daughters' playroom. Mathematicians being mathematicians, there were always a few of them gathered around the table, working on the puzzle. His favorite puzzle was hand-made: Instead of pieces having only the more common shapes, this one had a good sprinkling of shapes related to things he loved—mathematical ones like ellipses, spirals, everywhere concave pieces with cusps, as well as boots reminding one of mountain climbing. There were also a few animals, for which he always had a soft heart. Today, a scene printed on heavy cardboard rectangle is turned into a jigsaw puzzle by pressing, with several tons' force, a fancy cookie-cutter template over the scene to create separate pieces. Originally, however, a jigsaw puzzle was made exactly as the name implies: A jigsaw was used to cut apart the individual pieces, and that's how Hassler's favorite puzzle was made.

◇——◇

There is a beautiful pond at the south-west corner of the Institute campus:

Figure 22.5. The Institute pond.

One day Hassler decided to take his two daughters Sally and Emily to the pond to carry out "a little scientific experiment." He had his daughters find a few empty Kodak film canisters and the three headed for the pond, where the daughters' mission was to fill the cannisters with water taken from various parts of the pond. They collected samples reachable from the pond's edge, including the pond's surface, as well as underneath a lily pad, and the bottom of the pond's edge where there was scum. The cannisters were appropriately labeled, and once home, they set up the family microscope. The three of them compared microbial activity with pond location. They discovered that the greatest amount of activity came from the edges and at the bottom of the pond, and the least at the top and away from the pond's edges. For Sally, this experience began a lifetime interest in biology. Hass had also helped the girls with math, and in Sally's case the two subjects came together as her life's calling: She became a professor of biostatistics.

◇——◇

Hass felt that the life blood of mathematical progress is experimentation. All too often, schools reject experimentation because that sounds too much like guessing, which students aren't ever supposed to do. "It's nonsense to discourage reasonable guessing and estimating. One of the most important ways of making progress in mathematics is to make an educated guess, and then seeing if it works out. In fact, when I need to find the numerical size of something, I'll usually start with an estimate—call it a guess if you wish—and then calculate to see how close I was. Sometimes that estimate is way different from the calculation, and that's because I made a mistake in calculating! I might not have discovered that mistake if I hadn't made that initial guess. Estimating and making shrewd guesses is healthy science and should be encouraged early on in children."

◇——◇

Whitney attached tremendous importance to how kids were exposed to math in the earliest years. He once made this very concrete when he reminded me of something I had vividly experienced myself. He said, "If after a long absence you revisit your childhood home, you'll likely be struck at how much smaller it looks today. An 'Aha!' moment in discovering something as a kid can be remembered as a really big thing later in life and can be a very important psychological building block."

◇——◇

Whitney felt that one of the most useful things a math teacher can do for children is creating problems with an "Aha!" experience lurking within. He distinguished between tactical versus strategic math, and commiserated that so much of the math kids are exposed to is tactical—the answer is found by just grinding it out. In strategic math, a bit of imagination can lead to a quick answer and an "Aha!" moment. A series of such victories—even if they're small—can make a child feel powerful and have a lasting effect on his or her confidence. (One example of the kind of problem Hass had in mind is the handout shown in Figure 18.1 on p. 239.)

◇——◇

By the time Hass was 16, he was into sports in a big way. He played tennis and soccer, swam competitively (including underwater swimming), and learned to ski and ski-jump. Ice skating was always especially important to him, and later, when his son James was a small boy, they'd go to the frozen pond at the rear of their property and practice figure skating. Hass, looking at their tracks, would analyze what they'd done. Hass eventually became a judge at professional ice skating contests. Two decades later Hass similarly introduced his daughters Sally and Emily to ice skating, and they eventually took lessons in both figure and free skating. Ice skating grew to be an enjoyable and important part of their lives for several years. Later, Hass taught ice dancing.

◇——◇

Hassler received a number of honors and prizes in mathematics. From President Jimmy Carter he received The National Medal of Science in 1976 "…for founding and bringing to maturity the discipline of differential topology." Hass, Mary, and several other family members attended the White House ceremony held about a year later, and afterward all enjoyed a wonderful lunch hosted by the President. Hass had the award certificate framed but typical of his modesty, hung it in his home study's closet. In 1982, he received the Wolf Prize in mathematics which was considered, along with the Fields Medal and the Abel Prize, the closest equivalent to the Nobel Prize. (Myths notwithstanding, there's no Nobel in mathematics simply because it never occurred to Nobel to include mathematics.)

On the way to Israel where the prize was to be presented, Hass and his daughter Sally were in the John F. Kennedy International Airport in New York. Although Hass was then 75, he still had his youthful spirit, and when he noticed that the down escalator had no one on it, he impulsively decided to act on a fun challenge: He and daughter made a grand sprint up the down escalator to the next level. In 1985, he received the Leroy P. Steele Prize, awarded annually by the American Mathematical Society.[1] He also won, in 1969, the Mathematical Association of America's Lester Ford Prize for his paper on "The Mathematics of Physical Quantities" which appeared in the *American Mathematical Monthly*. He was elected to the National Academy of Sciences as well as to the American Philosophical Society.

◇——◇

Hass created the round in Figure 22.7 on p. 308 by composing music to go with an anonymous "Butterfly poem" that captured so much of his inner core. This poem fits in perfectly with his strong belief that life is no spectator sport—that you live and learn through involvement. That applied to children learning math as well: Let them actively test, explore, make mistakes, find, and correct them. It's what he did from his earliest years—using his wings to break out and fly.

◇——◇

Hass didn't mind mowing the lawn. But when it came to shoveling snow, that was a different matter. "Nature put the snow there. Nature can take it away!"

Figure 22.6. Hassler in 1981, shortly before receiving the Wolf prize.

◇——◇

The name Hassler comes from the German "hasel" meaning hazel, and "hasel-er" derives from one living in an area where hazelnuts grow.

◇——◇

In 1987 Hassler married Barbara Osterman, an artist. When he started talking marriage, she said she couldn't marry someone who didn't dance. "No problem," replied Hass, "I have taught ice dancing!" In his eighties, Hass would get up at dawn and jog about six miles, then bring her a cup of hot tea as she awoke. When they were first married, Barbara could walk perhaps half a mile, but Hass had a way of influencing people; in 2015 at nearly 90, she would regularly walk three miles, saying that this contributed to maintaining her excellent health. She once

Figure 22.7. Hass wrote this four-voice round based on an anonymous poem that spoke to his heart.

commented that Hassler's highly geometric mind influenced her artistic style, and found herself increasingly using the left side of her brain in artwork. When Hass ran math classes for young children, Barbara helped by making appealing manipulatives such as colorfully painted wooden tongue depressors. These creations made basic counting facts more concrete, and the kids loved her upbeat artistic touch. She and Hass would regularly take long walks to absorb the beauty

Figure 22.8. A four voice quartet: Mary, Emily, Sally, and Hass.

of nature. And he would end each day by playing on the piano Chopin's Berceuse in d-flat major, Op. 57, a set of sixteen variations on a hauntingly beautiful four-measure melody. The piece is like a stream of liquid tonalities. These golden years were happy ones for Hass—he knew a quietude and inner peace often missing in his earlier years. Unfortunately, however, there were too few of these years. Although he had apparently been in excellent health, in 1989 he suffered a severe stroke and died just two weeks later. Shortly before his death, his Institute colleague Freeman Dyson paid a visit, relaying news and gossip about the Institute. Hassler's eyes were closed and he didn't speak, but Hassler held Freeman's hand with such strength that Freeman vividly remembered that a quarter century later.

Hass died in Princeton, May 10, 1989 at age 82. He and Barbara had never bothered to talk about death, but Hass wouldn't ever have wanted anything fancy. Fate seemed to intervene: Hassler's Institute colleague Armand Borel and his wife Gaby wanted to "do a little something nice" for Barbara. Barbara recalled, "I had agreed to join the couple for dinner that night; earlier in the day I had received his ashes and had them in the car. Gaby, at dinner, insisted on helping somehow and said she was leaving for Switzerland the next morning. It suddenly occurred to me that it would be especially nice if Hassler were on his favorite mountain, Mont Dent Blanche, with all his friends. I asked her if she knew

Figure 22.9. Hass and Barbara in June of 1988.

anyone in the Swiss Alpine Club. 'Of course, my nephew Oscar!' she replied. I
gave her the container, asking if Oscar might scatter his ashes atop the mountain that held a lifetime of memories for Hass. Hass had climbed this peak many
times, and was his absolute favorite. It's a challenging climb, and it took several
tries before his fellow mathematician and mountaineer Oscar Burlet succeeded
in getting them to the top on August 20, 1989." Gaby included a heartfelt tribute
to Hass: She used a dentist's drill to carve out his name, birth and death dates on

a little stone, and had Oscar place it on Mont Dent Blanche among the scattered ashes.

Figure 22.10. Mt. Dent Blanche in the Pennine Alps, Valais, Switzerland.

CHAPTER 23

Parting Shots: A Gallery of Photos

Hundreds of photos of Hass and his family taken over more than four decades tell a story that words can't. They show Hass and various family members mountain climbing, music making, dancing, or Hass simply communing with Nature or enjoying young children. Most of these photos are informal, snapped by a family member to catch a moment in time. They give a glimpse of the tenderness, love, energy, and adventure that seemed to surround Hass and his family.

Hass cradles newborn Sally.

Hass greatly enjoyed his children, and vice versa. Sally is about two years old here.

Hassler is biking with precious cargo—Emily at four.

One year later, he's helping her get her wheels.

Right after Molly and Hugh's wedding ceremony, Emily and Sally wanted to visit the surf. They changed clothes for it but Hass, not so much—he's still in his suit from the wedding.

L to R: Molly, Hassler's mother Josepha, and Carol.

Molly, groom Hugh Melhuish, and Molly's approving mom Brock.

Hass does some bouldering, which is rock climbing close to the ground with no rope.

Carol, age 14, rock climbing at Quincy Quarry near Boston.

Molly rappelling off a Quincy Quarry climb. Hassler considered Molly to be the most athletic of his children. She took to rock and mountain climbing like a duck takes to water.

"Look Dad—no hands!" On a 1971 trip to the Sierra Nevada mountains, Molly shows her stuff.

Molly (top) and Emily rock climbing in the Sierras.

James did some rock and mountain climbing, too!

Like Hass, Carol's musical interest is intense. Here, she's playing the Flamenco guitar. She is also facile on the bonang (a set of tuned metal drums in the Javanese gamelan) and more recently, on the handpan. The handpan is a modern invention in the world of musical instruments; Carol's dates from about 2000 and is 21 inches wide. A handpan typically looks like a flying saucer with circular indentations distributed around its top half. Each indentation, when struck by the hand, emits a hollow-sounding, mellow pitch. She has a Ph.D. in ethnomusicology.

Molly caught the music bug, too. Here she is in 1954, playing the flute.

Brock in 1945 with her children Carol, James, Molly, and family dog.

Here are James, Carol, and Molly about seven years later.

A greatly magnified section of a landscape taken in 1945 of Carol, Brock, and Hass. The family collie shows his affection.

A happy day! Mary and Hass at their wedding in January, 1955.

Hass and Mary cut the wedding cake.

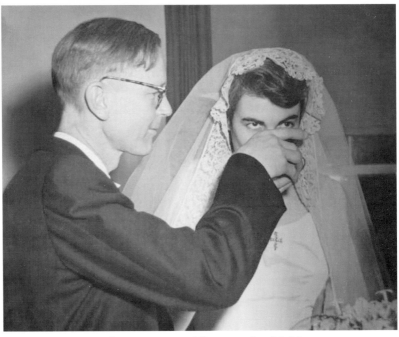

Hass shares some wedding punch with Mary.

In this 1962 photo, Sally, Mary, Hass, and Emily are outside the airport terminal, ready for a trip.

At the family dinner the night before Sally's wedding day: Hass, Barbara, Emily, Sally, groom George Thurston, Lillian, and James with their children Jon and Larisa.

Hass provides music at Sally and George Thurston's wedding ceremony in June, 1988.

Hass and Barbara at their wedding reception in February, 1986.

As Barbara's son Mark sings and plays the banjo, Hass and Emily dance at Hass and Barbara's wedding. The girl facing us is James's daughter Larisa.

Never a dull moment! At Hassler's home the day after marrying Barbara, Hassler's grandchild Amber (Emily's daughter) enjoys a game of chess.

Barbara and Hassler. His typical gestures when making a point remind us of the photo on p. 234.

Early on, a mutual fondness developed among Carol, Emily, and Sally. Carol found it gratifying to see the two sisters progress in life.

Carol and Sally—best buddies from way back.

Hass enjoying the beach with Molly's children Anne and Jamie.

Picnictime with Sally.

To Hass, seeing views like this was an important part of mountaineering. This photo was snapped by Mary; the children are Emily (middle) and Sally.

Hass was always attracted to the grandeur of Nature.

Throughout his life, Hass loved to be in inspired surroundings like this.

Notes

Chapter 1: *Some Snapshots*

1.1 [p. 6]. Lev Pontryagin was a Soviet mathematician and prominent contemporary of Hassler; their interests in topology and differential topology overlapped significantly. When Lev was 14 he lost his eyesight from an exploding pressurized kerosene heating stove. His mother supported his budding interest in mathematics and later read him books and papers, including those of Whitney. Pontryagin did foundational work in compact groups—groups supplied with a topology for which the groups were locally compact. Two familiar examples are $\mathbb{Z}$, the integers under addition, and $\mathbf{o}$, a circle made into a "continuous clock" by essentially identifying time with the angle of the hour hand. He studied continuous mappings of compact groups into the circle group. The set of all such mappings of a compact group G can itself be made into a compact group G^* known as the Pontryagin dual. The Pontrjagin dual of $\mathbb{Z}$ is topologically $\mathbf{o}$, and the Pontryagin dual of $\mathbf{o}$ is topologically $\mathbb{Z}$.

Chapter 3: *Growing Up*

3.1 [p. 27]. The "Law of the Cube" goes back to Galileo's 1638 work, *Two New Sciences*, where he called it the "Square-Cube law." He regarded it as one of his greatest discoveries, and in fact it does apply to an extraordinarily wide variety of natural phenomena. The law says that as the linear dimension of an object is multiplied by a factor m, the surface area varies as the square m^2 and the volume varies as the cube m^3. We can see this intuitively using a cube of edge length 1 and taking $m = 2$. If each edge of the cube is doubled to 2, the surface area of each side goes from 1 to $2^2 = 4$, and the volume goes from 1 to $2^3 = 8$. From this, one can see the general law: Divide the volume of a lump of coal into many tiny disjoint cubes, and similarly divide its surface into many disjoint squares. If the lump is uniformly magnified by a factor of 2, then every one of those cubes is increased in volume by a factor of 8, and each square's area goes up by a factor of 4. This applies just as well to airplanes as a lump of coal, and lift, being a function of wing surface area, increases more slowly than volume. Aeronautical engineers overcame this problem by redesigning wings to produce greater lift, and using lighter materials to decrease weight.

Galileo's law also applies to a rich variety of other physical phenomena. As an example, it says a lot about just how big living things can get. All other things being equal, why couldn't there be a human 60 feet tall instead of 6 feet? For one thing, 150 lb person would weigh $10^3 = 1000$ times as much, 150,000 lb. Muscle strength is more closely correlated with muscle cross-section than with

345

muscle mass, so one's strength would increase by only about $10^2 = 100$. Relative to the increased weight, this person would have only a tenth the strength as a normal human. Could this person walk? Even stand up? Since bones are only so strong, those would crumble under all that tremendous weight, making moot any question about walking or standing up! Analogous considerations apply to how big trees can get. Even aquatic animals like whales, aided by buoyancy, can grow only so large—Galileo's law would eventually catch up with them. Instead of 10 times taller, how about a tenth, or a hundredth as tall? A flea, with its spindly legs and relatively larger body, is famous for its high jumps. And many small bugs can lift many times their own weight—if their weight is $(\frac{1}{10})^3 = 0.001$ that of a larger animal, their strength is $(\frac{1}{10})^2 = 0.01$, making them relatively ten times stronger. A man can perhaps lift his own weight, while some dung beetles can easily pull over a thousand times their weight. It's safe to say that no 150 lb man could pull 150,000 lb, or some 75 tons.

The Law of the Cube applies to many other everyday situations. Take the heating up or cooling down of masses (volumes). An ice cube 1 inch on each edge will melt a lot faster than a cube of ice 10 inches on each side. Melting rate comes down to how fast heat is transferred from the room to the ice, and this transfer takes place across surface area. The more surface area there is per unit of volume of ice, the faster the melting. For the 1-inch cube, there's 6 square inches of area across which the room's heat can pass to melt 1 cubic inch. What about the 10-inch cube? That contains 1000 cubic inches, has 600 square inches of surface, so $\frac{600}{1000} = 0.6$ square inches of surface for each cubic inch of ice, just a tenth of an individual 1-inch cube. The big cube will take a lot longer to melt, and an iceberg can take months to melt. A snowflake might melt at room temperature in less than a minute. The same considerations apply to cooling: A big pot of tea will cool down more slowly than a small cup poured from the pot, and a teaspoon of tea will cool down even faster. Small animals are like a cup or teaspoon, so little puppies often sleep snuggled together to conserve heat—a bunch of puppies huddled together is like a pot of tea. At the opposite extreme, elephants have much less surface area compared to volume, and their large ears aren't primarily for extra keen hearing, but to increase surface area through which body heat can pass to prevent overheating.

The Law of the Cube famously applies to chemical reactions, too. For example, in combining with oxygen, a large surface area relative to volume means a faster reaction. In starting a campfire it makes sense to start with small twigs; they have a larger surface area per volume. In a gas motor, a carburetor turns fuel into a mist, increasing the fuel's surface area so much that a spark can ignite it explosively to suddenly heat up and expand the air above the cylinder, thus giving a push to turn the crankshaft. Gun powder is a powder for a good reason—the great surface area means a violently fast chemical reaction. Even mundane substances in powder form can be very explosive: Sawdust, flour, powdered sugar, or pollen, as a cloud in a confined space containing enough air, can explode with just a spark. The picture below shows one real-life consequence of Galileo's Law of the Cube.

A rare 1947 photograph capturing a Kansas mill exploding after a spark ignited clouds of suspended flour.

3.2 [p. 33]. Hass was certainly right—in the usual plane, we don't see points to the left or right of the circle because their y-coordinates are imaginary: Plugging any $|x| > 1$ into $x^2 + y^2 = 1$ leads to $y^2 < 0$, meaning y itself is imaginary. More generally, you can choose any complex value for x you wish, and use $x^2 + y^2 = 1$ to get corresponding values for y. That means above every point in the complex x-plane there are ordered pairs (x, y) in $\mathbb{C}^2$, and when limiting points at infinity are added in, all these points form a topological sphere. That is, the "complex circle" has genus 0. Figures 19.9 and 19.10 on p. 261, together with the explanations there, give a more detailed account of what happens for the curve $y^2 = (x + 1)(x)(x - 1)$. In this case, the ordered pairs plus the limiting points at infinity form a topological torus, and we say this curve, in the complex setting, has genus 1.

Chapter 4: *Hass Goes to College*

4.1 [p. 38]. *Karl Weierstrass* (1815–1897) was a Prussian-born mathematician, often called "The father of modern analysis." Upon entering the Gymnasium (high school) at 14, he was soon bringing home stellar marks and various awards.

Karl Weierstrass

His heart was already in mathematics, and his father, a tax inspector, began using Karl as the family bookkeeper. He formulated a life plan for Karl: The talented son would become an accountant. When it was time for university study, Karl's father, something of a tyrant, enrolled him in finance, economics, and law courses with no meaningful consultation with his son. Karl dutifully attended classes, but soon found the lectures insufferably boring, and eventually stopped working on his courses. Instead, he studied his love, mathematics, reading on his own some of the big masters like Laplace, Abel, Lie, and Jacobi. He did have other consuming interests: fencing with swords, partying, and drinking beer with friends. This lifestyle continued for four years, and Karl returned home with no degree. He eventually convinced his furious father to let him enroll in the Theological and Philosophical Academy of Münster, where he could pursue his interest in mathematics and gain certification as a secondary school teacher. This was successful, and Karl taught not only mathematics but physics, geography, history, botany, German, penmanship, and gymnastics. The pay, however, was so small that he could not afford the postage to communicate with some of his mathematical heros, so after school hours he would work alone on mathematics, mainly following his own instincts. He became increasingly uncomfortable with the fanciful handwaving he saw in calculus books. To Karl, it looked like calculus was regarded as a practical tool, but apparently nobody had a clear idea of the theoretical concepts used such as continuity and differentiability. How could you be sure this or that infinite series actually converged? Was it OK to differentiate term by term? Or multiply two different series? Even in the 1870s, many mathematicians, without giving the matter much thought, believed that continuous functions were differentiable. Later in his life, Weierstrass presented the world with an example of a function continuous everywhere and differentiable nowhere. This example shocked the mathematical community, which began to realize how porous and shaky the foundations of analysis were. His insistence on rigor and clarity has had an enormous effect on what we today consider appropriately rigorous mathematics.

But that very insistence on rigor meant he felt his own writings were never sound enough to be published, so his output in journals was small. At age 41, when he finally published an outline of his years-long musings about so-called abelian functions, readers were incredulous: "Who *is* this fellow? Out of nowhere comes this splendid paper full of original insights!" He was no longer in the shadows, and soon received an honorary doctorate from the University of Königsberg and a good-paying appointment at the University of Berlin. His clear lectures soon made him famous as a master teacher, with students from all over Europe flocking to his classes. At one point his class size exceeded 250 students. His clear, down-to-earth yet rigorous style tended to engender creativity, and many of his students are today household names in mathematics, including Felix Klein, Sophus Lie, Georg Cantor, Hermann Minkowski, and Gösta Mittag-Leffler. In all, Weierstrass was a teacher to over two dozen names that mathematicians recognize today. He also had a major impact on the growth and development of the Russian mathematician Sophie Kowalevski.

It is only fair to mention that besides his emphasis on careful definitions, proofs, and general rigor, Weierstrass also had a specialty and was a leader in it— the area of "abelian" and related functions. Without the benefit of today's cheap and fast computing power, in Weierstrass' day mathematicians needed formulas for integrals, and often used infinite series to get approximations when evaluating them. One basic integral formula was

$$\int \frac{dx}{\sqrt{1 - x^2}} = \arcsin x + C.$$

Choosing $C = 0$ and taking the inverse function gives $\sin x$, basic to innumerable problems in applied math and physics. It occurs in one of the earliest formulas in physics, going back to Galileo: The angular displacement of an ideal simple pendulum of length L is

$$\theta(t) = \theta_M \sin\left(\sqrt{\frac{g}{L}}\, t\right),$$

where g is gravitational strength and θ_M is maximum displacement. This, how-ever, is only an approximation, though it's quite good for small θ_M; the period increases for larger θ_M. For example, when θ_M is nearly 180°, it takes a long time for the pendulum to get up that high, then lose balance, and finally come down again. A natural question is, what function gives the *exact* motion of an ideal pendulum? Roughly speaking, in solving the problem exactly, the $\sqrt{1-x^2}$ in $\int \frac{dx}{\sqrt{1-x^2}}$ gets replaced by $\sqrt{1-(k\sin x)^2}$ $(0 < k^2 < 1)$. The inverse function of this isn't the sine function, but a sort of cousin to it, called an elliptic function of the first kind. And replacing the $\sqrt{1-x^2}$ in $\int \frac{dx}{\sqrt{1-x^2}}$ by $\sqrt{R(x)}$, where R is a polynomial of degree more than 4, gives inverse functions more general than elliptic functions, called "abelian" or "hyperelliptic" functions. Just as there's a power series expansion for $\sin x$, there turns out to be power series expansions of elliptic and abelian functions. Finding these expansions and exploring their gen-eral properties represented some of Weierstrass's most important research and initially led to his bursting out of obscurity.

Chapter 6: *The Four-Color Problem: Some History and Whitney's Contributions to It*

6.1 [p. 47]. A *topological arc* is a topological space C homeomorphic to $[0, 1]$, which is to say there exists a continuous, one-to-one, onto map F from $[0, 1]$ to C such that the inverse function F^{-1} from C to $[0, 1]$ is also continuous. (F^{-1} exists as a function because F is one-to-one and onto.) This means a topological arc has two distinct endpoints, and any of the arc's other points, together with an open neighborhood about it, looks topologically like a point in the open interval $(0, 1)$. This eliminates curves like a circle, which doesn't have distinct endpoints, and it also eliminates an alpha-shaped curve having two distinct endpoints because it also has a crosspoint; the part of the curve around that point locally looks instead like an ×.

6.2 [p. 47]. The four-color problem, which is today a theorem, is topological in nature. Although it's typically stated as a theorem about coloring maps drawn in a plane, it holds just as well for maps on a sphere. To see why, suppose we have a map on a sphere. Remove one point from the interior of any country; that leaves a topological plane map which we color with at most four colors. Now put the point back in and color that point the same as its surrounding country. The spherical map is therefore colored in at most four colors.

6.3 [p. 47]. In spreading the word about the four-color problem, De Morgan played an important role in its history. But he made basic contributions besides that, giving, for example, precise meaning to what we today call *mathematical induction*. In fact it was he who introduced this term. And in logic, he formulated the pair of laws connecting negation (overbar), $\wedge$ = AND, and $\vee$ = OR:

$$\overline{A \wedge B} = \overline{A} \vee \overline{B}, \qquad \overline{A \vee B} = \overline{A} \wedge \overline{B}.$$

To highlight the duality nature of negation, write $\vee = \overline{\wedge}$ and $\wedge = \overline{\vee}$. The equations then read

$$\overline{A \wedge B} = \overline{A} \,\overline{\wedge}\, \overline{B}, \qquad \overline{A \vee B} = \overline{A} \,\overline{\vee}\, \overline{B}.$$

In Boolean algebra, these become

$$\overline{A \cap B} = \overline{A} \,\overline{\cap}\, \overline{B}, \qquad \overline{A \cup B} = \overline{A} \,\overline{\cup}\, \overline{B}.$$

There are also analogs in electric circuit theory, and by 1886 Charles Peirce saw that these logical operations could be carried out by electrical switching circuits. This idea was used by John von Neumann in 1945 in formulating the ALU— Arithmetic Logic Unit—as the computational and decision-making heart of a digital computer.

Chapter 7: *Whitney and the Four-Color Problem: A Closer Look*

7.1 [p. 64]. $K_n, K_{n,m}, K_{n,m,p}, \ldots$ *graphs.*

- K_n denotes the graph with n vertices together with all possible edges connecting distinct vertices. In this and all graphs below, there are no loops or multiple edges. K_n is called "the complete graph on n points."
- $K_{n,m}$ denotes two disjoint sets of vertices, one having n points, the other m points, together with all possible edges connecting points in one vertex set with points in the other vertex set. No two vertices in the same set are connected. $K_{n,m}$ is called a "complete bipartite (= two parts) graph."
- $K_{n,m,p}$ denotes three disjoint vertex sets together with all edges connecting vertices in each set to all vertices in the other two sets. No two vertices in the same set are connected. $K_{n,m,p}$ is called a "complete tripartite graph." One can verify that $K_{1,1,1}$ is a triangle graph, while $K_{1,1,2}$ is a square graph together with one diagonal. $K_{2,2,2}$ consists of six vertices and twelve edges, looking like the plane projection of an octahedron.

7.2 [p. 64]. A graph G is *homeomorphic with G'* when G and G' have a common refinement: Any edge of a graph can be refined by adding a point to that edge, so that it gets replaced by two edges and a new vertex. In the picture below, graphs G and G' are not topologically the same, but edge e in graph G and edge e' in G' have been selected for refinement. After adding a point to each of these edges to refine them, the resulting graphs are each topologically the same as the bottom graph H.

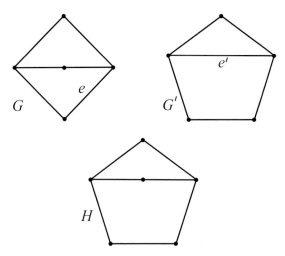

The top two graphs have the bottom graph
as a common refinement, so they are homeomorphic *with* each other, but not homeomorphic *to* each other.

7.3 [p. 72]. The plane is not big enough to draw in it arbitrary graphs with no accidental crossings—but 3-space *is* large enough for this. Even more, in 3-space we can make any graph lie with no accidental crossings on some closed topological manifold of genus g. Therefore there's a smallest g on which the graph lies, and that g is called the *genus* of the graph. As an example, the triangulation shown in Figure 10.10 on p. 120 has genus 1. Any planar graph can be drawn on a sphere and therefore has genus 0.

7.4 [p. 72]. *Alkanes* consist of only carbon and hydrogen atoms, and have the general chemical formula C_nH_{2n+2}. Their atoms are linked by single bonds. Unless forced into it, alkanes tend not to react with other elements. One force, however, is elevated temperature, and when that's high enough, alkanes can ignite in the presence of oxygen to form H_2O and CO_2—water and carbon dioxide. This type of reaction gives rise to a whole host of everyday applications. Here are some examples:

- Natural gas is composed mostly of CH_4 (methane) and C_2H_6 (ethane) and is used not only in homes for cooking and heating, but when compressed to form CNG (compressed natural gas), it can serve as fuel for buses and other vehicles.

- Propane (C_3H_8) and butane (C_4H_{10}) are very frequently used as LPG (liquefied petroleum gas). In this form, propane is popular in propane gas burners.
- Pentane (C_5H_{12}) through octane (C_8H_{18}) are often mixed in various proportions to form solvents, gasoline, and so on.
- As n increases in the general formula C_nH_{2n+2}, the alkanes get denser. In our listing so far, we've gone from gasses to volatile liquids. Alkanes C_9H_{20} through $C_{16}H_{34}$ serve as the main components of diesel fuel, which is more oily than gasoline.
- Alkanes having anywhere from 17 to 34 carbon atoms are more viscous, and because they don't mix with water, in this molecular range they can be used as oils and greases for lubricating and protection against rust or corrosion.
- For $n > 34$, the alkanes have waterproofing and hardness properties making them well suited for asphalt road surfacing.

Chapter 8: *Whitney Discovers a Big Brother to the Matrix: The Matroid*

8.1 [p. 89]. Matroids can also be useful in certain optimization problems: At the start of many decision-making processes having profit as the goal, if at each step you unfailingly choose the route offering the greatest profit, that purely local "walking in the fog" mentality often doesn't maximize profit, since other routes may offer less at the beginning but more toward the end of the process. However, if your possible decisions happen to form a decision graph—a graph with weights (say, profit margins) attached to each edge, then this weighed graph has an associated matroid, and in this case walking in the fog is always good enough. The total value of a basis in a weighted graph is the sum of the weights of the edges in the basis. Therefore to maximize profit, we look for a basis whose total value is the greatest. To construct such a basis, at the start of decision-making, choose the edge offering the greatest return. At the ith step, you have a partially constructed basis I of independent elements. At the next step, choose an e_i offering the greatest reward, ignoring any e_i for which $I + e_i$ is a cycle. This method is known as the greedy algorithm, and can be used equally well to minimize a quantity (such as time or cost) by choosing at each stage the edge with minimum weight.

Chapter 10: *Topology Grows Into a Branch of Mathematics*

10.1 [p. 125]. There's an interesting analogy between using ∂ to denote "boundary of" and using it for derivative: The area enclosed by a disk is πr^2, and the derivative of this is $(\pi r^2)' = 2\pi r$, the circumference of the disk's boundary. Going up a dimension, the volume of a ball is $\frac{4}{3}\pi r^3$; the derivative of this is $4\pi r^2$, the surface area of the ball's bounding sphere. This relationship holds in all dimensions.

Although the general formula
$$\frac{\pi^{n/2}r^n}{\Gamma\left(1+\frac{n}{2}\right)}$$
for the volume of an n-ball involves the gamma function (see Note 10.4 below), the derivative of this is nonetheless the formula for the $(n-1)$-volume of the ball's boundary. This is no coincidence: The ball's volume is the integral of the $(n-1)$-volumes of thin concentric shells, and our observation is essentially the reverse of this.

Analogies between the two uses of ∂ extend even further: Leibniz's rule $(fg)' = f'g+fg'$ for the product of functions works for the product of reasonable sets:
$$\partial(S \times T) = \partial(S) \times T + S \times \partial(T).$$
As an example, let I_x be an interval in the x-axis and I_y an interval in the y-axis. Then $I_x \times I_y$ is a filled-in rectangle, and Leibniz's rule gives
$$\partial(I_x \times I_y) = \partial(I_x) \times I_y + I_x \times \partial(I_y).$$
$\partial(I_x)$ consists of two points in the x-axis, so $\partial(I_x) \times I_y$ defines the two vertical sides of the rectangle. In a similar way, $I_x \times \partial I_y$ defines the two horizontal sides, so the sum of both terms is the entire boundary of the rectangle.

Try the rule on the product $\mathbf{o} \times I_z$, a cylinder. The product $\partial\mathbf{o} \times I_z = \varnothing \times I_z$ is the empty set, while $\mathbf{o} \times \partial I_z$ consists of two circles, which is indeed the cylinder's boundary. Similarly, applying the rule to the product $\Delta \times I_z$ of a disk and an interval gives the lateral sides for the first term, and the top and bottom end caps (disks) for the second term.

10.2 [p. 125]. There's more: Leibniz's rule generalizes to the product of any number of functions or sets. For the derivative of the product of n functions, write the product n times, and in the ith term, prime the ith function. If $n = 3$ for example, the rule becomes
$$(fgh)' = f'gh + fg'h + fgh'.$$
This idea works for sets, too. Applying it to the filled-in box $I_x \times I_y \times I_z$ produces, termwise, the three pairs of filled-in square sides perpendicular to the x-axis, to the y-axis, and to the z-axis. Their sum is the empty box. Such pairwise sides tell us that an n-cube has $2n$ sides, each an $(n-1)$-cube. This helps us visualize the eight sides of a tesseract (4-cube) $I_x \times I_y \times I_z \times I_t$, which like any n-cube may be inductively drawn by sketching two $(n-1)$-cubes and connecting corresponding vertices with line segments. Its four pairs of 3D-cube sides are perpendicular to each of the four orthogonal axes.

10.3 [p. 128]. If two groups G and G' have binary operators $\circ$ and $\cdot$, then a *homomorphism* $h : G \to G'$ is a map preserving the operations—that is, h satisfies

$$h(g_1 \circ g_2) = h(g_1) \cdot h(g_2)$$

for all g_1, g_2 in g. One can show that under h, the identity of G maps to the identity of G', and that inverses map to inverses—that is, for any $g \in G$, we have $h(g^{-1}) = (h(g))^{-1}$.

10.4 [p. 354]. About the gamma function: In the 1720s, the number theorist Christian Goldbach wondered if the factorial function $n! = 1 \cdot 2 \cdot \cdots n$, could be defined for *all* positive real values, not just for natural numbers. Since factorials arise in so many number-theoretic and combinatorial problems, it's not surprising that a mathematician in his area should eventually ask the question. His challenge was to make sense of expressions like $(\frac{1}{2})!$, $(\pi)!$, or $(x)!$. His question can be looked at geometrically: Find a nice, smooth function $y = F(x)$ whose graph goes through each of the infinitely many points $(n, n!)$ in the plane, as suggested in this figure:

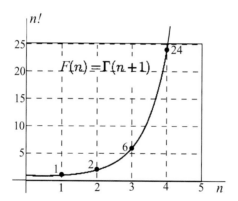

The gamma function curve.

The figure above depicts only one possibility, since for any $F(x)$ we might propose, adding $\sin(\pi x)$ to it is also such a curve because $\sin(\pi x)$ is zero whenever x is an integer. But the following two basic restrictions eliminate such problematic outsiders:

- The function should always grow *tremendously* fast—in fact, the factorial is one of the fastest-increasing functions commonly encountered. One way of looking at growth speed is seeing how convex upward it is. This can be gauged by giving it a stress test: Applying a logarithmic function to it puts severe brakes on growth—for example, applying ln to even the exponential

e^x results in $\ln(e^x) = x$, whose graph is just a straight line. If a graph remains convex even after applying a logarithmic function to it, it's called *super convex*, and that's what we demand of our Γ-function.

- The basic relation $(n + 1)! = (n + 1)n!$ should also hold when n is replaced by any positive real number x. This can be written suggestively as $(x + 1)! = (x + 1)x!$.

Goldbach corresponded with many mathematicians, one of them being Leonhard Euler, so often the "go to" man. Euler found that no finite combination of common functions worked, and eventually came up with an infinite product formula that seemed reasonable. By 1730 he had also found an integral formula much like the following standard formula used today to define the gamma function:

$$\Gamma(x) = \int_{t=0}^{\infty} t^{x-1} e^{-t}\, dt.$$

The notation Γ is due to Legendre, but is somewhat of a mixed blessing—the natural notation $x!$ becomes, with Legendre, $\Gamma(x + 1)$. So, for example, $\Gamma(4) = 3! = 6$.

The gamma function is considered a "special" function instead of one of the standard functions like exponential and trigonometric ones. Nonetheless, it's highly useful in many scientific areas, including physics, probability, and statistics. For even simple fractional values of x, the values are hardly ever correspondingly simple. The most famous noninteger example is $\Gamma(\frac{1}{2}) = \sqrt{\pi}$. Today, however, packages like Mathematica can produce values to a great number of digits in a tiny fraction of a second. For example, in Mathematica the command N[Gamma[1/3], 50] almost immediately gives $\Gamma(\frac{1}{3})$ accurate to 50 decimal places:

2.6789385347077476336556929409746776441286893779573.

Such a package tells us that the volume of a five-dimensional ball,

$$\frac{\pi^{\frac{5}{2}} r^5}{\Gamma\left(1 + \frac{5}{2}\right)},$$

is

$$5.263789 \cdots r^5.$$

Although Goldbach helped in the discovery of the gamma function, he is actually most famous for his Goldbach Conjecture stating that every even number greater than 2 is the sum of two primes—for example, $12 = 5 + 7$. For larger even numbers, there is usually more than one way: $24 = 11 + 13 = 17 + 7 = 19 + 5$. As of 2015, his conjecture has been established for all even n up to about 4×10^{18}— impressive, but not a proof.

Chapter 11: *Whitney Helped Revolutionize Algebraic Topology*

11.1 [p. 134]. The name "combinatorial topology" comes from the original method of dividing topological surfaces into vertices, edges, and faces, and counting them to arrive at constants associated with the surface. For example, Euler's formula $V - E + F = 2$ for a polyhedron drawn on a sphere, or $V - E + F = 2 - 2g$ for one drawn on a sphere with g handles, are theorems of combinatorial topology. As mathematicians considered higher dimensions, topological spaces got divided into standardized pieces—simplices, whose general definition is outlined on p. 121. Other topological properties of spaces were captured by Betti numbers (see p. 126) as well as the Euler characteristic—the alternating sum of a manifold's Betti numbers. All were ultimately defined using simplices and were shown to be independent of how the space was divided into a complex of simplices. In his paper "Analysis Situs" and supplements to it, written between 1895 and 1904, Poincaré helped clarify these ideas in combinatorial topology and made the day's intuitive arguments more rigorous. After Emmy Noether sparked a rethinking of combinatorial topology into group-theoretic terms at a dinner in 1925 with friends, her insights got absorbed into topology, which then began metamorphosizing into what we today call *algebraic topology*. This metamorphosis was fairly complete by 1944.

11.2 [p. 135]. A *group* consists of a set $G = \{g_i\}$ of elements and a binary operation ∘ on G, so that

- If g_1 and g_2 are any elements of G, then $g_1 \circ g_2$ is also an element of G;
- There is an identity element u in G satisfying $u \circ g = g \circ u = g$ for every $g \in G$;
- For every $g \in G$ there is an inverse g^{-1} for which $g \circ g^{-1} = g^{-1} \circ g = u$;
- The operation ∘ is associative: For any $g_1, g_2, g_3 \in G$, $(g_1 \circ g_2) \circ g_3 = g_1 \circ (g_2 \circ g_3)$.

The definition does not imply that the binary operation is commutative. If ∘ *is* commutative, then it's typically denoted by +, and then u is most often denoted by 0; the group is correspondingly called commutative or abelian.

The groups Noether had in mind were not only abelian, but *finitely generated*. One can look at these as special groups made up of simple pieces put together in a straightforward way.

The simple pieces are of two kinds:

Ordinary integers. One kind is $\mathbb{Z}$, the ordinary integers, together with the operation of addition. Addition actually includes subtraction, since $\mathbb{Z}$ also includes all the negative integers, so that $n - m$ is the same as adding n and $-m$. Addition is associative: $(n + m) + q = n + (m + q)$ for all integers n, m, q, and is also commutative: $n + m = m + n$ for all integers n, m.

Clock integers. The other kind is a clock together with clock arithmetic. The number of hours on any of these clocks is a prime power—for example, 2, 2^2, 3^5, 17^{1234}, $\cdots$. We'll call these groups "prime power cyclics." We number the hours starting from 0, so that the $7^2 = 49$-hour clock, denoted $\mathbb{Z}_{7^2}$, has hours $0, 1, 2, 3, \ldots, 48$. This more general clock arithmetic is similar to clock arithmetic on a 12-hour clock (calling 12 the 0-hour). So just as $10+5$ equals 3 in such a clock (because 5 hours after 10 o'clock is 3 o'clock), in $\mathbb{Z}_{7^2}$, we would have, for example, that 15 hours after 40 o'clock is 6 o'clock. ($40 + 15 = 55$, which is 6 hours past $49 = 0$ o'clock.) Clock arithmetic is commutative: In the 12-hour clock example, 5 hours after 10 is the same as 10 hours after 5; commutativity similarly holds in any of these prime-power clocks. Just as any integer n in $\mathbb{Z}$ has a negative $-n$ so that $n + (-n) = 0$, so too, for any prime power p^r, any hour (that is, element) h in $\mathbb{Z}_{p^r}$ has a negative $-h$ found by counting counterclockwise h hours from the 0-hour. Then, just as in $\mathbb{Z}$, $h + (-h) = 0$. As with $\mathbb{Z}$, clock addition is associative and commutative.

How are these building blocks put together?

These simple pieces are put together by using direct sum $\oplus$. As a familiar example, the plane $\mathbb{R}^2$ can be written $\mathbb{R} \oplus \mathbb{R}$ and $\mathbb{R}^3$ as $\mathbb{R} \oplus \mathbb{R} \oplus \mathbb{R}$. The direct sum effectively forms a vector with component entries, so that $\mathbb{R} \oplus \mathbb{R}$ consists of all ordered pairs (r_1, r_2), r_1, $r_2 \in \mathbb{R}$, and the direct sum $\mathbb{R} \oplus \mathbb{R}$ naturally endows $\mathbb{R} \oplus \mathbb{R}$ with componentwise addition: $(r_1, r_2) + (s_1, s_2) = (r_1 + s_1, r_2 + s_2)$. Such componentwise addition is, of course, ordinary vector addition. All this directly transfers over to our simple pieces $\mathbb{Z}$ and $\mathbb{Z}_{p^r}$. If we write $\mathbb{Z}^q$ for the direct sum of q copies of $\mathbb{Z}$ and use similar notation for the direct sum of copies of a prime power cyclic, then, for example, any element of the finitely generated abelian group

$$G = \mathbb{Z}^4 \oplus \mathbb{Z}_3^2 \oplus \mathbb{Z}_{5^2}^3 \oplus \mathbb{Z}_7$$

would be a 10-vector such as

$$(8, -3, 751, 21, 1, 2, 21, 13, 0, 5).$$

$\mathbb{Z}^4$ is the (finitely generated) infinite part of G, and $\mathbb{Z}_3^2 \oplus \mathbb{Z}_{5^2}^3 \oplus \mathbb{Z}_7$ is the finite part consisting of $3^2 \times 25^3 \times 7 = 984,375$ elements. Adding two of the 10-vectors would look like

$$(8, -3, 751, 21, 1, 2, 21, 13, 6, 5) + (-20, 50, 5, -19, 2, 0, 6, 12, -4, 4)$$
$$= (-12, 47, 756, 2, 0, 2, 2, 0, 2, 2).$$

Chapter 12: *Whitney's Extension Theorems*

12.1 [p. 145]. *One-sided derivative.* For a real valued function f defined at least on the interval $(a, b]$ ($a < b$), the left derivative of f at b is

$$\lim_{x \to b} \frac{f(b) - f(x)}{b - x},$$

with $x \in (a, b)$.

Similarly, for a real valued function g defined at least on the interval $[c, d)$ ($c < d$), the right derivative of g at c is

$$\lim_{x \to c} \frac{g(x) - g(c)}{x - c},$$

with $x \in (c, d)$.

As an example, the left derivative of $|x|$ at 0 is -1, while the right derivative there is $+1$. One-sided derivatives can easily be extended to partial derivatives of a function $F(x, y)$. For example, to get the left partial $\frac{\partial F(x,y)}{\partial x}$, hold a value of y fixed and take the left derivative of the resulting one-variable function. Other cases for left, right, and partials of several variables are all defined in the expected way.

12.2 [p. 147]. The name *Taylor series* was first used in 1786 by Antoine-Jean L'Huilier, whose story starts on p. 101. Brook Taylor (1685–1731) himself employed his series around 1712 as a way of solving Kepler's equation for the motion of a smaller heavenly body orbiting around a larger one. The equation has the general form $A = x - B \sin x$, where A and B are constants. Solving for x is an "inverse problem," and in this case you cannot solve for x using only a finite number of elementary operations. In a different day and for different reasons, several people came up with the idea of infinite series before Taylor did, including James Gregory, Isaac Newton, Gottfried Leibniz, Johann Bernoulli, and Abraham de Moivre—all born in the mid 1600s and within 30 years of each other. Note to history buffs: It was Taylor who discovered, around 1715, integration by parts. He and J. S. Bach were born the same year.

A Taylor series looks like this:

$$a_0 + a_1(x - c)^1 + a_2(x - c)^2 + a_3(x - c)^3 + \cdots,$$

where the a_n are constant coefficients and c is the center of expansion. In the best case, given a function $f(x)$ that is infinitely differentiable at $x = c$, the series should numerically represent the function in the sense that when you plug any value b for x in the series, the series converges to $f(b)$. Sometimes this works beautifully, other times it works somewhat, and other times it simply fails. One can always begin by writing

$$f(x) = a_0 + a_1(x - c)^1 + a_2(x - c)^2 + a_3(x - c)^3 + \cdots,$$

although it remains to be seen whether the "=" is justified for any particular $f(x)$. Then successively differentiating both sides of this purported equation and evaluating at $x = c$ will produce values for all the a_n, and therefore associate to $f(x)$ a unique Taylor series centered at $x = c$. When $n > 0$, the $(x - c)^n$ in the series is 0 when c is plugged in for x, so we get

$$f(c) = a_0,$$
$$f'(c) = 1 \cdot a_1,$$
$$f^{(2)}(c) = 1 \cdot 2 \cdot a_2,$$
$$f^{(3)}(c) = 1 \cdot 2 \cdot 3 \cdot a_3,$$

and so on. This leads right away to

$$a_n = \frac{f^{(n)}(c)}{n!},$$

meaning that at least formally,

$$f(x) = \sum_{n=0}^{\infty} \frac{f^{(n)}(c)}{n!}(x - c)^n.$$

The question is, how well does this formalism actually work?

- For "direct elementary functions" such as polynomials, sine, cosine, hyperbolic, and exponential functions, it works well. Even the Taylor series for a finite combination of elementary functions like $\cos(e^{1-x+3x^2-x^5})$ or $e^{\sin^2(x)}$ converges to the function throughout $\mathbb{R}$.
- For inverses to or ratios of the above elementary functions, the associated Taylor series typically represents the function only within a restricted range. For Taylor series centered $x = 0$, some examples of intervals of convergence to $f(x)$ are

$$
\begin{array}{lll}
\arcsin x & \text{converges in} & -1 < x < +1, \\
\arccos x & \text{converges in} & -1 < x < +1, \\
\arctan x & \text{converges in} & -1 < x < +1, \\
\ln(1 + x) & \text{converges in} & -1 < x \leq +1, \\
\dfrac{1}{(1 + x)} & \text{converges in} & -1 < x < +1, \\
\dfrac{\sin x}{\cos x} = \tan x & \text{converges in} & -\dfrac{\pi}{2} < x < +\dfrac{\pi}{2}.
\end{array}
$$

- There is a famous example of failure. It's

$$f(x) = e^{-1/x^2} \text{ if } x \neq 0, \qquad f(0) = 0.$$

This function is infinitely differentiable at each point of $\mathbb{R}$, and at $x = 0$ all the derivatives are 0. That means its Taylor series in x is identically zero and therefore converges to $f(x)$ at only one point. We look at this function in more detail starting on p. 148; this function and its relatives played a big role in some of Whitney's most important breakthroughs. Although mathematicians originally had to work a bit to discover and verify that this function is so badly behaved, that doesn't mean there aren't a lot like it. There's an analogy: Rational numbers are generally thought of as nicer, or better-behaved, than irrationals, but there are far more irrationals than rational numbers. Likewise, there are far more badly behaved functions like the above, compared to ones whose Taylor series actually equal the function. Just to give an idea, any nice function plus the famous bad one above is bad. That's akin to what happens with numbers: Any rational number plus an irrational one is irrational. Any nonzero scalar multiple of a bad function is bad. In the vector space of all functions that are infinitely differentiable at a fixed point $x = c$, if, from a probabilistic standpoint, you throw a dart at the vector space, the chance that it will land on a bad function is 100%, just as throwing a dart at the real line will, with probability 100%, land on an irrational point.

It is interesting to note that

$$a_n = \frac{f^{(n)}}{n!}(c)$$

involves the factorial $n!$, which grows *extremely* fast. One can turn this scenario around, in the sense that if the coefficients a_n are already known, then it's easy to determine the nth derivative, Take, say, the polynomial function

$$f(x) = 1 + x + x^2 + x^3 + \cdots + x^{20}.$$

What, for example, is $f^{(15)}(0)$? Regarding this as its own Taylor series, we see that

$$f^{(15)}(0) = 15!$$

In fact, successive nonzero derivatives of everyday polynomials can grow outrageously fast—something that most people are not aware of. In our case,

$$f^{(15)}(0) = 1, 307, 674, 368, 000,$$

which is over a trillion.

12.3 [p. 152]. Replacing x by $(x+\frac{1}{2})$ and y by $(y+\frac{1}{2})$ to translate the graph down and left is a special case of a much more general concept. The idea can actually be used to translate *any* object defined as the set of points satisfying an equation $f = 0$, f being a function in one or more variables. As a first example, consider the point $x = 5$ on the x-axis, and suppose we want to translate it one unit to the right. One obvious way is to just write $x = 6$, but a less obvious way turns out to be much more useful: Replace x in $x = 5$ by $(x - 1)$, getting $(x - 1) = 5$. This certainly simplifies to $x = 6$, but making the replacement $x \to (x-1)$ forces x to increase by 1 to maintain equality in the original equation, which in turn means the solution point moves right one unit. It would be natural to say, "So what?" But let's try another example, say the equation $x^2 + y^2 = 0$, whose only solution is $x = 0, y = 0$—the plane's origin. When we make the replacements $x \to (x-5)$ and $y \to (y - 3)$, what happens? The only solution to $(x - 5)^2 + (y - 3)^2 = 0$ is when both $x - 5$ and $y - 3$ are 0, so the only solution to $(x-5)^2 + (y-3)^2 = 0$ is the point $(5, 3)$. Our replacement has translated the origin to $(5, 3)$. As a more general example, suppose (x_0, y_0) is any point satisfying an equation $f(x, y) = 0$, so that $f(x_0, y_0) = 0$. Now replace $x \to (x-h), y \to (y-k)$, where h and k are (say, real) numbers. To get $f(x_0, y_0) = 0$, what do we plug into $f(x-h, y-k)$? Substituting $x_0 + h$ for x and $y_0 + k$ for y gives $f(x_0 + h - h, y_0 + k - k) = f(x_0, y_0) = 0$, so $(x_0 + h, y_0 + k)$ is the new point satisfying the new equation $f(x - h, y - k) = 0$. This new equation has moved the old solution point (x_0, y_0) to $(x_0 + h, y_0 + k)$.

There's a kind of "action-reaction" principle at work here: To translate in a positive direction by some amount, we *subtract* that amount from the corresponding variable; to translate in a negative direction by, say, 3 units, *add* 3 to the corresponding variable. This principle is quite general. For example, multiplying a variable x_i by some nonzero number m_i shrinks the entire space in the x_i-direction by the factor m_i, and the zero set of $f(x_1, \cdots, x_n)$ goes along for the ride. The reasoning is the same: To maintain equality, the variable must grow by the factor m_i. Likewise, dividing by m_i stretches the zero set by m_i. So, for example, suppose we wish to stretch the unit circle $x^2 + y^2 = 1$ by a factor of 5 in the x-direction and 3 in the y-direction. In the replacements, we divide by 5 and 3: $x \to \frac{x}{5}, y \to \frac{y}{3}$. Then $x^2 + y^2 = 1$ becomes

$$\left(\frac{x}{5}\right)^2 + \left(\frac{y}{3}\right)^2 = 1.$$

Does this look familiar? The standard form of an ellipse just says that a unit circle has been stretched by the factors you see in the denominator! This idea illuminates another familiar example: oscillation. One simple form is $y = \sin t$ describing oscillation in the y-direction with increasing time t; the oscillation has amplitude 1, frequency 1 radian per unit time, and phase shift 0. We can massage this into a more general form. Replace y by y/A to change the amplitude to A, and replace t by $t-\phi$ to introduce the phase shift ϕ. Multiply $t-\phi$ by ω to compress the graph by a factor of ω in the t-direction, which corresponds physically to speeding up the oscillation by the factor ω. Making these replacements and simplifying gives the familiar form

$$y = A \sin(\omega(t - \phi)).$$

The action-reaction principle also works for rotating any zero-set about the origin. In the (x, y)-plane, the matrix

$$R(\theta) = \begin{pmatrix} \cos\theta & \sin\theta \\ -\sin\theta & \cos\theta \end{pmatrix}$$

can be used to rotate each point around the origin through θ by sending the point (x, y) to $(x, y)R(\theta)$—that is, to

$$(x\cos\theta - y\sin\theta, x\sin\theta + y\cos\theta).$$

To rotate the zero-set $f(x, y) = 0$ by θ, the action-reaction principle tells us to replace (x, y) in $f(x, y)$ by $(x, y)R(-\theta)$. Since $\cos(-\theta) = \cos(\theta)$ and $\sin(-\theta) = -\sin(\theta)$, the replacements are

$$x \to x\cos\theta + y\sin\theta; \quad y \to -x\sin\theta + y\cos\theta.$$

Starting from the unit circle about the origin, you can successively apply stretching and/or shrinking, rotation, and translation to create an ellipse having any shape, tilt, and center you wish. You can do the same in three dimensions, starting from the unit sphere to get the equation of any shape of ellipsoid having desired tilt and center. (Any rotation in $\mathbb{R}^3$ can be written as a product of pure rotations about each of the three axes.) Although we have illustrated this using ellipses and ellipsoids, all these notions apply to the zero-sets of an arbitrary function defined on the space.

12.4 [p. 152]. More generally, a function $f(x)$ is called *odd* if it satisfies $f(-x) = -f(x)$—that is, if $f(x) + f(-x) = 0$. Analogously, a function is *even* if $f(-x) = +f(x)$, which is the same as $f(x) - f(-x) = 0$. Any odd function's graph is symmetric about the origin; any even function's graph is symmetric about the y-axis. Where do these names come from? Notice that $f(x) = x^n$ is odd whenever n is odd. So $y = x$, $y = x^3$, $y = x^5$, and so on, are all odd functions, and their familiar graphs are all symmetric about the origin. Similarly, $f(x) = x^n$ is even when n is even, so $y = x^0$, $y = x^2$, $y = x^4$, and so on, are all even functions, and their graphs are all symmetric about the y-axis. Although if n is negative the function isn't defined at $x = 0$, nonetheless in graphing what you can, you still get the expected symmetry about the origin or the y-axis. It's easy to check that any scalar multiple of an odd function is odd, any scalar multiple of an even function is even, the sum of odd functions is odd, and the sum of even functions is even. These sums may be infinite, as in the odd power series

$$\sin x = x - \frac{x^3}{3!} + \frac{x^5}{5!} - \cdots;$$

its graph is symmetric about the origin. Similarly, the series

$$\cos x = 1 - \frac{x^2}{2!} + \frac{x^4}{4!} - \cdots$$

is symmetric about the y-axis. Finally, notice that any function (continuous or not) is the sum of an even function and an odd one:

$$f(x) = \frac{f(x) + f(-x)}{2} + \frac{f(x) - f(-x)}{2}.$$

12.5 [p. 158]. Generalizing Taylor series from one variable to several variables follows the "Law of Minimum Astonishment," meaning things flow pretty much as expected. However in writing formulas for an arbitrary number of variables, the great number of subscripts, superscripts, and other paraphernalia can easily obscure the series' underlying simplicity and beauty. Because the basic ideas appear using just two variables, and since using the origin as center further simplifies formulas, we make these two assumptions. We therefore ask whether a two-variable function $f(x, y)$ can be represented as a power series in two variables:

$$f(x, y) = a_0 + (a_{10}x + a_{01}y) + (a_{20}x^2 + a_{11}xy + a_{02}y^2) + \cdots.$$

Take partials to get any particular coefficient as a factor of a lone constant term, with all remaining coefficients being multiplied by positive powers of x and y. Plugging in $x = 0$ and $y = 0$ then kills all terms except the one containing our particular coefficient, which we then solve for. The resulting Taylor series in two variables can be arranged in this suggestive form:

$$\frac{1}{0!} \left[f(0, 0) \cdot 1 \right]$$

$$+$$

$$\frac{1}{1!} \left[f_x(0, 0) \cdot 1x + f_y(0, 0) \cdot 1y \right]$$

$$+$$

$$\frac{1}{2!} \left[f_{xx}(0, 0) \cdot 1x^2 + f_{xy}(0, 0) \cdot 2xy + f_{yy}(0, 0) \cdot 1y^2 \right]$$

$$+$$

$$\frac{1}{3!} \left[f_{xxx}(0, 0) \cdot 1x^3 + f_{xxy}(0, 0) \cdot 3x^2y + f_{xyy}(0, 0) \cdot 3xy^2 + f_{yyy}(0, 0) \cdot 1y^3 \right]$$

$$+$$

$$\vdots$$

Notice that an old friend, the Pascal triangle, appears–not especially well-hidden– as coefficients of the x- and y-variables. Here are the first few lines:

$$
\begin{array}{ccccccccc}
 & & & & 1 & & & & \\
 & & & 1 & & 1 & & & \\
 & & 1 & & 2 & & 1 & & \\
 & 1 & & 3 & & 3 & & 1 & \\
1 & & 4 & & 6 & & 4 & & 1 \\
 & & & & \vdots & & & &
\end{array}
$$

Where does this Pascal triangle come from? For a differentiable function in two variables, the order of differentiating doesn't matter. So, for example, the $f_{xy}(0,0) \cdot 2xy$ appearing in the degree-2 row of the above series is a collapsed version of $f_{xy}(0,0) \cdot xy + f_{yx}(0,0) \cdot yx$. In the 4th derivative line of the series there are $\binom{4}{2} = \frac{4!}{2! \cdot 2!} = 6$ ways to choose two x's, so $f_{xxyy}(0,0) \cdot 6x^2y^2$ stands for the sum of all six of these partial derivatives.

As in the one variable case, a Taylor series obtained from a function f of several variables may or may not actually represent f. Series for direct elementary functions usually do represent the function; for example, the series for $\sin(x+y^2)$ or $\cos(x \cdot e^{xy})$ converge and represent the function throughout $\mathbb{R}^2$. Ratios or inverses of these functions may converge to the original function in just a rectangle of $\mathbb{R}^2$, and a function like

$$
z = e^{-1/(x^2+y^2)} \ \text{ if } \ xy \neq 0, \qquad z = 0 \ \text{ if } \ x = 0 \ \text{ and } \ y = 0
$$

is infinitely differentiable everywhere, with all derivatives 0 at $(0,0)$, so its Taylor series with center $(0,0)$ represents the function at only the origin.

Chapter 13: *Whitney's Weak Embedding Theorem*

13.1 [p. 162]. An *n-dimensional compact connected differentiable manifold* contains no boundary points since a manifold is a union of open sets. So a closed disk, although compact and connected, isn't a manifold because no small neighborhood about a boundary point topologically looks like an open disk. A sphere with g handles is a two-dimensional compact connected manifold, but if you remove an open disk from the surface, then it's no longer a manifold. If you remove a closed disk or a point, what's left is a manifold but not a compact one.

Chapter 16: *From Harvard to the Institute; Insights on Smooth Mappings*

16.1 [p. 199]. One of his projects was to expand into a book his well-received 41-page account of his work on sphere bundles, which appeared in *Lectures in Topology* under the title "On the topology of differentiable manifolds" [82]. His sphere bundles, splitting bundles into tangent and normal bundles, and so on, had their origins in his embedding theorems, since after embedding any smooth manifold in a Euclidean space, notions such as distance and orthogonality then make sense. This helped redefine the landscape of manifold theory—we touched on this in the section "Embedding a manifold has important consequences" starting on p. 182. More generally, applying topology to differential geometry uses the fibre bundle as a basic tool. Hass intended to write a book on sphere bundles, but he felt this first required a foundational theory of integration in embedded manifolds. Once that was achieved, cohomological questions on embedded manifolds could be addressed via de Rham's theory, which casts homology and cohomology in terms of differential forms and their integrals. Toward this end, he wrote the book *Geometric Integration Theory*, which appeared in 1957. One of its main accomplishments is extending Stokes's theorem to sets having certain types of singularities. The original edition is now out of print but has subsequently been reissued by Dover Publications ([**105**]). Although his book is full of original geometric ideas, he nevertheless felt there remained nontrivial difficulties in arriving at a satisfactory geometric foundation for the topological side of his proposed book on sphere bundles. Those nontrivial difficulties kept the project in limbo for years, until Norman Steenrod produced an outstanding book on fibre bundles, *The Topology of Fibre Bundles* ([**S1**]). Hass was enormously relieved, saying "Steenrod did a far better job than I could possibly have done." In fact, Steenrod's book, which appeared in 1951, was an instant classic. Although now an older book, its simple clarity, careful writing, and instructive examples set it apart from others that followed, and it is still uniquely useful since more recent books are generally more formal, less intuitive, and not as well motivated. Steenrod's book remains a very good starting point for those wishing to learn more about fibre bundles as they are used in differential as well as algebraic topology, and also differential geometry and algebraic geometry.

16.2 [p. 204]. Adding a cubic term, say, $10^{10}x^3$, to $y = ax + bx^2$ barely changes the shape of the parabola sufficiently near the origin—think of looking at the origin through a very powerful microscope. This is because successively multiplying $x < 1$ by itself produces ever smaller values. So, for example, $(0.1)^2 = 0.01$ and $(0.1)^3 = 0.001$. This effect becomes more dramatic for truly small values of x, so for x sufficiently small, the values of $10^{10}x^3$ in $y = ax + bx^2 + 10^{10}x^3$ can be less than the round-off error in a computer. Because of this, within a sufficiently small neighborhood of the origin, the computer will draw the same curve with and without the cubic term.

16.3 [p. 214]. Whitney's 1955 paper ([**102**]), catastrophe theory, and the areas of chaos and fractals, share some common threads. One is bifurcation, and another is the distinction between stability and instability. But just how these

are manifested in Whitney-Thom versus chaos and fractals can be very different. Philosophically, Whitney-Thom is more like the cosmos, in which most of
outer space is smooth, punctuated by critical points or catastrophes like black
holes, neutron stars, and so on. Chaos and fractals includes the micro, too. Figure 16.18 on p. 213 illustrates the first kind, with a manifold having a bifurcation,
and in more general applications there can be finitely many of these curves. (In
place of one dowel, there could be, say, all the interconnected steel I-beams in a
building.) The distribution of bifurcations is essentially macro in character. But
in chaos and fractals there are typically infinite cascades of bifurcations as well
as infinitely many cascades of cascades, with all the bifurcations getting progressively closer together. Cascades of bifurcations lead to cascades of stabilities as
well as cascades of instabilities. There will typically be infinitely many points P
so that in any of P's neighborhoods, you find cascades of cascades—very micro.
One also encounters periodicity and self-similarity.

We give only a brief overview of some of these ideas. The picture on p. 368
depicts one of the most familiar pictures in chaos and fractals: the bifurcation
diagram arising from the logistic population equation. Any equation leading to
chaos is nonlinear, and the logistic equation is an especially simple and symmetric example of this. As we'll see, the picture shows many period-doubling routes
to chaos as the governing parameter r increases. The logistic equation models
the year-to-year population of a species:

$$x_{n+1} = rx_n(1 - x_n).$$

In this equation, x_n represents the population size in year n, and the basic parameter r is the fecundity (here, the rate of annual reproduction) of the species.
Population size x ranges from 0 to 1—that is, 0% to 100%, where $1 = 100\%$ represents the maximum expected population. The maximum value of $rx(1 - x)$ is
$\frac{r}{4}$ (occuring at $x = \frac{1}{2}$), so the complete diagram ranges from $r = 0$ to $r = 4$ to
make x range from 0 to 1. To show more of the bifurcations and chaotic regions,
we start the diagram at $r = 2.4$.

Not surprisingly, there are similarities as well as differences between Whitney's work and catastrophe theory on the one hand, and chaos and fractals on
the other. We now compare some features of Figures 16.18 and the bifurcation
diagram. To bring out similarity, we make our comparisons more direct by re-
stricting Figure 16.18 to some fixed value of compression (distance between the
fixed blocks), so choose the compression corresponding to, say, the edge closest
to the viewer, the edge where we see the Start point. The force F in this picture corresponds to r in the above bifurcation diagram, and we choose $r = 2.4$.
From the Start point, increasing F brings the state closer to a critical point and
catastrophe. Increasing r from 2.4 leads us closer to the first bifurcation point
at $r = 3.0$. As for differences between Whitney-catastrophe and chaos-fractals,

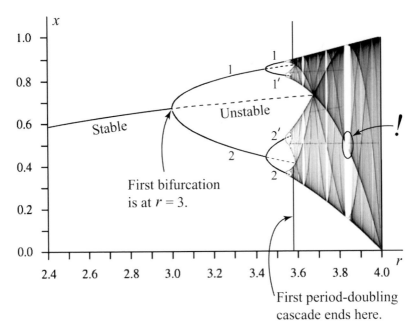

Bifurcation diagram.

in Figure 16.18 there's a discontinuity or catastrophe, while in the bifurcation diagram there isn't. Also, the catastrophe is irreversible in that after landing on the lower stable region, a small decrease in F won't put you back in the upper region—you're stuck there until you reach and pass a critical point on the lower region. In contrast, in the bifurcation diagram, if you cross a bifurcation point while increasing r, you can simply decrease r and return to the state you left. There are other differences as well. In Figure 16.18, increasing F corresponds to moving exactly on a curve toward a critical point. In the bifurcation diagram you are almost never on any of the curves in the diagram! The solidly drawn curves are only *attractors*. For example, fixing r at say, 2.5, some initial population size (value of x) will bounce around as n increases, tending toward the point of the curve above $r = 2.5$. Granted, if the initial population happened to be a point on the curve (unlikely as that would be), it would stay right there as n increases.

What's the story just after a bifurcation—say $r = 3.1$? The two solid branches are attractors, and after many generations (that is, for n large) the population will alternate, from one generation to the next, between being close to one branch, then close to the other. What about the dotted continuation of the original solid curve? Dotted corresponds to repelling: A point precisely on this curve corresponds to unstable equilibrium. If the point is off it, succeeding values of x_n will move away or be repelled from this curve, eventually getting alternatingly closer and closer to one solid branch, then the other, ...

Just as increasing F in Figure 16.18 has physical meaning—press down hard enough and the bent dowel will flip to bending the other way—so too, increasing r has physical meaning. Raising r from say 2.5 to 2.6 in the bifurcation diagram means the reproductive rate has increased (more offspring per year), and the diagram reflects that the logistic model says the total population rises somewhat. When r increases from 3.0 to 3.1 however, the reproductive rate is so high that the environment cannot long support such a mushrooming population, and there will be die-off, which means next year's population is smaller. The environment can now support this smaller population. Physically, the population bounces from year to year between larger and smaller, which at $r = 3.1$ eventually tends toward oscillating closely between the two x-values lying above $r = 3.1$. As r increases further to 3.2, 3.3, and 3.4, the die-off becomes progressively more severe, but because r gets larger, the year after a die-off year the population increases faster than ever.

It turns out that we encounter the second bifurcation when $r = 1 + \sqrt{6} \approx$ 3.4495. Beyond that, the reproductive rate is so high that the die-off from the population size on branch 1 is very severe, plunging to branch 2 below—so low that recovery the next year is only to branch 1′, followed by a less-severe die-off to branch 2′. This 4-cycle 1, 2, 1′, 2′, 1, ... repeats endlessly, the population sizes tending ever closer to points on the four solid branches above $r = 3.5$. We've already begun the first cascade! When we increase $r = 1 + \sqrt{6}$ by about 0.1 to $r = 3.5441 \cdots$ the diagram bifurcates once again, giving eight branches with a well-determined order of cycling through the points above that r. The rate of encountering bifurcations accelerates dramatically: Increasing $r = 3.5441$ by about 0.02 leads to the bifurcation into a total of 16 branches; increasing around another 0.004 brings us to the next bifurcation into 32 branches; about another 0.00094 brings us to 64 branches. Amazingly, in increasing only another 0.000255672, we blast through the entire infinity of bifurcations and enter a region of "deterministic chaos." Above this r in this chaotic region, the order can be calculated, but it follows no easily discernable pattern. All this highlights another hallmark of chaos: extreme sensitivity to initial conditions, in which small changes in the governing parameter can lead to wildly different outcomes.

Self-similarity is another common theme in chaos and fractals, and our figure showing period doubling is no exception. One can see several white vertical bands in the figure, and there are infinitely many of them, any one being visible when the picture is magnified enough. A new period-doubling cascade starts at the left side of each of these bands. The entire first cascade we've just looked at lives in the widest of these bands, spanning $r = 0$ to $r \approx 3.569945672$. In the second largest, we've drawn in a small oval enclosing a smaller copy of the first cascade of period-doubling. There are two other such copies in this band, one at its top and one at its bottom. For an r just to the right of the band's left edge, there are therefore three values of x, and these cycle with period three as n increments. As r increases, we encounter a cascade of period-doubling bifurcations leading to cycles of periods 3, 6, 12, 24, 48, ... Also visible is a thinner band to the left of this one, containing five smooth copies of the initial cascade, and we get within this band periods 5, 10, 20, 40, 80, ... Every one of these infinitely many bands leads to a chaotic region. In every case, as r increases, the chaos storm suddenly ends, followed by a fresh band starting off with some finite number of cycles which then period-double, ending in another region of chaos.

Chapter 17: *Are There Decomposition Theorems for Non-manifolds?*

17.1 [p. 227]. An *analytic variety* V in $\mathbb{R}^n$ can be defined this way: In some open neighborhood N_P of each point $P \in V$, $V \cap N_P$ is the set of common zeros of finitely many functions analytic at P, meaning each function is represented in N_P by a real Taylor series with center P.

Chapter 18: *After Research*

18.1 [p. 246]. A *complex-analytic variety* V in $\mathbb{C}^n$ can be defined as follows: In some open neighborhood N_P of each point $P \in V$, $V \cap N_P$ is the set of common zeros of finitely many functions analytic at P, meaning each function is represented in N_P by a Taylor series with center P.

Chapter 20: *Other Happenings at the Institute*

20.1 [p. 271]. *Walter Gieseking* (1895–1956) was perhaps the foremost interpreter of the piano music of Debussy, Ravel, and Mozart. Although German by heritage, he was born and raised in France and Italy, and that greatly influenced his musical sensibilities. Gieseking remains to this day a musical enigma. He started playing the piano when he was four with no teacher, disliked practicing, and preferred learning new repertoire away from the instrument. On the one hand, his absolute pitch combined with a phenomenal memory made this relatively easy, and on the other, he was free to form musical interpretations in his mind, unfettered by any physical considerations. After learning a composition away from the piano (and that included resolving many technical difficulties as well as interpretation), he would simply go to the piano and play the nearly finished product. In one respect he approached the piano the way some painters approach the canvas: Basic to his interpretation was chiaroscuro—using light and shade to bring out emotion and musical color, reminiscent of the way Rembrandt used the subtleties of natural light to such dramatic effect. In creating chiaroscuro, one of the tools Gieseking mastered to an almost unparalleled degree is the use of the pedals. "How did he do it?" has remained an unanswered question of music critics over the decades, and his only explanation was "The dreamer's intuition is far more sure than intellectual research." Yet, aside from the great refinement of French music, he could become wildly passionate and unbridled in virtuosic compositions by composers like Rachmaninoff or Beethoven. There is an extensive Gieseking discography, and many of his earlier recordings have been remastered.

20.2 [p. 277]. *Leo Sario* (1916–2009) was an important researcher in Riemann surfaces, guided 36 Ph.D. students, and wrote six books, the best known being *Riemann Surfaces* ([**AS**]) which he coauthored with Lars Ahlfors. After a temporary membership at the Institute for Advanced Study, he taught successively at MIT, Stanford, and Harvard before settling down into a long career at UCLA. In addition to his mathematical activities he was a tireless activist for social causes. He was instrumental in establishing the Finnish National Academy which funds scientific research. In 2015, for example, it awarded some 350 million euros to help support research activities of about 8,000 people. The statute establishing the Academy is named "Lex Sario," and he was knighted in 1957 by the Finnish government for his contribution.

Chapter 22: *Sometimes You Get to Know People Through the Little Things*

22.1 [p. 306]. The prize recognized his foundational work on geometric problems, the study of differentiable functions on closed sets, the theory of manifolds, geometric integration theory, and stratifications of analytic spaces. The prize represented a large chunk of his life's output.

Bibliography

[1] H. Whitney, Abstract for *A peculiar function*, Bull. Am. Math. Soc. **35** (1929), no. 4, 442–443. (Abstract only; unpublished.)

[2] H. Whitney, Abstract for *Note on central motions*, Bull. Am. Math. Soc. **36** (1930), no. 5, 352. (Abstract only; unpublished.)

[3] H. Whitney, Abstract for *A theory of graphs and their coloring*, Bull. Am. Math. Soc. **36** (1930), no. 11, 798. (Abstract only; unpublished.)

[4] H. Whitney, Abstract for *A normal form for maps*, Bull. Am. Math. Soc. **36** (1930), no. 3, 216–217. (Abstract only; unpublished.)

[5] H. Whitney, Abstract for *A logical expansion in mathematics*, Bull. Am. Math. Soc. **36** (1930), no. 11, 798. (Abstract only; article subsequently published in Bull. Am. Math. Soc. **38** (1932), no. 8, 572–579.)

[6] H. Whitney, *A theorem on graphs*, Ann. of Math. (2) **32** (1931), no. 2, 378–390, DOI 10.2307/1968197. MR1503003

[7] H. Whitney, *Non-separable and planar graphs*, Proc. Nat. Acad. Sci. U.S.A. **17** (February 1931), no. 2, 125–127.

[8] H. Whitney, *The coloring of graphs*, Proc. Natl. Acad. Sci. U.S.A. **17** (February 1931), no. 2, 122–125.

[9] H. Whitney, Abstract for *On homeomorphic graphs and the connectivity of graphs*, Bull. Am. Math. Soc. **37** (1931), no. 3, 168. (Abstract only; unpublished.)

[10] H. Whitney, Abstract for *A characterization of the closed 2-cell*, Bull. Am. Math. Soc. **37** (1931), no. 11, 820–821. (Abstract only; article subsequently published in Trans. Am. Math. Soc. **35** (1933), no. 1, 261–273.)

[11] H. Whitney, Abstract for *Basic graphs*, Bull. Am. Math. Soc. **38** (1932), no. 1, 37–38. (Abstract only; unpublished.)

[12] H. Whitney, Abstract for *A set of topological invariants for graphs*, Bull. Am. Math. Soc. **38** (1932), no. 1, 38. (Abstract only; article subsequently published in Am. J. Math. **55** (1933), nos. 1-4, 231–235.)

[13] H. Whitney, Abstract for *Conditions that a graph have a dual*, Bull. Am. Math. Soc. **38** (1932), no. 1, 37. (Abstract only; unpublished.)

[14] H. Whitney, *Regular families of curves, I*, Proc. Natl. Acad. Sci. U.S.A. **18** (March 1932), no. 3, 275–278.

[15] H. Whitney, Abstract for *On 2-congruent graphs*, Bull. Am. Math. Soc. **38** (1932), no. 5, 354. (Abstract only; unpublished.)

[16] H. Whitney, *Non-separable and planar graphs*, Trans. Amer. Math. Soc. **34** (1932), no. 2, 339–362, DOI 10.2307/1989545. MR1501641

[17] H. Whitney, *Note on Perron's solution of the Dirichlet problem*, Proc. Natl. Acad. Sci. U.S.A. **18** (January 1932), no. 1, 68–70.

[18] H. Whitney, Abstract for *Regular families of curves, I*, Bull. Am. Math. Soc. **38** (1932), no. 3, 183. (Abstract only; article subsequently published in Proc. Natl. Acad. Sci. U.S.A. **18** (1932), no. 3, 275–278.)

[19] H. Whitney, *Regular families of curves, II*, Proc. Natl. Acad. Sci. U.S.A. **18** (April 1932), no. 4, 340–342.

[20] H. Whitney, *Congruent graphs and the connectivity of graphs*, Amer. J. Math. **54** (1932), no. 1, 150–168, DOI 10.2307/2371086. MR1506881

[21] H. Whitney, *A logical expansion in mathematics*, Bull. Amer. Math. Soc. **38** (1932), no. 8, 572–579, DOI 10.1090/S0002-9904-1932-05460-X. MR1562461

[22] H. Whitney, Abstract for *Cross sections of curves in 3-space*, Bull. Am. Math. Soc. **38** (1932), no. 11, 808. (Abstract only; article subsequently published in Duke Math. J. **4** (1938), no. 1, 222–226.)

[23] H. Whitney, Abstract for *Characteristic functions and the algebra of logic*, Bull. Am. Math. Soc. **38** (1932), no. 1, 38. (Abstract only; article subsequently published in Ann. of Math. (2) **34** (1933), no. 3, 405–414.)

[24] H. Whitney, *The coloring of graphs*, Ann. of Math. (2) **33** (1932), no. 4, 688–718, DOI 10.2307/1968214. MR1503085

[25] H. Whitney, Abstract for *Note on Perron's solution of the Dirichlet problem*, Bull. Am. Math. Soc. **38** (1932), no. 1, 41. (Abstract only; article subsequently published in Proc. Natl. Acad. Sci. U.S.A. **18** (1932), no. 1, 68–70.)

[26] H. Whitney, Abstract for *Regular families of curves, II*, Bull. Am. Math. Soc. **38** (1932), no. 3, 183–184. (Abstract only; article subsequently published in Proc. Natl. Acad. Sci. U.S.A. **18** (1932), no. 4, 340–342.)

[27] H. Whitney, *The coloring of graphs*, Ph.D. thesis, Harvard University, 1932. Advised by G. D. Birkhoff. MR2936470

[28] H. Whitney, *2-Isomorphic graphs*, Amer. J. Math. **55** (1933), no. 1-4, 245–254, DOI 10.2307/2371127. MR1506961

[29] H. Whitney, *On the classification of graphs*, Amer. J. Math. **55** (1933), no. 1-4, 236–244, DOI 10.2307/2371126. MR1506960

[30] H. Whitney, *Characteristic functions and the algebra of logic*, Ann. of Math. (2) **34** (1933), no. 3, 405–414, DOI 10.2307/1968168. MR1503114

[31] H. Whitney, Abstract for *Differentiable functions defined on closed sets*, Bull. Am. Math. Soc. **39** (1933), no. 5, 352–353. (Abstract only; unpublished.)

[32] H. Whitney, Abstract for *Functions differentiable on the boundaries of regions*, Bull. Am. Math. Soc. **39** (1933), no. 11, 874. (Abstract only; article subsequently published in Ann. Math. (2) **35** (1934), no. 3, 482–485.)

[33] H. Whitney, Abstract for *Differentiable functions defined in closed sets, I*, Bull. Am. Math. Soc. **39** (1933), no. 9, 673. (Abstract only; article subsequently published in Trans. Am. Math. Soc. **36** (1934), no. 2, 369–387.)

[34] H. Whitney, *Regular families of curves*, Ann. of Math. (2) **34** (1933), no. 2, 244–270, DOI 10.2307/1968202. MR1503106

[35] H. Whitney, *Planar graphs*, Fundam. Math. **21** (1933), 73–84.

[36] H. Whitney, *A set of topological invariants for graphs*, Amer. J. Math. **55** (1933), no. 1-4, 231–235, DOI 10.2307/2371125. MR1506959

[37] H. Whitney, Abstract for *Analytic extensions of differentiable functions defined on closed sets*, Bull. Am. Math. Soc. **39** (1933), no. 1, 31. (Abstract only; article subsequently published in Trans. Am. Math. Soc. **36** (1934), no. 1, 63–89.)

[38] H. Whitney, *A characterization of the closed 2-cell*, Trans. Amer. Math. Soc. **35** (1933), no. 1, 261–273, DOI 10.2307/1989324. MR1501683

[39] H. Whitney, Abstract for *Derivatives, difference quotients, and Taylor's formula, I*, Bull. Am. Math. Soc. **39** (1933), no. 7, 508. (Abstract only; article subsequently published in Bull. Am. Math. Soc. **40** (1934), no. 2, pp. 89–94.)

[40] H. Whitney, Abstract for *Derivatives, difference quotients, and Taylor's formula, II*, Bull. Am. Math. Soc. **39** (1933), no. 11, 875. (Abstract only; article subsequently published in Ann. Math. (2) **35** (1934), no. 3, 476–481.)

[41] H. Whitney, Abstract for *On the abstract properties of linear dependence*, Bull. Am. Math. Soc. **40** (1934), no. 9, 663. (Abstract only; article subsequently published in Am. J. Math. **57** (1935), no. 3, 509–533.)

[42] H. Whitney, *Differentiable functions defined in closed sets. I*, Trans. Amer. Math. Soc. **36** (1934), no. 2, 369–387, DOI 10.2307/1989844. MR1501749

[43] H. Whitney, Abstract for *Analytic approximations to manifolds*, Bull. Am. Math. Soc. **40** (1934), no. 9, 663. (Abstract only; unpublished.)

[44] H. Whitney, *Analytic extensions of differentiable functions defined in closed sets*, Trans. Amer. Math. Soc. **36** (1934), no. 1, 63–89, DOI 10.2307/1989708. MR1501735

[45] H. Whitney, *Derivatives, difference quotients and Taylor's formula. II*, Ann. of Math. (2) **35** (1934), no. 3, 476–481, DOI 10.2307/1968744. MR1503173

[46] H. Whitney, *Functions differentiable on the boundaries of regions*, Ann. of Math. (2) **35** (1934), no. 3, 482–485, DOI 10.2307/1968745. MR1503174

[47] H. Whitney, *Erratum: Derivatives, difference quotients, and Taylor's formula*, Bull. Am. Math. Soc. **40** (1934), no. 12, 894.

[48] H. Whitney, *Derivatives, difference quotients, and Taylor's formula*, Bull. Amer. Math. Soc. **40** (1934), no. 2, 89–94, DOI 10.1090/S0002-9904-1934-05811-7. MR1562803

[49] H. Whitney, Abstract for *A numerical equivalent of the four-color problem*, Bull. Am. Math. Soc. **40** (1934), no. 1, 36. (Abstract only; article subsequently published in Monatsh. Math. Phys. **45** (1936), no. 1, 207–213.)

[50] H. Whitney, Abstract for *A function not constant on a connected set of critical points*, Bull. Am. Math. Soc. **41** (1935), no. 11, 796. (Abstract only; article subsequently published in Duke Math. J. **1** (1935), no. 1, 514–517.)

[51] H. Whitney, Abstract for *Sphere-spaces, with applications*, Bull. Am. Math. Soc. **41** (1935), no. 5, 337–338. (Abstract only; unpublished.)

[52] H. Whitney, *A function not constant on a connected set of critical points*, Duke Math. J. **1** (1935), no. 4, 514–517, DOI 10.1215/S0012-7094-35-00138-7. MR1545896

[53] H. Whitney, *On the abstract properties of linear dependence*, Amer. J. Math. **57** (1935), no. 3, 509–533, DOI 10.2307/2371182. MR1507091

[54] H. Whitney, *Sphere-spaces*, Proc. Natl. Acad. Sci. U.S.A. **21** (1935), no. 7, 464–468.

[55] H. Whitney, *Differentiable manifolds in Euclidean space*, Proc. Natl. Acad. Sci. U.S.A. **21** (July 1935), no. 7, 462–464.

[56] H. Whitney, Abstract for *Differentiable manifolds in Euclidean space*, Bull. Am. Math. Soc. **41** (1935), no. 9, 625–626. (Abstract only; article subsequently published in Proc. Natl. Acad. Sci. U.S.A. **21** (1935), no. 7, 462–464.)

[57] H. Whitney, Abstract for *On a theorem of H. Hopf*, Bull. Am. Math. Soc. **41** (1935), no. 11, 787. (Abstract only; unpublished.)

[58] H. Whitney, *Sphere-spaces*, Rec. Math. Moscou, n. Ser. **1** (1936), no. 5, 787–791.

[59] H. Whitney, *A numerical equivalent of the four color map Problem*, Monatsh. Math. Phys. **45** (1936), no. 1, 207–213, DOI 10.1007/BF01707988. MR1550643

[60] H. Whitney, Abstract for *Differentiable functions defined in arbitrary subsets of Euclidean space*, Bull. Am. Math. Soc. **42** (1936), no. 1, 23. (Abstract only; article subsequently published in Trans. Am. Math. Soc. **40** (1936), no. 2, 309–317.)

[61] H. Whitney, Abstract for *The maps of a 4-complex into a 2-sphere*, Bull. Am. Math. Soc. **42** (1936), no. 5, 338–339. (Abstract only; unpublished.)

[62] H. Whitney, *Differentiable manifolds in Euclidean space*, Rec. Math. Moscou, n. Ser. **1** (1936), no. 5, 783–786.

[63] H. Whitney, Abstract for *Matrices of integers and combinatorial topology*, Bull. Am. Math. Soc. **42** (1936), no. 11, 816. (Abstract only; article subsequently published in Duke Math. J. **3** (1937), no. 1, 35–45.)

[64] H. Whitney, Abstract for *On the maps of an n-sphere into another n-sphere*, Bull. Am. Math. Soc. **42** (1936), no. 11, 810. (Abstract only; article subsequently published in Duke Math. J. **3** (1937), no. 1, 46–50.)

[65] H. Whitney, *Differentiable functions defined in arbitrary subsets of Euclidean space*, Trans. Amer. Math. Soc. **40** (1936), no. 2, 309–317, DOI 10.2307/1989869. MR1501875

[66] H. Whitney, *The imbedding of manifolds in families of analytic manifolds*, Ann. of Math. (2) **37** (1936), no. 4, 865–878, DOI 10.2307/1968624. MR1503315

[67] H. Whitney, Abstract for *On regular closed curves in the plane*, Bull. Am. Math. Soc. **42** (1936), no. 9, 639. (Abstract only; article subsequently published in Compositio Math. **4** (1937), 276–284.)

[68] H. Whitney, *Differentiable manifolds*, Ann. of Math. (2) **37** (1936), no. 3, 645–680, DOI 10.2307/1968482. MR1503303

[69] H. Whitney, *On regular closed curves in the plane*, Compositio Math. **4** (1937), 276–284. MR1556973

[70] H. Whitney, *Topological properties of differentiable manifolds*, Bull. Amer. Math. Soc. **43** (1937), no. 12, 785–805, DOI 10.1090/S0002-9904-1937-06642-0. MR1563640

[71] H. Whitney, *The maps of an n-complex into an n-sphere*, Duke Math. J. **3** (1937), no. 1, 51–55, DOI 10.1215/S0012-7094-37-00306-5. MR1545972

[72] H. Whitney, *On the maps of an n-sphere into another n-sphere*, Duke Math. J. **3** (1937), no. 1, 46–50, DOI 10.1215/S0012-7094-37-00305-3. MR1545971

[73] H. Whitney, *On matrices of integers and combinatorial topology*, Duke Math. J. **3** (1937), no. 1, 35–45, DOI 10.1215/S0012-7094-37-00304-1. MR1545970

[74] H. Whitney, *Analytic coordinate systems and arcs in a manifold*, Ann. of Math. (2) **38** (1937), no. 4, 809–818, DOI 10.2307/1968837. MR1503372

[75] H. Whitney, *On products in a complex*, Proc. Natl. Acad. Sci. U.S.A. **23** (May 1937), no. 5, pp. 285–291.

[76] H. Whitney, *Tensor products of Abelian groups*, Duke Math. J. **4** (1938), no. 3, 495–528, DOI 10.1215/S0012-7094-38-00442-9. MR1546071

[77] H. Whitney, *Book Review: Leçons sur les Principes Topologiques de la Théorie des Fonctions Analytiques*, Bull. Amer. Math. Soc. **44** (1938), no. 11, 758–759, DOI 10.1090/S0002-9904-1938-06867-X. MR1563864

[78] H. Whitney, *On products in a complex*, Ann. of Math. (2) **39** (1938), no. 2, 397–432, DOI 10.2307/1968795. MR1503416

[79] H. Whitney, *Cross-sections of curves in 3-space*, Duke Math. J. **4** (1938), no. 1, 222–226, DOI 10.1215/S0012-7094-38-00416-8. MR1546045

[80] H. Whitney, *Some combinatorial properties of complexes*, Proc. Nat. Acad. Sci. U. S. A. **26** (1940), 143–148. MR0001337

[81] H. Whitney, *On the theory of sphere-bundles*, Proc. Nat. Acad. Sci. U. S. A. **26** (1940), 148–153. MR0001338

[82] H. Whitney, *On the topology of differentiable manifolds*, Lectures in Topology, University of Michigan Press, Ann Arbor, Mich., 1941, pp. 101–141. MR0005300

[83] H. Whitney, *On regular families of curves*, Bull. Amer. Math. Soc. **47** (1941), 145–147, DOI 10.1090/S0002-9904-1941-07395-7. MR0004115

[84] H. Whitney, *Differentiability of the remainder term in Taylor's formula*, Duke Math. J. **10** (1943), 153–158. MR0007782

[85] H. Whitney, *Differentiable even functions*, Duke Math. J. **10** (1943), 159–160. MR0007783

[86] H. Whitney, *The general type of singularity of a set of $2n - 1$ smooth functions of n variables*, Duke Math. J. **10** (1943), 161–172. MR0007784

[87] H. Whitney, *The self-intersections of a smooth n-manifold in 2n-space*, Ann. of Math. (2) **45** (1944), 220–246, DOI 10.2307/1969265. MR0010274

[88] H. Whitney, *Topics in the theory of Abelian groups. I. Divisibility of homomorphisms*, Bull. Amer. Math. Soc. **50** (1944), 129–134, DOI 10.1090/S0002-9904-1944-08101-9. MR0009404

[89] H. Whitney, *The singularities of a smooth n-manifold in $(2n - 1)$-space*, Ann. of Math. (2) **45** (1944), 247–293, DOI 10.2307/1969266. MR0010275

[90] H. Whitney, *On the extension of differentiable functions*, Bull. Amer. Math. Soc. **50** (1944), 76–81, DOI 10.1090/S0002-9904-1944-08082-8. MR0009785

[91] H. Whitney, *Complexes of manifolds*, Proc. Nat. Acad. Sci. U. S. A. **33** (1947), 10–11. MR0019306

[92] H. Whitney, *Geometric methods in cohomology theory*, Proc. Nat. Acad. Sci. U. S. A. **33** (1947), 7–9. MR0019305

[93] H. Whitney, *Algebraic topology and integration theory*, Proc. Nat. Acad. Sci. U. S. A. **33** (1947), 1–6. MR0019304

[94] H. Whitney, *On ideals of differentiable functions*, Amer. J. Math. **70** (1948), 635–658, DOI 10.2307/2372203. MR0026238

[95] L. H. Loomis and H. Whitney, *An inequality related to the isoperimetric inequality*, Bull. Amer. Math. Soc **55** (1949), 961–962, DOI 10.1090/S0002-9904-1949-09320-5. MR0031538

[96] H. Whitney, *Relations between the second and third homotopy groups of a simply connected space*, Ann. of Math. (2) **50** (1949), 180–202, DOI 10.2307/1969361. MR0034019

[97] H. Whitney, *La topologie algébrique et la théorie de l'intégration* [*Algebraic topology and the theory of integration*], in Topologie algébrique (Paris, June–July 1947) (A. Denjoy, editor), Colloques Internationaux du Centre National de la Recherche Scientifique 12. CNRS, Paris, 1949, 107–113. MR0034022

[98] H. Whitney, *An extension theorem for mappings into simply connected spaces*, Ann. of Math. (2) **50** (1949), 285–296, DOI 10.2307/1969453. MR0034021

[99] H. Whitney, *Classification of the mappings of a 3-complex into a simply connected space*, Ann. of Math. (2) **50** (1949), 270–284, DOI 10.2307/1969452. MR0034020

[100] H. Whitney, *On totally differentiable and smooth functions*, Pacific J. Math. **1** (1951), 143–159. MR0043878

[101] H. Whitney, *r-Dimensional integration in n-space*, Proceedings of the International Congress of Mathematicians, Cambridge, Mass., 1950, Vol. 1, Amer. Math. Soc., Providence, R. I., 1952, pp. 245–256. MR0043879

[102] H. Whitney, *On singularities of mappings of Euclidean spaces. I. Mappings of the plane into the plane*, Ann. of Math. (2) **62** (1955), 374–410, DOI 10.2307/1970070. MR0073980

[103] H. Whitney, *Elementary structure of real algebraic varieties*, Ann. of Math. (2) **66** (1957), 545–556, DOI 10.2307/1969908. MR0095844

[104] H. Whitney, *On functions with bounded nth differences*, J. Math. Pures Appl. (9) **36** (1957), 67–95. MR0084611

[105] H. Whitney, *Geometric integration theory*, Princeton Mathematical Series 21, Princeton University Press, 1957. (Out of print; reissued by Dover Publications.)

[106] H. Whitney, *Singularities of mappings of Euclidean spaces*, Symposium internacional de topología algebraica International symposium on algebraic topology, Universidad Nacional Autónoma de México and UNESCO, Mexico City, 1958, pp. 285–301. MR0098418

[107] A. Dold and H. Whitney, *Classification of oriented sphere bundles over a 4-complex*, Ann. of Math. (2) **69** (1959), 667–677, DOI 10.2307/1970030. MR0123331

[108] H. Whitney and F. Bruhat, *Quelques propriétés fondamentales des ensembles analytiques-réels* [*Some fundamental properties of real-analytic sets*] (French), Comment. Math. Helv. **33** (1959), 132–160, DOI 10.1007/BF02565913. MR0102094

[109] H. Whitney, *On bounded functions with bounded nth differences*, Proc. Amer. Math. Soc. **10** (1959), 480–481, DOI 10.2307/2032871. MR0106969

[110] H. Whitney, *Geometric integration theory*, (V. G. Boltyanski, editor), 1960.

[111] A. M. Gleason and H. Whitney, *The extension of linear functionals defined on H^∞*, Pacific J. Math. **12** (1962), 163–182. MR0142013

[112] H. Whitney, "The work of John W. Milnor", in *Proceedings of the International Congress of Mathematicians* (Stockholm, August 1962), Institut Mittag-Leffler, Djursholm, Sweden, 1963, XLVIII–L.

[113] H. Whitney, *Tangents to an analytic variety*, Ann. of Math. (2) **81** (1965), 496–549, DOI 10.2307/1970400. MR0192520

[114] H. Whitney, *Local properties of analytic varieties*, Differential and Combinatorial Topology (A Symposium in Honor of Marston Morse), Princeton Univ. Press, Princeton, N. J., 1965, pp. 205–244. MR0188486

[115] H. Whitney, *The mathematics of physical quantities. I. Mathematical models for measurement*, Amer. Math. Monthly **75** (1968), 115–138, DOI 10.2307/2315883. MR0228219

[116] H. Whitney, *The mathematics of physical quantities. II. Quantity structures and dimensional analysis*, Amer. Math. Monthly **75** (1968), 227–256, DOI 10.2307/2314953. MR0228220

[117] H. Whitney, *Complex analytic varieties*, Addison-Wesley Publishing Co., Reading, Mass.-London-Don Mills, Ont., 1972. MR0387634

[118] H. Whitney and W. T. Tutte, *Kempe chains and the four colour problem*, Utilitas Math. **2** (1972), 241–281. MR0309782

[119] H. Whitney, "Are we off the track in teaching mathematical concepts?", in *Developments in mathematical education: Proceedings of the Second International Congress on Mathematical Education* (A. G. Howson, editor), Cambridge University Press, Cambridge, UK, 1973, 283–296.

[120] H. Whitney and W. T. Tutte, *Kempe chains and the four colour problem*, Studies in graph theory, Part II, Math. Assoc. Amer., Washington, D.C., 1975, pp. 378–413. Studies in Math., Vol. 12. MR0392651

[121] H. Whitney, *Mathematical education: Comment on the division of the plane by lines*, Amer. Math. Monthly **86** (1979), no. 8, 700, DOI 10.2307/2321306. MR1539143

[122] H. Whitney, *Taking responsibility in school mathematics education*, J. Math. Behav. **4**:3 (December 1985), 219–235.

[123] H. Whitney, *Letting research come naturally*, Math. Chronicle **14** (1985), 1–19. MR826955

[124] A. Tucker and W. Aspray, *Hassler Whitney*, 1985. Online interview transcript, 10 April 1984.

[125] F. M. Hechinger, *Learning math by thinking*, New York Times (10 June 1986), C1. Article is based around an interview with Whitney.

[126] H. Whitney, *Coming alive in school math and beyond*, J. Math. Behav. **5**:2 (1986), 129–140.

[127] H. Whitney, *Coming alive in school math and beyond*, Educ. Stud. Math. **18**:3 (1987), 229–242.

[128] H. Whitney, *Moscow 1935: Topology moving toward America*, A century of mathematics in America, Part I, Hist. Math., vol. 1, Amer. Math. Soc., Providence, RI, 1988, pp. 97–117. MR1003166

[129] A. Shields, *Differentiable manifolds: Weyl and Whitney*, Math. Intelligencer **10** (1988), no. 2, 5–9, DOI 10.1007/BF03028349. MR932157

[130] U. D'Ambrosio, *The visits of Hassler Whitney to Brazil*, Humanistic Mathematics Network Newsletter **4** (1989), 8.

[131] A. Lax, *Hassler Whitney 1907–1989: Some recollections 1979–1989*, Humanistic Mathematics Network Newsletter **4** (1989), 2–7.

[132] H. Whitney, *Education is for the students' future (draft)*, Humanistic Mathematics Network Newsletter **4** (1989), 9–12.

[133] G. Fowler, *Obituary: Hassler Whitney, geometrician: He eased 'mathematics anxiety'*, New York Times (12 May 1989), B10.

[134] R. Thom, *La vie et l'œuvre de Hassler Whitney* [*The life and works of Hassler Whitney*] (French), C. R. Acad. Sci. Paris Sér. Gén. Vie Sci. **7** (1990), no. 6, 473–476. MR1105198

[135] H. Whitney, *Collected papers. Vol. I*, Contemporary Mathematicians, Birkhäuser Boston, Inc., Boston, MA, 1992. Edited and with a preface by J. Eells and D. Toledo. MR1138982

[136] H. Whitney, *Collected Papers, Vol. II*, Contemporary Mathematicians, Birkhäuser Boston, Inc., Boston, MA, 1992. Edited and with a foreword by J. Eells and D. Toledo.

[137] J. D. Zund, "Whitney, Hassler", in *American National Biography, Vol. 23* (J. A. Garraty and M. C. Carnes, editors), Oxford University Press, New York, 1999, 303–304.

Other References

[AH1] K. Appel and W. Haken, *Every planar map is four colorable. I. Discharging*, Illinois J. Math. **21** (1977), no. 3, 429–490. MR0543792

[AH2] K. Appel, W. Haken, and J. Koch, *Every planar map is four colorable. II. Reducibility*, Illinois J. Math. **21** (1977), no. 3, 491–567. MR0543793

[AS] L. V. Ahlfors and L. Sario, *Riemann surfaces*, Princeton Mathematical Series, No. 26, Princeton University Press, Princeton, N.J., 1960. MR0114911

[B1] L. P. Benezet, *The teaching of arithmetic I: The story of an experiment*, Journal of the National Educational Association **24** (November 1935), no. 8, 241–244.

[B2] L. P. Benezet, *The teaching of arithmetic II: The story of an experiment*, Journal of the National Educational Association **24** (December 1935), no. 9, 301–303.

[B3] L. P. Benezet, *The teaching of arithmetic III: The story of an experiment*, Journal of the National Educational Association **25** (January 1936), no. 1, 7–8.

[E] L. Euler, *Solutio problematis ad geometriam situs pertinentis*, Commentarii academiae scientiarum Petropolitanae **8** (1741), 128–140.

[K1] K. Kendig, *A guide to plane algebraic curves*, The Dolciani Mathematical Expositions, vol. 46, Mathematical Association of America, Washington, DC, 2011. MAA Guides, 7. MR2815937

[K2] K. Kendig, *Elementary algebraic geometry* 2nd ed., Dover Publications, Inc., Mineola, N.Y., 2015.

[MS] J. W. Milnor and J. D. Stasheff, *Characteristic classes*, Princeton University Press, Princeton, N. J.; University of Tokyo Press, Tokyo, 1974. Annals of Mathematics Studies, No. 76. MR0440554

[P] V. Paley, *On listening to what the children say*, Harvard Educational Review **56** (May 1986), no. 2, 122–131.

[S1] N. Steenrod, *The topology of fibre bundles*, Princeton Mathematical Series, Vol. 14, Princeton University Press, Princeton, N. J., 1951. MR0039258

[S2] S. H. Strogatz, *Nonlinear dynamics and chaos, with applications to physics, biology, chemistry and engineering* 2nd ed., Westview Press, Boulder, Co., 2015.

[T] R. Thom, *Structural stability and morphogenesis*, Advanced Books Classics Series, Perseus Books, New York, N.Y., 1994.

[W] W. M. Whyburn, *Non-isolated critical points of functions*, Bull. Amer. Math. Soc. **35** (1929), no. 5, 701–708, DOI 10.1090/S0002-9904-1929-04806-7. MR1561794

Index

381